Teacher Education, Learning Innovation and Accountability

Series editor

Claire Wyatt-Smith, Institute for Learning Sciences and Teacher Education, Australian Catholic University, Brisbane, QLD, Australia

This book series offers research-informed discussion and analysis of teacher preparation, certification and continuing professional learning and the related practice and policy drivers for change and reform. The series fosters and disseminates research about teaching as a profession of choice while offering a unique link to the realities of pre-service experience in workforce preparation. It takes account of research on teacher formation that opens up issues not routinely connected: what teachers need to know and be able to do, and who they are, namely the person of the teacher and their capabilities in contributing to students' personal development and wellbeing. This goal provides a current, practical and international view of the future of initial teacher education programs.

More information about this series at http://www.springer.com/series/15485

Claire Wyatt-Smith · Lenore Adie
Editors

Innovation and Accountability in Teacher Education

Setting Directions for New Cultures in Teacher Education

Springer

Editors
Claire Wyatt-Smith
Institute for Learning Sciences
  and Teacher Education
Australian Catholic University
Brisbane, QLD, Australia

Lenore Adie
Institute for Learning Sciences
  and Teacher Education
Australian Catholic University
Brisbane, QLD, Australia

ISSN 2524-5562   ISSN 2524-5570 (electronic)
Teacher Education, Learning Innovation and Accountability
ISBN 978-981-13-2025-5   ISBN 978-981-13-2026-2 (eBook)
https://doi.org/10.1007/978-981-13-2026-2

Library of Congress Control Number: 2018950957

© Springer Nature Singapore Pte Ltd. 2018
This work is subject to copyright. All rights are reserved by the Publisher, whether the whole or part of the material is concerned, specifically the rights of translation, reprinting, reuse of illustrations, recitation, broadcasting, reproduction on microfilms or in any other physical way, and transmission or information storage and retrieval, electronic adaptation, computer software, or by similar or dissimilar methodology now known or hereafter developed.
The use of general descriptive names, registered names, trademarks, service marks, etc. in this publication does not imply, even in the absence of a specific statement, that such names are exempt from the relevant protective laws and regulations and therefore free for general use.
The publisher, the authors and the editors are safe to assume that the advice and information in this book are believed to be true and accurate at the date of publication. Neither the publisher nor the authors or the editors give a warranty, express or implied, with respect to the material contained herein or for any errors or omissions that may have been made. The publisher remains neutral with regard to jurisdictional claims in published maps and institutional affiliations.

This Springer imprint is published by the registered company Springer Nature Singapore Pte Ltd.
The registered company address is: 152 Beach Road, #21-01/04 Gateway East, Singapore 189721, Singapore

This series is dedicated to the work of passionate teacher educators across the world. We recognize that they have a profound influence, not only on the times in which they live and work, but on the shaping of humanity. In particular, we pay tribute to Dr. Ann Sherman (1956–2017), Dean of the Faculty of Education at the University of New Brunswick, Canada. Ann was a great collaborator, educator, and friend to many. Her commitment to supporting student learning and teacher practice is carried forward through this book.

Foreword

In Wyatt-Smith and Adie's introduction to this book, they present a powerful case for the importance and urgency of the international spotlight on teacher education and student learning in this edited book. As editors, they set this case within the context of accelerating socio-economic and political changes, increasing calls from governments and parents for clear and consistent data on student learning outcomes, and the increasing recognition of the relevance of education to individual life chances. In firmly focusing the book on teacher education, they assert in their introductory chapter—'The logic is clear: improved teacher quality is the critical element for improved outcomes' (p. 2).

Wyatt-Smith and Adie outline three key components of current and pending change in teacher education. These include a wide range of international review reports on teacher education and reform initiatives, in particular those during the last decade. These have included official national reviews in Scotland, Wales, Northern Ireland, the Republic of Ireland, Australia, the USA, and England. Second is the increasing interest of governments in assessing the efficacy of schooling, as well as in assessing the quality of initial teacher education candidates (in Australia, both at entry, and in national testing prior to completion). The third element includes the increasing national calls for an improvement in the quality of the preparation of teachers. In particular, these authors argue that the evidence base which informs teacher education is limited in quantity and scale.

In presenting chapter contributors from Scotland, Norway, South Africa, Hong Kong, Singapore, Canada, the USA, New Zealand, and Australia, Wyatt-Smith and Adie emphasise what they term 'the complex ecologies of teacher education' (p. 13), noting that traditions and culture mediate the global imperatives in teacher education. The global perspectives offered in the book are underpinned by the motivation to generate a scholarly forum for key elements of teacher education's twenty-first century challenges and therefore generate new, evidence-informed thinking.

The book's 19 chapters are divided into three parts, with the first focusing on accountability and change, and the ongoing tension between trust, accountability systems, and quality. These chapters explore high stakes testing and emerging government control, the role of teacher professional standards, the challenges of curriculum content with the increasing drive for 'twenty-first century skills', and the attendant challenges in pedagogy for both experienced and beginning teachers. Within this accountability agenda, chapters also explore the concept of pre-service teachers' classroom readiness, with a focus on this emerging conceptualisation as critical to the reputation of initial teacher education, and the learning outcomes for students. This section also includes a chapter which describes the introduction of Teacher Performance Assessments in Australia as indicators of beginning teachers' preparedness for the classroom.

The second part of the book focuses on preparing teachers for learners in diverse contexts, with international contributions exploring early childhood education, inclusive education, preparing assessment capable teachers, and the challenges for teachers in their first placements, negotiating professional identities and the challenges of teaching in classrooms and in curriculum fields for which they feel unprepared. The complex and changing nature of teacher educator roles in universities, and the challenges for them in supporting pre-service teachers' learning, is also examined. This section of the book examines what teachers need to know and be able to do (teacher preparation), and perceptions and the person of the teacher (identity, formation), and their challenges in 'belongingness' in sites of development, that is initial teacher education programmes and schools.

The final part of the book focuses on teacher education and learning, and in particular how to connect academic learning and learning in the field through professional experience placements. Chapters in this section, drawn from experiences in Australia, South Africa, Ireland, and Hong Kong, affirm the challenge that ITE faces in developing new curriculum models which incorporate professional partnerships and not position these experiences as separate. What is evident in these chapters is the development of a new place for professional experience within the ITE programme, thereby reconstructing the relationships between theory and practice in teacher education.

In the final chapter of the book, Menter outlines the following global themes, emphasising that their importance transcends all cultures and contexts—professional status of teaching, partners, the place of research, governance, performability and accountability, and digitisation. What is important is that the profession works to develop a culture of research and inquiry to emphasise its self-renewing nature and proactively address the dearth of research evidence and research strength.

This edited volume is unique in its focus on the lifespan of teacher development, from initial professional preparation within the university and professional contexts, through induction into classroom practice and early professional development, and into continuing professional development within the culture of standards and quality. The existence of ITE, working to operate within a crucible of change, permeates throughout the book. Wyatt-Smith and Adie conclude their opening chapter by suggesting that the chapters can open new ways of thinking about the following fundamental questions: 'Who are the actors in teacher preparation and how do they interact? How can we know about the quality of teacher education? Where can we hear the voices of teacher educators and pre-service teachers, as well as school-based teacher educators? What are the new and emerging roles of others in teacher education who have not been involved previously, including employing authorities?' (p. 13).

Brisbane, Australia
Emeritus Professor Wendy Patton
Queensland University of Technology

Acknowledgements

The development of this book has been supported with the assistance of a strong editorial team. The editors wish to thank Donna Glase for her coordination and organisation, ensuring smooth progress in the production of this book. We thank Chantelle Day, Editorial Assistant, for her invaluable expertise and commitment to quality in formatting and final editing of the chapters and collating all sections of the book. We also wish to acknowledge Famena Staley and Megan Kimber for their excellent editorial work. Finally, we thank our chapter authors and the contributions that they made to thinking about teacher education together.

Contents

1. New Cultures in Teacher Education 1
   Claire Wyatt-Smith and Lenore Adie

Part I Accountability and Change in Teacher Education

2. Accountability in Teacher Education in Norway: A Case of Mistrust and Trust 19
   Kari Smith

3. Notes from a Small Country: Teacher Education, Learning Innovation and Accountability in Scotland 37
   Louise Hayward

4. Lost in Transition: Learning to Teach in the Era of Test-Based Accountability 51
   Jina Ro

5. The Explicit Nature of Educational Goals for the Twenty-first Century 65
   Esther Care and Helyn Kim

6. Challenges for Initial Teacher Education in the Context of 'Twenty-first Century' Learning Imperatives 81
   Rosemary Hipkins, Jo MacDonald and Jenny Whatman

7. Conceptions of Readiness in Initial Teacher Education: Quality, Impact, Standards and Evidence in Policy Directives 97
   Colette Alexander

8   Research-Informed Conceptualization and Design Principles of Teacher Performance Assessments: Wrestling with System and Site Validity 115
Lenore Adie and Claire Wyatt-Smith

Part II   Preparing Teachers for Diverse Learners and Contexts

9   Analyzing Curriculum Orientations of Kindergarten Curriculum 135
Barley Mak, Chrysa Keung and Alan Cheung

10   Engaging with Ambivalence: The Neglect of Early Childhood Teacher Education in Initial Teacher Education Reform in Australia 155
Joce Nuttall

11   Preparing Teachers for Assessment in Schools: The Influence of Teacher Educators 171
Christopher DeLuca, Andrew Coombs and Ann Sherman

12   Looking for Synergies to Meet the Challenges of Teacher Education 187
Bronwen Cowie and Beverley Cooper

13   Enhancing Inclusive Education Through Teacher Education Reforms 201
Joy Cumming, Megan Tones, Chantelle Day and Elizabeth Heck

14   Is Quality Initial Teacher Education Where the Music Stops? Conceptualizing the Becoming of a Teacher: Lessons from the Field 223
Anna E. Du Plessis

Part III   Partnerships and Professional Cultures

15   Early Career Teachers' Perceptions of Initial Teacher Education 243
Alex Kostogriz

16   Revisiting the Teaching Practicum: Effecting Innovation or Entrenching the Status Quo? Reflections from an ITE Program in South Africa 255
Anil Kanjee

17   School-Based Work in Initial Teacher Education: Responding to Policy in Practice 277
Bernadette Ní Áingléis and Anne Looney

18 Designing for Integration in Initial Teacher Education Curricula: The Hong Kong Postgraduate Diploma in Education 295
Susan Margaret Bridges, Stephen Andrews, Amy Bik May Tsui,
Carol Chan Kwai-kuen, Dan Wang, Tammy Yim Lin Kwan,
Joseph Wai Ip Lam, Gary James Harfitt, Cheri Chan, Wing-Wah Law,
Maurice Man Wai Cheng, Pui-sze Yeung, Wai Ming Cheung
and Rhoda Kuan Yun Wang

19 Teacher Education in a Crucible of Change 313
Ian Menter

Index 327

Editors and Contributors

About the Editors

Claire Wyatt-Smith is the Director of the Institute for Learning Sciences and Teacher Education (ILSTE) and Professor of Educational Assessment and Evaluation, Australian Catholic University. Her research is focused on teaching and evaluative expertise. It examines the role of standards, professional judgement, and moderation, as well as the use of data to inform teaching and improve learning. She acts as an advisor to various agencies within Australia and internationally, and is currently leading a large-scale Australian study involving a national collective of universities undertaking the Graduate Teacher Performance Assessment and cross-institutional standards-referenced moderation. Recent books include *Assessment for education: Standards, judgement and moderation* (Sage 2014) and *Designing assessment for quality learning* (Springer 2014). In addition to the series, *Teacher Education, Learning Innovation and Accountability*, she is the Foundation Editor of *The Enabling Power of Assessment Series*.

Lenore Adie is Associate Professor of Teacher Education and Assessment, and a Senior Research Fellow with the Assessment, Evaluation and Student Learning Research concentration in the Institute for Learning Sciences and Teacher Education (ILSTE), Australian Catholic University. Her research focuses on assessment and moderation processes as these contribute to supporting teachers' pedagogical practices and student learning. She has a further interest in the enactment of assessment policy and the validity of assessment processes. Her research has generated new knowledge in the field of assessment focussing on quality in assessment practices and processes, in particular within systems of standards-referenced assessment. This work addresses the alignment of curriculum, assessment and pedagogic practices through the design of assessment tasks, and the application of criteria and grading. She has extensive professional experience working in schools as a teacher and within leadership positions, and in teacher education for over 30 years.

Contributors

Lenore Adie Institute for Learning Sciences and Teacher Education, Australian Catholic University, Brisbane, Australia

Colette Alexander Institute for Learning Sciences and Teacher Education, Australian Catholic University, Brisbane, Australia

Stephen Andrews Faculty of Education, The University of Hong Kong, Hong Kong, China

Susan Margaret Bridges Faculty of Education/Centre for the Enhancement of Teaching and Learning, The University of Hong Kong, Hong Kong, China

Esther Care The Brookings Institution, Washington, DC, USA

Cheri Chan Faculty of Education, The University of Hong Kong, Hong Kong, China

Maurice Man Wai Cheng Faculty of Education, The University of Hong Kong, Hong Kong, China

Alan Cheung The Chinese University of Hong Kong, Hong Kong, China

Wai Ming Cheung Faculty of Education, The University of Hong Kong, Hong Kong, China

Andrew Coombs Faculty of Education, Queen's University, Kingston, Canada

Beverley Cooper University of Waikato, Hamilton, New Zealand

Bronwen Cowie University of Waikato, Hamilton, New Zealand

Joy Cumming Institute for Learning Sciences and Teacher Education, Australian Catholic University, Brisbane, Australia

Chantelle Day Institute for Learning Sciences and Teacher Education, Australian Catholic University, Brisbane, Australia

Christopher DeLuca Faculty of Education, Queen's University, Kingston, Canada

Anna E. Du Plessis Institute for Learning Sciences and Teacher Education, Australian Catholic University, Brisbane, Australia

Gary James Harfitt Faculty of Education, The University of Hong Kong, Hong Kong, China

Louise Hayward University of Glasgow, Glasgow, Scotland

Elizabeth Heck Institute for Learning Sciences and Teacher Education, Australian Catholic University, Brisbane, Australia

Rosemary Hipkins New Zealand Council for Educational Research (NZCER), Wellington, New Zealand

Anil Kanjee Tshwane University of Technology, Pretoria, South Africa

Chrysa Keung The Chinese University of Hong Kong, Hong Kong, China

Helyn Kim The Brookings Institution, Washington, DC, USA

Alex Kostogriz Monash University, Clayton, Australia

Carol Chan Kwai-kuen Faculty of Education, The University of Hong Kong, Hong Kong, China

Tammy Yim Lin Kwan Faculty of Education, The University of Hong Kong, Hong Kong, China

Joseph Wai Ip Lam Faculty of Education, The University of Hong Kong, Hong Kong, China

Wing-Wah Law Faculty of Education, The University of Hong Kong, Hong Kong, China

Anne Looney Dublin City University Institute of Education, Dublin, Ireland

Jo MacDonald New Zealand Council for Educational Research (NZCER), Wellington, New Zealand

Barley Mak The Chinese University of Hong Kong, Hong Kong, China

Ian Menter Department of Education, University of Oxford, Oxford, UK

Bernadette Ní Áingléis Dublin City University Institute of Education, Dublin, Ireland

Joce Nuttall Institute for Learning Sciences and Teacher Education, Australian Catholic University, Melbourne, Australia

Jina Ro National Institute of Education, Nanyang Technological University, Singapore, Singapore

Ann Sherman Faculty of Education, University of New Brunswick, Fredericton, Canada

Kari Smith Teacher Education Department, Norwegian University of Science and Technology (NTNU), Trondheim, Norway

Megan Tones Institute for Learning Sciences and Teacher Education, Australian Catholic University, Brisbane, Australia

Amy Bik May Tsui Faculty of Education, The University of Hong Kong, Hong Kong, China

Dan Wang Faculty of Education, The University of Hong Kong, Hong Kong, China

Rhoda Kuan Yun Wang Faculty of Education, The University of Hong Kong, Hong Kong, China

Jenny Whatman New Zealand Council for Educational Research (NZCER), Wellington, New Zealand

Claire Wyatt-Smith Institute for Learning Sciences and Teacher Education, Australian Catholic University, Brisbane, Australia

Pui-sze Yeung Faculty of Education, The University of Hong Kong, Hong Kong, China

List of Figures

Fig. 2.1	Norwegian teacher education	22
Fig. 5.1	Number of countries that meet the criterion in the four indicators	70
Fig. 8.1	Fidelity at the intersection of system and site validity, and responsive to tensions from system and site	125
Fig. 13.1	Diversity of students in Australian schools	202
Fig. 13.2	Coding density of identified key terms for the five international teacher education reform reports	209
Fig. 13.3	An illustration of the relationship between coding density and inclusion in international teacher education reform reports	210
Fig. 16.1	A programmatic approach to ITE	259
Fig. 18.1	Concept of a teacher	299
Fig. 18.2	PGDE integration	299
Fig. 18.3	Inquiry-based weekly cycles	300

List of Tables

Table 2.1	Tensions in teacher education at a master level	23
Table 2.2	Tensions in implementing a research based teacher education	25
Table 2.3	Tensions in the practicum	26
Table 2.4	Tensions between goal-orientation and bildung-orientation	28
Table 2.5	Tensions between control and accountability	30
Table 5.1	Description of the criteria established for the four indicators	69
Table 5.2	UNESCO's working definition of transversal competencies	72
Table 7.1	Count of conceptions of readiness across TEMAG review document	104
Table 9.1	Categorization of curriculum orientations from previous major studies	140
Table 9.2	Key characteristics of curriculum orientations to kindergarten education referring to the recommendations stated in the *2017 Guide*	144
Table 11.1	Assessment literacy themes and associated priority descriptions	178
Table 13.1	Overview of expectations in teacher professional standards regarding student diversity from six countries	204
Table 13.2	Overview of the selected sources	207
Table 16.1	Assessment for learning units and year introduced	262
Table 16.2	Sample of students responding to the questionnaire and participating in interviews	265
Table 16.3	Participant responses regarding the practicum assessment and feedback	267

Table 16.4	Participant responses regarding support received during the practicum	269
Table 16.5	Participant perceptions regarding their language assessment knowledge and skills gained	271
Table 16.6	Participant perceptions regarding their mathematics assessment knowledge and skills gained	272

Chapter 1
New Cultures in Teacher Education

Claire Wyatt-Smith and Lenore Adie

Introduction

Socio-economic and political changes as well as rapid technological advances are constant features of the present era. While many classrooms still appear more suited to models of learning and teaching practices adopted in the last century, there are loud calls for educational and assessment reform. There are also loud calls from outside education voicing concerns about the adequacy of current models of schooling and standards of teacher preparation. This is not new. It has, however, been accelerating in the context of what Sahlberg (2010) referred to as the Global Education Reform Movement (GERM). We introduce readers to this book by recognising potent forces outside education that have profound impact on human identities, how we communicate with one another locally and globally, and how we understand ourselves and our places in the world.

It is in this context of constant change that education assumes high priority in government policies, and in community and parental values in many societies. While the connections between education outcomes and economic productivity were heavily emphasised in the final decades of the last century, the twenty-first century has further intensified the interest in educational accountability and the related evidence of achievement outcomes. As part of this intensification, national and international standardised testing and reporting have become big business, with advances in machine marking offering unprecedented approaches to fast-track reporting. This is the era of the commodification of education and big data, where government appetites for

---

C. Wyatt-Smith (✉) · L. Adie
Institute for Learning Sciences and Teacher Education, Australian Catholic University, Brisbane, Australia
e-mail: Claire.Wyatt-Smith@acu.edu.au

© Springer Nature Singapore Pte Ltd. 2018
C. Wyatt-Smith and L. Adie (eds.), *Innovation and Accountability in Teacher Education*, Teacher Education, Learning Innovation and Accountability, https://doi.org/10.1007/978-981-13-2026-2_1

achievement data appear insatiable. Perhaps not surprisingly, in many countries the appetite for data extends beyond governments with parents having expectations about going online for a wide range of school and individual student performance information.

At the same time, there has been increasing recognition of the vital links between educational opportunities, youth learning and life chances. High quality and high equity have become latched together in the discourse of education policy with curriculum initiatives reflecting a broadened interest in developing young people's well-being, creativity, innovation and problem-solving skills, individually and in teams. In part, this movement reflects the increasing interest in student voice and agency in learning, and recognition of how the transfer and application of knowledge to solve new problems and pose new questions will be essential for young people's futures.

Within this complex mix of influences, teacher education and student learning have come to centre stage. The issue of schooling quality and more broadly the continuing relevance of schooling have been closely linked to the quality and impact of initial teacher education (ITE) programs on student outcomes. In what is undoubtedly a powerful policy driver in several countries, the illusive notion of teacher quality is regarded as a major determinant of the overall quality of a country's schooling system. The logic is clear: improved teacher quality is the critical element for improved learning outcomes.

Education systems characterised as high performing (or aspiring to be so classified) have invested in enhancing the initial education of teachers in a range of ways. For example, some countries have introduced the requirement for teaching to be studied at the advanced master's level as a postgraduate qualification. More commonly, 'student teachers' are educated in academic universities where the academic program and engagement with theory are integrated with school-based learning of teaching practice in a coordinated approach to teacher preparation. An additional pillar of these systems is the professional image of teaching as an attractive career choice: admission to teacher education is seen as highly competitive and intellectually demanding, offering stable and secure job opportunities.

Against the backdrop of global changes and national initiatives in teacher education, there is a need to grapple with the issues of evidence and quality in initial teacher education, and investigate how evidence may inform teacher education into the twenty-first century. Thus, we consider the role of (i) professional standards that promote deep reflection and advance the capacity of the profession; and (ii) authentic and situated teacher performance assessments that attempt to integrate theory and practice and recast teacher education as a practice of enacted collaboration. Following this, readers are introduced to the suite of chapters as portraits of change ecologies in initial teacher education.

Need for Research in Initial Teacher Education

In this foundation book, we recognise three forces that constitute a crucible of change in teacher education. First are the numerous national reviews and reform agendas that assert the need to improve quality in initial teacher education and, in turn, student learning and achievement. Importantly, the research evidence showing how to establish quality of ITE programs and their impact on student learning is in its infancy. However, the calls for action have been numerous and loud. In the last decade, official national reviews have taken place in countries including Scotland (Donaldson 2010), Wales (Furlong 2015), Northern Ireland (Sahlberg et al. 2014), the Republic of Ireland (Department of Education and Skills 2012), Australia (Craven et al. 2014), the USA (Cochran-Smith et al. 2013) and England (Carter 2014).

Second is the already strong and growing interest of government in evidence of the quality and effectiveness of schooling, together with advances in technologies for increasing the efficiency of testing, machine marking and the timeliness of reporting. Such advances make possible an immediacy of knowledge exchange about performance in ways not previously possible. Such testing is now being deployed in some countries as part of efforts to screen candidates on entry to teacher education as well as in various hurdle assessments or tests as prerequisites for program completion and initial registration for entering the workforce. For example, in 2016 Australia adopted as national education policy the requirement that beginning teachers must sit and pass a battery of online skills tests of 'personal' literacy and numeracy known as Literacy and Numeracy Test in Initial Teacher Education (LANTITE) before course completion (Australian Council for Educational Research [ACER] 2018).

Third are the repeated and increasingly loud calls for improving the quality of teachers' preparation. While the calls have some variation, they tend to highlight common issues. These include, for example, strengthening the evidence base that universities and those responsible for teacher education use in designing and implementing programs to integrate theory and practice. The optimum balance between academic programs and practicum or school-placement experiences is of high interest. In regard to the evidence base for teaching, it is worth noting that while there have been numerous research-informed reviews of teacher education, and seminal studies including meta-analyses of teacher preparation and certification (Cochran-Smith and Villegas 2015), as a field, teacher education research has tended to be dominated by small-scale studies. The potential of such work to respond to the current populist calls for evidence of 'what works' is limited, the simple reason being that generalisability beyond the sample of these small studies cannot be made. Added to this is the observation made more than two decades ago by Kennedy (1996) that:

> Primarily quantitative research on teacher education, intended to inform policy and policy makers, was often more familiar to sceptics and critics of teacher education, including economists and policy analysts, than to teacher educators themselves. (Kennedy, cited in Cochran-Smith and Villegas 2015, p. 8)

Teacher Professional Standards and Performance Assessments

Within this complex environment is the increasing interest of governments internationally in standards, performance assessments, recognition schemes and remuneration. Professional standards are considered the hallmark of a profession and associated with accreditation or entry into the guild of professional knowledge, skills and dispositions. Medical, legal and business communities have statements of standards that define what it means to be recognised within that community—what is necessary knowledge, how to use knowledge in practice, how to be and interact with others, and as an extension, how to address ethical practice requirements. In effect, the standards and related evidence are the linchpin for inferring that a practitioner is ready for safe, independent practice.

While teachers have always been regulated by codes of conduct, the articulation of professional standards places higher expectations for evidence-based practice. There are moves in several countries to strengthen the role of accreditation agencies with responsibilities for setting and monitoring professional standards for teaching and school leadership. This is reflected in the already strong and growing focus on professional standards and school and teacher performance data analytics. Teacher professional standards are now in place in many countries and represent a relatively recent arrival in initial teacher education in some.

Broadly speaking, the main purpose of professional standards is to formalise and communicate expectations of the profession at different career stages. While the nomenclature varies across contexts, essentially standards are intended to capture official expectations of the Beginning Teacher and, in some countries, the Advanced or Master Teacher through to leadership positions (see, e.g. DeLuca et al. 2015). Accompanying this development is a growing research interest in how standards represent teachers' work (Hayward and Wyse 2016; Wyatt-Smith and Looney 2016), and the developmental progression of a teacher's learning within the profession. It is irrefutable that teaching is complex; measures of teaching effectiveness are therefore difficult to identify and disentangle from other contextual factors. However, in attempts to establish an evidence base to show the effectiveness of ITE, it is arguable that professional standards (their nature and function) are fundamentally significant. Optimally, standards represent meaningful goals for preservice teachers and markers of quality for career progression for practicing teachers. The goal in standard-setting, as applied to performance assessment or at the program level, 'should not be to increase the failure rates of candidates but to improve the calibre of their preparation for the real tasks of teaching' (Darling-Hammond 2004, p. 46).

Criticisms of statements of professional standards are predominantly concerned with the promulgation of prescriptive lists of atomised knowledge and skills, with the expectation of replication across diverse contexts (Furlong 2015). The alternate perspective, and that endorsed in this chapter, is to view standards through a lens of intelligent accountability (O'Neill 2013). From this perspective, and referring to teaching, statements of standards can be understood to function as professional development tools that support reflection and that allow for the study of teaching as centring on student learning, interaction and knowledge: 'what teachers do, say, and think *with students, concerning knowledge*, in a particular social organisation of instruction' (Cohen and Ball 2001, cited in Darling-Hammond 2004, p. 47).

Participation in professional communities has been represented through various models of learning progression. For example, Miller's (1990) framework for clinical assessment represents successful participation in the medical community through levels of knowledge, competence, performance and action. We add to this framework by proposing that being a professional in the twenty-first century must also include skills of reflexivity—to learn from practice, and to act on that learning, which is in line with our conceptualisation of professional standards as guiding efforts to achieve intelligent accountability. Reflecting on practice with self and others 'stimulates professional learning through assisting educators to consider their values and to transform their practice through examining the implications of new theoretical perspectives' (Colmer 2017, p. 437). It also extends to a willingness to reflect on and monitor the impact of practice on others, in the case of teaching, colleagues and students.

When professional standards are understood as supporting the agency of the profession and individual teachers, then the focus in teacher education is on preparing teachers to be active professionals who are able to bring an inquiry approach to their practice and a willingness to 'see' its impact on student learning. Through connecting intelligent accountability into teacher education, preservice teachers would examine and provide evidence of their actions and decisions—that is, their thinking about their teaching—with an emphasis on why this is important for student learning, and how student learning has been progressed, or alternatively, met with barriers to progress. In teachers' reflexive practice, the focus is on promoting and progressing student learning, placing the student in the centre of decisions and actions. Thus, we position student classroom learning at the centre of teaching and assessment, and in turn, at the centre of the evidence required for effective practice.

We revisit this line of sight to possible teacher education futures after introducing the suite of chapters in the book in the following section. While each chapter in this book takes a particular focus within the broad field of teacher education, as a set they show how changes are underway in the contexts and cultures of teacher education.

Introducing the Chapters and Authors

Part 1 of the book takes up the topic of Accountability and Change in Teacher Education, with the chapters offering diverse perspectives on what this means in practice. Kari Smith, Norwegian University of Science and Technology (NTNU), Norway, presents an account of Accountability in Teacher Education in Norway, with a provocative title, *A Case of Mistrust and Trust*. Norwegian teacher education has been subject to numerous reforms in the last decade, the most recent one, requiring all teacher education programs to be at a master's level, took effect August

2017. The initiatives are policy instigated and heavily influenced by international trends characterised by an increasing demand for accountability, as raised earlier in this chapter. At the same time, society, including politicians, are apprehensive to explicitly talk about external control and accountability. Kari highlights the tension between accountability and responsibility that characterises the Norwegian case. There is also a tension between traditional values and international accountability, between external and internal accountability and responsibility. She posits that the concept of 'intelligent accountability' could be a way to balance accountability and responsibility requirements in Norway. This chapter sheds light on the tension between mistrust and trust, accountability and responsibility in Norwegian teacher education.

Louise Hayward's portrait of teacher education, learning innovation and accountability in Scotland highlights both global influences, policy issues and the mediating influences of the country's traditions and culture. In her chapter, *Notes from a Small Country*, her starting point, which is common across many of the chapters, is the observation that internationally, twenty-first century teacher education is enmeshed in a globalised world where the only constants are sociocultural and economic change. This chapter examines these ideas critically in the context of Teacher Education policy in Scotland. Although Scotland has not been immune to the influences of the Global Educational Reform Movement, its impact has been mediated by its traditions and culture. Louise concludes that consensual change in Teacher Education in Scotland has been possible for three reasons. First, the firm location of teacher education in higher education and within a series of complex stakeholder partnerships. Second, the generally respectful relationships across Scotland's educational communities and, third, the largely positive attitude to teaching and teachers in Scottish society, often sustained despite the media. However, although recent reports have praised the Professional Standards that lie at the heart of Teacher Education in Scotland, they have identified a remaining challenge—to ensure high-quality enactment across the country. If teacher education in Scotland is to continue to be trusted and accountability systems are to remain learning focused, then the challenge of high-quality, consistent enactment needs to be addressed. The chapter's connections across trust, accountability systems and quality resonate with the preceding discussion, pointing to some recurring themes across the chapters.

Jina Ro presents reflections on learning to teach in the era of test-based accountability in the USA, using a telling title, *Lost in Translation: Learning to Teach in the Era of Test-Based Accountability*. She offers a portrait of different levels of accountability and explores their implications for the experience of becoming a teacher. This chapter starts with the observation that neoliberalism has been increasing its impact on the educational policy landscapes in many nations in a way that leads to emphasise test-based accountability mandates. In the USA, the federal government has been gradually strengthening its accountability control by implementing high-stakes testing and using student performance data for teacher evaluation. She makes clear how teacher education programs are facing intense demands to produce high-quality teachers who are capable of improving student performance. Yet many teacher education programs in the USA tend to emphasise different pedagogy, such as culturally responsive teaching and constructivist methods that are often in conflict with the practices favoured by the accountability mandates. Acknowledging that this tendency may cause a significant challenge to beginning teachers who are new to the profession, this chapter analyses the preservice learning and current practices of three American beginning teachers who work in three different levels of accountability contexts: high, moderate and low accountability. A disconnection between the teachers' preservice education and their current practices, regardless of their accountability contexts and the preparation they experienced, is identified. The discussion suggests that developing teacher candidates' 'inquiry stance' is a necessary inclusion in teacher education. She proposes that this approach encourages them to lead their professional learning individually and collectively by questioning the taken-for-granted practices and deliberating on ways to improve their practices within and against the challenging accountability landscapes.

The preceding chapters set a strong backdrop for Esther Care's and Helyn Kim's exploration of *The Explicit Nature of Educational Goals for the Twenty-first Century*. The chapter includes evidence of a shift in education towards an endorsement of the value of acquisition of generalisable skills by students in their formal years of education. The skills of interest are often referred to as twenty-first century skills. The central question raised in this chapter concerns how education systems need to shift to accommodate an explicit focus on development of twenty-first century skills rather than adoption of broad frameworks. The position taken is that this shift cannot be successfully undertaken by a focus on curriculum alone. The issue is discussed through highlighting evidence of, and challenges to, the shift through a global mapping of education systems' adoption of skills' agenda; and a regional study which explored assessment of twenty-first century skills. Recommendations include the defining of key skills, development of practical approaches to early implementation through use of learning progressions and active pedagogies, and consideration of implications for teacher education. The chapter challenges readers to refocus discussions about accountability, narrowly defined, without a far broader frame of twenty-first century skills, learning progressions, pedagogical practices, teacher capacity and transversal competencies.

Rosemary Hipkins, Jo MacDonald and Jenny Whatman carry forward the theme of challenges in their discussion of educating beginning teachers to respond to twenty-first century learning imperatives. These challenges include: rethinking purposes for learning in response to the addition of new curriculum elements such as competencies or capabilities; using a wider range of pedagogies that respond more appropriately to diversity, including epistemic elements in curriculum knowledge; and making more effective use of e-learning, often in combination with working in 'modern learning environments' (Osborne 2013). They put forward the powerful point about what could be described as generational change in teaching: If established teachers are struggling to respond to these complex challenges, how are beginning teachers to learn to teach in ways they were not taught themselves? The chapter draws on evaluations of two recent teacher learning initiatives in New Zealand, and a recently completed literature scan, to explore the challenges of mentoring beginning teachers for today's classrooms. Overall, this chapter shines a spotlight on future-focused education and shows how mentoring beginning teachers involves futures thinking and practice.

While chapters can be read in any order, the editors have sequenced the chapters to build from discussions of accountability, through to consideration of twenty-first century learning and teacher preparation. Following this are chapters that take up different conceptions of 'readiness' in initial teacher education: What does it mean to say that a graduate of teacher education in the twenty-first century is ready—prepared and accountable—for classroom practice? Colette Alexander's chapter brings forward contested issues of quality and standards, how to discern the impact of teacher education preparation, and the notion of evidence in policy/political directives in the case of Australia. She presents a context where the quality and impact of ITE are increasingly being bound up with notions of evidence of graduate performance in relation to professional standards and evidence of the impact of graduates on school student performance. In this chapter, the conception of readiness and its relationship to ITE and educational concerns about the politically derived conception of readiness are examined. The analysis shows that there is a lack of consistent language or agreed definition of readiness which is manifested in competing discursive understandings and the misalignment of expectations for ITE. The chapter proposes a justification for the emerging conceptualisation of readiness for the profession as critical to quality initial teacher education that will impact positively on educational outcomes for all students. While Australia has had national standards in place for some years (Australian Professional Standards for Teachers, Australian Institute for Teaching and School Leadership 2011), the function of the standards in reshaping teaching, policy, preparation and practice remains a work-in-progress.

In a further presentation of ITE reform, Lenore Adie and Claire Wyatt-Smith open the discussion of the introduction in Australia of new Teaching Performance Assessments (TPAs). These are expected to function as summative, authentic assessments of beginning teachers' preparedness to enter the teaching profession. The chapter therefore is another angle on the policy-driven efforts to reshape teaching preparation and in turn, practice. The authors present a research-informed conceptualisation and design principles of Teaching Performance Assessments. This move to TPAs represents a new frontier in Australian teacher education. The authors explore the notion of system and site validity as integral to the conceptualisation and design of TPAs where they are expected to be embedded in diverse sociocultural contexts. Further, they examine the assessment notion of fidelity of implementation. Using the case of one Australian TPA, the Graduate Teacher Performance Assessment (GTPA), the authors locate fidelity at the intersection of the system and site validity and identify and bring into relief risks to fidelity of TPA implementation, as a policy reform. The contribution of this chapter in part is the linking of standards to notions of system and site validity and assessment fidelity at the point of implementation of reform.

In the second part of the book, attention turns to preparing teachers for diverse learners and contexts. Barley Mak, Chrysa Keung and Alan Cheung (The Chinese University of Hong Kong) lead readers through a critical review and analysis of *Curriculum Orientations of Kindergarten Curriculum*, with reference to the official document *Kindergarten Education Curriculum Guide* (Curriculum Development Council 2017) in Hong Kong. They use the concept of five curriculum orientations (academic, cognitive process, social reconstruction, humanistic and technological) as a lead analytical tool. The analysis covers the curriculum framework, curriculum planning, learning and teaching, and assessment. Their findings reveal that social reconstruction and cognitive process orientations are two main components identified in the current kindergarten curricula. With an increased focus on children's well-being, a humanistic orientation is also evident in the curricula. The authors point to the emphasis on providing each child with intrinsically rewarding experiences that contribute to their whole-person development. The study affirms the importance of curriculum orientations in formulating teachers' practices of curriculum design and corresponding curriculum decisions. The practical significances and policy implications of this orientation are discussed.

Continuing the focus on learners and each child, Joce Nuttall asserts that policy reforms in initial teacher education in Australia have typically omitted the early childhood sector. This chapter adopts a cultural-historical perspective to explain this persistent neglect. Obvious explanations, such as the location of early childhood education outside the compulsory education sector, are noted. It then argues that recent policy attention to early childhood education internationally makes this neglect increasingly difficult for teacher education policy-makers to sustain. Five emerging dimensions of teaching in the early childhood sector in Australia, including regulatory demands to increase the supply of degree-qualified teachers, are offered as evidence for the likelihood of teacher education policy reform reaching into early childhood education in the near future. The chapter concludes with proposals for research directions urgently needed to inform such reforms. The powerful message is that neglect of early childhood education cannot continue, but major questions remain about the type of actions needed for productive change in this phase of learning.

Presenting the contexts of Canada, Christopher DeLuca, Andrew Coombs and Ann Sherman take up the thorny issues of preparing teachers for assessment in schools. In this chapter, they shine the spotlight on the influence of teacher educators. The authors carefully connect the issues of influence and teacher candidates' learning and beliefs in educational assessment. They take up the notion of readiness, explored earlier in the context of Australian ITE reform, and consider how teacher educators shape teacher candidates' readiness for classroom assessment and how they might be mediating teacher candidates' classroom experiences. Despite their potential influence, there has been limited scholarship devoted to exploring teacher educators' approaches to assessment and the direct influence of accountability across schools in North America and in many other parts of the world. Studying how teachers are prepared in the area of assessment is both timely and critical. They present data on teacher educators' approaches to assessment with consideration for how these approaches might shape teacher candidates' readiness for practice. This chapter opens the space for considering how preservice teachers may well be required to learn how to teach, and indeed, how to unlearn some of the practices that they took for granted in how to interact with learners and knowledge in the classroom.

Bronwen Cowie and Beverley Cooper present their insights into the complex work of university-based teacher educators and the shifts that have occurred in expectations for student learning, of student teachers on graduation, and of teachers in New Zealand. They argue that university-based teacher educators need to be able to support teachers to respond to these changes, while simultaneously meeting the expectations associated with their university roles. They present New Zealand as a case study to explore some of the convergences across school curriculum goals, university graduate attributes and teacher performance standards for graduating and practicing teachers. They give readers insights into how making connections across contexts, ideas and activities is a sophisticated process, one that relies on high level skill, a disposition to make links, and sensitivity to occasions where this might be possible and productive. Drawing on their work and that of colleagues, they detail how mathematical thinking and an emphasis on lifelong learning can be seen as embedded in school goals, graduate attributes and teacher practicing standards. Kress (2000) asserted we just need to learn how to see; the examples are offered to illustrate how this seeing might be cultivated through initial teacher education and teacher learning.

Continuing the focus on learning and learners, Joy Cumming, Megan Tones, Chantelle Day and Elizabeth Heck take up the high-priority area of *Enhancing Inclusive Education through Teacher Education Reforms*. They examine the extent to which teacher education reforms identify preparation of teachers to engage with the diversity of students encountered in classrooms. The philosophical stance they take is a human rights equity perspective, where all students have the right to a quality education, endorsed through international treaties and conventions, as well as by legislation in many countries. The theoretical and conceptual stance they take in the chapter is the goal of inclusive education valuing all learners equally and enabling optimal learning for all. Two matters are identified in their review for future teacher education programs and research. First, there is a need to investigate the extent to which new teachers are prepared for inclusive education, including evidence-based practices to achieve the most effective preparation. Second, and perhaps more significantly, they put forward that there is a need to develop greater understanding of the emotions, beliefs, values and attitudes of teacher education staff and students. In advancing this they advocate for opportunities throughout programs to reflect on these dimensions to enable implementation of the spirit of inclusive education. In this piece, readers are invited to consider how pedagogical knowledge, and knowledge of curriculum and assessment practices can be extended to intersect with attitudes and dispositions, values, beliefs and emotions that not only shape, but some would argue constitute, teacher identity.

Anna Du Plessis's chapter takes a focus on conceptualising the becoming of a teacher. She argues that the challenge for education leaders who seek improvements in schooling is to adopt a holistic view of quality education in schooling and its alignment with ITE preparation and graduate teachers' first placements. In this portrait, the focus is on the complex employment conditions of graduate teachers and what it means in relation to their expected preparedness for the teaching profession. One of the topics explored is the implication of graduate teachers' placements in subject areas or year levels for which they are not suitably qualified. The research has shown that prospective teachers choose teaching as a career because of their passion and interest for a specific subject or context. Initial teacher education programs further prepare graduate teachers with specific content knowledge and pedagogical content knowledge. Graduate teachers struggle to develop a professional identity if they are placed in different out-of-field positions year after year. The chapter concludes with a reflection on views published in the national and international literature about quality teacher education and the realities of new graduates' entrance into the workforce.

In the third part of the book, the gaze shifts to focus on the critical contributions of partnerships and professional cultures. Using empirical data from a large-scale study, Alex Kostogriz takes a sharp focus on *Early Career Teachers' Perceptions of Initial Teacher Education*, addressing phenomenology of perceptions and transition from university to work. He discusses how beginning teachers perceive their preparedness for work, drawing on findings from the *Studying the Effectiveness of Teacher Education* (SETE) project (Mayer et al. 2017). The goal of this longitudinal project was to explore graduate teachers' experiences in Australia in order to understand their perceptions of teacher preparation and teaching in the early years of their career. In doing so, the study sought to understand: first, how graduates and principals perceived how effective teacher education programs were in preparing graduates for the diverse settings in which they take up teaching employment; second, whether there were any aspects of the teacher education programs that linked to their preparedness for teaching and their effectiveness as beginning teachers; and third, the career and employment pathways of the new teachers as well as retention and attrition. In this chapter, the focus is on the teachers' experience of perception as they transition across professional spaces between universities and schools. The transitional synthesis of perceptions has wide-ranging implications for understanding the utility of teacher education in and through situated experiences of beginning teachers in schools.

Professional experience school placements, sometimes referred to as the practicum, have been recognised as valuable elements of ITE. Anil Kanjee, Tshwane University of Technology, South Africa, calls readers to revisit the teaching practicum and examine whether they serve to effect innovation or entrench the status quo. His chapter presents reflections from an ITE program in South Africa. Referring to this context, he shows how developing programs that adequately prepare teachers to address the key challenges of quality and equity in schools remains an ongoing challenge in the new, democratic South Africa. While the positive effects resulting from program changes are reported and encouraging, he also notes several challenges regarding preservice teachers' preparedness to address issues of inclusivity and deal with the challenge of the different languages of learning and teaching at schools. In the conclusion of the chapter, readers are challenged to consider the durability of positive changes in ITE insofar as they impact on preservice teachers' practice as they enter the teaching profession: what remains unknown is whether newly acquired knowledge and skills learnt in initial teacher education, especially with regards to assessment, will impact on graduate classroom practices to address the challenges of improving learning for all.

Continuing the focus on professional experience placements, Bernadette Ní Áingléis and Anne Looney respond to policy in practice as it relates to what they refer to as school-based work in ITE. They start from the position that various constellations of school–university partnerships (SUPs) have long been part of the ITE landscape in Ireland. This situation is especially true in the context of ITE school-based work. While SUPs have been largely informal and unsystematic, recent policy changes have introduced structured roles and responsibilities for schools and for universities. Their chapter explores schools' and universities' responses to these policy changes. In common with the preceding chapter, this chapter serves to position student teachers within the complexity of school–university partnerships, initial teacher education academic program expectations, the national context where the role of the teacher is valued, and where the examination systems serve to mark key junctures in schooling. Once again, the emerging theme is of linking theory and practice and the roles and responsibilities in ITE, a theme that is clear in the next chapter.

Susan Bridges and her co-authors present their collective experience of *Designing for Integration in Initial Teacher Education (ITE) Curricula*: The Hong Kong Postgraduate Diploma in Education (PGDE). These authors recognise how discussions of ITE programs have indicated prevailing concerns regarding the linking of theory and practice with ongoing student criticisms that the theoretical, academic content of their degrees was the least helpful in preparing them for classroom teaching (Ure 2009). While competency-based movements underscored by craft-based, apprenticeship philosophies can offer much in 'training' teachers, they highlight that UK scholars, among others, perceive a general failure to connect teachers with theory and evidence (Menter 2013). They argue for the need for new curriculum models in ITE that can achieve practice-based outcomes as well as foster flexible thinkers able to design and adapt learning experiences in fluid and rapidly changing knowledge societies. In their chapter, they elaborate on the guiding philosophy and curriculum model of a new postgraduate ITE curriculum launched in the 2016–17 academic year by the Faculty of Education, The University of Hong Kong. Specifically, they articulate how an inquiry-based design was employed to address the central curriculum reform goal of integration of theory and practice.

In the final chapter of the book, Ian Menter explores some of the key underlying forces impacting on teacher education internationally. The effect of globalisation on curriculum and assessment processes with increased prescription and accountability, in particular on core skills such as literacy and numeracy, is evident. Menter connects this attention to the construct of teacher education as a policy problem and in urgent need of reform. In the competitive world of education with each nation vying for top position on international achievement measures, distinctive responses are evident, as illustrated in this book, yet the impact of globalisation reveals a similarity in the responses across nations. Menter draws on his experience of teacher education in the UK to illustrate how these common reform issues play out in a recognisable yet distinctive manner. In the final section of this chapter, Menter identifies six themes from which teacher education globally may be portrayed and evaluated—professional status, the place of research as an evidence base, partnerships, governance, performability and accountability, and digitisation. The themes present a common framework for teacher education on which international collaboration and comparative research can go forward to establish a needed evidence base.

Conclusion

Collectively, the chapters offer readers insider accounts of the complex ecologies of teacher education—different ways of seeing the preparation of teachers in times of global change. The chapters remind us that teacher preparation is situated practice. It is always and inextricably intertwined with culture and context and, by extension, attitudes, values and ways of thinking about schooling, communities, change and the place of teachers and students in efforts to shape the world. The editors invite readers to consider the accounts of ways of doing and ways of being in particular contexts (countries, states, institutions), with change being the common phenomenon across contexts.

In conclusion, we offer the chapters as opening new ways of thinking about fundamental questions: Who are the actors in teacher preparation and how do they interact? How can we know about the quality of teacher education? Where can we hear the voices of teacher educators and preservice teachers, as well as school-based teacher educators? What are the new and emerging roles of others in teacher education who have not been involved previously, including employing authorities? These questions need answers, reflecting how the field of teacher education research is in its infancy and represents a crucible of change. Moreover, they resonate with how Hargreaves and O'Connor (2017) described collaboration as 'the new chorus line for innovation and improvement' (p. 1). Joining these two authors, we propose that readers see in the chapters the challenges of achieving effectiveness in the collaboration that is of utmost importance in our present 'critical times' (Menter 2013), while addressing the thorny issues of evidence and quality in teacher education.

References

Australian Council for Educational Research [ACER]. (2018). *Literacy and numeracy test for initial teacher education students*. Retrieved March 22, 2018 from https://teacheredtest.acer.edu.au/.
Australian Institute for Teaching and School Leadership [AITSL]. (2011). *Australian professional standards for teachers*. Retrieved May 1, 2017 from https://www.aitsl.edu.au/australian-professional-standards-for-teachers/standards/overview/organisation-of-the-standards.
Carter, A. (2014). *Carter review of initial teacher training (England): Call for evidence*. Retrieved March 2, 2018 from https://www.gov.uk/government/uploads/system/uploads/attachment_data/file/346051/Consultation_Document_-_Carter_Review_Final.pdf.

Cochran-Smith, M., Piazza, P., & Power, C. (2013). The politics of accountability: Assessing teacher education in the United States. *The Educational Forum, 77,* 6–27. https://doi.org/10.1080/00131725.2013.73901.

Cochran-Smith, M., & Villegas, A. (2015). Framing teacher preparation research: An overview of the field, Part 1. *Journal of Teacher Education, 66*(1), 7–20. https://doi.org/10.1177/0022487114549072.

Colmer, K. (2017). Collaborative professional learning: Contributing to the growth of leadership, professional identity and professionalism. *European Early Childhood Education Research Journal, 25*(3), 436–449. https://doi.org/10.1080/1350293X.2017.1308167.

Craven, G., Beswick, K., Fleming, J., Fletcher, T., Green, M., Jensen, B., et al. (2014). *Action now: Classroom ready teachers.* Retrieved April 30, 2017 from https://docs.education.gov.au/system/files/doc/other/action_now_classroom_ready_teachers_print.pdf.

Curriculum Development Council [CDC]. (2017). *Kindergarten education curriculum guide [Draft].* Hong Kong: Government Printer. Retrieved October 26, 2017 from http://www.edb.gov.hk/attachment/en/curriculum-development/major-level-of-edu/preprimary/KGECG-En-Draft-2017.pdf.

Darling-Hammond, L. (2004). Reshaping teaching policy, preparation, and practice: Influences of the national board for professional teaching standards. In R. E. Stake, S. Kushner, L. Ingvarson, & J. Hattie (Eds.), *Assessing teachers for professional certification: The first decade of the National Board for Professional Teaching Standards (Advances in Program Evaluation)* (Vol. 11, pp. 25–53). Bradford, England: Emerald Group Publishing Limited.

DeLuca, C., LaPointe-McEwan, D., & Luhanga, U. (2015). Teacher assessment literacy: A review of international standards and measures. *Educational Assessment, Evaluation and Accountability,* 1–22. https://doi.org/10.1007/s11092-015-9233-6.

Department of Education and Skills [DES]. (2012). *Report of the international review panel on the structure of initial teacher education provision in Ireland: Review conducted on behalf of the Department of Education and Skills (Sahlberg Report).* Retrieved December 2, 2017 from https://www.education.ie/en/Press-Events/Press-Releases/2012-Press-Releases/Report-of-the-International-Review-Panel-on-the-Structure-of-Initial-Teacher-Education-Provision-in-Ireland.pdf.

Donaldson, G. (2010). *Teaching Scotland's future: Report of a review of teacher education in Scotland.* Edinburgh, Scotland: Scottish Government.

Furlong, J. (2015). *Teaching tomorrow's teachers. Options for the future of initial teacher education in Wales.* Retrieved January 16, 2018 from http://gov.wales/docs/dcells/publications/150309-teaching-tomorrows-teachers-final.pdf.

Hargreaves, A. & O'Connor, M. T. (2017). *Collaborative professionalism.* Retrieved from http://www.wise-qatar.org/sites/default/files/rr.12.2017_boston.pdf.

Hayward, L., & Wyse, D. (Eds.). (2016). *Handbook on curriculum, pedagogy and assessment.* London, England: Routledge.

Kress, G. (2000). "You've just got to learn how to see": Curriculum subjects, young people and schooled engagement with the world. *Linguistics and Education, 11*(4), 401–415. https://doi.org/10.1016/S0898-5898(00)00030-9.

Mayer, D., Dixon, M., Kline, J., Kostogriz, A., Moss, J., et al. (2017). *Studying the effectiveness of teacher education: Early career teachers in diverse settings.* Singapore: Springer.

Menter, I. (2013). From interesting times to critical times? Teacher education and educational research in England. *Research in Teacher Education, 3*(1), 38–40. Retrieved from http://hdl.handle.net/10552/1961.

Miller, G. E. (1990). The assessment of clinical skills/competence/performance. *Academic Medicine, 65*(9), 563–567.

O'Neill, O. (2013). Intelligent accountability in education. *Oxford Review of Education, 39*(1), 4–16. https://doi.org/10.1080/03054985.2013.764761.

Osborne, M. (2013). *Modern learning environments (CORE Education white paper)*. Christchurch, New Zealand: Core Education. Retrieved January 12, 2018 from http://www.core-ed.org/legacy/sites/core-ed.org/files/Modern-Learning-Environments-v.1.pdf?url=/sites/core-ed.org/files/Modern-Learning-Environments-v.1.pdf.

Sahlberg, P. (2010). *Finnish lessons*. Columbia, SC: Teachers' College Press.

Sahlberg, P., Broadfoot, P., Coolahan, J., Furlong, J., & Kirk, G. (2014). *Aspiring to excellence. Final report of the international review panel on the structure of initial teacher education in Northern Ireland (Report to the Minister for Employment and Learning)*. Belfast, Ireland: Department for Employment and Learning.

Ure, C. (2009). *Practicum partnerships: Exploring models of practicum organisation in teacher education for a standards-based profession*. Strawberry Hills, Australia: Australian Learning and Teaching Council.

Wyatt-Smith, C., & Looney, A. (2016). Professional standards and the assessment work of teachers. In L. Hayward & D. Wyse (Eds.), *Handbook on curriculum, pedagogy and assessment* (pp. 805–820). London, England: Routledge.

Claire Wyatt-Smith is the Director of the Institute for Learning Sciences and Teacher Education (ILSTE) and Professor of Educational Assessment and Evaluation, Australian Catholic University. Her research is focused on teaching and evaluative expertise. It examines the role of standards, professional judgement and moderation, as well as the use of data to inform teaching and improve learning. She acts as an advisor to various agencies within Australia and internationally, and is currently leading a large-scale Australian study involving a national collective of universities undertaking the Graduate Teacher Performance Assessment and cross-institutional standard-referenced moderation. Recent books include *Assessment for education: Standards, judgement and moderation* (Sage 2014), and *Designing assessment for quality learning* (Springer 2014). In addition to the Series, *Teacher Education, Learning Innovation and Accountability*, she is the Foundation Editor of *The Enabling Power of Assessment Series*.

Lenore Adie is Associate Professor of Teacher Education and Assessment, and a Senior Research Fellow with the Assessment, Evaluation and Student Learning Research concentration in the Institute for Learning Sciences and Teacher Education (ILSTE), Australian Catholic University. Her research focuses on assessment and moderation processes as these contribute to supporting teachers' pedagogical practices and student learning. She has a further interest in the enactment of assessment policy and the validity of assessment processes. Her research has generated new knowledge in the field of assessment focussing on quality in assessment practices and processes, in particular within systems of standard-referenced assessment. This work addresses the alignment of curriculum, assessment and pedagogic practices through the design of assessment tasks and the application of criteria and grading. She has extensive professional experience working in schools as a teacher and within leadership positions, and in teacher education for over 30 years.

Part I
Accountability and Change in Teacher Education

Chapter 2
Accountability in Teacher Education in Norway: A Case of Mistrust and Trust

Kari Smith

Introduction

When discussing *Assessment and Accountability in Teacher Education* in the Norwegian context it needs to be placed within the backdrop of international trends in teacher education, and more specifically, within the framework of European regulations and cooperation. Norway, as a small country of five million people, seeks inspiration and knowledge from other countries and eagerly adapts (or perhaps adopts) international trends to the national framework. This is also the case of assessment and accountability. At the same time, however, national educational traditions and beliefs are deeply rooted in the educational system, and policy makers seem to struggle to find a balance between international trends and the national context. Thus, the Norwegian case appears to be a description of a context which can best be characterized as a combination of trust and mistrust between teacher education institutions and the political system.

The most significant European motion for higher education throughout Europe is the Bologna process from 1999, which is a series of meetings and agreements between 29 European countries to ensure comparability in the standards and quality of higher-education qualifications. The process is grounded in the Sorbonne Conference and declaration from 1998. Today, the official signatory countries are 47, and the initiatives and agreements developed have truly changed higher education in the member countries. The most important motions noted by the European Commission/EACEA/Eurydice (2015) are:

- Developing a three cycles circle of higher education—most commonly explained as 3 + 2 + 3. The first cycle (Bachelor degree) consists of 180–240 European Credit

K. Smith (✉)
Teacher Education Department, Norwegian University of Science and Technology (NTNU), Trondheim, Norway
e-mail: Kari.smith@plu.ntnu.no

Transfer System (ECTS), 120 ECTS for the second cycle (master degree), and in 2003, the third cycle was added (doctoral degree).
- Developing a ECTS for study points which is acknowledged by all member states and therefore simplifies mobility and European accreditation of degrees.
- Developing a framework for quality assurance systems which includes internal, external and recently, also cross-national quality assurance activities.

For the purpose of this chapter, it is mainly the quality assurance directives which are of interest, and which to a certain extent reflects a picture of mistrust and trust also at the European level. This is the case even though it is clearly stated in the Bologna documents that the quality assurance standards are means to build up trusts between the countries (European Commission/EACEA/Eurydice 2015).

The quality assurance system can be said to have three, if not four levels. The first level is the internal level, and the institutions are encouraged to build up their own quality assurance systems in the form of ongoing self-evaluation. The second level of quality assurance is national and most often conducted by agencies which have been given the responsibility by the national government to accredit programs, evaluate existing programs, staff competence, research activity, and also, perhaps to a lesser degree, evaluate the quality of teaching. The latter is difficult to measure and therefore also difficult to assess. The third level is at the European level as the national agencies are expected to be registered in the European Assurance Register for Higher Education, and they are subjected to evaluation of their work to achieve registration. The increasing fourth level is the cross-country quality assurance activities, meaning that the agency of one country can evaluate the quality of institutions in another country (European Commission/EACEA/Eurydice 2015). So, it is a legitimate question to ask if this elaborated quality assurance system is a question of trust or mistrust. Norway is one of the countries which is most obedient to the European directives and has fully implemented them in its higher education system. This will be further discussed when presenting the Norwegian case.

Another European document which has impacted trends and reforms in teacher education is the OECD 2005 document *Teachers Matter*. Recommendations from this document are recognizable also beyond Europe, such as clear and precise statements of what teachers should know and are expected to do within a career-long perspective. This includes content knowledge, general knowledge, and reflective practice. Teacher learning is not restricted to initial teacher education, but a continuing process after graduation. Accomplishments of teaching are seen in relevance to student learning, most often in terms of measureable achievements. Field experience is a central component of teacher education, and the trend is to start it as early as possible, so there is a 'practice turn' in preparing teachers for the profession. A final thing to be mentioned here is the call for systematic induction of novice teachers. Similar recommendations for improving teacher education are found in the international literature, which also reports on the implementation of the above tendencies (Furlong et al. 2013; Sinnema and Aitkin 2013). Many of the more recent reforms in Norwegian teacher education reflect the above international trends (Smith 2016a, b).

A third, less well-known document which within the European teacher educator community has created interest and optimism for more policy attention to teacher educators and their work is the European Commission document from 2013, *Supporting Teacher Educators*. A key issue in this document is what is called the multifaceted teacher educator (Smith 2011). The concept includes the wide range of job responsibilities teacher educators in higher education hold, mainly in relation to teaching and research; responsibilities which often cause tensions and feelings of not serving both masters (Murray and Male 2005; Darling-Hammond 2016). However, the concept 'teacher educator' as presented in the European Commission document presents a broad definition of who a teacher educator is, and with more time spent in school during initial teacher education, school-based mentors of student teachers and novice teachers take on the role of teacher educators (Smith 2015). In Norway, the role of the school-based mentor is addressed by the teacher education community and by the policy makers, and centrally funded initiatives aiming to professionalize school-based mentors through specialized education programs are offered by most teacher education institutions.

With this backdrop I will move on to discuss the Norwegian case in more depth, focusing on mistrust and trust reflected in the adaptation (or perhaps simply adoption) of European motions and international trends.

The Norwegian Case

Norwegian teacher education is illustrated in Fig. 2.1. Pre-school teacher education is currently three years and mainly takes place at the university colleges; however, there are discussions underway to make this into a longer program requiring the same qualification for teaching in schools which is, from 2017, five years and at a master level. This means that all teacher education students have to submit a research-based master thesis, as this is required for all master degrees in Norway. Compulsory school is 10 years, and teachers are prepared to teach in grades 1–7 or in grades 5–10. Once they have started teacher education, they cannot switch between the programs. There is a stronger focus on content knowledge in the program for grades 5–10. Universities as well as university colleges offer these master programs, but the university colleges need to have their programs accredited by the Norwegian Agency for Quality Assurance in Education (NOKUT) which is the controlling authority for educational activity. The established universities do not need to apply for accreditation of new master programs. Secondary school teacher education mostly takes place at the universities which usually offer two programs. The first program is a five year integrated master degree where the students integrate educational, didactic courses, and field experience with their discipline studies from the very beginning. They can choose to write a master thesis in the discipline or to have more practice-oriented (didactics) topics. The disciplinary knowledge of these students will be at a master level in the discipline. A second program is a one-year postgraduate certificate in education (PGCE) offered by universities as well as university colleges. A prerequisite for this program is currently a bachelor or a master disciplinary degree (from 2018 only a master degree will be accepted), and the program focuses on educational and didactical courses, including a lengthy practicum.

The current picture of Norwegian teacher education as described above has been subject to multiple reforms in the last seven years, and the teacher education institutions have been busy at designing new programs according to governmental decisions and have not been able to focus on improving an established program. Norwegian teacher education can be said to be reform fatigue, and there are concerns about what might be the next reform in the government changes. In an increased accountability culture, there is a feeling of being made answerable for changes which are not yet institutionalized and resolved before new requirements are made accountable to redesign programs. The resultant perceived tension between mistrust and trust in the Norwegian teacher education system is the main focus of this chapter.

This not recent quote by O'Neill (2002), which draws on the English system, well illustrates the current situation in Norway:

> Perhaps the present revolution in accountability will make us all trustworthier. Perhaps we will be trusted once again. But I think this is a vain hope - not because accountability is undesirable or unnecessary, but because currently fashionable methods of accountability damage rather than repair trust. If we want greater accountability without damaging performance we need intelligent accountability.

The discussion will focus on the following issues, which are by no means intended to be an exhaustive list, but more a reflection of tensions in teacher education internationally: teacher education at a master level, research-based (informed) teacher education, practice turn in teacher education, content versus pedagogical knowledge, and control versus autonomy.

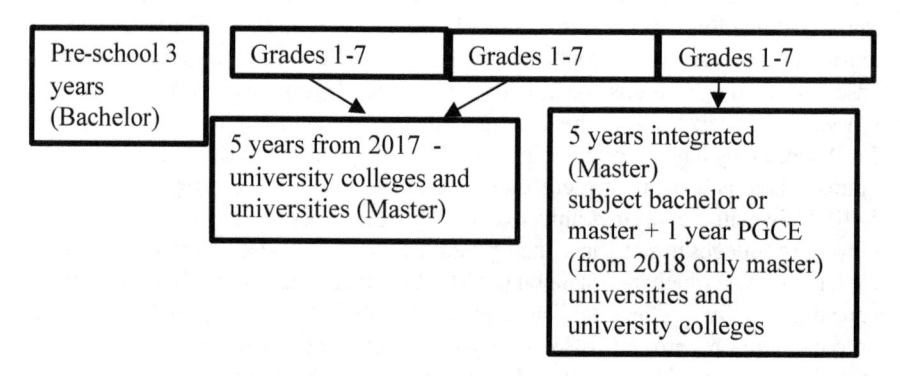

Fig. 2.1 Norwegian teacher education

Teacher Education at a Master Level

The main issues which cause tension between trust and mistrust related to the new reform of having all teacher education at a master level are listed in Table 2.1.

The university colleges have long experience in educating teachers for the lower grades, from seminar tradition to, in the last decades, a more academic level after the Bologna declaration. However, these colleges are not being trusted with developing their own programs without applying for accreditation from NOKUT. The universities do not need accreditation for their master programs. This creates tension in the system as the university colleges feel they are not being trusted and their long experience of educating teachers is not sufficiently appreciated to offer professional education at a master level. The tension is intensified as the criteria for accreditation is mainly on objective measures such as number of professors in the program and number of research competent staff with a doctorate. For graduate programs, at least 10% of the faculty should be at the professor level, and 40% must be research competent (Ph.D.). Moreover, for graduate programs, the faculty must document research competence at a high level (Ministry of Education and Research 2016, https://lovdata.no/dokument/LTI/forskrift/2013-02-28-237). The quality of teaching is not emphasized, yet this is more of a concern among teacher educators as well as students (Ulvik and Smith 2016). The university colleges feel mistrusted, especially because what they have been praised for, the quality of teaching, is not part of the accreditation process.

In relation to the new teacher education programs at a master level, there are clear top-down documents stating the scope and objective of the programs, followed by a long list of expected outcomes divided into knowledge, skills, and general competence in teaching. The national documents also clearly define the scope and the structure of the education, including the number of ECTS points required in the various subjects which might be perceived as an example of mistrust of the higher institutions. Yet, at the same time, there are no standards and there is no national external assessment of the learning outcomes listed in details for every subject in the national documents. The institutions are trusted to translate the framework into

Table 2.1 Tensions in teacher education at a master level

Mistrust	Trust
University colleges need accreditation	Universities do not need accreditation
Accreditation based on objective measures	Quality of teaching not questioned • Local implementation
National frameworks for programs • Scope and objective • Learning outcomes; knowledge, skills, general competence • Content and structure	• National guidelines, institutional adaptation • No national assessment—the Ministry may decide to hold part exams. • For example, master thesis may be a school subject, profession-oriented pedagogy, or special needs education

practice in their programs, and the assessment form is up to the institution to decide. Students' learning at the institution is assessed internally, and the form of assessment differs from institution to institution and from course to course. As a tradition in Norway, the internal assessment of students' exams is quality assured by an external assessor from another institution and the home institution chooses who the external assessor will be. Based on personal experience, it is often more a choice of convenience than looking for an objective expert in the field. Although the regulations state that the government may decide to have national exams, so far this has not been the case. Students have to submit a research-based master thesis as already mentioned, yet they, together with their institutional supervisors can decide on the project form (theoretical, disciplinary or practical research), and the institution is free to decide how many ECTS credits (within a range) the master thesis should have. A serious challenge, as regards the research-based master thesis, is that not all institutions have sufficient research competent teacher educators to supervise a master thesis and the NOKUT requirements of professors and faculty with a doctorate might well reflect this challenge. The above description has aimed to illuminate the ongoing tension between mistrust and trust in relation to the new requirement of having all teacher education at a master level in Norway. The reform is influenced by international trends, and in the Norwegian case, perhaps mainly by the successful Finnish teacher education (Niemi et al. 2012).

Research-Based Teacher Education

There is a variety of understandings of what a research-based teacher education means. Toom et al. (2010) claim that, in:

> Finland, research-based teacher education has four characteristics. First, the study program is structured according to the systematic analysis of education. Secondly, all teaching is based on research. Third, activities are organized in such a way that students can practise argumentation, decision making and justification while investigating and solving pedagogical problems. Fourth, students learn academic research skills. (p. 333)

This is, as I see it, a comprehensive definition of a research-based teacher education, and teacher educators as well as students become consumers as well as producers of research. When teacher education is at a master level and a research dissertation is required as in Finland, and now also in Norway, the research competence and activity of teacher educators is the foundation on which a research-based teacher education is built and evaluated during the accreditation processes. It can be questioned if teacher educators who do not actively engage in research can develop a disposition of inquiry within their students (Munthe and Haug 2010). In Norway, the research activity of teacher educators measured in number of publications has become part of the accountability and central funding scheme, and a tension between mistrust and trust develops, illustrated in Table 2.2.

In the Norwegian Higher Education Institutions (HEI) including teacher education, publications are measured in numbers and quality for promotion, funding, and

Table 2.2 Tensions in implementing a research based teacher education

Mistrust	Trust
Publications are counted (promotion, funding, accreditation)	Time for research not specified, varies among institutions—little practice of perishing with low publications rate
Research competence—Ph.D. required	TEs without a Ph.D. employed, not all research competent
Research informed programs	Syllabi freedom
Specified outcomes	Institutional assessment
Research-based master thesis	Supervision decided at institutional level

accreditation purposes. The challenge is, however, that not all members of staff have equal opportunities for conducting research and the writing of quality publications in refereed journals. University staff with a Ph.D. will normally have 50% of their job responsibilities and time dedicated to research, and they can 'buy' more time through externally funded research projects. In University colleges, however, the research time differs from institution to institution, and in some institutions, members of staff need to apply for research time. If staff members do not hold a Ph.D., their basic rights for time to conduct research is nil. Thus, those who are established researchers have time and can more easily fulfill requirements for promotion and funding, whereas it is more difficult for beginning researchers to find time to engage in research, especially when they do not hold a Ph.D. This causes tension within an institution and also between institutions, especially since some institutions demand a doctorate to be employed in teacher education whereas other institutions are not able to set similar demands. In an international study of teacher educators' preferences for professional development, it was found that learning more about research and time to conduct research and write it up was high on the list internationally (Czerniawski et al. 2017). Norway was part of this study, and even though the Norwegian teacher educators were more positive as regards their research opportunities than their international colleagues, research and academic writing were still high on the list. The well-established universities are trusted to employ research active staff, whereas newer and smaller institutions have to be accountable to NOKUT to document research competence and activity to be accredited with a master degree. Some of these, however, have a long tradition of educating elementary school teachers, and they do not have long research traditions.

Another example of mistrust is that in the national steering documents there is a claim that Norwegian teacher education shall be research based (NOKUT 2006; Ministry of Education and Research 2010). There are specified learning outcomes for teacher education graduates, but on the other hand, there is syllabi freedom, including reading lists and institutional-based assessment of the learning outcomes. In this respect, the institutions are trusted to create quality programs and when accreditation has been granted, there is little external interference with the implementation. The same can be said about supervision of the master dissertations, once the institution has documented it holds the required numbers of professors and doctorates, there is no control of who actually supervises the dissertations. The assessment of students' work is, as already said, internal in cooperation with an external assessor appointed by the institution.

Practice Turn in Teacher Education

Another international trend in teacher education is the increased emphasis on practice, what is often called as the practice turn in teacher education. The overwhelming evidence of a decade of research on teacher knowledge is that 'knowledge of teaching is acquired and developed by the personal experience of teaching' (Munby et al. 2001, p. 897). The practicum often reveals the notorious gap between theory acquired at the university and practical skills, knowledge of teaching. Solstad (2010) documents in a small scale qualitative study that theory is viewed as increasingly more important as the students proceed in their education. Theory serves as a foundation for reflection, and it provides the students with a language to analyze and understand practice. Bhabha (1990) talked about the need to create a hybrid space in teacher education, the space where theory and practice meets, where university and school staff members become equal colleagues. More recently, this space is also called the third space which, according to Zeichner (2010), is the hybrid space where theory and practice meet and new knowledge about, and of, teaching, is created and made accessible to teachers-to-be. The need to create third spaces in teacher education is also highlighted in Norwegian steering documents (White paper 2009), and there are requirements for extended practicum in the most recent reforms. However, regarding the practicum, teacher education institutions also experience a tension between mistrust and trust as illustrated in Table 2.3.

The national steering documents clearly specify the number of field days each teacher education program has to include, and when redesigning the institutional programs, it was a difficult challenge to fit the increased number of field days into an already packed schedule (personal experience). Once the number of field days have been programmed, there are few guidelines of how the days shall be spent, how many

Table 2.3 Tensions in the practicum

Mistrust	Trust
Number of field days specified in national frameworks	Content of the field experience at an institutional level
Mentor education recommended	Mentors without mentor education
Partnerships with schools required	Implementation at the institutional level, new initiatives, e.g., university schools
Learning outcomes specified as skills, competence	No specific criteria for 'passing' the practicum

hours the students have to be in school and what the focus should be, e.g., observation, participating in staff meetings, actually teaching, planning assessment. Heggen and Thorsen (2015) report that it is still the higher education institution which, to a large extent, provides information to the school of how practice is to be structured and its content. Further, there is little dialogue between the university/university college and the schools about how to plan the practicum, as specified in the steering documents, which also indicate that the school principal has the overall responsibility for the practical component of the teacher education. Here, there is a sign of mistrust from the institutions regarding the ability of schools to take on full responsibility for the practicum.

The same documents also strongly recommend mentor education. In Norway, there is central funding to the institutions to offer 30 ECTS education for school-based mentors with the purpose of assuring the quality of the practicum and in acknowledgment of the fact that mentoring student teachers differs from teaching school children (Smith 2015). At the same time, there is institutional freedom regarding the content of mentor education, and this differs from institution to institution. There is, however, communication across institutions, including exchange of teaching staff. It seems that in the case of school-based mentoring, there is a lot of trust by the authorities in the ability of the institutions and the schools to develop a good practicum, yet Heggen and Thorsen's (2015) study suggests that this is not really the case. Smith (2016a, b) presents the various types of cooperation between schools and the HEIs as a continuum ranging from schools being practice schools which are 'told' by the HEI what to do, to selected partner schools which have made an agreement of cooperation and mutual responsibilities with the HEI, to the most recent developments of a few selected university schools which function like a university hospital with dual employment and mutual agreements about Research and Development projects for students and for staff. These developments are made independently of national steering documents, and the trust put in the institutions to quality assure the practicum needs to be supported by mutual trust between the HEIs and the practice field.

Finally, the practicum has to be assessed according to national steering documents, and passing the practical component of teacher education is a requirement for qualification, as it should be. The learning outcomes are specified in the national steering documents; however, how to assess, or who should be the assessors, is all left to the individual institution and differs from institution to institution. In this respect, much trust is put on the teacher education institutions, yet they do not fully trust schools to make the final assessment, even though the school-based mentor would have most information about a student teacher's teaching skills.

Content Knowledge Versus Bildung Perspective

There is an increased understanding internationally of the importance of teachers' content knowledge as well as the knowledge about how to teach the content to improve the quality of student learning (Shulman 1986; Baumert et al. 2010; Kleickmann et al. 2013). The role of content knowledge and didactical knowledge, what Shulman (1986) calls Pedagogical Content Knowledge (PCK), has also caught the attention of Norwegian policy makers, and in the 2010 reform for elementary school education (grades 1–10), higher requirements for teaching the core subjects, Norwegian, Mathematics and English were made, and the same counts for the teaching of other subjects. The new requirements were perceived to be a direct response to Norway's disappointing ranking on international tests. The international trend is therefore clearly implemented in Norwegian steering documents, and many experienced teachers felt that their ability to teach the core (and other subjects) was questioned by the government. Intensive in-service courses were centrally funded to upgrade teachers' content knowledge, and the government decided on a transition period of 10 years, starting from 2010. Table 2.4 illustrates the tension between mistrust and trust in relation to teachers' content knowledge.

The mistrust of teachers' content knowledge as well as of teacher education programs to provide teachers with sufficient content knowledge is reflected in the very specific demands required for ECTS to teach the core and other subjects in the younger grades (1–7), and higher demands to teach grades 5–10. Secondary school teaching has always had high demands for teaching a subject, and this is historically related to the fact that teacher education for grades 8–13 was under the responsibility of the universities. The design of the courses and the content of the discipline courses are, however, left to the institutions, and once the program has been accepted, there is little external interference with the implementation, which can be taken as a sign of trust. Having said that, though, there is a need to look at the national curricula for the many school subjects, and these are to a certain extent rather detailed, and there is a strong focus on the three core subjects in school at the expense of more practical/aesthetical subjects. National tests play a central role in the Norwegian school system, mainly for accountability purposes, but also, according to steering documents, to be used formatively by school principals and teachers. Stornes et al. (2013) found that external testing does not work as well as assessment for learning and might have a harmful effect on students' motivation and learning outcomes. An accountability system in education which involves increased disciplinary testing and measurement does not align with the long tradition of the concept 'dannelse' in the Norwegian context. 'Dannelse' can best be defined as the forming of the human

Table 2.4 Tensions between goal-orientation and bildung-orientation

Mistrust	Trust
Number of required ECTS (European Credit Transfer System) in teaching subject	Design of courses/programs at institutional level
Subject-specific knowledge formed by detailed curricular for schools	'Bildung'—perspective, embodied in Norwegian tradition
Specified outcomes	Institutional decisions on how to assess outcomes

personality, behavior, and moral through upbringing, environment, and education. It is one of the classical themes of pedagogy and reflects to a certain extent the antique concept 'paideia' or German 'Bildung'. But 'dannelse' also entails a normative and cultural dimension which the other concepts are missing (Store norske leksikon 2017). The requirement of developing 'dannelse' in students is included in the overall law for Norwegian education (Opplæringsloven 1998, https://lovdata.no/dokument/NL/lov/1998-07-17-61#KAPITTEL_1). For many schools and teachers, the increased focus on the core subjects accompanied by extensive testing creates a tension between teaching the subjects and preparing for tests and at the same time addressing the 'dannelse' requirement which is mainly rooted in the pedagogy of teaching. The schools and teachers are not told how to implement 'dannelse' education, yet there is less time to deal with it as the external content demands are increased. Ulvik et al. (2017) examined ethical dilemmas novice teachers experienced in the first year of teaching. Few dilemmas were related to content knowledge, and the novices felt that they had not been sufficiently prepared to handle ethical dilemmas in their teacher education. As previously related to the other tensions discussed above, we can also see here a tension between mistrust and trust as the steering documents state in detail the knowledge, skills, and competencies teachers shall have in the various subjects; however, teacher education institutions are trusted to assess whether their graduates have acquired the national goals.

Control Versus Autonomy

Teacher education is a policy problem. This seems to be an international trend and a frequently discussed issue in the global teacher education literature (Darling-Hammond 2010; Cochran-Smith et al. 2013; Conroy et al. 2013). Sahlberg (2012) claims that there is a cross-national education reform movement which has led to a standardized education and accountability process by the means of tests. Norway is not different, and in 2003, NOKUT was established under the Ministry of Education and Research. NOKUT is 'the controlling authority for educational activity at all Norwegian universities, special field universities, university colleges, and institutions with single accredited higher-education programs' (http://www.nokut.no/en/Universities-and-university-colleges/). The main task of NOKUT is to document and inform on the status of Norwegian Higher Education, professional education and recognition of foreign qualifications. NOKUT is, to a certain extent, perceived to be a means of control more than a means to improve higher education, and as such, it might symbolize the mistrust that the government has in its HEIs. On the other hand, one could also say that NOKUT is a means to quality assure higher education and its work should be viewed in a formative and less summative perspective. This tension is illustrated in Table 2.5.

The fact that NOKUT was established could be seen as a sign of mistrust, especially since academic institutions in Norway enjoyed a great deal of academic free-

Table 2.5 Tensions between control and accountability

Mistrust	Trust
The fact that NOKUT exists	Cooperates with institutions
Evaluation of internal quality assurance system (every 6 years)	Institutions decide on their own quality systems
Accreditation of study programs (graduate and postgraduate level)	Established universities exempted
National evaluations of study programs (nursing, engineering, teacher education)	No sanctions, mostly formative, based on self-evaluation and quantifiable measures such as publications, Ph.D. graduates, etc.

dom prior to NOKUT. But in reality, NOKUT intends to and strives to cooperate with the institutions, and only in very severe situations would NOKUT require that a program or course is removed (personal communication). NOKUT claims that from their experience the fact that there is a monitor system suffices to pinpoint weaknesses which are then repaired. The quality assurance system implemented by NOKUT is based on institutional quality assurance systems which are controlled every six years. In other words, it is not the institution which is controlled every six years, but the institutions' internal quality assurance activities. New universities and university colleges have to be accredited to introduce new programs, and they are evaluated, as previously said, by countable measures, as if a fixed number of professors in a program are sufficient to guarantee the quality teaching in the program. When preparing for accreditation, much work and time is put into studying the requirements and finding ways, sometimes creative ways, of meeting the stipulated numbers of professors, staff with doctorates, and publications, as well as the number of practice days, and the number of ECTS provided in the core contents. An atmosphere of mistrust can easily develop in such situations. The established universities are exempted for accreditation, and they are, to my knowledge, rarely controlled if they meet the stipulated requirements. Finally, there are national evaluations of study programs in professional education (e.g., nursing, engineering, and teacher education) with the evaluation report made public. Yet, there are few or no sanctions, and the evaluations are again mainly based on institutional self-evaluations and number of publications, Ph.D. graduates, etc. In this respect, the institutions are trusted not to present 'alternative facts'. In the Norwegian educational system, a tension between mistrust and trust of control versus autonomy seems to be a core around which the system is working.

Summary and Conclusions

The above discussion can be summarized in the following points:

- Norwegian higher education is strongly framed by European initiatives such as the Bologna declaration.
- Norwegian teacher education is strongly affected by international trends, and in the current paper, five international trends which have influenced Norwegian teacher education are discussed; teacher education at a master level, research-based teacher education, practice turn in teacher education, focus on content knowledge, and an increased control system.
- Norwegian teacher education is increasingly being centralized. Policy decisions translated into national steering documents are addressed in the planning and implementation of the frequent reforms teacher education programs are subjected to.
- Per today, there is a balanced approach to accountability versus autonomy, between mistrust and trust in Norwegian teacher education. There is a national quality assurance system, which controls the institutional accreditation system. Currently, the process of seeking accreditation to offer the required teacher education at a master level which many institutions have to do might be experienced as an uneven balance between control and autonomy. The big question is: Where are we heading?

The answer might be found in what Terry Crooks (2007) from New Zealand calls *intelligent accountability* (IA). He argues for a recognition of the need for accountability but claims it has to be practiced with intelligence and not technically. There are seven main features of IA Crooks highlights.

1. *IA preserves and enhances trust among the key participants in the accountability process.* Much has been said about trust in the current chapter; and the question is if Norway will be able to find an optimal balance between mistrust and trust, between accountability and personal/institutional responsibility and autonomy. This could be done if policy makers, NOKUT, HEIs, and the practice field, could develop a shared language of teacher education and shared understanding of the ultimate goals.
2. *IA involves participants in the process, offering them a strong sense of professional responsibility and initiative.* This feature of IA argues against a top-down approach in relation to forming educational policies, in decision making and not least in the implementation of decisions made. Are the professionals sufficiently involved in the process, do the policy makers draw on a variety of research, and not only research supporting their views when deciding on policy strategies? Is sufficient attention given to the national and local context in full realization that copy and paste from other contexts does not work? Perhaps Norway, like most countries, would benefit from listening to the national professionals in addition to the many international experts who generously share their knowledge and views with Norwegian authorities and colleagues.

3. *IA encourages deep, worthwhile responses rather than surface window dressing.* When reforms are frequent, such as Norwegian teacher education has experienced, a kind of reform fatigue might easily develop (Day et al. 2007). Norwegian teacher education underwent a major reform in 2010 in the four year teacher education program for elementary school, and in 2017, a new major reform, upgrading all teacher education to a master level with extensive requirements of staff competence, was introduced. Teacher education institutions have not yet had time to settle into and evaluate their revisions from 2010 before they were forced to engage in a new planning and accreditation process. This might lead to window dressing of the external requirements, at least in the beginning, and the process of implementing deep worthwhile responses takes time.
4. *IA recognizes and attempts to compensate for the severe limitations of our ability to judge performance through the use of performance indicators.* When quality is merely assessed by quantifiable measures, such as, for example, the accreditation of new master programs, the teaching quality of the programs is not taken into consideration. It is still a question if a professor with a doctorate is a better teacher educator than an experienced school teacher? The answer is probably that the best teacher educator would be an experienced teacher with a doctorate who actively engages in research, but these people are not easy to find in big numbers. Norwegian accreditation criteria as well as promotion criteria might benefit from being revisited, introducing more qualitative non-measurable aspects of the profession than the norm is today.
5. *IA provides well-founded effective feedback that promotes insights into performance.* The external quality assurance organization in Norway, NOKUT, does, in principle and intention, meet this criterion for IA. The system is built on an internal quality assurance system which receives feedback every six years, and the main purpose is, according to NOKUT, formative, to provide feedback which can be used in the future activity of the institution.
6. *IA is that as a consequence of the accountability process the majority of participants are more enthusiastic and motivated in their work.* External demands and control serve as the lever of change in Norwegian teacher education, yet it might appear that it does not necessarily increase enthusiasm and motivation within the professional community. An example could be the promotion and funding system based on publications—it is a lever for research, but do the researchers mostly engage in research and writing out of enthusiasm, or because they have no other choice, and try to squeeze as many publications out of the same data material? Does the accountability pressure have a negative impact on the enthusiasm for academic work, and thereby also the quality? The other side of the coin is the quality of teaching, how motivated are teacher educators to invest in their teaching when they get less academic credit for it? It might seem that in Norway the pressure of the accountability lever is becoming too strong, and it is, perhaps, time to stop and revisit if accountability as a means to improvement has become the end in itself.

7. *IA is flexible, the intensity of the accountability process can be adjusted for different participants.* This final point in Crooks' list of intelligent accountability features suggests that national, regional, and local considerations have to be taken into consideration when making Norwegian teacher education institutions accountable for their activities, especially the university colleges. They differ in size, they differ in geographical locations, and they serve various social purposes. As the situation is now, a 'one size fits all' accreditation and accountability system does not pay attention to the diversity of the institutions, and it does not address the various types of teacher educators working in the system. In full acknowledgment of the complexity of addressing this diversity, it might, in the long-term interest of Norwegian teacher education, be a wise thing to do.

Norway has, perhaps more than many other countries, developed a more balanced approach between accountability and autonomy, between mistrust and trust in its teacher education system. We are, however, heavily influenced by global trends, and at times, it might seem that the policy makers too eagerly adopt accountability systems from elsewhere without sufficient consideration of the national and local context. There is little adaptation. Therefore, it would be useful to have Terry Crooks' (2007) work on intelligent accountability as a backdrop in our ongoing efforts to improve Norwegian teacher education.

References

Baumert, J., Kunter, M., Blum, W., Brunner, M., Voss, T., Jordan, A., et al. (2010). Teachers' mathematical knowledge, cognitive activation in the classroom, and student progress. *American Educational Research Journal, 47*, 133–180. https://doi.org/10.3102/0002831209345157.

Bhabha, H. (1990). The third space. In J. Rutherford (Ed.), *Identity, community, culture and difference* (pp. 207–221). London, England: Lawrence and Wishart.

Cochran-Smith, M., Piazza, P., & Power, C. (2013). The politics of accountability: Assessing teacher education in the United States. *The Educational Forum, 77*(1), 6–27.

Conroy, J., Hulme, M., & Menter, I. (2013). Developing a 'clinical' model for teacher education. *Journal of Education for Teaching, 39*(5), 557–573.

Crooks, T. (2007, October). *Principles for intelligent accountability with illustrations from education.* New Zealand: Inaugural professorial lecture presented at the University of Otago.

Czerniawski, G., Guberman, A., & MacPhail, A. (2017). The professional developmental needs of higher education-based teacher educators: An international comparative needs analysis. *European Journal of Teacher Education, 40*(1), 127–140.

Darling-Hammond, L. (2010). Teacher education and the American future. *Journal of Teacher Education, 61*(1–2), 35–47.

Darling-Hammond, L. (2016). Research on teaching and teacher education and its influences on policy and practice. *Educational Researcher, 45*(2), 83–91.

Day, C., Flores, M. A., & Viana, I. (2007). Effects of national policies on teachers' sense of professionalism: Findings from an empirical study in Portugal and in England. *European Journal of Teacher Education, 30*(3), 249–265.

Det store norske leksikon. (2017). Foreningen for det store norske leksikon. Oslo, Norway. Retrieved April 12, 2017 from https://snl.no/dannelse.

European Commission/EACEA/Eurydice. (2015). *The European higher education area in 2015: Bologna process implementation report*. Luxembourg: Publications Office in the European Union.
Furlong, J., Cochran-Smith, M., & Brennan, M. (2013). *Policy and politics in teacher education: International perspectives*. Oxfordshire, England: Routledge.
Heggen, K., & Thorsen, K. E. (2015). Praksisopplæring-et felles prosjekt mellom høgskole og praksisskole? *Norsk pedagogisk tidsskrift, 99*(05), 362–374.
Kleickmann, T., Richter, D., Kunter, M., Elsner, J., Besser, M., Krauss, S., et al. (2013). Teachers' content knowledge and pedagogical content knowledge: The role of structural differences in teacher education. *Journal of Teacher Education, 64*(1), 90–106. https://doi.org/10.1177/00224 87112460398.
Ministry of Education and Research. (1998). *Opplæringsloven*. Retrieved April 12, 2017 from https://lovdata.no/dokument/NL/lov/1998-07-17-61#KAPITTEL_1.
Ministry of Education and Research (2009). *Læreren Rollen og utdanningen*. (Norwegian White Paper 11, 2008–2009). Oslo, Norway: Ministry of Education and Research.
Ministry of Education and Research. (2010). *Rundskriv F-05-10: Forskrift om rammeplan for grunnskolelærerutdanningene for 1.–7. trinn og 5.–10. trinn, vedtatt 01. mars 2010*. Retrieved February 3, 2017 from http://www.regjeringen.no/nb/dep/kd/dok/rundskriv/2010/Rundskriv-F-05-10-Forskrifter-om-ny-grunnskolelarerutdanning.html?id=598615.
Ministry of Education and Research. (2016). *Forskrift om tilsyn med utdanningskvaliteten i høyere utdanning (studietilsynsforskriften)*. Retrieved March 27, 2017 from https://lovdata.no/dokumen t/LTI/forskrift/2013-02-28-237.
Munby, H., Russell, T., & Martin, A. K. (2001). Teachers' knowledge and how it develops. In V. Richardson (Ed.), *Handbook of research on teaching* (4th ed., pp. 877–904). Washington, DC: American Educational Research Association.
Munthe, E., & Haug, P. (2010). En integrert, profesjonsrettet og forskningsbasert grunnskolelærerutdanning. *Norsk pedagogisk tidsskrift, 94*(03), 188–203.
Murray, J., & Male, T. (2005). Becoming a teacher educator: Evidence from the field. *Teaching and Teacher Education, 21*(2), 125–142.
Niemi, H., Toom, A., & Kallioniemi, A. (2012). *Miracle of education: The principles and practices of teaching and learning in Finnish schools*. Rotterdam, The Netherlands: Sense Publishers.
Norwegian Agency for Quality Assurance in Education [NOKUT]. (2006). *Evaluering av allmennlærerutdanningen i Norge 2006. Del 1: Hovedrappport. Rapport fra ekstern komité*. Oslo, Norway: Nasjonalt organ for kvalitet i utdanningen.
O'Neill, O. (2002). *BBC Reith lecture: A question of trust*. Retrieved March 26, 2017 from http://www.bbc.co.uk/radio4/reith2002/.
Sahlberg, P. (2012). *Finnish lessons: What can the world learn from educational change in Finland?*. New York, NY: Teachers' College Press.
Shulman, L. S. (1986). Those who understand: Knowledge growth in teaching. *Educational Researcher, 15*(2), 4–14. https://doi.org/10.3102/0013189X015002004.
Sinnema, C., & Aitken, G. (2013). Trends in international curriculum development. In M. Priestley & G. J. J. Biesta (Eds.), *Reinventing the curriculum: New trends in curriculum policy and practice* (pp. 141–164). London, England: Bloomsbury.
Smith, K. (2011). The multi-faceted teacher educator—A Norwegian perspective. *Journal of Education for Teaching, 37*(3), 337–349.
Smith, K. (2015). Mentoring—A profession within a profession. In H. Tillema, G. van Westhuisen, & K. Smith (Eds.), *Mentoring for learning—Climbing the mountain* (pp. 283–298). Rotterdam, The Netherlands: Sense publishers.
Smith, K. (2016a). Partnerships in teacher education—Going beyond the rhetoric, with reference to the Norwegian context. *CEPS Journal: Center for Educational Policy Studies Journal, 6*(3), 17.
Smith, K. (2016b, April). *Recent developments in Norwegian teacher education*. Paper Presented at the Symposium: Policy, Governance and Quality in Teacher Education: Four Cases, Washington, D.C.

Solstad, A. G. S. (2010). Praksisnær teori og teorinær praksis–den nødvendige relasjonen. *Norsk pedagogisk tidsskrift, 94*(03), 203–218.

Stornes, T., Tvedt, M. S., & Bru, E. (2013). Best med test?—Et motivasjonsteoretisk perspektiv på bruk av normative tester i grunnskolen. *Norsk pedagogisk tidsskrift, 97*(04–05), 315–325.

Toom, A., Kynäslahti, H., Krokfors, L., Jyrhämä, R., Byman, R., Stenberg, K., et al. (2010). Experiences of a research-based approach to teacher education: Suggestions for future policies. *European Journal of Education, 45*(2), 331–344.

Ulvik, M., & Smith, K. (2016). Å undervise om å undervise. Lærerutdanneres kompetansen sett fra deres eget og studenters perspektiv. (Teaching about teaching. Teachers' competence from their own and student teachers' perspectives). *UniPed, 9*(1), 61–77.

Ulvik, M., Smith, K., & Helleve, I. (2017). Ethical aspects of professional dilemmas in the first year of teaching. *Professional Development in Education, 43*(2), 236–252. https://doi.org/10.1080/19415257.2016.1178163.

Zeichner, K. (2010). Rethinking the connections between campus courses and field experiences in college- and university-based education. *Journal of Teacher Education, 61*(1–2), 89–99. https://doi.org/10.1177/0022487109347671.

Kari Smith is a Professor (Ph.D.) of education at the Department of Teacher Education, Norwegian University of Science and Technology (NTNU). Her main research interests are teacher education, professional development, mentoring novice teachers and assessment for and of learning. She has acted as the Head of Teacher Education programs abroad as well as at the University of Bergen, Norway. Currently, she is the Head of the Norwegian National Research School in Teacher Education (NAFOL) and serves as a scientific advisor to the European Doctorate in Teacher Education (EDITE). She is the project leader of the International Forum for Teacher Educator Development (InFo-TED). She has been involved with evaluation of teacher education programs in Norway and abroad. She has published widely, internationally and in Norway, and has given invited talks in all continents.

Chapter 3
Notes from a Small Country: Teacher Education, Learning Innovation and Accountability in Scotland

Louise Hayward

Introduction

A central purpose of this book is to explore the trajectory of Teacher Education for the twenty-first century as it emerges in different countries in what Wyatt-Smith and Adie (see Chap. 1 of this book, p. 3) describe as 'a crucible of change in teacher education' impacted by unprecedented sociocultural and economic change and technological advances. This chapter focuses on Scotland. My thesis is that, by exploring teacher education policy in Scotland, we can begin to identify the dominant values at that time within that society (Menter 2016) and thus begin to understand how teacher education in Scotland is positioned in a global context. I argue that

- although Scotland has not been immune to the influences of the Global Educational Reform Movement, its impact has been mediated by its traditions and culture
- teacher education is firmly located in higher education and enmeshed in a series of complex partnerships with a range of stakeholders
- the closeness of Scotland's educational communities, combined with a generally positive attitude to teaching and teachers, often sustained despite the media, has led to change in teacher education remaining consensual
- Scotland's teacher accountability is standards based, contextualized in a model of continuing professional learning for beginning teachers, growing teachers and educational leaders
- recent reports on evaluations of education in Scotland praise the Professional Standards. OECD (2015) described them as 'inspirational' (p. 119), yet identified a remaining challenge—to ensure high quality enactment across the country

L. Hayward (✉)
University of Glasgow, Glasgow, Scotland
e-mail: louise.hayward@glasgow.ac.uk

- if teacher education in Scotland is to continue to be trusted and accountability systems are to remain learning focused, then the challenge of high quality, consistent enactment needs to be addressed.

This chapter is divided into two sections. The first section offers background into the context in Scotland and the historical influences on current accountability policy and societal values; the second considers teacher education, related educational accountability systems and the impact of global, international and national influences on teacher education policy. Ball (2015) argues that although policies are complex:

> differentially represented by different actors in different contexts (policy as text), but on the other hand, at the same time produced and formed by taken-for-granted and implicit knowledges and assumptions about the world and ourselves (policy as discourse). (p. 6)

Most policy analysis focuses only on what is written and said rather than on how statements are formed and made possible. Using the framework of knowledge as text and knowledge as discourse, this chapter will offer an analysis of the policy context in Scotland using evidence from an exploration of Scotland's *'taken-for-granted and implicit knowledges and assumptions about the world and ourselves'* policy texts (policy as discourse) and a policy analysis of three seminal documents interrogated through the lens of teacher education and accountability (policy as text). The three texts are as follows:

- *Teaching Scotland's Future* (2011), a national review of Teacher Education in Scotland, commonly known as the Donaldson Report
- The report of the *Evaluation of the Implementation of Impact of Teaching Scotland's Future* (2016) carried out by Ipsos MORI and
- *Improving Schools in Scotland* (2015), the OECD review of Scotland's National Curriculum Framework, Curriculum for Excellence.

The Scottish Context

Scotland, one of the four countries within the UK, has always had an independent education system and takes pride in that fact. Three contextual factors are crucial to explain the current relationship between teacher education and accountability: Scotland's educational history; its educational political stability; and the nature of School Education in Scotland where market forces have had comparatively little impact.

Scotland's Educational History

The devolution settlement of the late 1990s and the establishment of the Scottish Parliament in 1999 give full legal responsibility for education law, policy, and practice to the Scottish Parliament and Government (The Stationery Office 1998, s. 28, 29, 53 and Schedule 5). Education is a key part of what gives Scotland, as a nation, identity. It is a small country (area 78,000 km^2, population 5.3 million) made up of densely populated urban areas, thinly populated rural areas and many islands. The concept of social justice matters to most Scots and having an education system that is socially just has been a long term national aspiration. For centuries, Scotland has been committed to education and to its power of transformation. Although it is more than possible to challenge the depth of this commitment in practice (Bryce et al. 2013), there is evidence to support the intention. For example, in 1496, during the reign of King James IV, the Estates of Scotland passed the country's first education act intended to reflect ideals of the Renaissance. In 1560, immediately after the Reformation, the First Book of Discipline established the principle that there should be a teacher (schoolmaster) in every parish and a college in larger towns (Knox 1560, Fifth Head). The practice proved more challenging to achieve. Universal compulsory primary education was established in 1872, and since then, the school system has worked to become ever more inclusive. Secondary education became compulsory in 1945 (HMSO 1945, s. 1, 23), and the strong commitment in Scotland to the democratic intellect and to comprehensive education (Davie 1961) meant that by the early 1970s all secondary schools had become comprehensive taking children from local catchment areas. Legislation in 2000 established that children and young people would only attend special schools in exceptional circumstances and considering the views of the child and the child's parents (Scottish Parliament 2000, s. 15). Teachers, in Scotland, have always been regarded as important figures in the lives of communities (Kerr 1910).

The history of education in Scotland matters: commitment to community and the right of every child to be part of that respect for education and for teachers; and a desire for social justice are key factors in understanding the current context for teacher education and the ways in which the accountability agenda has developed. In common with other countries internationally, Scotland has experienced the pressures of neoliberal agendas and, in particular, the impact of the global reform movement. However, a number of factors have combined to soften its impact—the country's concern for social justice, its historical belief in the power of education as a force for social change and the centrality of the teacher in that process. International debates around standardization, choice, competition, teacher education and data-driven accountability have been present in the educational discourse in Scotland (Croxford and Raffe 2007; Peters and Besley 2014) but have been mediated by the power of tradition and history (Grek 2012). Scotland has remained something of an outlier in the world of global educational reform (Hayward et al. 2016) with a distinctive 'vernacular' form of globalisation (Rizvi and Lingard 2010). Teacher education is part of Scotland's 'vernacular' repertoire.

Scotland's Political Context

National education policy in Scotland is established by the Scottish Government through the Cabinet Secretary for Education and Lifelong Learning within the legal framework of the Scottish Parliament. Re-established in 1999, after a recess of three hundred years, Parliament has given fresh impetus to the distinctiveness of Scottish Education (Raffe 2005). Although different political parties have been in power (Labour/Liberal Democrat coalitions, Scottish National Party (SNP) minority and majority administrations), an educational consensus has been maintained. All political administrations have shared key educational commitments:

- public primary and secondary schools should be comprehensive with a common curriculum for all learners and
- privatization and market forces, certainly during compulsory education, lead to less equitable provision.

School Education in Scotland

Education is compulsory for all children and young people between the ages of 5 and 16. It is largely a public enterprise (Hayward 2007). Ninety-six per cent of children and young people attend state schools, 4% go to private schools and a small number are educated at home. Most young people in Scotland attend school in their local community. Parents can choose to send their children to a school outside their local catchment area, but the numbers who choose to do so are comparatively small. State schools, primary and secondary, are provided, funded and staffed by Scotland's 32 local authorities; these vary greatly in population and area. Councils have considerable autonomy and can make their own decisions about the proportion of local tax revenue and of the funding provided to them by government that will be allocated to education.

The value system within which Local Councils is expected to operate is explicit and contextualized in international convention. They must ensure that education is designed to address the needs of all individuals: using the words of the United Nations Convention on the Rights of the Child (UNCRC), 'it shall be the duty of the authority to secure that the education is directed to the development of the personality, talents and mental and physical abilities of the child or young person to their fullest potential' (Scottish Parliament 2000, s. 2).

The curriculum in Scotland (Curriculum for Excellence) is not enshrined in law but is a framework based on a set of values and principles (Curriculum Review Group 2004). Young people at all stages from 3 to 18 are intended to become 'successful learners, confident individuals, effective contributors and responsible citizens' (Curriculum Review Group 2004, p. 12). These four purposes, with echoes in the twenty-first century aspirations of many other countries, recognize that learning must focus on bodies of knowledge and skills but recognize that personal, interpersonal, intrapersonal and social skills and affective dimensions are also essential elements of education in Scotland.

Educational policy in Scotland also makes high demands of teachers in assessment. It aspires to have an assessment system for young people aged 3–15 in which teachers' professional judgement, supported by rigorous moderation processes, is the basis of all decision making. Education Scotland, an Executive Agency of the Scottish Government, is charged with supporting quality and improvement in Scottish Education through support for curriculum and assessment professional learning and a program of inspection to support school self-evaluation (Education Scotland 2012). It has played a major role in seeking to develop teachers' professional judgement, working with practitioners and local authorities. Whilst progress has been made, achieving dependable teachers' professional judgements nationally is a complex process and issues remain about how dependable teachers' professional judgements are in relation to the relatively new curriculum (Hayward and Hutchinson 2013). In 2016, the Government advocated the introduction of Standardized Testing as one source of evidence to be used to support Teachers' Professional Judgement (Scottish Government 2016). This was highly contentious. It was not the Government's intention that the tests dominate. Having recognized that test results or data emerging from tests were being used for purposes of accountability, with likely unintended consequences on classroom learning, the Cabinet Secretary in a statement at the Scottish Learning Festival (2017), announced that the tests would be available as a resource for teachers and that test data would not be collected nationally.

This broad definition of what matters in the curriculum, the central role that teachers play in the assessment system, the importance of local context and self-evaluation are all important features in attempting to understand attitudes in Scotland to Teacher Education. Although different local authorities in Scotland have different approaches to accountability, accountability is most commonly intended to support the growth of teachers rather than to control them as is evident in other parts of the UK, particularly in England (Beauchamp et al. 2015).

Teacher Education and the Impact of Global, International, and National Influences on Teacher Education Policy: Policy as Text

Teaching in Scotland is an all-graduate profession, now moving towards master-level (Dickson 2011). Teacher Education is situated in a partnership between universities, local schools and local authorities. Subject-based studies accompany education in pedagogy through concurrent and postgraduate models of education, ensuring that newly qualified teachers are well prepared in both content knowledge and teaching and learning methodologies. There is no prescribed curriculum for teacher education, but there is a broad framework of guidance that recognizes the professional autonomy of the eight universities who offer initial teacher education.

The General Teaching Council for Scotland is an independent professional body with responsibility for setting and monitoring teachers' professional standards. There are three sets of standards:

- Standards for Beginning Teachers—Registration as a gate-keeping function for entry into teaching in Scotland and Full Registration, the standard for a fully qualified teacher: the baseline Professional Standard for Competence.
- The Standard for Career-Long Professional Learning—designed as a framework for teachers to use as the basis of their reflections as part of their professional learning.
- The Standards for Leadership and Management—developed to support the self-evaluation and professional learning of those in, or aspiring to, formal leadership roles in schools. (GTCS 2012)

All Professional Standards for teachers in Scotland are based on values of social justice, integrity, trust and respect and professional commitment demonstrated through practitioner enquiry. These professional values form the core of the standards.

Principles of practitioner enquiry underpin the Standard for Career-Long Professional Learning, requiring teachers to have an enquiring disposition at the core of their professional practice. Teachers are encouraged to think critically and to question their own educational beliefs, assumptions, values and practices. Teachers are encouraged to be adaptive experts who remain open to change, to engage with new ideas about teaching and learning and to work collaboratively. This self-reflective professional, reminiscent of Hoyle's (1974) extended professional, lies at the heart of the Scottish model of accountability in teacher education.

Professional Update is the formal mechanism for the continuing accreditation of teachers and is also the responsibility of the General Teaching Council for Scotland. Every teacher in Scotland must be registered with the General Teaching Council. The Council also deals with the removal of teachers from the register. Since 2012, the General Teaching Council has become the world's first independent, self-regulating professional body of teaching (Matheson 2015). Teachers in Scotland are obliged to take part in professional learning and must self-evaluate using the GTCS Professional Standards. They must maintain a record of their learning using an online profile, and every five years, there is a process to confirm that engagement.

Teaching Scotland's Future—The Donaldson Report

In 2009, the Scottish Government invited Graham Donaldson, previously the Chief Inspector of Schools in Scotland, to conduct a fundamental review of Teacher Education. The investigation was wide ranging and included visits to each of the eight universities providing teacher education, to a selection of local authorities and schools and meetings with a wide range of stakeholder groups and individuals. The study also included a commissioned literature review to look at evidence on teacher education worldwide and, where interesting practice was identified, this was followed up by discussions with colleagues in that country. Finally, the review team issued a call for evidence (receiving 100 responses) and developed a questionnaire for teachers (approximately 2500 responses).

The extensive body of evidence gathered through these various sources provided the base from which the findings and recommendations for *Teaching Scotland's Future* (2011) emerged. The methodology used was included as an Appendix of Chap. 13 in the report. This approach sought to build consensus through the process of policy development and to be transparent: making explicit the methodology used in the collection of evidence and the link between evidence and recommendations including an acknowledgement of the contested nature of views on Teacher Education.

> Understandably, there were strongly held and often divergent views about the best way to proceed. However, the response from individuals and organisations alike has invariably been open, thoughtful and constructive. (Foreword, p. iii)

The report was received positively.

The literature review (Menter et al. 2010) that underpinned the study reflected on the international context. The authors argued that, since the 1980s, the focus on 'effectiveness' had led to attention being focused on measurement and measurable outcomes, on education as a driver for economic growth, management processes and governance arrangements. The implications for Teacher Education had been to stress the importance of practical competence. Donaldson argued, however, that the most successful education systems had taken a different view. They had sought to move beyond standards of competence and conceptualized teachers *as 'reflective, accomplished and enquiring professionals…key actors in shaping and leading educational change'* (Donaldson 2011, p. 4).

Teaching Scotland's Future (2011) offered a radical vision for the future of the profession in Scotland. Teachers were not to be driven by forces of external change but were 'prime agents' (p. 4) in the change process. Teacher Education was a lifelong process and should seek to develop a profession where teachers saw themselves not only as educators of children, but also of their colleagues, locally, nationally and internationally. This vision for teacher education, with professionals as leaders in their fields, had implications for approaches to accountability. A word count of key terms in the policy offers an interesting insight into what matters in terms of Teacher Education and accountability. The word accountability appears twice in the document. Accountability is part of one of the eight statements of future direction:

- a call to reinvigorate the profession linked to a reconceptualization of teacher education
- more rigorous selection into teacher education and improvements in curricular relevance, use of time and consistency in assessment
- greater coherence across lifelong teacher education underpinned by a framework of standards
- development of leadership qualities throughout a career
- a new concept of partnership across stakeholder groups setting practical experience in a more reflective and enquiring culture
- better use of existing contracts and structures
- better alignment of policy, practice, theory and accountability to serve the needs of learners

- national and local infrastructure to promote and evaluate teacher education in ways that connect practice and innovation to beneficial impact on learning. (Teaching Scotland's Future 2011, p. 11)

Two issues are worthy of consideration. The first is that when the term accountability is used, it is linked to serving the needs of learners and to the need for alignment across policy, practice and theory. The second is that although the term accountability is used sparingly, the framework for evaluation is an intrinsic part of the agenda for action, most noticeably the statements of direction that refer to the framework of standards and to the evaluation of teacher education. Again, this is directly linked to impact on learning.

The second use of the term accountability in the Donaldson Report (2011) relates to how other professions have addressed the issue. The example cited is medicine (p. 42).

> It is not enough for a clinician to act as a practitioner in their own discipline. They must act as partners to their colleagues, accepting shared accountability for the service provided to patients. They are also expected to offer leadership, and to work with others to change systems when it is necessary for the benefit of patients.
>
> The roles of Doctor as a scientist and scholar, as a practitioner and as a professional should not be considered in isolation from each other. Doctors need to link them routinely in clinical practice. (General Medical Council 2009)

This example serves to highlight key aspects of the Donaldson vision—teachers as mentors, as self and peer evaluators, as agents of change and as professionals who integrate theory and practice into their everyday activities.

However, whilst the term accountability appears only twice, there are 148 references to professionalism and professional standards and 33 references to professionalism. Donaldson's intention is clear: to build teacher professionalism and to develop a self-regulating professionally accountable system for Teacher Education. This argument is supported by his recommendation that a set of Professional Standards for lifelong Teacher Education should be developed.

Evaluation of the Impact of Teaching Scotland's Future

Five years after the publication of the Donaldson Report (2011), the Scottish Government commissioned an evaluation of the impact of *Teaching Scotland's Future*. It was carried out by Ipsos MORI, an independent company, perhaps chosen to ensure that the evaluation was both independent and was seen to be independent. Ipsos MORI (2016, p. 6) reported that the teaching profession had 'risen to the challenge' of *Teaching Scotland's Future*. The evaluation detected significant shifts in the culture: teachers were more engaged in professional learning more broadly defined and saw professional learning as part of what it was to be a teacher; better partnerships existed between universities, local authorities and schools; professional learning was more closely linked to pupil learning; professional dialogue was common and teachers were more open to sharing experience and discussing pedagogy; teachers were more willing to try new approaches; fewer teachers reported barriers to accessing professional learning; there was far more evidence of mentoring and coaching and increased activity around leadership. Significantly, Ipsos MORI argued that the Standard for Leadership and Management had helped to make the pathway for leadership clearer.

Insights from the qualitative evidence gathered as part of the Ipsos MORI study identified several factors perceived to have influenced the cultural change. From the perspective of this chapter, the most interesting features related to the Standards. They argued that the use of the Standards as part of Professional Update:

> played a very important role in increasing engagement with professional learning. It was felt that the new Standards provided coherence to CLPL through all career stages. It was also noted that they promoted a shared language around CLPL and pedagogy. (Ipsos MORI 2016, p. 7)

There was also evidence of changes in initial teacher education. The evaluation reported a pervasive view that teachers recently emerging from initial teacher education had been influential in changing the more general teaching culture. This next generation of teachers was self-reflective, engaged routinely in professional dialogue, shared practices as a matter of course and sought to work collaboratively.

There were four references to accountability in the *Evaluation of the Impact of Teaching Scotland's Future* (Ipsos MORI 2016). The evaluators suggested that they had found evidence of the profession having risen to the challenge of transformational change at both school and system levels, driven not by external accountability or by the central development of guidance and resources, but by the professional capacity of teachers. As with *Teaching Scotland's Future*, there were significantly more references to professional standards ($n = 104$) and to professionalism ($n = 6$). Teachers were comfortable with the educational values on which the Standards are based but a major challenge remained: policy enactment was not consistent across the country and some teachers had had better experiences than others. There was, the evaluators recognized, still some way to go—Scotland was '*On the path—but not there yet*' (p. 91).

The OECD Report 'Improving Schools in Scotland'

The final policy text analyzed in this section is the OECD review of Scotland's National Curriculum Framework, Curriculum for Excellence (2015). This review was not focused on Teacher Education but reference was made to teacher education. As with the other two policy documents, a word count was undertaken of key terms. The balance between the use of the terms, professional standards, professionalism and accountability was different in this document. Whilst differences might be expected in the number of references to professional standards, given the different focus of the OECD report, even allowing for the differing lengths of the overall policy documents, there was a major difference. There were 35 references to accountability in the international review (OECD 2015) as opposed to two references in *Teaching Scotland's Future* (Donaldson 2011).

The OECD described both the call for a stronger profession in the Donaldson Report on Teacher Education as 'inspiring' (p. 126) and the GTCS Professional Standards as 'inspiring' (p. 17). They supported the conceptualization of the teaching profession in the Standards but argued for an increased focus on 'collaborative professionalism and leadership' (p. 22). They suggested that the approach taken to Professional Standards and Appraisal was consistent with international best practice (O'Day 2002; Klinger et al. 2008).

Their main critique of the Professional Standards lay not in the Standards themselves, but reflecting the *Evaluation of the Impact of Teaching Scotland's Future* (Ipsos MORI 2016), the OECD questioned 'how deeply the GTCS standards have moved from the theory to the practice and become embedded in the professional culture of the Scottish educational system' (p. 126). A second suggestion from OECD was to focus attention more on improving pupil outcomes.

Reflections

The vision of teacher education as a lifelong enterprise as envisioned in the Donaldson Report was well received by the profession. Its recommendations were taken forward by Government. The success of this radical review of teacher education may have been influenced by several factors. First, Scotland is a small country with a sense of shared values and the report ran with the grain of Scottish society. Its commitment to education, to high-quality professionalism and to the central role of the teacher was consistent with attitudes to education throughout Scotland's history. Second, among teacher educators, there may have been a sense of relief that the Donaldson Report (2011) had taken a strong line on continued partnerships between universities, local authorities and schools in contrast to the proliferation of routes into Teacher Education in England, e.g., to private organizations and to school-based training. Smithers et al. (2013) found 348 providers catering for 35,790 students who were admitted to Initial teacher education courses in England.

Third, the model used in the development of the report was highly inclusive, using the policy process as a means of building consensus. But perhaps most importantly, Donaldson left control of the profession with the profession and supported a model of accountability that sought not only to set high entry standards, but also to enhance career-long professional development, to promote high-quality leadership and to encourage a standards-based approach to professional engagement for all teachers.

The Review of the Impact of the Donaldson report (Ipsos MORI 2016) demonstrated progress—the profession had 'risen to the challenge' (p. 6). The standards-based approach to professional accountability was beginning to make a positive difference and given the radical nature of the changes proposed in the Donaldson review, it was not surprising that the evaluators reported that, five years on, Scotland was on the road but not there yet.

The OECD report (2015) also recognized the journey towards enhanced Teacher Professionalism in Scotland. They praised the approach to reflective practice being taken and argued that it was consistent with other high-quality international practices. They highlighted the challenge of the enactment of the standards-based approach across the education system and provided a series of helpful recommendations to support the Scottish system to realize its aspirations. However, the accountability focus in the OECD Review was stronger than in the other two policy papers. The report cautioned against the collection of certain kinds of data without being confident of the ability of individuals and groups to interpret, and more importantly to use, data to enhance learning:

> the different types of testing and assessment – local, national and international - have led to an explosion in the evidence available to decision-makers at all levels, putting a premium on the capacity to understand what they mean. (p. 98)

Whilst advocating the need for an accountability system to be able to discern differences across local authorities, the report also highlighted the danger of accountability measures that might bring with them unintended consequences.

> To achieve this goal, an important step during the consultation process will be to identify key principles on which to base the new assessment system that captures both the intended purposes, such as high-quality information, and the possibilities for unintended consequences, such as reducing rather than promoting teachers' assessment capacities. (p. 155)

However, following the visit of OECD, the Scottish Government committed to introduce online adaptive National Tests, following what they believed was a recommendation from OECD. There is international evidence that if tests become high stakes (Eggen and Stobart 2014) they are likely to have a negative effect on the development of teachers' professional judgement and in their views of themselves as professionals. Further dangers exist if data from tests are used by others in the education system in ways that the Government does not intend. The Scottish Government consistently argued that it was not their intention to use Standardized Tests for accountability purposes. Scotland is a small country and relationships across policy, research and practice are strong. It is testament to the strength of those relationships that, influenced by evidence from practice and from national and international research, the National Testing Policy was changed and the potential use or misuse of test data for high stakes purposes was averted.

The evidence emerging from the evaluation of Teaching Scotland's Future suggests that the Professional Standards and the model of accountability that they promote are beginning to be effective. However, the model where such confidence is shown in teachers and teacher educators as collaborative professionals is relatively rare in a world where accountability all too often has a much harder edge (Cochran-Smith et al. 2016). It has to be guarded with care. One aspect of guarding with care is to ensure that the profession faces up to the challenges the model presents and, as a profession, is actively involved in resolving tensions.

Teaching Scotland's Future, the Donaldson Report (2011) offers a powerful vision for the future of teacher education. The Ipsos MORI evaluation (2016) provides some reassurance that progress is being made towards that vision. The OECD report (2015), whilst very positive about the vision, provides an agenda for action that the profession has to address. In Teacher Education, Scotland's history, values and culture have provided some protection against the worst excesses of the Global Educational Reform Movement, but as hard, rather than intelligent, accountability (O'Neill 2002) systems continue to grow internationally, Scotland cannot be complacent. Although there is a strong commitment amongst politicians to engage in policy learning through collaboration with countries internationally, Scotland is not immune to the world of policy borrowing (Lingard 2010). It will take more than a commitment to values to keep the accountability tiger tamed.

References

Ball, S. J. (2015). What is policy? 21 years later: Reflections on the possibilities of policy research. *Discourse: Studies in the Cultural Politics of Education, 36*(3), 306–313. https://doi.org/10.1080/01596306.2015.1015279.

Beauchamp, G., Clarke, L., Hulme, M., & Murray, J. (2015). Teacher education in the United Kingdom post devolution: Convergences and divergences. *Oxford Review of Education, 41*(2), 154–170. https://doi.org/10.1080/03054985.2015.1017403.

Bryce, T. G. K., Humes, W. M., Gillies, D., & Kennedy, A. (Eds.). (2013). *Scottish education* (4th ed.). Edinburgh, Scotland: Edinburgh University Press.

Cochran-Smith, M., Stern, R., Sánchez, J. G., Miller, A., Keefe, E. S., Fernández, M. B., et al. (2016). *Holding teacher preparation accountable: A review of claims and evidence*. Boulder, CO: National Education Policy Center. Retrieved January 14, 2018 from http://nepc.colorado.edu/files/pb_cochran-smith_teacher_prep_0.pdf.

Croxford, L., & Raffe, D. (2007). Education markets and social class inequality: A comparison of trends in England, Wales and Scotland. In R. Teese, S. Lamb, M. Duru-Bellat, & S. Helme (Eds.), *International studies in educational inequality, theory and policy* (pp. 710–737). Dordrecht, The Netherlands: Springer. https://doi.org/10.1007/978-1-4020-5916-2_28.

Curriculum Review Group. (2004). *A curriculum for excellence*. Edinburgh, Scotland: Scottish Government. Retrieved from January 19, 2018 from http://www.gov.scot/Resource/Doc/26800/0023690.pdf.

Davie, G. E. (1961). *The democratic intellect*. Edinburgh, Scotland: Edinburgh University Press.

Dickson, B. (2011). Beginning teachers as enquirers: M-level work in initial teacher education. *European Journal of Teacher Education, 34*(3), 259–276. https://doi.org/10.1080/02619768.2010.538676.

Donaldson, G. (2011). *Teaching Scotland's future: Report of a review of teacher education in Scotland*. Edinburgh, Scotland: Scottish Government.

Education Scotland. (2012). *Framework document*. Glasgow, Scotland: Author. Retrieved January 18, 2018 from http://www.educationscotland.gov.uk/Images/EducationScotlandFrameworkDocument_tcm4-745890.pdf.

Eggen, T. J. H. M., & Stobart, G. (Eds.). (2014). *High stakes testing in education: Value, fairness and consequences*. London, England: Routledge.

General Medical Council. (2009). *Tomorrow's doctors-outcomes and standards for undergraduate medical education*. London, England: GMC.

Grek, S. (2012). What PISA knows and can do: Studying the role of national actors in the making of PISA. *European Educational Research Journal, 11*(2), 243–254. https://doi.org/10.2304/eerj.2012.11.2.243.

GTCS [General Teaching Council of Scotland]. (2012). *The standard for career-long professional learning: Supporting the development of teacher professional learning*. Retrieved April 10, 2017 from http://www.gtcs.org.uk/web/FILES/the-standards/standard-for-career-long-professional-learning-1212.pdf.

Hayward, E. L. (2007). Curriculum, pedagogies and assessment in Scotland: The quest for social justice 'Ah kent yir faither'. *Assessment in Education: Principles, Policy and Practice, 14*(2), 251–268. https://doi.org/10.1080/09695940701480178.

Hayward, L., & Hutchinson, C. (2013). Exactly what do you mean by consistency? Exploring concepts of consistency and standards in curriculum for excellence in Scotland. *Assessment in Education: Principles, Policy and Practice, 20*(1), 53–68. https://doi.org/10.1080/0969594X.2012.742423.

Hayward, L., MacBride, G., & Spencer, E. (2016). Scotland: The intersection of international student assessment and educational policy development. In L. Volante (Ed.), *The intersection of international achievement testing and educational reform* (pp. 58–74). New York, NY: Routledge.

HMSO. (1945). *Education (Scotland) Act 1945*. London, England: Author.

Hoyle, E. (1974). Professionality, professionalism and control in teaching. *London Educational Review, 3*(2), 13–19.

Ipsos MORI. (2016). *Evaluation of the impact of teaching Scotland's future*. Retrieved January 14, 2018 from https://www.ipsos.com/ipsos-mori/en-uk/evaluation-teaching-scotlands-future.

Kerr, J. (1910). *Scottish education—Schools and universities: From early times to 1908*. Retrieved April 10, 2017 from http://www.electricscotland.com/education/edu.htm.

Klinger, D. A., Shulha, L. M., & DeLuca, C. (2008). Teacher evaluation, accountability, and professional learning: The Canadian perspective. *Rev. Pensamiento Educativo, 43*, 209–222.

Lingard, B. (2010). Policy borrowing, policy learning: Testing times in Australian schooling. *Critical Studies in Education, 51*(2), 129–147.

Matheson, I. (2015). *Milestones and minefields—A history of GTC Scotland*. Edinburgh, Scotland: GTCS Publication.

Menter, I. (2016). Introduction. In G. Beauchamp, L. Clarke, M. Hulme, M. Jephcote, A. Kennedy, G. Magennis, et al. (Eds.), *Teacher education in times of change* (pp. 3–17). Bristol, England: Policy Press.

Menter, I., Hulme, M., Elliot, J., & Lewin, J. (2010). *Literature review on teacher education in the twenty first century*. Glasgow, Scotland: University of Glasgow.

O'Day, J. (2002). Complexity, accountability and school improvement. *Harvard Education Review, 72*(3), 293–329.

OECD [The Organisation for Economic Co-operation and Development]. (2015). *Improving Schools in Scotland*. Paris, France: OECD. Retrieved January 14, 2018 from http://www.oecd.org/education/school/Improving-Schools-in-Scotland-An-OECD-Perspective.pdf.

O'Neill, O. (2002). *BBC Reith lecture: A question of trust—Called to account (Lecture 3)*. Retrieved January 18, 2017 from http://www.bbc.co.uk/radio4/reith2002/lecture3.shtml.

Peters, M. A., & Besley, T. (2014). What is global studies in education? *Policy Futures in Education, 12*(7), 850–854. https://doi.org/10.2304/pfie.2014.12.7.850.

Raffe, D. (2005). Devolution and divergence in education policy. In J. Adams & K. Schmuecker (Eds.), *Devolution in practice: Public policy differences within the UK* (pp. 52–69). Newcastle, England: IPPR North.

Rizvi, F., & Lingard, B. (2010). *Globalizing education policy*. London, England: Routledge.

Scottish Government. (2016). *A national improvement framework for Scotland—Excellence and equity*. Edinburgh, Scotland: Scottish Government.

Scottish Parliament. (2000). *Standards in Scotland's schools etc. Act 2000*. Edinburgh, Scotland: Author.

Smithers, A., Robinson, J., & Coughlin, M. D. (2013). *The good teacher training guide 2013*. Buckingham, England: Centre for Education and Employment Research, University of Buckingham. Retrieved March 30, 2017 from http://www.alansmithers.com/reports/The_Good_Teacher_Training_Guide_2012.pdf.

The Stationery Office. (1998). *Scotland Act 1998*. London, England: Author.

Louise Hayward is Professor of Educational Assessment and Innovation at the University of Glasgow, Scotland. She has a particular interest in social justice and how decisions taken about curriculum, assessment and pedagogy might be enhanced by collaboration across research, policy and practice communities. Currently, Louise is working with the Scottish, Welsh and Norwegian Governments. She is a founder member of the International Assessment in Education Network bringing together researchers and policy makers from small nations and states to tackle some of the more intransigent international assessment challenges. She is one of four executive editors of the Curriculum Journal. Louise was a member of the internationally renowned Assessment Reform Group and has written extensively on assessment and learning and on national change processes.

Chapter 4
Lost in Transition: Learning to Teach in the Era of Test-Based Accountability

Jina Ro

Introduction

Neoliberal ideology is leading educational policies and practices in many nations around the world today. In the context of schooling, it puts greater emphasis on teacher quality and accountability based on the assumption that teachers are the key performants who educate the nation's future workforce (Apple 2006; Spring 2010). Observable and measurable outcomes and indicators, such as test score data, have become more significant to estimate not only the current state of students' academic performance but also the performance of teachers as well as the nation. In some countries, such as in the USA, the federal government has been strengthening its accountability control by supporting the implementation of high-stakes testing and evaluating teachers based on student performance data (Kumashiro 2012; Tuck 2013).

The recent trend of the dominance of neoliberalism is also affecting teacher education significantly. Just as teachers are expected to contribute to improving student performance, teacher education programs are facing intense demand for producing high-quality teachers who are capable of improving the performance of students (Cochran-Smith et al. 2013; Lewis and Young 2013; Tuck 2013). In the case of the USA, this demand has pushed teacher education to reduce its length, offer diverse pathways to becoming teachers besides university-based programs, and eliminate any elements of such programs that are not immediately useful to teachers (Cochran-Smith et al. 2013; Lewis and Young 2013).

The challenges facing teacher education at this time are intense and complex. In a test-based accountability context, there exists a 'practice-practice gap' between preservice teacher education and schools. In schools affected by test-based accountability, teaching to the test is taken for granted. It often takes the form of

J. Ro (✉)
National Institute of Education, Nanyang Technological University, Singapore, Singapore
e-mail: jina.ro@nie.edu.sg

© Springer Nature Singapore Pte Ltd. 2018
C. Wyatt-Smith and L. Adie (eds.), *Innovation and Accountability in Teacher Education*, Teacher Education, Learning Innovation and Accountability, https://doi.org/10.1007/978-981-13-2026-2_4

teacher-directed instruction focusing on mastering the content and drilling students on their test-taking skills (Valli and Chambliss 2007; Watanabe 2007). In this condition, teachers are expected to be content masters who faithfully deliver the accurate tested content (Imig and Imig 2006). Therefore, teachers in a test-based accountability context must be prepared to teach in this manner. However, preparation programs often promote different practices that largely conflict with teaching to the test. In the case of the USA, many preparation programs promote equity, diversity, and social justice as their mission and aim to reflect these values in their curricular and practices in teacher education. Aligned to these values, teacher candidates learn the practices, methods, and pedagogies of culturally responsive teaching and the constructivist approach, which emphasizes teachers' attention on students' interests, prior learning experiences, and backgrounds (Achinstein and Ogawa 2012; Agee 2004). However, the problem here is that such practices are not favored and encouraged within an accountability system where teachers are expected to meet demands through the performance of their students.

If the practices valued in preparation programs and schools are substantially different and conflict with each other, it is obvious that beginning teachers are those who would be most disadvantaged by and who would suffer because of this disjuncture. This chapter explores how teacher education can and ought to prepare teacher candidates to teach in the era of test-based accountability that enforces practices that are often poles apart from their preservice learning. Using the framework of the relationships of knowledge and practice by Cochran-Smith and Lytle (1999), I analyze the preservice learning and current practices of three American beginning teachers who work in three different levels of accountability contexts: high, moderate, and low accountability. Based on the analysis results, I suggest that one way for teacher education to resolve the issue of disconnected preservice learning and teachers' struggle of learning to teach in a test-based accountability context is to build teacher candidates' capacity for change by establishing their 'inquiry stance' (Cochran-Smith and Lytle 1999, 2009), which will promote critical thinking, active roles in leading professional learning, and contributions toward transforming the school system.

The Three Conceptions of Teacher Learning

This chapter is grounded in two assumptions, the first of which is that teacher learning is a continual process. To become a teacher, every candidate undertakes preservice education, but the completion of it does not mean the end of his or her learning. In fact, teacher learning still continues on the job. Therefore, the role of preparation programs should be to support smooth transition and build the foundation of teacher learning for continuous professional growth (Feiman-Nemser 2001; Ulvik et al. 2009).

Another assumption is that the role of preservice education in the era of test-based accountability is not to educate teachers to be mere executors of accountability demands. If test-based accountability is found to have many limitations and side effects, as indicated by numerous educators, teachers need to be able to challenge this situation and play a role in transforming the problematic schooling caused by accountability mandates. Teachers are also required to have greater abilities beyond just implementing a set of practices (Hargreaves and Fullan 2012; Imig and Imig 2006). Thus, building teachers' capacity for change needs to be a significant part of preservice education.

In line with these two assumptions, Cochran-Smith and Lytle (1999) suggested a framework that synthesizes and categorizes previous discourses about teacher learning into three conceptions: knowledge *for* practice, knowledge *in* practice, and knowledge *of* practice. The first conception, knowledge *for* practice, is grounded in the assumption that there exists a formal knowledge base. Shulman's (1987) notion of the knowledge base for teaching, which involves various domains of teacher knowledge—such as content knowledge, knowledge about learners, classroom management, and assessment—is an exemplar of this conception. In the conception of knowledge for practice, teachers are expected to master the best practices of such a formal knowledge base that are typically developed by experts in the field. Professional learning of teachers involves becoming skillful in such practices and implementing them successfully in teachers' own work settings. In this conception, what Lampert (2009) called the 'rehearsal' (p. 27) becomes the central pedagogy of preservice education: 'a focus on rehearsing and becoming proficient at the routine aspects of teaching can provide a backdrop for learning how to make the more complex interactive judgments that are required in the context of an activity' (p. 27). Understanding preservice education in this respect, however, raises the question of whether more complex activities of teaching that are context-specific or that involve interactions with pupils could also be learned in this way (Zeichner 2012).

The second conception, knowledge *in* practice, assumes that teacher learning evolves and progresses through experience. Instead of a formal knowledge base, it assumes that teacher knowledge is situated in and established from teachers' working context. Such knowledge is identified and developed through individual teachers' reflection on practice and learning of the exemplary practices of expert teachers (Cochran-Smith and Lytle 1999). The mentoring of novices by an experienced teacher is an example that illustrates this conception. Through mentoring, novice teachers can gain the wise, experiential, and practical knowledge of the mentor and become more proficient by repeating the application of this practical knowledge to their own contexts (Ingersoll and Strong 2011; Wang and Fulton 2012). In recognizing the significance of context in teacher learning, this conception shares a similar view with the first conception by assuming that the knowledge teachers need to know is predetermined and established and that teachers become proficient through the experience of repetitive practice and reflection (Cochran-Smith and Lytle 1999).

The third conception, knowledge *of* practice, is differentiated from the first two in that it considers teachers as co-constructors and generators of knowledge that is not only useful in their own specific contexts but can also be influential in other contexts. Instead of mastering a set of predetermined knowledge or modeling the exemplar practices of an expert teacher, teachers can learn by, 'challenging their own assumptions; identifying salient issues of practice; posing problems; studying their own students, classrooms, and schools; constructing and reconstructing curriculum; and taking on roles of leadership and activism in efforts to transform classrooms, schools, and societies' (Cochran-Smith and Lytle 1999, p. 278). Moreover, teacher learning is facilitated when they collaboratively participate in systematic inquiry about practice through communities or networks (Cochran-Smith and Lytle 1999, 2009; McLaughlin and Talbert 2006; Paugh 2006). These are ideal structures for teachers to investigate, understand, and theorize on their own as well as others' knowledge and to co-construct knowledge that can alter their individual practices in classrooms as well as inform broader changes in schooling (Cochran-Smith and Lytle 2009; Paugh 2006).

Understanding Teacher Learning in the Era of Test-Based Accountability: The Cases of Three American Teachers

In this section, three American teachers' experiences of learning from preservice education to their current working contexts is examined to understand the impact of their preparation on their current practice of teaching and professional learning and to identify issues regarding preparing teachers in the context of test-based accountability. The teachers were drawn from a larger research project that looked into the lived experiences of beginning teachers' professional learning in the context of test-based accountability. Each beginning teacher in this project participated in a series of three in-depth interviews that explored his or her journey of learning to teach. The three teachers were particularly selected for this chapter because each of their school contexts represented high-, moderate-, and low-stakes test-based accountability that may have a different impact on their learning to teach. They also went to different university-based preparation programs located in the same area (Boston, Massachusetts).

The Learning of a Teacher from a High-Stakes Accountability Context

Jim was a second-year middle school English teacher who worked in a high-stakes accountability context because his school district used student performance data on the state standardized test for teacher evaluation, which was called 'student growth percentile' (SGP). According to this measure, the new cohort's scores on the standardized test were compared with the last year's cohort every year. For example, if the new cohort showed a higher performance than 70% of the students from the last year, their SGP was 70%. If a teacher's SGP was below 50%, the teacher was identified as 'needs improvement' and had to provide additional materials or do extra work to meet the guidelines for promotion and tenure. For that reason, Jim felt intense pressure to show his teaching capability. He explained the pressure as follows:

> I have always put a lot of pressure on myself to achieve well. I think, when you look at it, this is the only test that I take all year. I know it's my 75 kids taking the test, but my SGP score feels like it's a grade to me. If I get a 70, it's supposed to be good, but I think it should be better. I think I've done a better job than what shows. I guess that kind of bothers me a little bit.

Because his evaluation results were tied to his student performance, Jim had no choice but to practise teaching to the test. However, Jim complained that this prevented him from teaching in the way that he had wished to teach before he started teaching: 'I definitely wanted to be engaging; I wanted to bring a lot of different lesson plan ideas that kids had not really seen, [and] get them thinking in different ways.' In reality, however, the time was always too limited for him to even teach all the necessary knowledge and skills for the test.

The most frustrating thing for Jim was to see some of his students, who were mostly English language learners and had special needs, giving up on taking the test. Because the test was too long and had too many questions, the students were not able to complete it in time. Jim said this was not because his students were incapable, but because the test was not a proper measure to assess their potential. Jim felt frustrated that he still needed to drill them although they were discouraged and scared by the test:

> There's a mix between drilling at the end and calming them down, because they'll start to freak out a little bit or get tired of writing. (…) I don't try to overdrill them, because then when the day comes, they're sick and tired of writing. It's trying to find this balance of making sure they know what to do and making sure that they might actually do it. I've had kids—even this year, I had kids who go to the test and they just handed it in blank because they knew it didn't count for them and they didn't feel like writing again, so they'll just hand it in blank. There's that.

Because of the high-stakes accountability system in his district, Jim struggled with too many tasks: worrying about his evaluation results, drilling his students on the test, securing the time to teach them other materials, and calming down nervous students. It was daunting for a second-year teacher to handle all these matters, which he had never expected to encounter. In this regard, Jim said it would have been helpful for him to have a prior understanding of the significance of test-based accountability during preservice education:

> You don't really get the full picture of how much standardized testing there is [until you started to teach]. It still shocks me how much. We did MCAS [the state standardized test] two weeks ago. I've got a district-wide assessment coming up. I just did two open responses last week, district-wide assessment this week. It's constant. Just constant, constant, constant testing.

Although Jim was generally satisfied with his preparation program, because he could have abundant practicum experiences during four entire semesters in three different schools, he felt he was not prepared well for the significance of an accountability system that greatly affected his current practice. When he started to teach, Jim thought he had the knowledge and skills for teaching English, as well as his own ideas about what and how to teach, but he did not realize that these could be greatly constrained by the accountability system. Jim's case suggests that just equipping novice teachers with the knowledge and skills of teaching without much consideration of future working contexts is insufficient for such teachers to survive and navigate the high-stakes accountability context.

The Learning of a Teacher from a Moderate-Accountability Context

Chelsey was a second-year high-school math teacher who worked in an average-performing urban school that had diverse students from various cultural and socioeconomic backgrounds. Unlike Jim, her school district did not have a teacher evaluation system based on state test results. However, she was teaching a tested grade and subject (Algebra I and Geometry), and so she felt responsible for preparing her students for the test. Chelsey complained that she had to rush to cover all the content before the test; and this time constraint pushed her to make her classes more teacher directed, which she did not like:

> The fastest way to get through the most material is to have it be teacher-centered, where I am lecturing at them 95% of the time. They come in. I'm teaching them how to do X, Y, and Z, [and] they are doing X, Y and Z at home because I need to cover so much material. The MCAS [the state standardized test] wants us to get through 12 chapters before the school year is done, which is ridiculous. The advanced classes don't even get through a whole book. It's impossible. The quickest way to deliver that so that they can at least be shown and experience all the mathematics contents on the MCAS, is for me to stand in front of them and talk, which I hate because that's going to get boring. It's going to get tedious, 'Are we doing notes again today, Ms. P.?' 'Of course.'

Instead of teacher-directed lessons, Chelsey had been aspiring to use the discovery learning approach, which she had learned from one of her teaching methods courses during her preservice education. In this course, the professor taught by letting students discover their own ways to resolve a math problem. By experiencing the discovery learning approach themselves, the students could learn how to teach it. Chelsey was fascinated by this method and came to have a strong wish to use this approach when she became a teacher:

> It was just a really new way of being taught and of someone teaching me that I had never seen before. It just made me think in a completely new way. That really affected the rest of my college career. It taught me that everything doesn't have to be cookie cutter, and I don't need to have a recipe for mathematics. Like, let's just go crazy and figure out something new. I think that's what really blew my mind that first class.

After she started to teach, however, Chelsey realized that she was not able to use the method as often as she had wished because she had to teach to the test. Instead of discovery learning, she said she was mostly 'shoveling' mathematics content into her students' brains. Chelsey was frustrated that she might bore her students and diminish their interests in learning mathematics, although she had never wanted and expected to do so: 'It bugs me a bit because I would love to just do those big discovery learning activities like I got to do when I was in college, but we have to get through so much material so fast that it is like I barely have time to breathe.'

Although Chelsey strongly believed in the value and effect of the discovery approach, she needed to accept that this practice was not encouraged under the accountability system to which she belonged. There was a huge discrepancy between the practice she learned and found to be meaningful from her preservice education and the practice—teaching to the test—that was prioritized in her current working context. Chelsey still maintained her wish to use discovery learning because she believed in its effects for meaningful student learning, but she struggled with carrying it out along with teaching to the test. Although her preservice education taught her a wonderful method, it seemed to fail to prepare her to deal with such a conflicting situation.

The Learning of a Teacher from a Low-Accountability Context

Dana was a second-year high school English teacher working in a low-stakes context because, unlike Jim and Chelsey, she was not teaching a tested grade or subject. Therefore, Dana had more flexibility to teach in the way she liked, taking into account her students' academic backgrounds, abilities, and interests. Many of her students were English language learners from immigrant families or had special needs, so they struggled with reading and writing. Hence, Dana tried to include various kinds of learning activities, provide positive and constructive feedback on students' work, and offer enough time to let students finish a task during the lesson. She was aware that her lessons could reflect the students' needs more than the lessons of other teachers in her school because she was not teaching the tested grade. Dana said she was 'lucky' that she did not have the same pressure to teach to the test as the other colleagues and thus felt content about her teaching: 'I have full freedom. I am given a book and they say 'make your units around that book.' Everything is completely up to me on what I teach, how I teach it. That's amazing. That's why … I love this school so much.'

While she liked to teach in her current school, Dana was very critical about her preservice education. She said, 'I don't think my [preservice] education came into play. I think it's something that come[s] with experience.' Being interested in teaching high school students, Dana had enrolled in a secondary English education program, expecting to learn about teaching English as well as classroom management at the high-school level. However, she found that:

> In one class, I was one of two high-school teachers. It was difficult because the majority, like I said, were elementary, so when it came to doing projects and stuff, everything was too fine-tuned to elementary. Even, like, taking classes on theories, teaching theories, they were more relevant to children transitioning into adolescence. My kids are pretty much, I mean, they've transitioned. It's not relevant to them, transitioning now into adulthood. It was very child-based. Again, yeah, I think it's because we were extremely outnumbered.

Besides the irrelevant coursework, Dana pointed out that she did not learn much about the accountability-related matters that affect her current work, such as standardized tests, curriculum standards, and teacher evaluation. She only realized their significance after she became a teacher. She specifically referred to the Common Core Standards, which is a set of curriculum standards in English language arts/litcracy and math developed by the majority of states in the United States for kindergarten through 12th-grade learners. It is currently adopted and implemented by 42 states and the District of Columbia (The Common Core State Standards Initiative 2016). She said, 'In my classes [in preservice education], they talked about the Common Core Standards but not in depth, and they never told you really how to apply them. I thought that was a huge disservice to teachers.' For that reason, Dana needed to spend much time and effort during her first year to develop her lessons according to the standards, as she had never learned about them. She said, 'I was just given a book [that included the curriculum standards] and they said 'We teach around the book.' That's basically how I start[ed].'

The only positive experience Dana had during preservice education was the practicum, because she had a chance to practise teaching, and develop many strategies and skills that she could start using in her second year. Because of her negative experience in preservice education, Dana was skeptical about the necessity and effect of preparation programs. She said:

> I don't think that anybody is actually prepared [through preservice education]. You can take 1,500 teaching courses and not know. I mean, next year, maybe I won't be prepared. Maybe I won't be prepared for teaching because I'll have a whole different student body that I'm working with, a whole different group of personalities that I'll have to get to know.

For Dana, learning by doing was the way she had been learning to teach. Much of her learning had been established in her current context of experiencing teaching, but she had not gained much foundational knowledge and support from elsewhere. Although Dana was hopeful that she could continue to learn and grow year by year, it was uncertain whether sustainable learning would be possible if she encountered more difficult challenges when, for example, teaching the tested cohorts and when she was subjected to higher-stakes accountability control.

The Role and Meaning of Preservice Education for Constant Teacher Learning in the Test-Based Accountability Context

Looking at the three teachers' cases, it becomes evident that there was a disconnection between their preservice education and their current practice of teaching, regardless of the accountability contexts and the preparation programs they went through. Jim and Chelsey struggled with teaching to the test, which conflicted with their prior goals and expectations for teaching. Dana had to create everything on her own from the beginning because her preservice education was not relevant to her classroom practice. The job of bridging the gap between preservice learning and actual classroom practice was solely left to the novice teachers. They were still in the stage of figuring out how to do it and what to do to continue to learn to teach without much support. This raises the question of how to promote novice teachers' constant learning and growth when they are placed in different accountability contexts and what contribution preservice education can particularly make in this regard.

By applying the framework of teacher learning, several approaches can be considered in preservice education. One way is teaching candidates about accountability matters by aligning to the conception of knowledge *for* practice. Specifically, the topics of how to incorporate curriculum standards into lessons and the process of teacher evaluation (including its significance for promotion and tips for obtaining good results) and how to provide effective test preparation could be included in the coursework of preparation programs. This may be particularly useful if the goal and purpose of preservice education is to prepare candidates for their future performance by equipping them with a set of knowledge and skills that is most relevant and applicable to their current work. However, this manner of support has limitations because, as Dana mentioned, every teacher's classroom is different and changes every year. In fact, the three cases considered in this chapter show that most preservice learning is not directly relevant to or applied in teachers' classrooms. Even a strong, research-based practice may not be utilized in every case; instead, it may require some modification or adaptation by the teacher. Therefore, teachers themselves still need to play a substantial role in adjusting their preservice learning in the classrooms (Korthagen 2017; Zeichner 2012).

Another way is to offer ongoing support during teachers' early years in the form of mentoring or induction programs based on the conception of knowledge *in* practice. Many studies have found that this is an effective way of providing support for novice teachers' transition and retention (Ingersoll and Strong 2011; Wang and Fulton 2012). Coaching from expert teachers can be helpful if learning to teach is concerned with learning 'how.' However, learning 'what to be' is also a significant part of teacher learning because teachers are more than technicians who deliver a set of practices. In fact, teachers are autonomous practitioners who are capable of pursuing their own professional visions and leading their professional learning and growth (Hargreaves and Fullan 2012; Imig and Imig 2006; Lampert 2009; Zeichner 2012). This capacity of teachers becomes more significant in a test-based accountability context in which teaching becomes reduced to test preparation and teachers' role is minimized as deliverers of tested content (Hargreaves and Fullan 2012; Imig and Imig 2006; Zeichner 2012). The first two ways, which are respectively grounded in the ideas of knowledge *for* and *in* practice, neglect this point by treating teachers merely as targets of intervention and passive receivers and implementors of knowledge, similar to the way they are treated by accountability mandates.

The precondition to provide meaningful support for novice teachers' constant learning in the context of test-based accountability is to acknowledge teachers as active learners who are capable of leading their professional growth. Based on this assumption, it is necessary to understand the learning needs of novice teachers. What Jim, Chelsey, and Dana wanted to learn was not a technique or skill that helped them conform to the accountability mandates better by effectively teaching to the test. In fact, they were all critical about this practice, and Jim and Chelsey particularly struggled with it because it conflicted with their vision about good teaching, which they had established during preservice education. Instead of learning such practices that make them mere executors of the accountability mandates, the teachers may have needed to learn problem-solving skills that would enable them to find ways to survive and grow within the accountability system, especially when it constrains their realization of their visions and goals in teaching. Learning and being prepared to exercise knowledge *of* practice would have been helpful, as it would have encouraged their active role in bridging the gap in leading their own professional learning and transforming their practice and schooling. This knowledge needs to be established from the preservice education stage so that the teachers are confident about playing their role when they start to teach and are capable of building on it further on the job.

According to Cochran-Smith and Lytle (2009), the knowledge of practice can be developed through teachers having *inquiry as stance*. This means that teachers uphold inquiry 'as a critical habit of mind' (p. 121) and have it inform their practice. However, inquiry in this sense is strictly differentiated from inquiry as a classroom-based research project that is typically bounded by time and place and that aims to derive immediate solutions for individual teachers' problems. Instead, Cochran-Smith and Lytle (2009) argued:

> Fundamental to the notion of inquiry as stance is the idea that educational practice is not simply instrumental in the sense of figuring out how to get things done, but also and more importantly, it is social and political in the sense of deliberating about what to get done, why to get it done, who decides, and whose interests are served. Working from and with an inquiry stance, then, involves a continual process of making current arrangements problematic; questioning the ways knowledge and practice are constructed, evaluated, and used; and assuming that part of the work of practitioners individually and collectively is to participate in educational and social change. (p. 121)

As Cochran-Smith and Lytle (2009) argued, inquiry as stance emphasizes that teachers should have a critical perspective that problematizes and questions every aspect of their practice, rather than just accepting and modeling certain practices. Teachers who have such a stance would continuously question the taken-for-granted practices in their working contexts and deliberate on various data concerning those problematized practices with a clear purpose of participating in transforming the school system. This idea aligns to the view that considers teachers as change agents whose work aims to contribute to enhancing the conditions of society that affect student learning and well-being (Carr and Kemmis 1986; Hargreaves and Fullan 2012).

Despite being novices, it was obvious that Jim, Chelsey, and Dana all possessed change mind-sets. They did not want to be teachers who merely complied with accountability mandates. Rather, they had their own ideas about teaching that were centered on student interests and learning, and they hoped to practise these ideas more within the accountability system. In other words, they wanted to know 'something' that helped them work both 'within and against the system' (Cochran-Smith and Lytle 2009, p. 146) to establish their knowledge *of* practice. Common to all three cases was their vision of teaching and contributing to meaningful student learning and transforming current schooling. Inquiry as a stance could be a way of building such teachers' capacities as change agents, continuing from preservice education.

Implications for Teacher Education and the Next Step

Most preparation and induction programs have been inclined to provide support grounded in the first two conceptions, knowledge *for* and *in* practice. This chapter illustrates that in the context of test-based accountability, these two approaches have limitations in supporting novice teachers' constant learning and promoting their efforts for change. However, the third conception, knowledge *of* practice, has potential in this context, and so preservice education could consider to address it significantly in their curriculum and practices. A common misunderstanding is that this conception may neglect building the foundational knowledge and skills of candidates in teaching. It should be noted that these foundations are still important and teacher candidates need to learn them, but they should also be open to questions, critiques, and deliberations and be encouraged to take inquiry as a stance (Cochran-Smith and Lytle 2009). With this stance, candidates can actively participate in raising questions and deliberating on the taken-for-granted practices in their education system. The so-called best practices or core practices in teaching are also called into question as candidates attempt to problematize and challenge such practices.

Developing knowledge of practice in preservice education does not only involve questioning and critiquing. If some discrepancies or holes are detected in this process, candidates need to find ways to resolve these issues through systematic inquiry and collaboration among diverse bodies, such as teacher educators, experienced teachers, and peers. It is not only teacher educators and experienced teachers (e.g., the cooperative teacher of their practicum) whom candidates can seek help from but also their peers. The peers can provide alternative perspectives and collaborate with and support one another in learning to teach. This reflects how in the conception of knowledge *of* practice, teacher learning is facilitated by collaborative participation in inquiry, and every member's backgrounds, viewpoints, opinions, and expertise are equally valued (Cochran-Smith and Lytle 2009; Paugh 2006). Thus, turning every preparation program classroom into an inquiry community could be an ideal structure for learning to teach.

Although the conception of knowledge *of* practice and inquiry as a stance has potential for enhancing teacher learning and growth in the context of test-based accountability, how it can be reflected and developed in preservice education is still ambiguous. To be considered as an alternative approach to teacher education, more investigation and evidence of this conception are necessary. What is it like developing a preparation program grounded in this perspective? What are the specific practices of teacher education that address and promote this idea? What are the results of such a program or practices, including its effects and limitations, particularly regarding preparing candidates to teach in a test-based accountability context?

Further research is also needed that examines whether and how teacher education based on this conception can truly bridge the gap between preservice learning and current practice and promote teachers' active participation in their own learning and change. Moreover, how teachers continue to utilize and build on their knowledge *of* practice in a challenging working context, such as in a test-based accountability system, needs to be investigated.

References

Achinstein, B., & Ogawa, R. (2012). New teachers of color and culturally responsive teaching in an era of educational accountability: Caught in a double bind. *Journal of Educational Change, 13*(1), 1–39. https://doi.org/10.1007/s10833-011-9165-y.

Agee, J. (2004). Negotiating a teaching identity: An African American teacher's struggle to teach in test-driven contexts. *Teachers College Record, 106*(4), 747–774. https://doi.org/10.1111/j.1467-9620.2004.00357.x.

Apple, M. W. (2006). *Educating the 'right' way: Markets, standards, God, and inequality*. New York, NY: Taylor & Francis.

Carr, W., & Kemmis, S. (1986). *Becomming critical: Education, knowledge and action research*. London, England: Falmer.

Cochran-Smith, M., & Lytle, S. L. (1999). Relationships of knowledge and practice: Teacher learning in communities. *Review of Research in Education, 24*(1), 249–305.

Cochran-Smith, M., & Lytle, S. L. (2009). *Inquiry as stance: Practitioner research for the next generation*. New York, NY: Teachers College Press.

Cochran-Smith, M., Piazza, P., & Power, C. (2013). The politics of accountability: Assessing teacher education in the United States. *The Educational Forum, 77*(1), 6–27.

Feiman-Nemser, S. (2001). From preparation to practice: Designing a continuum to strengthen and sustain teaching. *Teachers College Record, 103*(6), 1013–1055.

Hargreaves, A., & Fullan, M. (2012). *Professional capital: Transforming teaching in every school*. New York, NY: Teachers College Press.

Imig, D. G., & Imig, S. R. (2006). What do beginning teachers need to know? An essay. *Journal of Teacher Education, 57*(3), 286–291.

Ingersoll, R. M., & Strong, M. (2011). The impact of induction and mentoring programs for beginning teachers: A critical review of the research. *Review of Educational Research, 81*(2), 201–233. https://doi.org/10.3102/0034654311403323.

Korthagen, F. (2017). Inconvenient truths about teacher learning: Towards professional development 3.0. *Teachers and Teaching, 23*(4), 387–405.

Kumashiro, K. K. (2012). *Bad teacher!: How blaming teachers distorts the bigger picture*. New York, NY: Teachers College Press.

Lampert, M. (2009). Learning teaching in, from, and for practice: What do we mean? *Journal of Teacher Education, 61*(1–2), 21–34.

Lewis, W. D., & Young, T. V. (2013). The politics of accountability: Teacher education policy. *Educational Policy, 27*(2), 190–216.

McLaughlin, M. W., & Talbert, J. E. (2006). *Building school-based teacher learning communities: Professional strategies to improve student achievement.* New York, NY: Teachers College Press.

Paugh, P. C. (2006). Making sense of 'conflicting observations': Teachers, tests, and the power of collaborative inquiry in urban schools. *New Educator, 2*(1), 15–31.

Shulman, L. (1987). Knowledge and teaching: Foundations of the new reform. *Harvard Educational Review, 57*(1), 1–23.

Spring, J. (2010). *The politics of American education.* New York, NY: Routledge.

The Common Core State Standards Initiative. (2016). *About the standards.* Retrieved January 13, 2018 from http://www.corestandards.org/about-the-standards/.

Tuck, E. (2013). Neoliberalism as nihilism? A commentary on educational accountability, teacher education and school reform. *Journal for Critical Education Policy Studies, 11*(2), 324–347.

Ulvik, M., Smith, K., & Helleve, I. (2009). Novice in secondary school—The coin has two sides. *Teaching and Teacher Education, 25*(6), 835–842.

Valli, L., & Chambliss, M. (2007). Creating classroom cultures: One teacher, two lessons, and a high-stakes test. *Anthropology & Education Quarterly, 38*(1), 57–75.

Wang, J., & Fulton, L. A. (2012). Mentor-novice relationships and learning to teach in teacher induction: A critical review of research. *REMIE-Multidisciplinary Journal of Educational Research, 2*(1), 56–104.

Watanabe, M. (2007). Displaced teacher and state priorities in a high-stakes accountability context. *Educational Policy, 21*(2), 311–368.

Zeichner, K. (2012). The turn once again toward practice-based teacher education. *Journal of Teacher Education, 63*(5), 376–382.

Jina Ro is a post-doctoral fellow in Curriculum, Teaching, and Learning Academic Group at National Institute of Education, Nanyang Technological University, Singapore. Her research focuses on teacher learning and professionalism in the context of high-stakes testing. She is interested in researching this area further with qualitative methodologies. Prior to joining NIE, she taught English at a low-performing middle school in Korea and worked as an intern in the section for Teacher Education, United Nations Educational, Scientific and Cultural Organization. These experiences led her to pursue her doctoral degree in Curriculum and Instruction at Boston College, USA, focusing on teacher education. At NIE, she is conducting research on teacher learning and teaching courses about teacher learning, practitioner inquiry, and curriculum implementation to in-service teachers and professionals from the educational field.

Chapter 5
The Explicit Nature of Educational Goals for the Twenty-first Century

Esther Care and Helyn Kim

Introduction

Statements by OECD (2018) concerning the need for development of global competency are re-framing educators' vision of the goals of education. The identification of global citizenship as a target area within the Sustainable Development Goals (UN General Assembly 2015) is similarly a stimulus for the monitoring of skills as well as knowledge, values and attitudes. Against this backdrop, countries are shaping their individual reform efforts, often starting with curriculum. Curriculum reform is just one of several needed steps. Where the explicit promotion of skills is valued, review of pedagogical approaches and assessment methods is also required. This raises major issues for teachers and for teacher training. One issue concerns educators' knowledge of skills and teachers' capacity to model these skills; a second concern is the consequences of focus on skills, as well as on knowledge content, for pedagogical strategies.

What Are Twenty-first Century Skills?

For the current purpose, twenty-first century skills refer to those generic skills that are highly valued in our twenty-first century societies. Most of these skills are not idiosyncratic to this century; rather, they have been valued over the centuries, but not necessarily in terms of a formal education focus. Since the 1980s, there has been increasing global attention focussed on expectations of education systems. These expectations have been framed by a number of reports, including the Delors' Report (1996) which marked the beginning of UNESCO's twenty-first century competence

E. Care (✉) · H. Kim
The Brookings Institution, Washington, DC, USA
e-mail: ECare@brookings.edu

© Springer Nature Singapore Pte Ltd. 2018
C. Wyatt-Smith and L. Adie (eds.), *Innovation and Accountability in Teacher Education*, Teacher Education, Learning Innovation and Accountability,
https://doi.org/10.1007/978-981-13-2026-2_5

learning discourse—with learning to know, learning to do, learning to be and learning to live together—forming the four pillars of learning. In turn, the OECD supported the DeSeCo Project (Definition and Selection of Competencies; Rychen and Salganik 2003) classifying key competencies in three broad categories: first, individuals using a wide range of tools for interacting effectively; second, being able to engage with others; and third, taking responsibility for managing self within the broader social context. Translating the generic aspirations of the UNESCO and OECD visions into specific skills, Pellegrino and Hilton (2012) reported a classification scheme clustering competencies across cognitive, intrapersonal and interpersonal. They identified as "deeper learning" the concept of transfer of learning from one situation to another, characterising this as twenty-first century competency when blended with knowledge. A major recommendation of the National Research Council report was to support programs of research that would illuminate whether teaching for transfer of competencies was possible. The report also identified conditions that would support such transfer—primarily that the individual understands the general principles underlying the particular learning and that the transfer situation involves the same principles—in other words a quite explicit approach. Another perspective from the report was that cognitive competencies were reasonably well represented across multiple disciplines, while the interpersonal and intrapersonal were less distributed. The implication of this is that there may be fewer learning opportunities within the education curricula for these latter clusters of skills (Scoular and Care 2018).

Instrumental in directing attention to the changing demands on education, twenty-first century education frameworks such as OECD's (Rychen and Salganik 2003) and UNESCO's (Delors et al. 1996) are very broad and aspirational. They are not implementation frameworks or models, and there has been a gradual movement towards more specificity in succeeding models, such as that developed by Partnerships 21, and the Assessment and Teaching of 21st Century Skills project (Griffin et al. 2012; Care et al. 2018). These have also embraced a framework approach but developed more detail in populating them. Some countries have similarly developed both aspirational and implementation frameworks (e.g. Singapore, Australia), but a large number of countries are currently confronting the challenge of making sense of both the breadth and the depth of this movement.

Pellegrino and Hilton (2012) identified four challenges to implementation of deeper learning:

1. The diversity of constructs, many of which lack clear definition
2. Psychometric issues particularly in the assessment of intrapersonal and interpersonal competencies
3. Political and economic forces that favour standardised summative tests
4. Teacher capacity in terms of new understandings of subjects in the context of twenty-first century competencies.

In this discussion, the definitional issue and teacher capacity are the focus. The remaining two issues are no less salient, but are not informed strongly by the data drawn upon here.

Factors Impacting on Roll-Out of Twenty-first Century Skills Education

In order for nations to be competitive in today's society, a twenty-first century education that prepares citizens with a broad range of skills for future success is critical. Skills frequently mentioned include creativity, critical thinking, social and interpersonal skills, problem-solving, collaboration and communication. Acknowledgement that these generalising competencies, or twenty-first century skills, are essential for individuals to function constructively, is placing demands on education systems to support students' abilities to apply and demonstrate knowledge rather than focus on its accumulation. Countries all over the world are acknowledging that the traditional education model focusing primarily on academic domains is insufficient.

The majority of education systems have relied on a transmission style of education delivery throughout the twentieth century and into the twenty-first. Education systems have relied on a content-based knowledge approach to teaching and learning, where the emphasis has been on memorising and recalling facts. Associated with this pedagogical style has been a focus on academic disciplines—language, mathematics, natural sciences and history. The approach has been that children must acquire a basic competency in language and that this provides access for learning within the disciplines. Learning within mathematics and the sciences has necessarily followed a hierarchical approach, where simple processes and concepts are first learnt followed by increasingly sophisticated understandings. In the primary and lower secondary school years, information acquisition has been valued. This has been demonstrated through tests and examination practices, which tend to reward correct answers. Correct answers could comprise production of the correct facts, or at times reasoning with those facts. The assumption of this education style has been that equipped with language facility and facts, the student will be able to go out into the world as a functioning member of society.

Now this assumption is being questioned. Rather than assume that these skills will develop through the years of formal education, the demand is for these skills to be addressed explicitly. This shift raises issues concerning the education infrastructure that has been built to support twentieth century perceptions of education, and the degree to which this can equally well support twenty-first century education.

Acquisition of skills is different from acquisition of knowledge. Simply, the first is dynamic and the second is static. Skills acquisition enables the individual to activate those skills where the stimulus environment requires it. The activation will vary across situation, and the particular activation response cannot invariably be learned in advance. The essence of skills is therefore about generalisability and adaptability. Historically, the acquisition of knowledge in education is centred around its constancy. For example, regardless of the stimulus environment, the answer to a knowledge question remains the same. The implications of the nature of the two areas of learning are that it is impossible to teach or to assess skills acquisition comprehensively because its activation will have multiple and infinite variations, while teaching and assessment of knowledge acquisition is possible through the correct/incorrect approaches seen in traditional assessment. This basic difference between the two has repercussions for education system infrastructure.

Different learning domains require different teaching and learning approaches. Mathematics is not taught in the same way as drama; science cannot be taught in the same way as a sport. And these different learning domains demand different modes of assessment—some learning domains can be assessed appropriately using pen and paper tests; others require different behavioural modes. Accordingly, when the goals of education are changed to reflect inclusion of different learning domains, not only the curriculum needs to be considered, but also pedagogical strategies and assessment methods. The degree to which this reality is well understood is unclear. For systemic change, all three education system elements of curriculum, assessment and pedagogy (Wyse et al. 2016) need to be considered.

Global and Regional Evidence

To reflect on the global adoption of an education agenda that explicitly acknowledges twenty-first century skills, two sources of data are drawn upon. Apart from demonstrating the ubiquity of the movement, the data also demonstrate the challenges identified by Pellegrino and Hilton (2012).

Global Mapping

As part of the Skills for a Changing World[1] project at the Center for Universal Education at the Brookings Institution, which seeks to ensure all children, have high-quality learning opportunities to develop the breadth of skills needed to meet the challenges of the twenty-first century, a scan of 131 countries was conducted to visualise the global breadth of skills movement. The overall purpose was to investigate the degree to which a range of skills, beyond traditional academic learning domains, is reflected at various levels of education systems, from the aspirational level described in vision and mission statements to a grounded level within curricula.

Specifically, four indicators were examined as evidence of the degree to which aspirations to cultivate a broad range of skills in students have translated into implementation within systems. These four indicators include:

1. Reference to breadth of skills in a country's educational mission and vision statements
2. Identification of specific skills or competencies in national policy documents
3. Embedding of skills within the curriculum
4. Evidence of progression of skills from basic to more sophisticated levels.

---

[1] https://www.brookings.edu/series/skills-for-a-changing-world/.

Countries state aspirations of their education systems in mission and vision statements. These aspirations may identify the characteristics that are emphasised and valued for individual learners or may refer to social, economic, or values goals. Similarly, identifying specific skills in national policy documents suggests that governments value these skills. That identified skills are embedded in the curriculum confirms the intention to develop these and that opportunities for doing so have been explored. However, it is insufficient simply to acknowledge that a skill is important or to include a skill in the curriculum. In order to teach these skills, there must be recognition that skills develop and progress over time and that students need to move from one level to another, in order to gain expertise. Therefore, identification of skills progression is essential for implementation. These four indicators are of course not mutually exclusive categories. For instance, countries which articulate specific skills in their vision and mission statements may also have skills embedded within the curriculum. In fact, meeting criteria for multiple indicators may indicate consistency across the education system, as well as demonstrate how far along a country is in the process of implementation "from aspiration to planning for actual education change, to thinking through an approach to integrate competencies in the curriculum, and to initiating a process of delineating growing sets of competencies" (Care et al. 2016, p. 5).

Official government websites, as well as websites of national agencies responsible for curriculum development, were explored by the research team between May 2016 and April 2017. The raw data (i.e., excerpts taken from the national websites) were analysed and coded as "meets criterion", "does not meet criterion", or "no data found", based on the set of criteria established for each of the four indicators (Table 5.1). A visual mapping of the results can be accessed at skills.brookings.edu.

Variability in the degree to which these indicators exist across education systems is expected, given that not all education systems approach implementation in the same way. For example, many education systems mention within their education policies a variety of skills that they plan for individual learners to acquire, whereas others

Table 5.1 Description of the criteria established for the four indicators (adapted from Care et al. 2016, p. 5)

Indicators	Criteria description
Mission and vision statements	Identification of individual characteristics of aspirations for the individual learner, as opposed to for the society or nation as a whole, such as promotion of peace for the country
Skills identified	National policy documents have specific skills, beyond literacy and numeracy, identified within, such as collaboration, problem-solving, communication, and social skills. Explanation or definition of skills is not necessary to meet this criterion
Skills within the curriculum	The curriculum, or description of the curriculum, includes how or where the skills will be addressed within the education system
Progression of skills	Description of how specific skills develop over time, from basic to more complex, and across different education levels

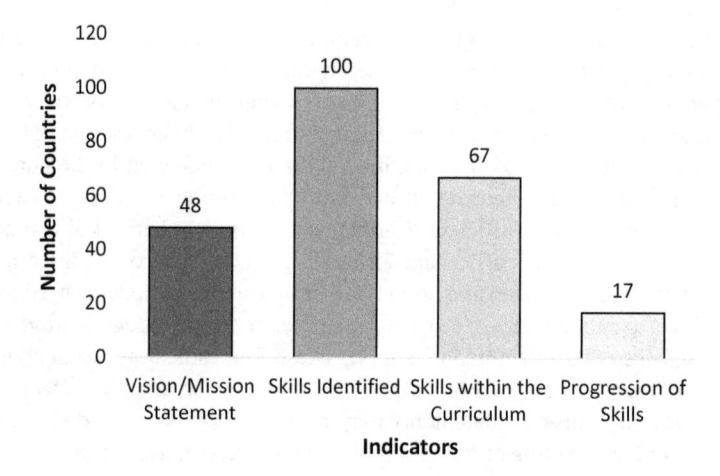

Fig. 5.1 Number of countries that meet the criterion in the four indicators

only refer to them in the mission and vision statements. Therefore, whether countries meet just some or all four indicators—from the national vision, to identifying the competencies needed to fulfil that vision, to embedding them in the curriculum, and finally, to signifying how they progress over time—is of particular interest, as it can provide useful information on how nations approach integrating skills through their education system.

Overall, the analysis of the four indicators from 131 countries indicates that national education systems are broadening their educational provision to include skills beyond literacy and numeracy. The four most frequently identified skills were communication, creativity, critical thinking and problem-solving. The majority of the countries (76%) identify specific skills somewhere within their policy documents (Fig. 5.1). Notably, there are more countries that list skills within the curriculum (51%) than articulate these in their vision and mission statements (37%). For example, the mission and vision statements of Uganda do not identify skills, competencies, or characteristics for an individual learner, but rather focus on the nation as a whole (Republic of Uganda, Ministry of Education and Sports, n.d.[2]). Still, there is evidence of a broad range of skills within their curriculum. The new Lower Secondary curriculum,[3] for instance, emphasises both thinking skills and applied skills, such as critical thinking, problem-solving, creativity, communication, calculation and information and communication technology. Despite the fact that 100 countries mentioned specific skills within policy documents, only 17 countries out of 131 (13%) provided any documentation of skills progression.

---

[2] The Republic of Uganda, Ministry of Education and Sports. (n.d.). *About the ministry*. Retrieved from http://education.go.ug/data/smenu/47/About%20the%20Ministry%20.html.

[3] http://education.go.ug/files/downloads/NCDC%202-%20The%20aims%20of%20the%20new%20Lower%20Secondary%20curriculum.pdf.

Countries vary in the degree to which skills have been integrated through their education systems. For example, although 81% of the countries met the criterion in at least one of the indicators listed in Table 5.1, only 7% met the criterion for all four indicators. That is, only nine out of the 131 countries showed evidence of consistently incorporating a breadth of skills throughout their national policy documents, as well as including progression of skills. These national or provincial education systems include Australia, Canada (Ontario), Hong Kong, Kosrae (Federated States of Micronesia), Mauritius, Peru, Qatar, Scotland and Singapore. A total of 25 countries did not meet the criterion in any of the four indicators.

The study provides evidence of a global shift towards inclusion of breadth of skills, at least in terms of national aspirations. Educational systems are broadening their educational provision to equip students with the skills and competencies to succeed both in and out of school. This supports recent research on teaching and learning of twenty-first century skills in six different countries (Reimers and Chung 2016). However, aspirations at the policy level do not necessarily indicate that these skills are being learned and taught in schools and classrooms. These findings reveal that there is no universal systematic approach to integrating breadth of skills through the education system. While the majority of countries identify specific skills somewhere within their policy documents, a little over a half identify skills within their curriculum, and only one-eighth of the countries in the study provide evidence of an understanding that skills develop over time. Therefore, despite indications that a skills approach has been underway in many countries around the world, implementation seems to lag behind as countries explore how to integrate these skills into the teaching and learning systems across grade levels.

Regional Studies

The assessment of transversal competencies[4] study (Care and Luo 2016) undertaken through the Network on Education Quality Monitoring in the Asia-Pacific (NEQMAP), a regional network coordinated by UNESCO's Education Bureau in Bangkok, followed a series of three studies undertaken by the Asia-Pacific Education Research Institutes Network (ERI-Net). The four studies each drew upon the same 9–11 countries, varying slightly: Australia, China (Shanghai; Beijing), Hong Kong SAR, India, Japan, Republic of Korea, Malaysia, Mongolia, Thailand, Vietnam, Philippines. The research aimed to document and consolidate reform initiatives for knowledge dissemination and policy consideration in the Asia-Pacific region and beyond. All four studies were designed to understand the degree to which twenty-first century skills are embedded in formal education systems. ERI-Net participating countries made the decision to refer to these skills as transversal competencies and that is the terminology adopted for the following discussion. The ERI-Net framework

---

[4]Twenty-first century skills are referred to by many labels; in the Asia Pacific studies, they are frequently referred to as transversal competencies.

Table 5.2 UNESCO's working definition of transversal competencies (adapted from UNESCO 2015)

Domains	Examples of key skills, competencies, values, and attitudes
Critical and innovative thinking	Creativity, entrepreneurship, resourcefulness, application skills, reflective thinking, reasoned decision-making
Interpersonal skills	Communication skills, organisational skills, teamwork, collaboration, sociability, collegiality, empathy, compassion
Intrapersonal skills	Self-discipline, ability to learn independently, flexibility and adaptability, self-awareness, perseverance, self-motivation, compassion, integrity, self-respect
Global citizenship	Awareness, tolerance, openness, responsibility, respect for diversity, ethical understanding, intercultural understanding, democratic participation, conflict resolution, respect for the environment, national identity, sense of belonging
Media and information literacy	Ability to obtain and analyse information through ICTs, ability to critically evaluate information and media content, ethical use of ICTs
Others (e.g. physical health, religions)	Appreciation of healthy lifestyle, respect for religious values

(Table 5.2) is comprehensive but not prescriptive. The approach taken within ERI-Net, and later NEQMAP, was that this framework could comprehend the qualities that participating countries valued, but that these would vary across countries. The first study (UNESCO 2015) explored how different countries and economies in the region define and apply "non-academic" skills in their education policies, practices and curriculum.

In terms of curriculum integration, three modes were identified: specific subject, where learning of transversal competencies is included as a specific subject; cross subject, where learning of the competencies underpins traditional subjects; and extra-curricular, where transversal competencies are highlighted in non-classroom activities. The three modes were not seen as mutually exclusive, and examples of this from Australia, Thailand, Malaysia and Mongolia, among others were outlined. The key findings from this study were that:

- Skills and competencies were referred to in education policy of all ten countries and economies (participants)
- Creative and innovative thinking was particularly endorsed by all participants
- Valuing of interpersonal skills varied across participants

- The concept of global citizenship varied, as did the importance and definition of physical and psychological health
- ICT literacies were highly valued.

Some skills and qualities were differentially valued across participants, reflecting different national cultures and contexts. For example, global spirituality was identified by the Philippines, while yoga and health were identified by India. Independent learning was mentioned by Australia and Japan while Malaysia and Hong Kong SAR named risk-taking. These elements draw attention to the very broad and different perspectives that exist concerning the nature of skills, supporting Pellegrino and Hilton's (2012) point concerning lack of definition. This broadness itself poses a challenge to teaching and learning in a formal education system.

The study identified three types of challenges to implementation: definitional, operational and systemic. These three challenges were reflected upon in the fourth study in the series, on assessment of transversal competencies (Care and Luo 2016). Definitional refers to lack of clarity in scope of transversal competencies (as illustrated by the examples from the first study above), which translate into lack of clear goals within the teaching and learning process. Operational refers to the logistics of implementation—human and physical resources. Systemic refers to system wide issues that are not specific to the particular transversal competencies phenomenon, but which act as hurdles to its implementation. For example, if the operating paradigm in the system is that performance in traditional examinations is the epitomy of success, then integrating into the system a set of competencies that is not aligned with this provides a conundrum. Pellegrino and Hilton's (2012) challenges are clearly reflected in the challenges identified in the first ERI-Net study and through to the fourth study in the series.

In the second report (UNESCO 2016a), School and Teaching Practices for Twenty-First Century Challenges were explored. Taking a non-representative, small case study approach, the study found that policies were filtering down to school level. However, there was little evidence that transversal competencies were comprehensively represented in the curricular materials used in schools. Similarly, pedagogical practices in the main had not shifted. Particular examples of innovative classroom structures designed to facilitate teaching and learning of the competencies were identified, but the majority of classes maintained traditional teacher-led structures. The third report (UNESCO 2016b) focussed on Preparing and Supporting Teachers. It drew on nine countries and 2621 educators to explore how teachers felt supported to integrate learning of transversal competencies in the classroom and the challenges they faced. Findings indicated some gaps between the skills teachers felt they possessed and those they felt were needed such as creativity and assessment skills. In addition, responses indicated some different understandings of transversal competencies, supporting the centrality of the definitional challenge highlighted both in other ERI-Net reports and by Pellegrino and Hilton (2012). Teachers identified operational challenges such as lack of resources, curricula that do not clarify methods to integrate the competencies, concerns about time available in already congested curricula, and lack of assessment frameworks. Reflecting systemic issues, also identified were parent and student concerns about the benefits of the competencies in comparison to the examination assessment culture associated with traditional subjects.

In the NEQMAP Assessment of Transversal Competencies: Policy and Practice study, Care and Luo (2016) reported, analogous to the second and third ERI-Net reports, that schools and teachers were very much aware of transversal competencies and specific to assessment that no systematic approaches were being promulgated or practiced. The prime obstacles to implementation were analysed across the definitional, operational and systemic categories used in UNESCO (2015). The study targeted alignment of awareness and understandings about assessment of transversal competencies across system, school and teacher levels, since consistency would imply coherence across the system. Lack of alignment might signify lack of communication structures or recency of change. Lack of alignment within school and teacher level might imply lack of "whole school" responsibility for transversal competencies.

Of the three types of challenge, the definitional have implications for everything else—they are the first "blocker". There needs to be common understandings of what the skills might "look like", how they might be demonstrated at different levels of competence and quality, and how assessment might be used functionally to promote them. Without these understandings, effective implementation is impossible. In the NEQMAP study, school and teacher responses made it clear that these understandings were not ubiquitously held; and as a natural consequence, teachers stated that they needed more resources, more training and more support. The authenticity of the needs was also substantiated by teacher responses. For example, although more than 60% of the teachers across all countries reported including transversal competencies in their teaching and assessment, not all of these teachers reported that their teaching and assessment practices had changed. The very nature of the teaching and learning skills demands change from traditional teacher-directed instruction and student independent work, so this inconsistency demonstrated a very real lack of understanding on the part of many of the teachers concerning the nature of what was confronting them.

Although operational issues in the education shift, the second "blocker", were most frequently identified, these need to be seen as symptomatic of the over-arching issue, which is the lack of understanding of the skills and consequences for their teachability (Rotherham and Willingham 2010). The third "blocker" is the systemic challenges including long-held beliefs in examinations approaches to identifying student quality, and systems of promotion based on these, and concerns that traditional curricula will be disregarded if additional educational goals are valued.

Discussion

From both data sources, it is evident that the skills movement is in train. The key issue is implementation. Implementation relies on understanding of the nature of the skills. Through the Brookings study, a very small number of the countries identified provided information about learning progressions. This is one indicator of a possible lack of development of skills curricula, in the sense of providing information about how the skills might be expected to develop through the different phases of schooling. The lack of such information implies that targeting of teaching of the skills at appropriate levels throughout the years of schooling is not occurring. A reasonable hypothesis for this is that knowledge about the development of skills is inadequate. The information provided by teachers in the third ERI-Net study (UNESCO 2016b) and the NEQMAP study (Care and Luo 2016) noting the lack of resources which inhibit their implementation of teaching and of assessment of skills is another signifier of a major impediment to implementation. Again, a reasonable hypothesis is that these resources do not exist due to lack of knowledge about development of the skills that can inform how these can be made explicit in curricular, teaching and assessment materials. And this lack of resources means that teachers are not provided with examples of appropriate teaching approaches. These findings point to two immediate solutions: first, development of learning progressions for valued skills which will provide a "curriculum" for teachers, a roadmap of what they might expect to see in students as they demonstrate increasing levels of competency; and second, encouragement of use of active pedagogies in the classroom that will be congruent with the nature of the skills being developed.

The use of learning progressions to support teaching and assessment of twenty-first century skills is well documented (Wilson et al. 2016; Pitman and Broomhall 2009; Hoffman 1998) but less well disseminated in the literature which reaches many teachers. The development of these progressions poses another task for educators, and taking the model provided by the ERI-Net and NEQMAP studies, it is suggested that networks of countries could reasonably pool their resources and expertise to work on this development. All countries in the ERI-Net and NEQMAP studies identified critical thinking, problem-solving, creativity, collaboration, communication, for example, as highly valued. Starting to develop learning progressions for just a few of these, particularly those that are more easily integrated into current curricula, such as problem-solving and collaboration for example, would provide useful examples for teachers.

The second solution brings the issue of teacher training to the fore. It has been suggested that although teacher education should serve education by being consistent with current curricular, pedagogical and assessment approaches, it can also constitute an effective source of change (Menter 2016). Current practice demonstrates that not only is much of the pre-service teacher education inconsistent with education delivery, it certainly does not act as a dynamic change factor. Where late in the twentieth century pre-service education moved to including psychology and philosophy to provide teachers with perspectives and understandings beyond their discipline areas, we do not see a similar adjustment today to including a twenty-first century values perspective and its associated areas of knowledge and skills. Many pre-service teacher education courses have not shifted to accommodate the need to move beyond transmission styles of education (Saavedra and Opfer 2012). These styles focus on knowledge transfer and storage and typically do not focus on application of skills, or manipulation of the knowledge. In addition, many of the skills that characterise the learnings we desire for students are the same skills that need to characterise the teaching process—metacognition, collaboration, critical thinking. Yet, teacher education courses remain typically organised around academic disciplines such as mathematics, science, language. Therefore, the focus on teaching and learning twenty-first century skills needs to explicitly consider the alignment of teacher training with the other components of the education system.

The use of active pedagogies, that is having teachers engage more dynamically with individual and groups of students, in order to provide the opportunity for all participants in the classroom to practice and model the skills, is an authentic way to promote the skills. This perspective is not far removed from the approach taken in recent years in science teaching in particular (e.g. Hokayem and Gotwals 2016). For example, Windschitl (2010) compared the need for learning reform in science teaching and the learning goals of twenty-first century skills, identifying their congruence. Windschitl's approach relies on identifying processes that need to be carried out by students. It features learning how to solve problems collaboratively by having students engage in metacognitive activities. This puts responsibility on students to make learning decisions and requires monitoring of students in order to target instruction—formative assessment. Although his suggestions were derived from a focus on the teaching of science inquiry, the approach is relevant for other disciplines in which skills goals are embedded. Windschitl emphasised the importance of teachers having strong content knowledge, in order for them to display the agility to provoke questioning and problem-solving; as well as understanding of child development and learning, in order to target activity appropriately. Introduction of twenty-first century approaches to teaching and teacher practice is well recognised in the literature (e.g. Rotherham and Willingham 2010). However, the degree to which these approaches have influenced pre-service teacher education courses is less clear. The interest in lesson study provides an example of recognition by education systems of the need for continuous teacher professional development (Lewis et al. 2012), notwithstanding the absence of major pre-service teacher education change.

Recommendations

A particular conclusion of note in the first ERI-Net study (UNESCO 2015) was that "there is not singular or coherent movement" (p. 21) across the countries and that each had initiated movement stimulated by their idiosyncratic circumstances. Given the strong commonalities of interest and need in the Asia-Pacific region, as well as demonstration of countries already working together through the ERI-Net and NEQMAP groups, the benefits of common research to develop progressions and test active pedagogies would include efficiency, economy and capacity-building across the region. Similar networks could be established in other locations such as sub-Saharan Africa or the MENA region, where countries are similarly exploring the skills agenda (e.g. Kenya Institute of Curriculum Development [KICD] 2015) and skills curricula (e.g. South Africa [Department of Basic Education 2011]).

The concept of using learning progressions to describe skills acquisition would provide teachers with a practical approach to teaching and modelling the skills. The behaviours indicative of skills at different proficiency levels would be contextualised within and across different subjects. The active pedagogies to be used would be commensurate with the nature and level of skills being targeted.

What is clear is that there is consensus in intent—there is a global endorsement of the need for education to include an explicit focus on twenty-first century skills development. What is also clear is that the curricular, pedagogical and assessment shifts required to achieve this focus are enormous. The position taken in this chapter is that the key to achievement is through active pedagogies—modelling of twenty-first century skills as part of classroom discourse and practice provides a natural learning environment for skills development. In order for this to occur, the skills themselves need definition; educators need to understand how these skills develop and how to nurture them; and teachers need to be provided with the resources to shift their practices to more active teaching and learning pedagogies.

Conclusion

As more countries embrace the need to equip their youth differently, we are lacking evidence of implementation. What might that evidence look like? One source of evidence of teaching of transversal competencies could be both summative and formative assessment resources. For example, at national or regional levels, large-scale assessment data might be available; at school level, student report cards; and at classroom level, student records. Indications that assessment is used formatively would include student records, assessment tasks and classroom observation data. From these sources of evidence, the competencies of students could be evaluated, and movement in those competencies could be identified. This leads of course to the unanswered question of whether explicit teaching and modelling of twenty-first century skills will in fact lead to improved competencies. This has not yet been established at large scale.

In this chapter, we suggest that the global movement towards valuing of twenty-first century skills is not currently met with clear implementation pathways. The magnitude of the movement, not only globally, but for any individual education system, challenges the resources of educators, particularly in the light of a lack of deep understanding of the implications of adoption of skills for pedagogy and assessment, quite apart from curriculum. We suggest a simple approach of regional initiatives designed to define and describe learning progressions of a few highly valued skills and to make concrete the active pedagogical strategies that teachers can use to model the skills with students at varying levels of competency.

References

Care, E., Anderson, K., & Kim, H. (2016). *Visualizing the breadth of skills movement across education systems*. Washington, D.C.: Brookings Institution.

Care, E., Griffin, P., & Wilson, M. (2018). *Assessment and teaching of 21st century skills: Research and applications*. Dordrecht, The Netherlands: Springer.

Care, E., & Luo, R. (2016). *Assessment of transversal competencies: Policy and practice in the Asia-Pacific region*. Bangkok, Thailand: UNESCO.

Delors, J., Al Mufti, I., Amagai, I. A., Carneiro, R., Chung, F., Geremek, B., et al. (1996). *Learning: The treasure within*. Paris, France: UNESCO.

Department of Basic Education. (2011). *National curriculum statement: English life skills foundation phase grades R-3*. Cape Town, South Africa: Department of Basic Education. Retrieved July 17, 2017 from http://www.education.gov.za/Portals/0/CD/National%20Curriculum%20Statements%20and%20Vocational/CAPS%20Life%20Skills%20%20English%20_%20Gr%20R-3%20FS.pdf?ver=2015-01-27-162204-953.

Griffin, P., McGaw, B., & Care, E. (Eds.). (2012). *Assessment and teaching of 21st century skills*. Dordrecht, The Netherlands: Springer.

Hoffman, R. R. (1998). How can expertise be defined? Implications of research from cognitive psychology. In R. Williams, W. Faulkner, & J. Fleck (Eds.), *Exploring expertise* (pp. 81–100). New York, NY: Macmillan.

Hokayem, H., & Gotwals, A. W. (2016). Early elementary students' understanding of complex ecosystems: A learning progression approach. *Journal of Research in Science Teaching, 53*(10), 1524–1545.

Kenya Institute of Curriculum Development [KICD]. (2015). *National curriculum policy*. Kenya: Ministry of Education, Science and Technology. Retrieved January 12, 2018 from https://www.kicd.ac.ke/images/PDF/national-curriculum-policy.pdf.

Lewis, C. C., Perry, R. R., Friedkin, S., & Roth, J. R. (2012). Improving teaching does improve teachers: Evidence from lesson study. *Journal of Teacher Education, 63*(5), 368–375.

Menter, I. (2016). Teacher education—Making connections with curriculum, pedagogy and assessment. In D. Wyse, L. Hayward, & J. Pandya (Eds.), *The Sage handbook of curriculum, pedagogy and assessment* (pp. 1015–1028). London, England: Sage Publications.

OECD [Organisation for Economic Co-operation and Development]. (2018). *Preparing our youth for an inclusive and sustainable world: The OECD Pisa global competence framework*. Paris, France: OECD. Retrieved from https://www.oecd.org/education/Global-competency-for-an-inclusive-world.pdf.

Pellegrino, J. W., & Hilton, M. (2012). *Education for life and work: Developing transferable knowledge and skills in the 21st century*. Washington, D.C.: National Research Council.

Pitman, T., & Broomhall, S. (2009). Australian universities, generic skills and lifelong learning. *International Journal of Lifelong Education, 28*(4), 439–458.

Reimers, F. M., & Chung, C. K. (2016). *Teaching and learning for the twenty-first century: Educational goals, policies, and curricula from six nations*. Cambridge, MA: Harvard Education Press.

Rotherham, A. J., & Willingham, D. (2010). 21st century skills: The challenges ahead. *Best of Educational Leadership, 67,* 16–21.

Rychen, D. S., & Salganik, L. H. (Eds.). (2003). *Key competencies for a successful life and a well-functioning society*. Cambridge, MA: Hogrefe and Huber Publishers.

Saavedra, A. R., & Opfer, V. D. (2012). Learning 21st-century skills requires 21st-century teaching. *Kappan, 94*(2), 8–13.

Scoular, C., & Care, E. (2018). Teaching 21st century skills: Implications at system levels in Australia. In E. Care, P. Griffin, & M. Wilson (Eds.), *Assessment and teaching of 21st century skills: Research and applications*. Dordrecht, The Netherlands: Springer.

UNESCO [United Nations Educational, Scientific and Cultural Organization]. (2015). *Transversal competencies in education policy and practice (Phase I): Regional synthesis report*. Paris, France:

UNESCO. Retrieved August 14, 2015 from http://unesdoc.unesco.org/images/0023/002319/231907E.pdf.

UNESCO [United Nations Educational, Scientific and Cultural Organization]. (2016a). *School and teaching practices for twenty-first century challenges: Lessons from the Asia-Pacific region (Phase II): Regional synthesis report*. Paris, France: UNESCO. Retrieved October 17, 2016 from http://unesdoc.unesco.org/images/0024/002440/244022E.pdf.

UNESCO [United Nations Educational, Scientific and Cultural Organization]. (2016b). *Preparing and supporting teachers in the Asia-Pacific to meet the challenges of twenty-first century learning (Phase III): Regional synthesis report*. Paris, France: UNESCO. Retrieved June 5, 2017 from http://unesdoc.unesco.org/images/0024/002468/246852E.pdf.

UN [United Nations] General Assembly. (2015). *Transforming our world: The 2030 agenda for sustainable development*. Retrieved from http://www.refworld.org/docid/57b6e3e44.html.

Wilson, M., Gochyyev, P., & Scalise, K. (2016). Assessment of learning in digital interactive social networks: A learning analytics approach. *Online Learning, 20*(2), 97–119.

Windschitl, M. (2010). How teacher education will have to evolve. In M. Hilton (Ed.), *Exploring the intersection of science education and 21st century skills: A workshop summary*. Washington, D.C.: The National Academies Press.

Wyse, D., Hayward, L., & Pandya, J. (Eds.). (2016). *The Sage handbook of curriculum, assessment and pedagogy*. London, England: Sage Publications.

Esther Care is a Senior Fellow at the Brookings Institution, Washington DC, and there leads projects designed to explore the educational implications of the twenty-first century skills movement. These include Skills for a Changing World and Optimizing Assessment for All, projects which draw on countries' experiences as they integrate twenty-first century skills into their education policy and practice. Working through two regional networks, NEQMAP in Asia and TALENT in Africa, from 2017, Esther is leading an initiative to build assessment capacity in the context of countries monitoring their education progress against the Sustainable Development Goals. Esther is also a Professor at the University of Melbourne and directs the Assessment Curriculum and Technology Research Centre, funded by the Australian Government to undertake research in the Philippines to inform that country's K–12 education reform. She maintains her interest and research in the assessment of twenty-first century skills, an area in which she publishes widely.

Helyn Kim is a Post-Doctoral Fellow at the Center for Universal Education at the Brookings Institution. Her primary interest is in ensuring all children have high-quality learning opportunities that build the breadth of skills necessary to succeed in the current global economy. Her research focuses on understanding and assessing a broad range of skills that contribute to learning and development. Her current work, Optimizing Assessment for All, seeks to improve assessment literacy, build capacity among regional and national stakeholders for measuring and teaching twenty-first century skills, address the alignment of assessment of skills with curriculum and pedagogy and change perceptions regarding educational assessment for measuring learning and twenty-first century skills. Helyn received her Ph.D. in Education from the University of Virginia, where she studied multi-dimensional approaches to understanding the nature and interplay among the foundations of learning.

Chapter 6
Challenges for Initial Teacher Education in the Context of 'Twenty-first Century' Learning Imperatives

Rosemary Hipkins, Jo MacDonald and Jenny Whatman

Introduction

This chapter addresses a complex challenge that has yet to be widely debated in studies of initial teacher education. How might teacher educators more effectively educate beginning teachers to respond to so-called 'twenty-first century' learning imperatives? This is a deceptively simple question to which we respond by drawing on a study of 'future focused' trends in education, commissioned by New Zealand's Ministry of Education (Bolstad et al. 2012). The chapter draws on the six principles identified in this review to highlight the profound nature of changes to practice envisaged by futures thinkers in education. Future-oriented practice makes major demands on teachers, requiring them 'to do—and be—very different' from in the past (Gilbert et al. 2015, p. 2). Gilbert (2013) also notes that there has been little work on what future-oriented teaching practice means for individual teachers. And if existing teachers struggle, who will show the way to those who are only just setting out?

The first two sections outline several commonly advocated types of change in curriculum and pedagogy. We discuss the role that competencies/capabilities should play in the curriculum, with associated pedagogical implications. The third section then addresses e-learning and the challenge of teaching in flexible learning spaces and innovative learning environments (ILEs). In New Zealand, ILEs refer to pedagogical elements, and flexible learning spaces refer to infrastructural elements and physical space. These spaces and technologies require investments in infrastructure that are foundational for a twenty-first century education system, but they also need a twenty-first century teaching workforce that thinks differently (Gilbert et al. 2015).

Woven through all three of these early sections are research-based indications that it is not easy for many teachers to evolve their established practice in response to

R. Hipkins (✉) · J. MacDonald · J. Whatman
New Zealand Council for Educational Research (NZCER), Wellington, New Zealand
e-mail: Rose.Hipkins@nzcer.org.nz

© Springer Nature Singapore Pte Ltd. 2018
C. Wyatt-Smith and L. Adie (eds.), *Innovation and Accountability in Teacher Education*, Teacher Education, Learning Innovation and Accountability,
https://doi.org/10.1007/978-981-13-2026-2_6

the changes described. We then turn our attention to two recent initiatives that have proactively addressed challenges for changing teachers' ways of being and doing in twenty-first century classrooms. Neither of these initiatives is straightforwardly 'initial teacher education'. However, they both speak to the dilemma of educating beginning teachers to respond to twenty-first century learning imperatives.

The first initiative we discuss is the Manaiakalani Digital Teacher Academy (MDTA). MDTA was born out of frustration that a cluster of schools, supported by the Manaiakalani Trust (see http://www.manaiakalani.org/), could not find beginning teachers who were ready and equipped to work in their settings. The Trust supports a group of schools in a low socioeconomic area in Auckland, by ensuring every child has access to a digital device and by supporting teachers to evolve their pedagogies to make sure these are used to good effect. In brief, the MDTA initiative paired a beginning teacher with an experienced mentor teacher for their full first year following graduation from initial teacher education.

The second initiative we discuss is professional development for teachers offered by collaboration between a tertiary provider and a specialist education laboratory. A partnership with a philanthropic foundation provides scholarships to support teachers with tuition fees. This collaboration, The Mind Lab by Unitec (see http://themindlab.com/) offers an applied, blended postgraduate qualification specialising in digital and collaborative learning. We include it here as one response to the dilemma of educating teachers for the twenty-first century, even though it is not initial teacher education or even for beginning teachers. Our reasoning is that teachers who have experienced the type of learning aspired to by Mind Lab by Unitec will bring this to their role as mentors for pre-service and early career teachers. Unless teacher education students and beginning teachers have opportunities to experience 'twenty-first century learning' while they are still learning how to be teachers, they will most likely teach as they were taught.

These case studies then provide the basis for a broader discussion of the challenges of initiating beginning teachers into different sorts of classrooms and practices. We pick up the call for professional learning—in initial teacher education and beyond—to be transformative. We conclude by briefly outlining three big ideas about the conditions under which such transformation might be productively achieved.

Reframing Purposes for Learning

> The role that knowledge plays in learning should be rethought: It is no longer sufficient to absorb and reproduce existing knowledge; students need to develop their capabilities to work with disciplinary knowledge to create new knowledge that addresses specific real-world issues and challenges. (principle summarized from Bolstad et al. 2012)
>
> Learning should be personalised: The 'logic' of the system is reversed so that learning programs are built around the specific learning needs of the student rather than requiring them to fit into the existing system (principle summarised from Bolstad et al. 2012).

Contemporary debates about the purposes and outcomes envisaged for learning confront teachers with profound philosophical questions about who they hope their students can be and become and how their teaching might enable that growth (Biesta 2014). Such questions sit at the heart of innovative framework curricula such as the *New Zealand Curriculum* (*NZC*), where they are specifically bound up with the introduction of key competencies, values and an aspirational vision statement (Hipkins 2005).

Competences, or capabilities, or key competencies (depending on which curriculum framework is being considered) are a defining feature of so-called twenty-first century curriculum frameworks. One recent meta-analysis of twenty-first century competency-based frameworks identified four sets of outcomes mentioned in all the twenty-first century frameworks located: collaboration; communication; ICT literacy; and social and/or cultural skills and citizenship (Voogt and Pareja Roblin 2012). Most twenty-first century frameworks also mentioned: creativity; critical thinking; problem-solving; and development of quality products/productivity (Voogt and Pareja Roblin 2012). Thus, despite ongoing debate about which of these elements to emphasise in specific national curriculum documents, there does seem to be a degree of consensus about the scope of the intended outcomes.

Educating for any of these outcomes arguably demands a rethinking of how a teacher's knowledge and expertise should be deployed. The first of the principles cited above implies that students should undertake active investigations and that they should be supported to build their epistemic awareness of how different disciplines work to build new knowledge. These things are easier said than done and are certainly easily misunderstood. A recent two-nation analysis asked why curriculum innovation in the senior secondary school might come to be misunderstood as necessitating a binary choice between knowledge development and other types of outcomes such as those signalled above. In this commentary, Zohar and Hipkins (2017) identified teachers' lack of epistemic awareness as a significant stumbling block to productive implementation of the types of changes actually intended by the curriculum policy-makers.

The second of the above principles introduces the concept of personalisation. A common misunderstanding also positions this as a binary choice—in this case about which knowledge counts. Either students are introduced to disciplinary knowledge or they are denied access to powerful ways of knowing, restricted instead to having all their learning framed in relation to what is already known and familiar (e.g. Riley 2016). This binary is unhelpful in both directions. Personalisation is a response to *sociological* concerns about the potentially alienating nature of disciplinary knowledge. The imperative is to build bridges between students' lived experiences and meaningful encounters with powerful disciplinary ways of knowing. *Epistemic* concerns are less visible but equally complex. Here, the focus turns to the other side of the binary and the seeming assumption that disciplinary knowledge presents as a relatively stable and uncontested curriculum. Yates and Millar (2016) use the discipline of physics to demonstrate that there are tensions within the physics community when curriculum matters are being debated. In any case, knowledge in physics is changing so fast that physicists themselves can struggle to keep up with sub-fields outside their own areas of expertise. Furthermore, the ever-growing computational power of computers is radically changing the way much science is actually done. Weinberger (2011) uses the term 'intertwingly' to describe new knowledge about the 'complexly interdependent and entangled' nature of the world as it is revealed through new methods of science inquiry (p. 115).

Epistemic challenges constitute a powerful common thread between these two principles. However, many teachers do not seem to have the epistemic awareness that could help them make sense of curriculum debates concerning the knowledge that students should learn and for what purposes (Zohar and Hipkins 2017). In any case, as long as high-stakes assessments continue to focus on traditional curriculum outcomes, many teachers will see no compelling reason to engage with these complex and unsettling questions about how knowledge should contribute to twenty-first century curricula (Hipkins et al. 2016).

Whole books can and have been written about these curriculum challenges. Despite contested views about how change should unfold, there is no denying that profoundly changing social conditions do now require something more than superficial responses to be made within education systems. Teachers need to be able to work with disciplinary knowledge in ways many of them are unlikely to have experienced during their own education. How can more experienced teachers support beginning teachers to make sense of such knowledge challenges if they are struggling themselves to understand the profound shifts in practice signalled by just these two principles?

Working with a Wider Repertoire of Pedagogies

> Roles and relationships between teachers and learners are restructured: Teachers work with students to draw out and develop the strengths and interests that students bring to their learning. This entails learning for both sides of the partnership. (principle summarized from Bolstad et al. 2012)
>
> Ideas about equity and diversity also need to be rethought: Instead of a problem to be managed in the interests of offering an equitable education to all students, diversity should be seen as a learning resource to be fostered. Working constructively with diversity should be seen as an important outcome of learning. (principle summarized from Bolstad et al. 2012)

Both these principles have pedagogical implications. To some extent, the first of them has already been addressed in the discussion about how teachers deploy their expertise to support students' knowledge gains. However, an additional challenge is highlighted by the second of this pair of principles. How, if at all, should teachers aim to deliberately foster competencies such as those needed to work productively with diverse others? How might students be supported to have respectful conversations across cultural and experiential differences, without being left with the relativist impression that 'anything goes'? Essentially, the same dilemmas are raised by the related curriculum goal of fostering capabilities for citizenship. Yet recent research in New Zealand in social studies (Wood et al. 2017) and in physical education (Hart

2014) has shown that teachers can be reluctant to take up opportunities to support students to explore and take action on controversial issues, especially when doing so requires students to confront issues of power and social injustice.

There is another layer to the 'diversity' dilemma, as Sue McDowall describes in this moment of personal epiphany: 'But now I can see we hardly ever used diverse ideas in our class and community for real purposes. The activities I set up *made space* for diversity *but they did not require* diversity to do the work' (Hipkins et al. 2014, p. 26, emphasis added). Similarly, Sara Murray describes her search for better ways to equitably mentor student teachers from Asian cultures during their practicum in a New Zealand early childhood centre. Noting that the student teachers' experiences of being educated were very different from what was now being asked of them, she reflects on her own struggle towards intercultural understanding and the associated awareness of how and why she needed to change her mentoring practices in these circumstances (Murray 2016). What is clear in both commentaries is that coming to a deeper understanding of the seemingly simple idea of 'working constructively with diversity' is personal and confronting. It changes a teacher's ways of being with their students, not just their knowing about diversity. We will come back to this dilemma in the context of the MDTA initiative.

How do ideas about working productively with diversity and ideas about fostering competencies/capabilities fit together? In our own curriculum research, we have found it useful to encourage school leaders and teachers to think about the *NZC* key competencies as 'ideas to think with' when they are designing rich learning experiences (Hipkins et al. 2014). Students' immediate learning experiences need to help them envision and reach towards aspirational future selves, with all the known and unknown challenges entailed. How they come to know themselves and the world around them is a key to helping them realise their capabilities as they live their lives, both during and beyond their school years (Barnett 2004). It is easy to agree with the fine-sounding aspirations just outlined, but realizing the profound changes in pedagogy needed to bring them to life is another matter entirely. If the sorts of pedagogies needed are not being modelled by their mentor teachers, how are beginning teachers going to even start on the sorts of intense personal learning journeys indicated by McDowall and Murray?

Ongoing Learning in an Interconnected World

> A culture of continuous learning is fostered for everyone: Teachers' needs as adult learners are also appropriately addressed, so that they are well supported to address the changes implied in the other five principles. (principle summarized from Bolstad et al. 2012)
>
> Strong school–community connections need to be fostered: The support of many others is needed if students are to be offered the sorts of authentic learning experiences valued in 21st century approaches such as capability building. At the same time, communities need to understand and value the sorts of shifts that schools are attempting to make. (principle summarized from Bolstad et al. 2012)

This section introduces e-learning and the complex mix of challenges that accompany this profound global shift in ways that knowledge and information circulate and are used. Again, whole books have already been written about these matters, and we only have space to broadly signal some areas where more experienced teachers need to show beginning teachers different ways of doing and being, especially but not only in ILEs.

Within an ILE, learners typically have ready personal access to a digital device. Blended learning approaches can then be used to provide a rich mix of activities that are responsive to specific learning demands as these arise. Learning might be teacher-led, individual or collaborative, both online and offline. There will also be rich collaboration between the teachers working in the ILE. They typically have a home group for whom they have pastoral oversight, but they also plan together, mix groups differently for different parts of their learning, and generally, all take responsibility for the overall work program that unfolds within the space. There is a strong emphasis on self-directed learning where relevant, with students kept on track by the strong planning and tracking frameworks that guide the unfolding learning action. An account written by two senior leaders in one of the schools in the Manaiakalani cluster (Martin and Bradbeer 2016) emphasises the importance of deliberately fostering strong interpersonal capabilities, so that teachers can work together in conditions where their pedagogy—and their ongoing professional learning—is on display to other teachers and adults to observe.

Working in ILEs also adds acuity to the curriculum/epistemic challenges outlined above. The affordances of e-learning technologies can be used for traditional knowledge transmission purposes, or they can be used to help students become more literate in the ways they access and work with knowledge claims made in online environments. Recall that developing 'IT literacy' is one of the outcomes shared by twenty-first century curriculum frameworks (Voogt and Pareja Roblin 2012). However, this appears to be an area where many teachers have been slow to rethink their curriculum assumptions and their pedagogy. For example, a recent investigation of New Zealand teachers' use of e-learning in science suggested that support for traditional knowledge transmission goals is still the most commonly conceived purpose for using the affordances of information technologies (Buntting and Bolstad 2013). Important curriculum/epistemic questions are also raised when learning is integrated across subjects, as is becoming more common in ILE practice. How can specific disciplines be kept in sight when addressing complex issues that cross disciplinary boundaries? Turning outwards to the community and the wider world beyond the classroom (sixth principle above), surfaces another set of personal learning challenges. These are nicely encapsulated in the Manaiakalani cluster's overarching pedagogy of 'learn, create, share'. Students are supported as appropriate in the initial stages of learning. They then use their new knowledge in a meaningful activity that creates something new (for them), and they share some of this with a wider audience. The model is intended to provide the impetus to make the outcomes of learning visible to learners and all those who support them (including their parents and wider family); to encourage ubiquitous learning (anytime, anywhere); and to foster strong learner agency and connectedness. In the MDTA initiative outlined next, beginning teachers were encouraged to experience the power of this model as they created blogs to share their own digital and pedagogical learning with a wider teacher audience. Here are glimpses of new possibilities for knowledge-building in teacher education. The 'intertwingly' connections now leading to new insights in science (Weinberger 2011, p. 115) also have the potential to build new pedagogical and curriculum knowledge—but only if experienced teachers lead the way for those who are just setting out on the journey of learning to be a teacher in complex and fast-changing times.

How Two Teacher Education Initiatives Have Responded to These Dilemmas

We now highlight the two teacher education initiatives briefly introduced at the start of the chapter as responses to the challenges of twenty-first century learning. MDTA focuses on initiating beginning teachers into digital-rich classrooms, while Mind Lab by Unitec offers digital and collaborative learning for teachers at any stage of their career to complete part-time. We undertook small evaluative research projects of both MDTA and the Mind Lab by Unitec initiatives. One common thread is the complex and demanding challenge entailed in becoming a teacher who is able to work in ways that are totally unfamiliar from one's own schooling experiences. In highlighting these features, we are not claiming that these initiatives have worked perfectly. Our evaluations showed the mixed results to be expected when the changes being sought are so demanding. Our purpose in introducing these two cases is simply to show what is possible.

Introducing the MDTA Initiative

Manaiakalani's approach is predicated on accelerating the learning of every child or young person who attends a school in the Manaiakalani cluster, while at the same time transforming their practice for the digital era. The MDTA pilot was conceived as a proactive response to a growing frustration from leaders of the Manaiakalani schools. From their perspective, initial teacher education programs have not kept up with twenty-first century changes in education. Newly qualified teachers have been employed in Manaiakalani schools without adequate skills and knowledge for the types of digital pedagogies the schools now employ, or for working collaboratively in ILEs. Coupled with this was the need to attract and retain effective beginning teachers in schools serving low socioeconomic communities. It can be very confronting for white middle-class beginning teachers to encounter children from families living in very different cultural and economic circumstances to their own.

During 2014, ten newly qualified beginning teachers were each paired with a mentor teacher, working alongside each other in the same learning space. The aim was to accelerate the progress of these first-year teachers to becoming the sorts of highly effective teachers needed by the schools in the cluster. There were three strands to the initiative. For most of the week, each beginning teacher and their mentor shared a class or a group of students within an ILE. In the late afternoon on Wednesdays, both the beginning teachers and their mentors attended a postgraduate course designed specifically for them by the University of Auckland. The course explored challenges in accelerating learning for students from their schools. Earlier that same day, the beginning teachers all attended a digital learning academy at one of the Manaiakalani schools so that they could become fluent in using a wide range of technologies in their teaching.

The university component built intellectual tools for surfacing the beliefs, assumptions and values that teachers need to draw on to bring past experience to present action (Hipkins et al. 2015). When seeking to build agency in a complex action context, such intellectual tools allow teachers to recognise dynamics that might otherwise go unnoticed—they make the resources from past experience 'reflectively available' in the present (Priestley et al. 2015, p. 139). The digital learning component provided a range of future-oriented learning experiences that simultaneously served to bolster material aspects of agency in the present. Knowing how to use apps, solve practical problems, etc., makes it easier to see oneself using these in the thick of the classroom action. The mentor/beginning teacher pairing supported reflective leveraging of rich experiences across a spectrum of professional challenges. These included modelling of: appropriate routines of behaviour management; cultural responsiveness; pedagogical strategies for accelerating learning; and pedagogies for a 1:1 learning environment (Hipkins et al. 2015).

In the strongest pairings, both the mentor and the mentee were comfortable in the role of learner. They worked together on their university assignments, and sometimes the mentees, freshly out of university, needed to take the academic lead. Mentors and mentees worked together in the classroom, and mentors sometimes had to dig deep to surface tacit thinking about their own practice as they shaped support and guidance for the mentee. In turn, the beginning teachers brought new digital knowledge and skills to their wider school teams. In the very best of the partnerships, there were win/wins all around and clear evidence that there had been a positive impact on students' learning progress (Hipkins et al. 2015; Whatman et al. 2016).

The beginning teachers all learned to teach in ways they had not personally experienced as learners themselves. Doing so was challenging and stressful and took a great deal of time. Everyone found it hard to juggle the university component with the other parts of the pilot, but they all agreed that it was important that they did persevere and that the study brought deeper insights that enriched the overall experience. The effectiveness of the overall whole was very apparent throughout the evaluation.

MDTA is unique in New Zealand and, as far as we can ascertain, internationally. It is unique in pairing beginning teachers (who have completed their initial teacher education) and mentors in classrooms, all day every day, for a year. The classroom pairing is central to the conception of the first year of MDTA as an 'apprenticeship' for working successfully in a digitally-enabled, low decile school (i.e. schools in low socioeconomic areas). The general consensus was that this apprenticeship was much more successful in preparing beginning teachers for independent teaching than the traditional practice of allocating teachers sole responsibility for a class right from the start of their first year.

Those involved in MDTA were very aware that this is a high-cost option compared to more traditional programs for supporting beginning teachers. But they were also aware of the hidden negative costs of other options (e.g. higher dropout rates when teachers struggle to successfully begin their careers in low decile schools; Whatman et al. 2016).

Introducing the Mind Lab by Unitec program

We now briefly consider the Mind Lab by Unitec postgraduate certificate in applied practice (digital and collaborative learning) as another considered response to the multiple professional learning challenges outlined in the first three sections of this chapter. Parsons et al. (2015) outlined various drivers for change that underpinned the development of the postgraduate certificate. These included the ideas that the existing system is failing to meet the needs of young people that new generations of learners have different requirements and expectations due to their formative experiences with digital technologies and that technological change in education needs to be supported by deliberate changes in pedagogy. The three complementary themes of digital tools, collaboration and leadership underpin the program. The 32-week part-time postgraduate certificate is based upon the completion of four compulsory courses over a year. Teachers doing the certificate continue to teach while they study. The first half comprises weekly four-hour face-to-face sessions at one of The Mind Lab by Unitec labs at multiple sites around New Zealand. The second half is primarily online.

The goal of the postgraduate certificate program is to influence teachers' thinking and practice in ways that lead to transformation of teaching and learning. Our research based on teachers' self-reports in participant blogs and in-depth interviews concluded that participation in the postgraduate certificate had impacted on teachers' thinking, both about their practice and themselves as teaching practitioners (Bolstad and MacDonald 2016). Some used words like 'disruption' or 'mind-shift' to summarise their overall experience. The breadth of ideas, theories and concepts explored in the postgraduate certificate meant that teachers had to think their way through and across a lot of different ideas over the course of the program (Bolstad and MacDonald 2016).

The teachers felt positive about trying new practices and continuing to explore and learn, even if they had only made tentative first steps so far. The evaluation identified six themes in teachers' descriptions of their practice in relation to the postgraduate certificate: using reflection, theory and evidence to guide changes in practice; trying out new ideas, and finding the ones that 'resonate'; giving learners more agency and sharing power; fostering collaborative learning; working towards more culturally responsive practice; and exposure to a range of digital tools and an intention to keep exploring these in practice (Bolstad and MacDonald 2016, p. ix).

ITE and In-service Professional Learning Co-relate

The Mind Lab by Unitec is a response to the dilemma of educating teachers to respond to twenty-first century learning imperatives and to the question we posed in the introduction. If existing teachers struggle, who will show the way to those who are only just setting out? Given this question, we believe that the problems of educating beginning teachers cannot be separated from challenges faced by other teachers as learners. We wonder what longer-term impacts might emerge if a 'critical mass' of more experienced teachers could take part in learning that is designed to be transformative—and has indeed been transformative for many participants in the two initiatives we have outlined.

A recent literature scan completed for the Educational Council of Aotearoa New Zealand focused on ways to ensure high quality practicum experiences during initial teacher education (Whatman and MacDonald 2017). The literature reviewed demonstrated a clear recognition of the need to involve whole communities in accepting responsibility for new teacher preparation and of the need to establish genuine and authentic partnerships between institutions. Multiple studies also showed that mentor teachers and visiting lecturers are pivotal in providing rich learning experiences for student teachers (e.g. Le Cornu 2012). However, established teachers need to be modelling new approaches so that beginning teachers can learn to teach in ways they were not taught themselves and to assess learning in ways that they were not themselves assessed. That is the dilemma we have addressed in this chapter, and to which MDTA and the postgraduate certificate in applied practice (digital and collaborative learning) are responses.

Transforming Initial Teacher Education

The twenty-first century teacher learning challenges addressed in this chapter have been organised in relation to six future-focused principles (Bolstad et al. 2012), which highlight the profound nature of changes to practice envisaged by futures thinkers in education. Each of them has implications for what twenty-first century teachers need to be and do, and therefore implications for twenty-first century initial teacher education. Gilbert (2013) asks 'What should initial teacher education programs for 2022 look like and why?'. Features she discusses map onto the future-focused principles: personalizing initial teacher education to develop individual strengths; productively using diversity; moving away from the current model of standardised 'generalist' teachers (because of the epistemic challenges we outlined above); focusing on relationship skills; selecting candidates who demonstrate potential to make cognitive shifts and 'work with knowledge'; and supporting teacher educators to engage in their own forms of transformational learning (Gilbert 2013, pp. 113–114).

Picking up on the call for professional learning to be transformative, we draw the threads of the chapter together by briefly outlining three different sets of ideas about the conditions under which such transformation might be achieved. All three ideas can be aligned with the learning conditions that were fostered in the MDTA and Mind Lab by Unitec initiatives. It is hard to escape the conclusion that 'doing more of the same but better' will not be a sufficient response to the challenges that confront initial teacher education for the twenty-first century.

Teaching as an Embodied Act

Ord and Nuttall (2016) argue that the concept of embodiment provides useful insights for supporting student teachers during practica. They argue that what is often described as 'practice' is in fact the felt experience of becoming knowledgeable, of grasping 'important concepts through their enactment in the messier, more complex reality of practice settings' (p. 359). The authors contend that teacher educators should pay attention to how 'the body *feels* during the experience of learning to teach' (p. 361, emphasis in original). In the school setting, student teachers should closely observe their mentor teachers and talk to them about 'how they negotiate space, time, resources, concepts and feelings in the "real time" of classroom practice' (p. 361).

The MDTA model made space for these types of interchanges because mentees were almost always alongside their mentors as the classroom action unfolded. Both mentees and mentors valued the learning insights prompted by the felt intensity of difficult moments. Mentors needed to dig deep to shape reasons for tacit (embodied) responses, while mentees got on-the-spot advice as they learned new ways of being (Hipkins et al. 2015). Similar conditions could be achieved on a shorter practicum, but our evaluation suggested that the sustained nature of interactions over time allowed for gradually deepening insights to form and grow.

Vocational Thresholds

Vaughan et al. (2015a) developed the concept of vocational thresholds, building on the idea of threshold concepts within a discipline that are significant for transformative student learning (Meyer and Land 2003). They studied practice-based learning for general practice registrars, carpentry apprentices and engineering cadets. Their insights about practice-based learning transfer readily to considerations of practicum, as well as the support given to beginning teachers. They are also useful for reflecting on the impact for both of these groups when other teachers also experience transformative learning as an integral part of their ongoing practice.

Vocational thresholds are 'significant shifts for learner-practitioners that are ontological (about their way of being), as well as epistemological (about what, and how, they know things)' (p. 61). Crossing such thresholds involves 'transformational learning experiences, sometimes troublesome, of existing beliefs and knowledge, that open up a new set of spaces in which people can not only know, and do, but "be" as practitioners' (p. 61). Vaughan et al. (2015b) argue that:

> once someone has crossed a vocational threshold they see their work and its purpose in a new light. They are likely to move to a new level of capability and vocational identity that integrates what they know, what they can do, and *how they are* as practitioners. (p. 1, emphasis in original)

Threshold experiences are personal to each individual, but Vaughan et al. (2015b) identify three characteristics of systemic learning arrangements that are likely to shift meaningful experiences into a vocational threshold zone. Aspects of all three of the following can be seen in the case studies above:

1. recognition and cultivation of a practice landscape where practitioners engage in a range of authentic relationships and are deliberately inducted into a community
2. opportunities to practise and reflect through activities with real meaning, real consequences, real challenges and rewards, and space for critical reflection
3. people in designated support roles (i.e. mentors) who 'focus on development of independent work and judgement through practice … [and draw] learner-practitioners into a "community of practice" where they [can] *inhabit* the practice landscape' (Vaughan et al. 2015b, p. 6, emphasis in original).

Towards a More 'Virtuous' Conception of Teacher Education

> Our educational actions are never just a repetition of what has happened in the past but are always radically open to the future. We need judgment rather than recipes in order to be able to engage with this openness and do so in an educational way. (Biesta 2014, p. 137)

Biesta (2014) discusses the challenges of supporting beginning and early career teachers to make the *educationally wise* judgements needed to teach today's young people well. He calls for 'more virtuous' models of initial teacher education. Such models go beyond evidence-based 'what works' approaches which look back to past practice. They also go beyond competency-based approaches which emphasise what teachers can do, but do not necessarily address the *purposes* to be served by new learning. Biesta identifies three broad sets of purposes: qualification (knowing and doing new things); socialisation (learning to fit into existing social structures); and subjectification (coming to be one's own person). These three types of purpose can amplify each other, or they can conflict. For this reason, teaching is always a balancing act that requires moment-by-moment decision-making as competing priorities are juggled. One important but often neglected aspect of this balancing act is to judge if changes are actually improving learning for students.

Substitute beginning teachers for school students, and it should be apparent that all three types of purposes can also amplify or conflict within their professional learning experiences. In particular, this chapter has highlighted challenges for learning to embody new ways of being a teacher (i.e. subjectification in Biesta's terms). Educating a new generation of more virtuous teachers requires the most experienced teachers to bring the wisdom that comes with deep experience to bear, in conditions where their moment-by-moment knowing, doing and being can be accessed and discussed. The initiatives we have introduced indicate that there are different ways in which such learning conditions might be achieved, but also that intended shifts in practice must be deliberately supported by thoughtfully designed, new types of professional learning opportunities.

Next Questions

In this chapter, we have explored the complex challenge of how teacher education programs might more effectively support beginning teachers to respond to so-called twenty-first century learning imperatives. Evidence from a range of studies shows that experienced teachers can struggle to make the transformative pedagogical changes advocated in future-focused commentary, which suggests that these will not yet be routine in their own practice. Nevertheless, initial teacher education programs rely on experienced teachers to mentor beginning teachers into the profession, so this is a dilemma that needs to be proactively addressed.

The two case studies we have outlined suggest new approaches that could help address the challenges we have described. The extended one-to-one mentoring employed in the MDTA initiative did successfully support a small number of beginning teachers to begin their careers in the complex collaborative teaching conditions that pertain in ILE contexts. But there are several critical limitations to this model, not least its cost. Additionally, this could never constitute a widespread solution for the very reason the dilemma exists in the first place—many experienced teachers are only just making this transition, and it is one that they tend to find very demanding. There would not be enough mentors to go around. In a new project, with initial field work just underway as we were finalising this chapter, one experienced teacher pondered whether beginning teachers could be expected to go straight into ILEs. She did not think she could have made the transition without a 'solid foundation' of traditional practice on which to build. Our evidence in MDTA suggests that an argument about building more traditional experience at the start of a teaching career does not necessarily hold; some of the beginning teachers in the MDTA initiative did learn to thrive in ILEs, even though they found the experience rather shocking at first. However, we do not have enough examples to be confident of making generalisations. New types of mentoring programs constitute one area in need of systematic investigation and further innovation.

Our other case study concerns conditions under which any teachers might make transformative changes to their practice. The Mind Lab by Unitec initiative seems able to successfully trigger threshold experiences that support at least some teachers to transform their practice. Can the combination of influences and learning experiences that worked for them be more deliberately leveraged at scale? What combinations of learning conditions make transformative change more likely? Why are some teachers drawn to tackle pedagogical challenges while others resist? These broad questions hold for both beginning teachers and their mentors. The answers are likely to be complex. Again larger, more systemic programs of research are needed to address these urgent and intriguing questions.

References

Barnett, R. (2004). Learning for an unknown future. *Higher Education Research and Development, 23*(3), 247–260. Retrieved January 12, 2018 from https://ieprojekt.sites.ku.dk/files/2014/07/Learning_for_an_unknown_future_-_Barnett_2004.pdf.

Biesta, G. (2014). *The beautiful risk of education.* London, England: Paradigm.

Bolstad, R., Gilbert, J., McDowall, S., Bull, A., Boyd, S., & Hipkins, R. (2012). *Supporting future-oriented learning and teaching: A New Zealand perspective.* Wellington, New Zealand: Ministry of Education. Retrieved January 12, 2018 from http://www.educationcounts.govt.nz/publications/schooling/109306.

Bolstad, R., & MacDonald, J. (2016). *Research for The Mind Lab by Unitec—Postgraduate certificate in applied practice (Digital and collaborative learning): An analysis of participant blogs supplemented by teacher interviews.* Wellington, New Zealand: NZCER. Retrieved January 12, 2018 from http://themindlab.com/wp-content/uploads/2015/09/An-analysis-of-participant-blogs-supplemented-by-teacher-interviews.pdf.

Buntting, C., & Bolstad, R. (2013). *E-learning in science: Future-oriented science learning.* Wellington, New Zealand: Ministry of Education. Retrieved January 12, 2018 from http://www.nzcer.org.nz/system/files/EinscienceFuture_orientedscience.pdf.

Gilbert, J. (2013). What should initial teacher education programmes for 2022 look like and why? *Waikato Journal of Education, 18*(1), 105–116.

Gilbert, J., Bull, A., Stevens, L., & Giroux, M. (2015). *On the edge: Shifting teachers' paradigms for the future.* Wellington, New Zealand: Teaching and Learning Research Initiative. Retrieved January 12, 2018 from http://www.tlri.org.nz/sites/default/files/projects/TLRI_Gilbert_Summary.pdf.

Hart, S. (2014). *Investigating socio-critical discourses in assessment of senior physical education in New Zealand* (Unpublished master's thesis). University of Waikato, Hamilton, New Zealand. Retrieved January 12, 2018 from http://researchcommons.waikato.ac.nz/handle/10289/8984.

Hipkins, R. (2005). Learning to 'be' in a new century: Reflections on a curriculum in transition. *Curriculum Matters, 1,* 71–86.

Hipkins, R., Bolstad, R., McDowall, S., & Boyd, S. (2014). *Key competencies for the future.* Wellington, New Zealand: NZCER Press.

Hipkins, R., Whatman, J., & MacDonald, J. (2015). *Evaluation of the Manaiakalani digital teaching academy.* Wellington, New Zealand: Ministry of Education. Retrieved January 12, 2018 from https://www.educationcounts.govt.nz/publications/e-Learning/evaluation-of-the-manaiakalani-digital-teaching-academy.

Hipkins, R., Johnston, M., & Sheehan, M. (2016). *NCEA in context.* Wellington, New Zealand: NZCER Press.

Le Cornu, R. (2012). Leaders of learning in professional practice. *Australian Journal of Education, 37*(3), 18–33.

Martin, S., & Bradbeer, C. (2016). Creating collaborative effectiveness: One school's approach. *Set: Research Information for Teachers, 2,* 48–52. https://doi.org/10.18296/set.0046.

Meyer, J. H. F., & Land, R. (2003). *Threshold concepts and troublesome knowledge: Linkages to ways of thinking and practising within the disciplines.* London, England: Economic and Social Research Council.

Murray, S. (2016). Finding the third space: Successful intercultural practicum. *Early Education, 59,* 6–10. Retrieved January 12, 2018 from http://www.aut.ac.nz/__data/assets/pdf_file/0018/710451/EE-59.pdf.

Ord, K., & Nuttall, J. (2016). Bodies of knowledge: The concept of embodiment as an alternative to theory/practice debates in the preparation of teachers. *Teaching and Teacher Education, 60,* 355–362. https://doi.org/10.1016/j.tate.2016.05.019.

Parsons, D., Thomas, M., Inkila, M., Antipas, P. N., Valintine, F., Pham, T., et al. (2015). Transforming teacher education with digital and collaborative learning and leadership. *International Journal of Digital Literacy and Digital Competence, 64*(4), 30–47. https://doi.org/10.4018/IJDLDC.2015100103.

Priestley, M., Biesta, G., & Robinson, S. (2015). Teacher agency: What is it and why does it matter? In R. Kneyber & J. Evers (Eds.), *Flip the system: Changing education from the ground up* (pp. 134–148). London, England: Routledge.

Riley, B. (2016). *Science, data and decisions in New Zealand's education system.* Wellington, New Zealand: Fulbright New Zealand. Retrieved January 12, 2018 from http://fulbright.org.nz/portfolio/benjamin-riley-ian-axford-new-zealand-fellow/.

Vaughan, K., Bonne, L., & Eyre, J. (2015a). *Knowing practice: Vocational thresholds for GPs, carpenters, and engineering technicians.* Wellington, New Zealand: NZCER. Retrieved January 12, 2018 from http://www.nzcer.org.nz/research/publications/knowing-practice-vocational-thresholds-gps-carpenters-and-engineering.

Vaughan, K., Bonne, L., & Eyre, J. (2015b). *Knowing practice: Vocational thresholds for GPs, carpenters, and engineering technicians: Summary.* Wellington, New Zealand: Ako Aotearoa and NZCER. Retrieved January 12, 2018 from https://akoaotearoa.ac.nz/download/ng/file/group-9519/knowing-practice-vocational-thresholds-for-gps-carpenters-and-engineering-technicians-summary.pdf.

Voogt, J., & Pareja Roblin, N. (2012). A comparative analysis of international frameworks for 21st-century competences: Implications for national curriculum policies. *Journal of Curriculum Studies, 44*(3), 299–321. https://doi.org/10.1080/00220272.2012.668938.

Weinberger, D. (2011). *Too big to know: Rethinking knowledge now that the facts aren't the facts, experts are everywhere, and the smartest person in the room is the room.* New York, NY: Basic Books, Perseus.

Whatman, J., Hipkins, R., & MacDonald, J. (2016). *Follow-up evaluation of the Manaiakalani digital teaching academy.* Wellington, New Zealand: Ministry of Education. Retrieved January 12, 2018 from https://www.educationcounts.govt.nz/__data/assets/pdf_file/0008/173915/MDTA-Evaluation-addendum.pdf.

Whatman, J., & MacDonald, J. (2017). *High quality practica and the integration of theory and practice in initial teacher education: A literature review prepared for the Education Council.* Wellington, New Zealand: NZCER. Retrieved January 12, 2018 from https://educationcouncil.org.nz/sites/default/files/Practica_Review_Full_Report.pdf.

Wood, B., Taylor, R., Atkins, R., Johnston, M., Wilson, J., Grey, K., et al. (2017). *Creating active citizens: Interpreting, implementing, and assessing 'personal social action' in social studies.* Wellington, New Zealand: Teaching and Learning Research Initiative. Retrieved January 12, 2018 from http://www.tlri.org.nz/sites/default/files/projects/TLRISummary_Woodv2.pdf.

Yates, L., & Millar, V. (2016). 'Powerful knowledge' curriculum theories and the case of physics. *The Curriculum Journal, 27*(3), 298–312. https://doi.org/10.1080/09585176.2016.1174141. (Accessed September 2017).

Zohar, A. & Hipkins, R. (June, 2017). *How 'tight/loose' curriculum dynamics, combined with teachers' epistemic understanding, impact the treatment of knowledge in two national contexts.* Paper presented at the Third European Conference for Curriculum Studies, Stirling University, Scotland.

Rosemary (Rose) Hipkins was a science teacher for over 20 years, followed by six years as a teacher educator. For the last 16 years, she has been at the New Zealand Council for Educational Research (NZCER), most recently as a Chief Researcher. Rose maintains a strong interest in the complex space at the intersection of curriculum and assessment practices. She was actively involved in the development of both the New Zealand Curriculum (NZC) and the National Certificates of Educational Achievement (NCEA assessment system). Over the 16 years, she has been at NZCER; she has lead national research projects related to both curriculum and assessment innovation in New Zealand, with a particular focus on how the NZC key competencies have been understood and enacted. Rose often works in close partnership with teachers and school leaders. She has supported a number of practitioner-led projects funded by the Teacher-Led Innovation Fund and is often invited to speak at conferences and workshops for school practitioners. With her co-authors Jo and Jenny, Rose has also recently explored the complexities of beginning to teach.

Jo MacDonald is a Senior Researcher at the New Zealand Council for Educational Research (NZCER). She has a keen interest and expertise in policy and program evaluation across diverse contexts. In recent years, much of her work has been in the area of initial teacher education and early career teaching. A common thread is how people (particularly teachers) are prepared for and supported to do their work through initial and ongoing training, mentoring and communities of practice. In addition to her role as a senior researcher and evaluator, Jo leads NZCER's coordination of the Teaching and Learning Research Initiative (TLRI), a contestable research program funded by the New Zealand government. Jo has over 20 years' experience in education and educational research, including a decade working in research and evaluation in the government sector in New Zealand and Scotland.

Jenny Whatman is an education consultant who until recently was a Senior Researcher at the New Zealand Council for Educational Research (NZCER). She has a keen interest and expertise in policy and program evaluation across diverse contexts. In recent years, much of her work has been leading research projects in initial teacher education, early career teaching and professional learning and development. She has a strong interest in and knowledge of mentoring and adults as teachers and learners. She has also worked extensively in the area of adult numeracy and literacy and in developing assessment tools and criteria. Jenny has over 40 years' experience in education and prior to NZCER worked as a senior policy analyst for the Ministry of Education in Wellington and as a teacher educator at Wellington College of Education (now Victoria University of Wellington).

Chapter 7
Conceptions of Readiness in Initial Teacher Education: Quality, Impact, Standards and Evidence in Policy Directives

Colette Alexander

Introduction

It is internationally claimed in educational and political contexts that the most important school-based factor in student learning is the quality of the teacher (Darling-Hammond 2010; Hattie 2009). While some academics question the evidence underpinning such an assumption (Cochran-Smith 2009; Cochran-Smith et al. 2016), its danger is not in the accuracy of the statement as much as in the consequential policies and practices that emerge in response. Most troubling are contemporary policies across international jurisdictions that presume to improve education and the educational experience of learners through the assessment of teacher performance for the purposes of eliminating or retaining and remunerating teachers on the basis of assessed quality or effectiveness (Elliott 2015).

Initial teacher education (ITE) is not impervious to the implications of this focus on the quality of teachers and teaching. Recent political engagement in the review and regulation or accreditation of ITE across many international contexts has strongly focussed on the impact of teacher preparation programs on the quality of the teachers produced (see, e.g. Furlong 2015, referring to Wales; Sahlberg et al. 2014, referring to Northern Ireland; Craven et al. 2014, referring to Australia). At the heart of these political discourses are concerns about the standard of graduates and their readiness or preparedness for teaching. Two common policy responses are (1) a focus on the quality of entrants to teacher preparation programs and (2) the assessment of the quality of graduates at the conclusion of their studies. While the issue of entrance standards and the social justice implications of excluding prospective teachers on the

---

C. Alexander (✉)
Institute for Learning Sciences and Teacher Education, Australian Catholic University, Brisbane, Australia
e-mail: Colette.Alexander@acu.edu.au

© Springer Nature Singapore Pte Ltd. 2018
C. Wyatt-Smith and L. Adie (eds.), *Innovation and Accountability in Teacher Education*, Teacher Education, Learning Innovation and Accountability,
https://doi.org/10.1007/978-981-13-2026-2_7

basis of prior educational advantage or disadvantage is important (Cochran-Smith et al. 2017), the focus in this chapter is on issues surrounding the assessment of teachers at the point of transition from preparation to employment in the profession.

Critical to discussions about transition into teaching is the assumption that the purpose of teacher preparation is to ensure that graduates are ready to teach and that teacher education programs should have assessed 'readiness' as a condition of graduation (Craven et al. 2014; Conway et al. 2009). Yet, there is a lack of agreement in relation to what is evidence of readiness (Rowe and Skourdoumbis 2017), whether readiness as an end-point is achievable, and how readiness is perceived by various participants and stakeholders in teacher preparation (Craven et al. 2014). The purpose of this chapter is to consider how readiness might be conceptualised in ITE and how that conception of readiness might be productively used in teacher preparation.

Background

The discourse of readiness has permeated recent educational research into the assessment of teacher performance in ITE. Internationally, there is a plethora of research and regulatory practices being used to assess teacher performance. Across the professional lifespan, these can be summarised into just a handful of tools, which provide different lenses, inwards and outwards, on the performance of teaching (Goe et al. 2008). Some examples of uses of tools include individual tasks or groups thereof (Henry et al. 2013), portfolios of tasks or evidence (Allard et al. 2013), engagement with and observation by other professionals (Strong et al. 2011), measures of student achievement (Brady et al. 2016), and questionnaires or surveys of participants and clients (Kyriakides 2005). Judgements about teaching performance are made on the basis of one or more of these tools.

In the initial phase of professional learning, the tools for assessing teacher performance described in the literature represent varying conceptions of performance as an outworking of the knowledge base for teaching. This ranges from Finland's conceptually complex teacher research inquiry approach, to the knowledge-driven Praxis Examination in the USA. Recently, efforts have also been made to include evidence of student learning or achievement in the assessment of performance in ITE. Brady et al. (2016) designed a 'value-added model' (VAM) that used pre- and post-tested student achievement data in a selected reading test across the span of 8–10 weeks of instruction by the pre-service teacher as evidence of teaching performance. Ostensibly, these various means of assessing teacher performance in ITE are designed to quality assure graduates and instil political and community confidence in teachers entering the profession. However, ongoing questions about the quality of teachers across international boundaries has served to sharpen attention on perceptions of the readiness of graduates and the effectiveness of various measures of teacher performance to determine the readiness of graduates.

A case example is the edTPA conducted and validated by Stanford Center for Assessment, Learning and Equity (SCALE). Exploratory and confirmatory factorial analysis of the edTPA has shown that it assesses a single latent factor which is then described as 'readiness to teach' (Nayfeld et al. 2015). Despite this, little is said in the reports about what is actually meant by the term, and in the context of the edTPA it is assumed to be self-evident in the performance of the practices of teaching measured by this portfolio-based assessment task. Critiques of the edTPA have considered its capacity to assess teaching practice across a divergent range of alternative conceptions of teaching (Sato 2014), which by association point to alternative conceptions of 'readiness to teach'. Yet, the presence and implications of alternative conceptions about teaching and readiness remain largely unchallenged in the literature surrounding the edTPA.

In the Australian context, the focus of ITE on readiness has intensified in recent years. Notable in this intensification was the release of the final report of the recent national review of teacher education. The Teacher Education Ministerial Advisory Group (TEMAG) report titled, *Action now: Classroom ready teachers* (Craven et al. 2014), included five key proposals and 38 recommendations formulated to assure the quality of teacher education and its graduates through transparent, integrated processes grounded in evidence of readiness as measured by outcomes for graduate teachers and their students. The report identified an apparent vacuum created by a lack of data and evidence of the quality of teacher preparation across various pathways into teaching. In the context of this vacuum, the report concluded that evidence of successful achievement of the Graduate Teacher Standards should be taken as, 'a sufficient and up-to-date benchmark of the expectations of graduates entering the profession' (Craven et al. 2014, p. 39). The Graduate Teacher Standards are the first of four levels of standards within the *Australian Professional Standards for Teachers* (Australian Institute for Teaching and School Leadership [AITSL] 2011), that are applied to teacher registration in all states and territories.

The policy initiatives that resulted from the TEMAG report led to a review of the national guidelines for the accreditation of ITE programs. Foundational in this review was the establishment of national program standards for the assessment of pre-service teachers prior to graduation and the collection and analysis of the resulting assessment data as evidence of the readiness of graduates and the impact of the program. These assessment initiatives included: (i) strengthening the role of the Graduate Teacher Standards in determining readiness for graduation through the academic program (see Program Standard (PS) 1.1, AITSL 2016, p. 6); (ii) incorporating a teaching performance assessment in the final year of a program to determine meeting the Graduate Teacher Standards (see PS 1.2, AITSL 2016, p. 8); (iii) measuring academic and non-academic selection criteria for entry (see PS 3.2, AITSL 2016, p. 18); (iv) testing for personal literacy and numeracy against a benchmark of the top 30% of the population (see PS 3.5, AITSL 2016, p. 22); and (v) mandating a role for supervising teachers in reporting achievement against the Graduate Teacher Standards (see PS 5.4, AITSL 2016, p. 39). Critical to these initiatives is the role given to the Graduate Teacher Standards in assessing pre-service teachers' progressive and culminating performance through the academic and professional experience components of all ITE programs. As such, accreditation requirements in the Australian context have established the Graduate Teacher Standards as a proxy for 'readiness' in alignment with the assumptions made about these standards in the TEMAG report. What is missing from these policy directives is a critical analysis of the conceptions of readiness that have underpinned the reform agenda.

Methods

In order to interrogate conceptions of readiness and their relationship to performance in ITE, an investigative process that used textual analysis of documentation was developed. The selected focus for investigation was the reform agenda in ITE in the Australian context, which has been overtly focussed on the preparation of 'classroom ready teachers' (Craven et al. 2014). The processes used involved the selection and reading of documents and the application of quantitative and qualitative analytical strategies to interrogate the use of the term 'readiness' across the selected documentation.

First, all included documents were selected on the basis of a direct relationship to the processes of the TEMAG review. This relationship was determined by inclusion of the document on the Australian Government's dedicated website, *The Teacher Education Ministerial Advisory Group* (Australian Government: Department of Education and Training [DET] 2017). A total of 145 documents were downloaded and included in the analysis:

- Teacher Education Ministerial Advisory Group: *Issues Paper* (Australian Government DET 2014);
- *Best Practice Teacher Education programs and Australia's Own programs* (Ingvarson et al. 2014), research conducted by Australian Council for Education Research (ACER) as commissioned by TEMAG;
- all 141 publically available submissions made in response to the issues paper;
- the final report, *Action now: Classroom ready teachers* (Craven et al. 2014); and
- Teacher Education Ministerial Advisory Group: *Action now: Classroom ready teachers. Australian Government Response* Response (Australian Government DET 2015).

Second, all selected documents were reviewed to determine content and themes related to readiness. This involved the reading of the document, searching for specific terms that would identify the concept of readiness and its relationship to ITE, and analysing the conceptual themes present in the selected portions of text. The search terms used included 'read', 'train', 'initial' and 'prepare', in order to capture as many forms of the various terms as related to ITE. For example, 'read' allowed for the identification of both ready and readiness. Irrelevant references were then ignored. In the case of 'read', the search also captured reading, breadth and the readiness of learners or school students for transitioning between educational contexts, all of which were eliminated. Thematic analysis was used to identify and articulate alternative conceptions of readiness present across the documents, and references to readiness were categorised and quantified in order to consider how the different conceptions of readiness were used within and across the documents.

Findings

The analysis of the inclusion and intent of the term readiness within the documentation selected in relation to the TEMAG report led to four findings, as follows.

Finding 1: Prevalence of 'Ready' and 'Readiness' Across the TEMAG Review

Despite the use of the term *classroom ready teachers* in the title of the final TEMAG report, the terms *ready* and *readiness* were identified in just 20 (13%) of the 145 documents reviewed. Importantly, this included all four of the core political review documents, namely the issues paper, commissioned research paper, final report and Australian government response. This showed that the concept of readiness was present throughout the political review processes. In articulating the issues to be investigated, the *TEMAG: Issues Paper* (2014) stated that 'New teachers need to be *ready* for the rigour and demands of teaching in classrooms that are more challenging and diverse than ever before' (p. 3), and, 'the rigour of the assessment of pre-service teachers undertaking professional experience across different higher education institutions has been criticised with some arguing for greater consistency in assessment of *classroom readiness*' (p. 9; italics added). This focus on rigour and pre-service teachers' readiness for classrooms can be traced through to the government's response to the TEMAG recommendations. This document (DET 2015) states that 'universities will need to clearly show that their graduates are *classroom ready*' (p. 5) and that this will be facilitated by universities and schools able to, 'undertake rigorous, continuous and consistent assessment of teacher education students for *classroom readiness*' (p. 7). As such, one of the five core themes of the government's response is the 'Robust assessment of graduates to ensure classroom readiness' (p. 8).

In contrast, the terms *ready* and *readiness* were found in just 16 (11%) of the 141 publically available submissions to the TEMAG review. All submissions that included these terms were identified as institutional rather than individual submissions. These institutions included: employers (6), universities (3), regulatory authorities (2), education unions (2), and educational associations or stakeholders (3). Across the submissions, a wide range of phrases were used, including *work ready, school ready, job ready, readiness to be a competent good beginning teacher, teacher ready, ready to teach, readiness to transition, readiness to begin their careers, readiness for employment* and *readiness to be admitted to the profession.* This showed that participants and stakeholders with different contextual purposes and relationships to the field of teacher education used different phrases with different emphases when discussing readiness.

The broad range of terms used demonstrated a lack of consistency in the language and definition of the conception of readiness in the submissions that points to diverse discursive understandings of the role and purpose of readiness in ITE. The text surrounding the terms points to different perspectives of the meaning or qualities of readiness. For example, a Department of Education submission claimed a survey of Principals showed that 'It is clear that there are areas of the ITE program that are not currently adequately preparing graduate teachers to be *work ready* upon graduation'. This view contrasts with a university claim that it 'aims for *work ready* graduates with pedagogic knowledge and skills as well as personal qualities to work in such a challenging and inspiring environment'. These types of contradictions demonstrate that there are different, idiosyncratic interpretations of what constitutes readiness that can be linked to the roles and responsibilities of the different participants in the processes and practices of teacher education.

Finding 2: Definitional Dissonance in Considerations of Readiness

No clear definition of readiness was provided in any of the documents reviewed. As described above, the TEMAG report identified that performance against the Graduate Teacher Standards could be assumed to be an appropriate measure of readiness (Craven et al. 2014, p. 39). Considerations of the context and quality of the performance of the Graduate Teacher Standards and the assessment there of is not provided in the report. Rather, this is assumed to be the work that must be undertaken by AITSL and ITE providers as a consequence of the TEMAG review. Across the public submissions, the reference that comes closest to defining readiness was made by an educational stakeholder group which stated that 'The role of teacher education institutions is to prepare graduates for readiness to be a competent, good beginning teacher'. However, another educational stakeholder cautioned against the definitional notion of competence stating that it is 'naïve to expect that novice teachers will be fully competent in all areas of the role from their first day on the job'.

The lack of definitional clarity about readiness was also evident in different levels of expectation and perceptions of the readiness of graduates in the stakeholders' public submissions. A Department of Education submission directly referenced this dissonance stating that 'a considerable gap exists between the perspectives of providers and employers with regard to *graduate teacher readiness* and capabilities'. This was further explained by a union submission that pointed out that, 'government, schools and the community had unrealistically high expectations of what a *teacher ready graduate* might be'. This was further articulated in the submission of a regulatory body that reflected faculty concerns about the 'unrealistic expectations by schools of the *classroom readiness* of graduates unsupported by strong induction practices'. As such, the presence of differences in the conception of readiness by different stakeholders in teacher education was overtly identified as a core dissonance in the practices of ITE.

Finding 3: Three Thematic Conceptions of Readiness

Given that the documents demonstrate variation in the use and definitions of readiness, a thematic analysis of the use of the terms *ready* and *readiness* was applied. Unlike the divergent use of terms in the public submissions, the four core documents used a small number of phrases that were categorised into themes. Across the four core political review documents, the 74 uses of *ready* or *readiness* can be categorised into three thematically different conceptions of readiness as represented by phrases that qualify the nature of that readiness. The three phrases used were *classroom readiness* (59, 70%), *readiness for teaching* (6, 8%) and *readiness for the profession* (9, 12%). The phrases 'classroom ready' and 'ready for the classroom' were categorised as *classroom readiness*. *Readiness for teaching* was also described as 'readiness for independent teaching', 'teacher readiness' and 'ready to teach'. *Readiness for the profession* was connected to the phrases 'readiness to be admitted to the profession' and 'readiness for full entry to the profession'.

These three core phrases exemplify alternate conceptions of readiness at the point of graduation. First, comments that referenced *classroom readiness* implied that readiness needed to predictively quality assure future performance in any or all possible classroom contexts. The purpose of working towards and assessing readiness was to identify graduates capable of performing competently as the teacher in any classroom to which they might be allocated. Within this conception, the core focus is on the capacity of the graduate teacher to successfully adapt to, and positively impact, the full breadth of possible classrooms across the Australian context.

Second, comments on *readiness for teaching* shift the focus towards the performance of the knowledge, skills and practices that are expected of a teacher irrespective of classroom context. It assumes that teacher performance is independent of classroom context, and that graduates who are ready for teaching will be capable of having a positive impact on learning regardless of context. As such, it assesses readiness to safeguard the public by preventing teachers with poor skills from entering the classroom.

Third, comments related to *readiness for the profession* focused on eligibility for entry to the teaching profession as assessed by the profession and exemplified by the knowledge, practices and dispositions of the profession. The purpose of assessing readiness was to identify the core capabilities and dispositions needed to cope with and thrive among the contextual challenges of teaching. The goal was to identify graduates who are ready to work towards effectively applying these core capabilities and dispositions to the independent practice of teaching.

While the public submissions used more divergent language, as described above, the same thematic phraseology was also identified. For example, discussion in the submissions about the assessment of the readiness of graduates specifically referenced two of these themes. A union submission stated that 'Australia needs a systemic approach to preparing teachers for a successful career in the classroom and a more rigorous threshold to ensure that every teacher is actually *ready to teach*'. By comparison, a regulatory body made a similar point stating, 'We need to strengthen our ability to measure the knowledge and skills graduate teachers are mastering at key junctures through their course and their *readiness to be admitted to the profession*'. Both of these statements establish a high expectation of the role of assessment for ensuring and measuring the readiness of graduates. Yet, the phraseology selected provides a striking difference to the tone and intent of the comment. While the *readiness to teach* theme invokes a 'rigorous threshold' that might be used to identify successful and, by association, unsuccessful teachers at the point of graduation, the *readiness for the profession* theme establishes developmental understandings of the process of becoming a teacher. Importantly, these differences demonstrate that these language choices are not superficial but indicative of theoretically and practically different conceptions of readiness.

Finding 4: Patterns in the Use of the Conceptions of Readiness

Two core patterns were identified in the use of the phrases that conceptualise readiness in ITE. These related to: (i) the roles and relationships of participants in ITE and (ii) the progression of the TEMAG review. Effectively, the language selected to describe readiness related to institutional roles and relationships to ITE of the authors of a specific document. This is most clearly seen in the four core political review documents. Table 7.1 quantifies the thematic references to the three conceptions of readiness in each document.

The political review process started and concluded with documents prepared by the Australian Government's Department of Education. In both cases, all references to readiness fell within the *classroom readiness* theme. This theme also dominates the discourse of the final report prepared by the ostensibly independent Teacher Education Ministerial Advisory Group through both its title, *Action Now: Classroom*

Table 7.1 Count of conceptions of readiness across TEMAG review document

	Issues paper (DET)	Research paper (ACER)	TEMAG report (TEMAG)	Response paper (DET)
Classroom readiness	2	2	45	10
Readiness for teaching	0	2	3	0
Readiness for the profession	0	5	4	0

Ready Teachers, and the content of the report. Interestingly, the research paper that was commissioned by TEMAG and written by six teacher education academics for ACER did not present this same predilection for *classroom readiness*. Rather, more than half the time this report used phrases related to *readiness for the profession*, and all three conceptions were identified.

Over time, it is shown that the variation in conceptions of readiness shown in the ACER research paper and other submissions was intensified towards *classroom readiness* in the final report and then wholly focussed on that theme in the culminating government response. It is notable that this government response document prompted the contemporary reform agenda in the accreditation and provision of ITE in the Australian context. This demonstrates the significant role that the conception of *classroom readiness* is playing in the outworking of the revised national program standards. This problematises the issue and its impact on the practices of teacher education in making a contribution to the provision of quality teachers for the education of all.

Discussion

The presence of wide-ranging linguistic choices across the analysed documentation has highlighted a lack of definitional and conceptual clarity about readiness in the context of ITE. Without a clear and common understanding of readiness, various expectations regarding the level of knowledge and skill of graduates have been shown to abound. This has contributed to ongoing concerns about unrealistic expectations of beginning teachers that fuel criticisms of ITE (Bahr and Mellor 2016). Additionally, the narrowing of the conception of readiness towards *classroom readiness* in the ongoing political reform of ITE in the Australian context is problematised for its role in objectifying and de-professionalising the work of teachers, teacher educators and teacher education (Rowe and Skourdoumbis 2017).

The problematising of *classroom readiness* does not negate the importance of readiness to the processes and practices of ITE. Logically, graduates do need to be ready to transition into employment at the end of their qualification. Equally, ITE providers need effective means to assess readiness to assure that graduates are ready to begin. However, this analysis has shown that we do not know what readiness means in relation to the professional learning and development of teachers. Consequently, the application of *classroom readiness* to the processes and practices of ITE through the current reform agenda is built upon divergent conceptions of readiness reliant on the tacit knowledge and experience base of employers, members of the teaching profession and other educational stakeholders.

Therefore, it is necessary to engage with and negotiate the dissonances between the divergent conceptions of readiness in the educational community and the capacities and limitations of higher education in preparing teachers (Alexander 2016). This work will need to develop collaborative understandings of the meaning and intent of readiness to work towards more realistic expectations of graduates and ITE programs.

From this platform, higher education providers will be able to work on the project of effectively preparing for and assessing readiness, and the educational community will be in a much better position to design effective inductive practices supportive of the next-step needs of beginning teachers. While this analysis focussed on evidence from the political reform agenda in the Australian context, continuing and growing reform initiatives internationally highlight the significance of these issues more broadly.

As such, the analysis undertaken for this chapter makes an introductory contribution to the complex task of theorising readiness within the context of ITE. The findings, described above, provided a perspective on the breadth of conceptualisation of readiness across a range of participants and stakeholders in the educational community. However, there were also some notable similarities among the three identified conceptions that might be productively employed towards identifying common ground in seeking to negotiate meaning in relation to readiness. First, all three conceptions assumed that readiness required understanding of a body of knowledge related to teaching; this was most often described in relation to one or more of content knowledge, pedagogical knowledge and pedagogical content knowledge. Second, they all included the performance of a range of teacher skills and practices in an authentic classroom context as essential for demonstrating readiness. Third, they all acknowledged that the building of required knowledge, skills and practices for readiness was developmental from entry into an ITE program through to graduation, and that this development continued into the classroom through induction and continued professional learning. Together, these similarities across the conceptions of readiness point to three proposals for the ongoing project of theorising readiness. These are that readiness is a *professional outcome* and as a consequence readiness is a *shared responsibility* and an *initial milestone* in professional learning.

Readiness as a Professional Outcome

An important distinction that can be made in relation to the three conceptions of readiness is that they represent increasingly sophisticated understandings of the practices of teachers. The conceptions of readiness each identify a particular conception of teaching, which places limitations on the development and assessment of teaching performance from within that conception of readiness. Both *classroom readiness* and *readiness for teaching* limit teaching by focusing on training in a pre-defined set of skills or practices that make up the craft of teaching. In contrast, a professional conception of readiness acknowledges that the integrated role of professional knowledge, practices and dispositions in context relies upon the making of and acting on professional judgements grounded in a complex array of possibilities and consequences where no definitive correct action can be predetermined (Sachs 2000; Southwick 1997). Thus, acknowledging teaching as a profession makes room for a multiplicity of conceptions of teaching and actively promotes knowledge and practice across this range of possibilities in the identification and assessment of readiness through teacher performance (Sato 2014).

There is a deeper understanding and appreciation of the complexity of teaching from one conception to the next. This results in more realistic expectations of the beginner, in that *classroom readiness* assumes it is possible to be ready for any classroom in any context, but, *readiness for the profession* appreciates that the complexity of both practice and context means that readiness is not a guarantee of classroom performance or of success in subsequent development towards proficiency. Despite this apparent reduction in the anticipated capabilities of the beginning teacher, the deepening of the conception actually leads to greater quality assurance.

Readiness for the profession can be shown to facilitate the intent of all three conceptions, but the same cannot be said of taking a perspective from the other way. This is because *readiness for the profession* lifts teacher performance beyond the conception of a skill or craft to be mastered, towards a focus on service to students (Kane 1992; Sachs 2000), such that teaching must impact student learning. It also links readiness to the development of capabilities that contribute to resilience, retention and continued learning (Southwick 1997). In doing so, identifying *readiness for the profession* as the purpose of ITE works to both safeguard the public from poor quality teachers and increase the likelihood of success across a divergent range of classroom contexts.

Readiness as a Shared Responsibility

Across the TEMAG documentation, the comments made about readiness were consistently associated with the term 'quality'. First, this was observed in relation to defining what constitutes a quality teacher as a means of thinking about what constitutes readiness. Interestingly, definitions of quality teachers were much closer to each other across the various stakeholders than was evident in the conceptions of readiness. For example, a Department of Education submission described quality in terms of the 'highest-performing teachers have high-quality pedagogical skills, a thorough understanding of the content and curriculum, a passion for student learning and the subject itself'. Similarly, a Deans' council, representing higher education, stated that 'The balance of content and pedagogical knowledge throughout university courses is critical for pre-service teachers to develop the skills, knowledge and attributes for quality teaching and life-long contribution to the profession', and an education union identified that 'Quality teachers employ a wide range of dynamic, flexible teaching strategies in response to the differing needs of individual students and cohorts'. As such, these shared understandings of the nature of quality teachers and quality teaching might be mined for their potential to contribute to conceptions of readiness on which various stakeholders might agree.

Second, the development of quality teachers was strongly linked across the submissions to opportunities for pre-service teachers to experience quality professional experience placements as a precursor to readiness. As stated in another Department of Education submission 'Opportunities to undertake practicums in progressively more diverse, complex and challenging school contexts … will lead to increased capacity and *classroom readiness* in beginning teachers'. This emphasis on the quality of professional experience was taken up in the TEMAG report in terms of its key proposal for the 'integration of theory and practice' and the role of professional experience in school contexts in achieving that integration (Craven et al. 2014, pp. 3, 26–33), and the need for effectively 'supporting beginning teachers through induction' as a key finding (Craven et al. 2014, pp. xvii, 40–45).

The reform agenda to strengthen professional experience in ITE as a means of improving quality and assuring readiness has been pivotal in the broader re-framing of the national standards (see PS 5—Professional Experience, AITSL 2016, pp. 35–41). Critically, these new requirements have continued to place the onus of responsibility over the quality of professional experience in schools with the ITE provider, a position that is not without some irony. In relation to the recommendations for more effective workforce planning and induction practices to support beginning teachers, the Australian Government response and the subsequent national reform agenda has been silent. Despite this silence in the political context of teacher education, shared responsibility for quality and readiness through effective professional experience has continued to motivate educators and educational research (Kriewaldt et al. 2018; Le Cornu 2015). Within this work is the potential to shift the focus of the responsibility for readiness away from the individual teacher or ITE provider towards a collective, shared understanding of the responsibility of the profession and the educational community to provide classrooms and schools ready to productively contribute to beginning teachers' professional learning, readiness and ongoing induction.

Readiness as a Milestone of Professional Learning

The conception of *readiness for the profession*, if taken as the most productive expression of the conception of readiness, leads to the conclusion that readiness should be viewed as an initial milestone in a life-long process of professional learning. Again, this conception of readiness has some support in the reform agenda surrounding teachers and teaching. The Graduate Teacher Standards (AITSL 2011) that were taken up as a proxy for readiness in the TEMAG report are in fact the first of a set of four levels of standards for Australian teachers. The other levels are the proficient, highly accomplished and lead teacher standards that have been correlated to progressive phases of employment. For example, graduate teachers should attain the Proficient Teacher Standards through induction and the completion of at least 80 days of successful teaching (AITSL 2017). As a consequence, continuums of learning or development for teachers are often developed in terms of phases of employment that include steps such as preparation, induction, teaching and professional development (Alexander 2016).

However, the conception of *readiness for the profession* shifts the discourse of professional learning towards a professionally oriented rather than an employment-oriented continuum of development. Across a range of professions and practices, a common continuum of learning used in this way is the Dreyfus (2004) model that describes the trajectory for developing expertise as moving from novice to expert. This is a five-stage model of development including novice, advanced beginner, competent, proficient and expert that has been applied to a diverse range of fields including physics, nursing, pedagogical and even criminal expertise (Benner 2004; Larkin et al. 1980; Lyon 2015; Ward 1999). As a developmental continuum, this model recognises the overt, cognitive and practical challenges of early development of practice that gives way to the intuitive tacit practice of an expert. As such, it shifts the focus from what is done to the teacher to what the teacher does and is closely aligned to the intent of the theorising of readiness as a professional pursuit.

Importantly, Dreyfus' (2004) model actively acknowledges that the development of expertise to the level of an expert is not a given for all practitioners. Rather, it posits that there are many capable, proficient practitioners who will never attain the intuitive tacit practice of an expert. The assumption that ITE can or should be developing experts guaranteed of success in any classroom context is shown to be theoretically and practically impossible. The level identified as suitable to begin independent practice is that described as 'competent' (Benner 2004). Competence is experienced as a conscious activity of making, assessing and re-making decisions. In the case of teaching, this must be in response to the actions of learners in a classroom context. It is comprised of both an observable embodied experience and an internalised cognitive activity. Interestingly, this definition of competence links well to the definitions of readiness that were identified in the TEMAG documentation. This model of learning might be productively employed in the work of identifying and defining what we mean by *classroom ready teachers*.

Conclusion

This chapter has identified a growing emphasis, internationally, on the concept of readiness in ITE that has been intensified in the Australian context through the work of the TEMAG review (Craven et al. 2014). It used the documentation from this political review process to analyse three conceptions of readiness and their implications for the processes and practices of ITE. This showed that the conception of readiness has a significant impact on conceptions of teaching, the expectations of graduate competence, and the means by which that competence, and thus readiness, is assessed. It was proposed that the educational community needs to negotiate the dissonances between alternative conceptions to theorise readiness and its application to ITE.

Significantly, the conception of readiness was shown to play a critical role in establishing the point at which beginning teachers are suitably prepared for the rigours of working in contemporary classrooms. The role of theorising readiness must have a dual focus that identifies both what readiness is and how we know. In considering the purpose and impact of the three conceptions of readiness in the TEMAG documentation, it was proposed that the conception of *readiness for the profession* was the most productive avenue for theorising readiness and the assessment thereof.

The conception of *readiness for the profession* is considered powerful because it facilitates accessing models and theories about professions in identifying what readiness is (Sachs 2000; Southwick 1997). As such, it provides an open platform for conceptualising teaching as critical reflective practice that considers a range of pedagogical options grounded in models and theories of learning. It acknowledges the complexity present in the act of teaching and focuses attention on its core purpose, service to and impact on student learning. This contrasts sharply with the discourses surrounding *classroom readiness* and *readiness for teaching* that hold that readiness is a single, uniform concept understood by external observers of the process that can be definitively identified, or not, by observing the beginning teacher.

Additionally, *readiness for the profession* can be shown to be related to the other conceptions through the features of readiness that were shown to be held in common across them. First, it theorises the need for engagement with a unique body of knowledge by the professional teacher (Southwick 1997). That is, it calls for a broad and deep understanding of a complex body of knowledge that is applied in decision-making and problem-solving to meet the needs of learners. Second, it theorises that readiness to enter the profession requires a foundational level of competence in the knowledge, skills and dispositions of teaching practice (Freidson 1994). In order to be ready for the profession a teacher must have developed a range of critical capabilities needed for safe and ethical independent practice (Benner 2004). Importantly, this shows that readiness is connected to the expertise needed to competently begin teaching practice. Beginners do not need to be experts.

In the context of ongoing negotiations about conceptions of the purpose and intent of readiness, the second issue to be considered is how we might make judgements about readiness in the context of ITE. Theorising from the perspective of professional learning and development has led to the proposal that competence, as a step in the development from novice to expert, might be an appropriate target for assessing readiness (Dreyfus 2004). The next step is to identify ways that performance of teaching at this stage is experienced and demonstrated, and how this connects to methods used to assess teacher performance. Together, the educational community needs to identify the point in the continuum of professional learning where there is sufficient development of the critical capabilities of the profession to have confidence in a beginning teacher's capacity to operate independently within a context of supportive induction. We need to develop understandings of how that level of development is experienced, demonstrated and evidenced, and how to make judgements about the qualities of that evidence and how that reflects the identified qualities of readiness.

The significance of this work in ITE in the Australian context is clear. Given the propensity for political reform in Australia, there have been over 110 reviews in the last 40 years (Alexander 2016), failure to engage productively in the outworking of the TEMAG report is likely to leave the work of teacher education and teacher educators at the whim of the next wave of political review. At the same time, engaging educatively in defining and then garnering evidence of the readiness of graduates carries the potential to contribute positively to professionalising teaching and teacher education and raising the standard of evidence of the readiness of graduates. Given the strong penchant for policy advisors and bureaucrats to closely observe reforms across international borders, this work is also important to the teaching profession more broadly. In it lies an opportunity to stake a claim for teaching as a profession and the professionalisation of teachers.

References

Alexander, C. R. (2016). *Reforming the reform of teacher education: A critical grounded theory of a social approach to change and continuity* (Unpublished doctoral thesis). University of Adelaide, Adelaide, Australia. Retrieved February 21, 2018 from https://digital.library.adelaide.edu.au/dspace/bitstream/2440/101568/2/02whole.pdf.

Allard, A. C., Mayer, D., & Moss, J. (2013). Authentically assessing graduate teaching: Outside and beyond neo-liberal constructs. *The Australian Educational Researcher, 41*(4), 425–443. https://doi.org/10.1007/s13384-013-0140-x.

Australian Institute for Teaching and School Leadership [AITSL]. (2011). *Australian professional standards for teachers*. Carlton South, Australia: Education Services Australia. Retrieved February 21, 2018 from https://www.aitsl.edu.au/docs/default-source/apst-resources/australian_professional_standard_for_teachers_final.pdf.

Australian Institute for Teaching and School Leadership [AITSL]. (2016). *Guidelines for the accreditation of initial teacher education programs in Australia*. Melbourne, Australia: Author. Retrieved February 21, 2018 from https://www.aitsl.edu.au/docs/default-source/initial-teacher-education-resources/guidance-for-the-accreditation-of-initial-teacher-education-in-australia.pdf.

Australian Institute for Teaching and School Leadership [AITSL]. (2017). *Becoming a registered teacher*. Retrieved February 21, 2018 from https://www.aitsl.edu.au/prepare-to-be-a-teacher/become-a-registered-teacher.

Australian Government: Department of Education and Training [DET]. (2014). *Teacher Education Ministerial Advisory Group Issues paper.* Retrieved February 21, 2018 from https://docs.education.gov.au/system/files/doc/other/temag_issues_paper_-_april_2014.pdf.

Australian Government: Department of Education and Training [DET]. (2015). *Action now: Classroom ready teachers. Australian Government response.* Retrieved February 21, 2018 from https://docs.education.gov.au/system/files/doc/other/150212_ag_response_-_final.pdf.

Australian Government: Department of Education and Training [DET]. (2017). *Teacher Education Ministerial Advisory Group.* Retrieved February 7, 2017 from https://www.education.gov.au/teacher-education-ministerial-advisory-group.

Bahr, N., & Mellor, S. (2016). Building quality in teaching and teacher education. *Australian Education Review, 61.* Melbourne, Australia: Australian Council for Educational Research. Retrieved February 21, 2018 from https://research.acer.edu.au/cgi/viewcontent.cgi?article=1025&context=aer.

Benner, P. (2004). Using the Dreyfus model of skill acquisition to describe and interpret skill acquisition and clinical judgment in nursing practice and education. *Bulletin of Science, Technology & Society, 24*(3), 188–199. https://doi.org/10.1177/0270467604265061.

Brady, M. P., Heiser, L. A., McCormick, J. K., & Forgan, J. (2016). Value-added models for teacher preparation programs: Validity and reliability threats, and a manageable alternative. *The Educational Forum, 80*(3), 339–352. https://doi.org/10.1080/00131725.2016.1173150.

Cochran-Smith, M. (2009). The new teacher education in the United States: Directions forwards. In J. Furlong, M. Cochran-Smith, & M. Brennan (Eds.), *Policy and politics in teacher education: International perspectives*. Oxfordshire, England: Routledge.

Cochran-Smith, M., Stern, R., Sánchez, J. G., Miller, A., Keefe, E. S, Fernández, M. B., et al. (2016). *Holding teacher preparation accountable: A review of claims and evidence.* Boulder, CO: National Education Policy Center. Retrieved February 21, 2018 from http://nepc.colorado.edu/publication/teacher-prep.

Cochran-Smith, M., Baker, M., Chang, W., Fernández, M. B., & Keefe, E. S. (2017). *Review of within our grasp: Achieving higher admissions standards in teacher prep*. Boulder, CO: National Education Policy Center. Retrieved February 21, 2018 from http://greatlakescenter.org/docs/Think_Twice/TT-CochranSmith-NCTQ-Teacher-Prep.pdf.

Conway, P. F., Murphy, R., Rath, A., & Hall, K. (2009). *Learning to teach and its implications for the continuum of teacher education: A nine-country cross-national study*. Ireland: Teaching Council. Retrieved February 21, 2018 from http://www.teachingcouncil.ie/en/Publications/Research/Documents/Learning-to-Teach-and-its-Implications-for-the-Continuum-of-Teacher-Education.pdf.

Craven, G., Beswick, K., Fleming, J., Fletcher, T., Green, M., Jensen, B., et al. (2014). *Action now: Classroom ready teachers*. Retrieved February 21, 2018 from https://docs.education.gov.au/system/files/doc/other/action_now_classroom_ready_teachers_print.pdf.

Darling-Hammond, L. (2010). *Evaluating teacher effectiveness: How teacher performance assessments can measure and improve teaching*. Washington, DC: Center for American Progress.

Dreyfus, S. E. (2004). The five-stage model of adult skill acquisition. *Bulletin of Science, Technology & Society, 24*(3), 177–181. https://doi.org/10.1177/0270467604264992.

Elliott, K. (2015). Teacher performance appraisal: More about performance or development? *Australian Journal of Teacher Education, 40*(9), 102–116. https://doi.org/10.14221/ajte.2015v40n9.6.

Freidson, E. (1994). *Professionalism reborn: Theory, prophecy and policy*. Cambridge, England: Polity Press.

Furlong, J. (2015). *Teaching tomorrow's teachers. Options for the future of initial teacher education in Wales (Report to Huw Lewis, Minister for Education and Skills)*. Oxford, England: Oxford University.

Goe, L., Bell, C., & Little, O. (2008). *Approaches to evaluating teacher effectiveness: A research synthesis*. Washington, DC: The National Comprehensive Center for Teacher Quality. Retrieved February 21, 2018 from https://files.eric.ed.gov/fulltext/ED521228.pdf.

Hattie, J. (2009). *Visible learning: A synthesis of over 800 meta-analyses relating to achievement*. London, England: Routledge.

Henry, G. T., Campbell, S. L., Thompson, C. L., Patriarca, L. A., Luterbach, K. J., Lys, D. B., et al. (2013). The predictive validity of measures of teacher candidate programs and performance: Toward an evidence-based approach to teacher preparation. *Journal of Teacher Education, 64*(5), 439–453. https://doi.org/10.1177/0022487113496431.

Ingvarson, L., Reid, K., Buckley, S., Kleinhenz, E., Masters, G., & Rowley, G. (2014). *Best practice teacher education programs and Australia's own programs*. Australian Council for Educational Research. Retrieved February 21, 2018 from https://research.acer.edu.au/cgi/viewcontent.cgi?article=1014&context=teacher_education.

Kane, M. T. (1992). The assessment of professional competence. *Evaluation and the Health Professions, 15*(2), 163–182. https://doi.org/10.1177/016327879201500203.

Kriewaldt, J., Ambrosetti, A., Rorrison, D., & Capeness, R. (Ed.). (2018). *Educating future teachers: Innovative perspectives in professional experience*. Singapore: Springer.

Kyriakides, L. (2005). Drawing from teacher effectiveness research and research into teacher interpersonal behaviour to establish a teacher evaluation system: A study on the use of student ratings to evaluate teacher behaviour. *Journal of Classroom Interaction, 40*(2), 44–66.

Larkin, J., McDermott, J., Simon, D. P., & Simon, H. A. (1980). Expert and novice performance in solving physics problems. *Science 208*(4450), 1335–1342. Retrieved from http://www.jstor.org/stable/1684057.

Le Cornu, R. (2015). *Key components of effective professional experience in initial teacher education in Australia: A paper prepared for the Australian Institute for Teachers and School Leaders*. Melbourne, Australia: AITSL. Retrieved February 21, 2018 from https://www.aitsl.edu.au/docs/default-source/default-document-library/aitsl_key-components-of-effective-professional-experience.pdf?sfvrsn=aec9ec3c_0.

Lyon, L. J. (2015). Development of teaching expertise viewed through the Dreyfus model of skill acquisition. *Journal of the Scholarship of Teaching and Learning, 15*(1), 88–105. https://doi.org/10.14434/josotl.v15i1.12866.

Nayfeld, I., Pecheone, R. L., Whittaker, A., Shear, B., & Klesch, H. (2015). *Educative assessment and meaningful support: 2014 edTPA administrative report*. Stanford, CA: Stanford Center for Assessment, Learning and Equity.

Rowe, E. E., & Skourdoumbis, A. (2017). Calling for 'urgent national action to improve the quality of initial teacher education': The reification of evidence and accountability in reform agendas. *Journal of Education Policy*, 1–17. https://doi.org/10.1080/02680939.2017.1410577.

Sahlberg, P., Broadfoot, P., Coolahan, J., Furlong, J., & Kirk, G. (2014). *Aspiring to excellence. Final report of the international review panel on the structure of initial teacher education in Northern Ireland (Report to the Minister for Employment and Learning)*. Belfast, Ireland: Department for Employment and Learning.

Sachs, J. (2000). Rethinking the practice of teacher professionalism. In C. Day, A. Fernandez, T. E. Hauge, & J. Moller (Eds.), *The Life and work of teachers: International perspectives in changing times* (pp. 76–90). Abingdon, England: Routledge Farmer.

Sato, M. (2014). What is the underlying conception of teaching of the edTPA? *Journal of Teacher Education, 65*(5), 421–434. https://doi.org/10.1177/0022487114542518.

Southwick, J. (1997). *National competition policy and the professions: Can the professions survive under a national competition policy?* Retrieved February 21, 2018 from http://www.professions.com.au/advocacy/archives/item/national-competition-policy-the-professions-1997.

Strong, M., Gargani, J., & Hacifazlioğlu, O. (2011). Do we know a successful teacher when we see one? Experiments in the identification of effective teachers. *Journal of Teacher Education, 62*(4), 367–383. https://doi.org/10.1177/0022487110390221.

Ward, T. (1999). Competency and deficit models in the understanding and treatment of sexual offenders. *The Journal of Sex Research, 36*(3), 298–305. https://doi.org/10.1080/00224499909552000.

Colette Alexander is Coordinator Accreditation in the School of Education at Australian Catholic University. Colette has worked as a teacher educator for 14 years. Colette has recently completed her doctorate in the area of policy and reform in teacher preparation. As an early career researcher, she participates in the Teacher Education, Quality and Professional Practice Research concentration in the Institute for Learning Sciences and Teacher Education (ILSTE). Her research interests are in policy and practice for initial and continuing teacher education and the influence of these on the work of teachers and teacher educators. This includes interest in the impact of policy and reform on curriculum, pedagogy and assessment in teacher education as enacted within the context of higher education. Colette is working towards addressing issues of data, evidence and quality in teacher education as generated by contemporary agendas related to standards and quality.

Chapter 8
Research-Informed Conceptualization and Design Principles of Teacher Performance Assessments: Wrestling with System and Site Validity

Lenore Adie and Claire Wyatt-Smith

Introduction

The proposition offered in this chapter is that *standards* (statements of expected professional competence) and *evidence* requirements (demonstrations of how standards are met) must be conjointly addressed in Initial Teacher Education (ITE) reform. We apply this proposition to the move in Australia to introduce teacher performance assessments (TPAs). In exploring the idea of connecting standards and evidence in a new form of ITE assessment, we draw on the distinction between system and site validity (Freebody and Wyatt-Smith 2004) and the allied notion of assessment fidelity (Sadler 2010). First, our interest in these dual levels—system and site—reflects decades of research in various fields of education research showing that context matters and that examining both the generalizable (system level) and the salience of the particular (site level) can generate insights not otherwise possible. In the following discussion, we sketch the international and Australian policy context in which the *Graduate Teacher Performance Assessment* (GTPA)[1] had its genesis and consider expectations for *system validity*, where the interest is in generalizable implementation, and for *site* validity, that addresses how a reform comes to be operationalized and experienced in local contexts.

---

[1] The Graduate Teacher Performance Assessment (GTPA) is one teaching performance assessment in use in Australian universities. It was developed by the Institute for Learning Sciences and Teacher Education, Australian Catholic University in 2015, piloted in 2016 and trialed across a consortium of 13 Australian universities in 2017.

L. Adie (✉) · C. Wyatt-Smith
Institute for Learning Sciences and Teacher Education, Australian Catholic University, Brisbane, Australia
e-mail: Lenore.adie@acu.edu.au

Second, we examine the introduction of TPAs through the lens of assessment fidelity where fidelity relates to 'the extent to which something actually is what it purports to be' (Sadler 2010, p. 728). We propose that fidelity of assessment implementation is a critical phenomenon located at the intersection of system and site validity. This intersection reflects how, in Australia and other countries including the USA and Germany, federal and state governments exert considerable authority in education policy, putting downward pressure on practice. In these circumstances, responses to national regulatory requirements coexist within state, jurisdictional, university, and other local contextualized requirements. By locating assessment fidelity at the intersection of system and site validity, we focus attention on the dichotomy of (1) the stability of teacher performance assessments as an instrument and (2) their responsiveness to particular contexts in implementation. This dichotomy can be understood as the distinction between a standardized assessment and intelligent accountability, which is explored later in the chapter. We propose that an examination of the intersection of system and site validity enables us to understand the tensions generated as a result of multiple levels of demand on initial teacher education. These tensions in turn bring risks to the assessment reform agenda, and to fidelity in particular. We argue that the sourcing of tensions and risk back to the intersection of system and site is key to productive management of change in ITE reform.

Drawing on international research and relevant policy sources, the chapter first presents background information on the introduction of teaching performance assessments in ITE internationally. Following this is a discussion of professional standards as the official referent for ITE programs and for designing the GTPA in Australia. Next, the response to regulatory requirements for reform in initial teacher education is considered in terms of the design features of a teaching performance assessment. Finally, we identify three main risks to the fidelity of implementation of TPAs visible as tensions between the achievement of system validity and that of site validity.

Background: Preservice Teaching Performance Assessments

In a context where international and national test results are used as catalysts for education reforms, it is not surprising to see a strengthening focus in many countries on the quality of teaching and teacher education (Akiba 2017), and increased accountability and transparency across all levels of education (Cochran-Smith et al. 2013; Duckor et al. 2014). In countries such as Australia, England and the USA, there has been criticism of the lack of rigour in teacher education programs, and a lack of evidence of the factors related to producing quality graduates (Ingvarson and Rowley 2017). This criticism has resulted in numerous reviews of initial teacher education undertaken in the last few years; in Australia alone, there have been over 110 reviews (Alexander 2016). While each national review is necessarily interested in and takes up particular contextual considerations, broadly speaking they present some common issues. These include the processes by which candidates are selected for entry into ITE programs, the relationship between the academic component and the school-based component of initial teacher education, the relationship between theory and practice in opportunities to learn how to be a teacher, and the assessments intended to determine professional competence. The latter includes those assessments completed over the course of an academic program, those undertaken in schools as part of practicum or professional experience placements, and terminal assessments that occur at the exit or juncture point of completing initial teacher preparation, and that are linked to licensure or professional registration requirements.

Assessment in teacher education is understood to function as 'a *gatekeeper* and quality measure to ensure that graduates are competent to take on the huge responsibility of educating future generations and to function in, and contribute to, the development of the nation and the world' (emphasis in original, Smith 2016, p. 411). Evidentiary practices used as gatekeepers to teaching that have been trialled include portfolios, written tests, observations of practice, interviews, and performance assessments. These types of assessments have been used individually or combined to provide evidence of practice and to show teacher dispositions or 'attitudes to learning and learners' (Wyatt-Smith et al. 2017, p. 2). For example, in Chinese Taipei, graduates undergo a written test, as well as observation of classroom practice and an interview (Ingvarson and Rowley 2017). In the USA, the edTPA (Teacher Performance Assessment) developed by Stanford University has been designed to assess 'readiness to teach' (Nayfield et al. 2015, p. 4). The range of evidence, and in particular performance assessments, are intended to generate proof of competence—graduate knowledge, skills and dispositions—in essential components of teaching (Darling-Hammond and Snyder 2000; Flowers 2006; Mandinach and Gummer 2016), as well as being evidence of the impact of ITE programs on teaching quality (Ingvarson and Rowley 2017).

While higher education institutes (HEIs) that offer ITE are subject to regulation and quality control mechanisms through program design and alignment with professional standards, they are now, in many nations, being held accountable for the quality of teacher graduates and their knowledge and skills to improve student learning and achievement (Cochran-Smith et al. 2013). In England, this call for accountability has resulted in school-led programs of initial teacher education being developed (Brown et al. 2015). In Australia, teacher professional standards have provided key indexes to quality assure and guide the accreditation of ITE programs however, to date the review focus has typically been on the standards as 'inputs'. That is, the programs have been checked to discern where the aspects of the standards are taught or covered off in the teaching program, including the professional experience placements or school-based learning program. There has been no common or agreed evidence base showing that the competences have actually been developed at program completion or exit from the program, the critical juncture at which preservice teachers enter the classroom and are registered for independent classroom practice. Moreover, there has been no requirement for universities to demonstrate the overall quality and impact of ITE programs.

In Australia, the increasingly loud criticisms of teacher quality led to a major review of ITE conducted by the Teacher Education Ministerial Advisory Group (TEMAG) led by Professor Greg Craven (2014). This review acknowledged the need for 'robust evidence of successful graduate outcomes against the Professional Standards' (p. vii) within an integrated system of professional partnership between higher education institutes and school systems. Similar to other nations' reviews into ITE, the authors of the TEMAG report concluded that the Australian Professional Standards for Teachers (AITSL 2011) and the standards and procedures for the accreditation of ITE programs in Australia (AITSL 2015) needed to be more rigorously applied as a 'foundation for quality assurance and improvement to initial teacher education' (p. viii); that there needed to be a closer alignment and cooperation between the theoretical learning occurring in universities and the professional experience component occurring in schools; and there needed to be a way to assess classroom readiness of graduates (Craven et al. 2014).

As a result of this significant strengthening of accountability, recommendations of particular significance to this discussion include:

- Recommendation 6: … final assessments that ensure preservice teachers are classroom ready. Higher education providers provide a set of measures that assess the effectiveness of their programs in achieving successful graduate outcomes (p. xii).
- Recommendation 14: Higher education providers deliver evidence-based content focused on the depth of subject knowledge and range of pedagogical approaches that enable preservice teachers to make a positive impact on the learning of all students (p. xiii).
- Recommendation 15: Higher education providers equip preservice teachers with data collection and analysis skills to assess the learning needs of all students (p. xiii).
- Recommendation 27: Preservice teachers develop a portfolio of evidence to demonstrate their achievement of the graduate level of the professional Standards[2] (p. xv).
- Recommendation 28: Higher education providers and schools work together to assist preservice teachers to develop and collect sophisticated evidence of their teaching ability and their impact on student learning for their portfolio of evidence (p. xv).

The Australian Government accepted the TEMAG report recommendations in full and agreed that robust evidence of successful graduate outcomes made against the Professional Standards for Teachers was necessary to ensure that preservice teachers were prepared for teaching (Australian Government Department of Education and Training 2015). This included skills in collecting, analysing and using data to improve student learning. The emphasis on teacher capability in using evidence to improve teaching and learning was already included in the Professional Standards (Standard 5.4). However, recent research (Wyatt-Smith et al. 2017) showed there are no common expectations about data analysis or use in classroom practice; few universities are well placed to access authentic student performance data, and few

---

[2] The Australian Professional Standards for Teachers (graduate level) are also referred to as Graduate Standards and Graduate Teacher Standards (e.g. see https://www.aitsl.edu.au/teach/teacher-standards/career-stages).

offer systematic studies in assessment and evaluation in teacher education. A related finding was that there was no agreed evidence base or validated approach to demonstrating preservice teachers' instructional quality and their related ability to positively impact on the learning of all students. This observation is of direct relevance to the call for reform that included the requirement that ITE providers are to 'identify how their pre-service teachers demonstrate a positive impact on student learning' (p. 10) against the Graduate Teacher Standards (AITSL 2015: Program Standard 1.3).

The agency charged with leading the reform in Australia is the national regulator of teaching standards, the Australian Institute for Teaching and School Leadership (AITSL). This body actioned the Government response to the TEMAG report through a policy position that required the strengthening of standards and procedures for the Accreditation of Initial Teacher Education programs in Australia (AITSL 2015). In particular, Program Standard 1.2 requires, in part, that preservice teachers complete 'a final-year teaching performance assessment prior to graduation that is shown to:

(a) be a reflection of classroom teaching practice including the elements of planning, teaching, assessing and reflecting
(b) be a valid assessment that clearly assesses the content of the Graduate Teacher Standards
(c) have clear, measurable and justifiable achievement criteria that discriminate between meeting and not meeting the Graduate Teacher Standards
(d) be a reliable assessment in which there are appropriate processes in place for ensuring consistent scoring between assessors
(e) include moderation processes that support consistent decision-making against the achievement criteria' (p. 10).

The above requirements make clear that a TPA is expected to function as summative or terminal assessment, which is understood as a 'summing up or summarizing the achievement status of a student, … geared towards reporting at the end of a course of study especially for the purposes of certification' which 'often influences decisions which may have profound educational and personal consequences for the student' (Sadler 1989, p. 120). The introduction of a teacher performance summative assessment is intended to represent graduate readiness to teach, or in the terms of the TEMAG report, *classroom readiness* (Craven et al. 2014, p. xiii).

The GTPA was designed to contribute to efforts to build an evidentiary base for ITE in Australia. This design work required consideration of the types or form of assessment necessary to generate robust evidence of the preparedness of the graduate for professional practice. It also required validation of the assessment instrument against the identified Australian Professional Standards for Teachers (AITSL 2011) and the application of standard-setting procedures that discriminate between meeting and not meeting the standard. Each level of decision has important consequences for preservice teacher graduation, program design, program accreditation, workforce planning and teacher standards.

Professional Standards, Teacher Performance Assessments and Active Professionalism

Lists that identify the qualities or characteristics of a good teacher are not new to education. Historical lists of the characteristics of teachers as model citizens as well as good disciplinarians are frequently called on to illustrate the progress of the profession (Wyatt-Smith and Looney 2016). In 1929, Charters and Waples called on teacher education programs to be structured around the development of identified characteristics. Over time, professional standards have been developed and adopted across many nations to identify the knowledge and skills that are valued within a contextual teaching practice. Three common features of professional standards for teachers, across national and international jurisdictions, have been identified as: (i) a multiplicity of codified components of the task of teaching; (ii) an identification of incremental steps in the proficiency of practice of the standards as progression markers; and (iii) a degree of quality captured in the terms used to convey the standards (Wyatt-Smith et al. 2017). Professional standards are used as the basis for professional development and goal setting, teacher evaluations, and ITE program design.

Evidencing readiness for the profession against professional standards, however, is a contentious issue and is dependent on the approach taken towards formulating and promulgating standards. Criticisms and concern about professional standards typically raise issues of performativity, technicism, reductionism and reification where the standards become a set of separate, atomized skills that valorise a particular set of professional knowledge rather than taken as representative of the nature and complexity of teaching (Beck 2009; Beyer 2002; Delandshere and Arens 2001; Furlong 2015). Furlong (2015), referring to Wales, described this issue as 'a set of behaviourally based 'competencies': things that newly qualified teachers 'must know and do' (p. 12) which then became the 'de facto curriculum in many teacher education programs' (p. 12). The issue, according to Beyer (2002) is that teachers' work is represented as technical skills rather than an acknowledgement of 'teacher-scholars' (p. 310). Delandshere and Arrens (2001) questioned the evidence base on which claims of essential knowledge and skills are based. In discussing the trap of performativity, Biesta (2010) warned of measuring only that which is easily measured, 'and thus end up valuing what we (can) measure' (p. 13).

An alternative conceptualization of using standards is for teachers 'to be active professionals, with their own judgements to make and with their own responsibilities as leaders of children's learning' (Furlong 2015, p. 12). This stance is one of *intelligent accountability* which includes features of professional trust, self-evaluation, performance measures related to the purposes of schooling, and measures that encourage development to the highest level (Cowie et al. 2007). In intelligent accountability, standards are viewed as the basis for critical reflective practice in which teachers inquire into, and reflect on, their practices and consider alternate actions that are contextually, temporally and individualistically appropriate (Sinnema et al. 2017; Wyatt-Smith et al. 2017). This emphasis on principles of practice, professional judgement and action supports a view of teachers who have the necessary competence to act on evidence and are able to justify their actions in response to it.

The Australian Professional Standards for Teachers (AITSL 2011) are designed as descriptions of performance across four levels or developmental career stages: graduate, proficient, highly accomplished and lead. Another design feature is that requisite knowledge and skills are grouped into three domains, namely professional knowledge, practice and engagement, which are then captured across seven Standards understood to be interdependent. The intent is that teachers will be 'able to integrate and apply knowledge, practice and professional engagement as outlined in the descriptors to create teaching environments in which learning is valued' (AITSL 2011, p. 5). However, while seeking to illustrate the complexity of teaching practice, the standards fall short in capturing professional identity and disposition, the professional 'who'. Wyatt-Smith and Looney (2016) contrast this limitation in the Australian Professional Standards for Teachers with medical and judicial professional standards, which use second person, direct address and imperative (e.g., you must keep your professional learning up to date) to signal an expectation of responsibility for action, and the adoption of a professional identity or disposition to act. In Australia, preservice teachers are required to meet all 51 aspects of the Australian Professional Standards for Teachers at the graduate level (Australian Institute for Teaching and School Leadership [AITSL] 2011).

In countries where professional standards for teachers have been established, these can form a construct for teacher performance assessments. A stance of active professionalism will engage with professional standards in ways that move beyond standards as static descriptors of practice. According to Ball (2016), professionalism is evident as teachers make informed judgements based on 'principles, set within the contexts of practice' (p. 1052). He warned of defining professionalism within a set of skills and competences and recommended positioning assessment as 'a form of reflection, a relationship between principles and judgment' (p. 1050). A challenge for designing TPAs is how to capture the metacognitive actions and processes of a preservice teacher's decision-making in the act of planning, teaching and assessing their own class, or in real terms, the messiness of teaching practice (Cowie et al. 2007; Klenowski and Wyatt-Smith 2014; Newton and Shaw 2014). This stance reflects the view that teaching does not flow in a linear manner from planning to teaching to the assessment of students; rather it is an iterative process of data collection that continuously informs and modifies planning and teaching.

Keeping in mind the features of intelligent accountability and the related tensions of confining the profession to a set of skills and competences, the GTPA has been designed to elicit preservice teacher knowledge and skills, along with identity and disposition. Underpinning this is the expectation that the core purpose of teaching is learning, and a positive disposition towards the growth of all learners, including informed collection and use of evidence to support self-growth, is not an optional extra in teacher preparation. Successful completion of a TPA assessment would therefore require teacher education faculties to prepare preservice teachers for this role of active professionalism, that is, a reflective practitioner who researches their own practice with the aim of improving their practice and student learning.

Designing an Australian Teacher Performance Assessment

Consistent with the TEMAG report, the Graduate Teacher Performance Assessment (GTPA) is designed to generate evidence of preservice teachers' core pedagogic knowledge and practices of planning, teaching, assessing and reflecting. These practices involve professional judgement that draws on the preservice teacher's pedagogical, curricula, content, theoretical and contextual knowledge as well as knowledge of the range of students in the class and how to meet their diverse needs (Shulman 2013).

In completing the GTPA, preservice teachers demonstrate their teaching practices and show how their instructional decision-making is based on student data and evidence of learning. The value of selecting and incorporating data and evidence from a range of possible sources, and using this to plan, review, modify and improve teaching and learning has been identified as an important skill for contemporary teachers (Hamilton et al. 2009; Little et al. 2003; Matters 2006). Cowie and Cooper (2016) describe this as 'the growing imperative for teachers (student teachers, mentor teachers and initial teacher educators) to be assessment and data literate' (p. 159). Mandinach and Gummer (2016) have proposed a conceptual framework identifying a vast array of knowledge, skills and dispositions that teachers require for data literacy. Teaching decisions are made based on an interpretation of prior data and evidence of learning as well as on-the-spot evidence as teaching occurs in response to student answers and actions. Thus, a teaching performance assessment needs to provide evidence that preservice teachers are discerning in how they plan, taking account of students' learning needs and trajectories. Furthermore, how data that are fit-for-purpose in promoting student growth are selected and used needs to be explicated.

The evidence collected by the preservice teacher in undertaking the GTPA is recognized as situated within a particular school, education authority system or sector, and community. The intention is to achieve integration of multiple sources of evidence and multiple kinds of knowledge and skills as used in classroom practice. For this reason, it is important not to restrict the evidence collected to a wholly prespecified set of requirements. Within a broad framing of evidence categories, practice and related evidence may vary, even considerably, as preservice teachers, establish contextualized learning goals for the whole class and for individual students, provide feedback, and consider next-step teaching.

In addition, teachers in Australia are responsible for the design and grading of assessments, and the use of stated achievement standards for reporting. While there is no agreed statement of required assessment content knowledge, there is support in published research (Livingston and Hutchinson 2017; Looney et al. 2017; Stobart 2014) for teachers to have knowledge and understanding of assessment purposes, traditional assessment canons (e.g., validity, reliability), feedback, fairness, the use of standards, and the related use of data and evidence for monitoring learning and promoting growth. Further, pressing on this aspect of teacher preparation is the growing and already strong recognition of the role of teachers in aligning curriculum, teaching and assessment (Wyatt-Smith and Gunn 2009) and promoting students' engagement in their learning through assessment practices (Hattie 2009; Mory 2004; Sadler 1989). Teachers bring together this combination of knowledge in the GTPA to demonstrate how they provide feedback, make judgements, determine next-step teaching and develop students' evaluative knowledge and expertise.

An expected core feature of a TPA, and a main challenge in its design, is to capture decision-making in progress through the response and the accompanied relevant artefacts that evidence the planning, teaching and assessing components. Korthagen and Vasalos (2005) describe this process as activating reflection during teaching 'to make contact with the core qualities which are of importance at that particular moment' (p. 68). Reflective practice involves preservice teachers critically analysing, justifying and defending their pedagogic decision-making in context. The focus here is on the 'why' of teaching—Why is one strategy/practice better to use than another for this child or group of children? When asking 'why', preservice teachers are required to not only articulate their practice but justify their pedagogic decisions by connecting research, theory and practice. This perspective on reflective practice offers 'a lens that can usefully link the background experiences and beliefs of a teacher to his understandings of his own practice' (Edwards and Edwards 2017, p. 191).

The production of the GTPA as an account of a preservice teacher's decision-making related to the context of their professional placement was a purposeful move away from teaching portfolios that tend to represent a compilation of artefacts rather than showing the deliberately interconnected and iterative cycles of planning, teaching and assessing. The critical element of data collection and decisions based on a range of evidence types establishes the conditions to demonstrate learning and the application of theory to the complex decision-making processes within classrooms which research has shown is an important feature of performance assessments (van der Vleuten et al. 2010).

By design, the GTPA is deliberately located at the nexus of the academic program of teacher preparation and the school-based component. Going beyond the demonstration of how to teach, the GTPA calls forth evidence of how preservice teachers appraise the impact of their teaching on student learning over the period of the placement. They are in effect evidencing the learning experience for both their students and themselves at the point of entry to the profession. In this assessment, they draw on planning documents and student work examples and show the intellectual work of teaching. That is to say, preservice teachers are called on to make explicit their teaching as a complex *social and metacognitive act*.

Authenticity as a Design Feature

Teaching performance assessments need to function as a *window into practice as inquiry*, and therefore, the assessment itself must be authentic. An authentic assessment has been described as one that can assist preservice teachers to link 'generalizations about practice to apparently idiosyncratic, contextualized instances of learning' and 'include opportunities for developing and examining teachers' thinking and actions in situations that are experience based and problem oriented' (Darling-Hammond and Snyder 2000, p. 524). The authenticity of the assessment is inherent in its ability to capture pedagogic decision-making such that it is ecologically valid and 'representative of the way knowledge and skills are used in real-world contexts' (Stobart and Gipps 2010, p. 204). Authenticity is recognized through the specific knowledge and ways of working within a discipline or specialization from initial planning decisions based on collected data and evidence of student learning to on-the-spot teaching decisions to continue with, adapt or alter a teaching plan by revising, differentiating or accelerating learning according to students' specific learning needs and dependent on the continuous flow of information gathered throughout a lesson. Darling-Hammond and Synder (2000) outlined four aspects of authentic assessments of teaching:

1. Assessments sample the actual knowledge, skills and dispositions desired of teachers as they are used in teaching and learning contexts, rather than relying on more remote proxies.
2. Assessments require the integration of multiple kinds of knowledge and skill as they are used in practice.
3. Multiple sources of evidence are collected over time and in diverse contexts.
4. Assessment evidence is evaluated by individuals with relevant expertise against criteria that matter for performance in the field (p. 527).

While the identified aspects of an authentic assessment are necessarily broad, they give priority to evidence that has ecological validity, that is to say, connected to classroom and school sites as real-world contexts. The design principle for the GTPA is that it has both system and site validity. System validity is addressed when the assessment and accompanying criteria is recognized as fit-for-purpose, as discussed earlier. Thus, the assessment should generate evidence of teaching quality that can be assessed against the Australian Professional Standards for Teachers. To achieve site validity, the assessment should provide evidence of enacted practices that are particular to a site, and potentially, the impact of practice on student learning. The GTPA is, therefore, intended to show the teaching, learning and assessment cycle as it occurs in real time, and involves the deliberate design, use, analysis and refinements of teaching and learning artefacts. It is therefore distinct from microteaching or other simulations of practice that have historically been a recognized part of ITE in some countries including Australia.

Fidelity of Implementation at the Intersection of System and Site Validity

The design of a teacher performance assessment and the conditions of its implementation are central to issues of fidelity and opportunities to demonstrate achievement. We position fidelity of assessment implementation at the intersection of system and

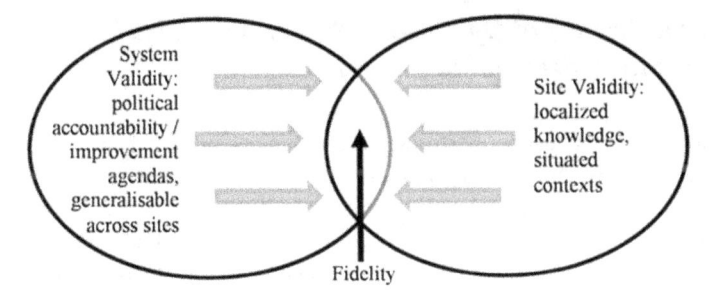

Fig. 8.1 Fidelity at the intersection of system and site validity, and responsive to tensions from system and site

site validity (Fig. 8.1) and identify three main risks to the fidelity of teacher performance assessments. It is at the point of intersection that the tensions between system validity and site validity become apparent and can manifest as 'blockers' to change.

Risk 1: Sufficiency of Opportunity to Learn and Practise

Of specific relevance to the fidelity of teacher performance assessments is the structure of the university program to provide opportunity for preservice teachers to learn and practise the relevant skills and knowledge they are required to demonstrate in a final teacher performance assessment. This includes the focussed development of metacognitive capabilities in the program. Here fidelity is linked to issues of fairness. Ewell (2013) stated that university courses should be successively developed to build towards students' successful completion of a 'culminating demonstration of mastery' (p. 17). As applied to the GTPA, Ewell's observation opens the space for considering the actions that participating universities would take to ensure the necessary build of knowledge, skills and dispositions over the course of the academic program. Much of the writing in this area recommends focused interrogation of teaching practice within the academic program that links to application in professional field experience (Hiebert et al. 2007; Hill et al. 2017; Huston 2016; Ord and Nuttall 2016). Hiebert et al. (2007) suggest a critical inquiry approach into teaching practice where teaching is the object of study and the focus is on student learning, evidence of impact and improving teaching. Ord and Nuttall (2016) go further to suggest that learning to teach should include 'Interrogation of the felt experience of learning to teach in the teacher education classroom… [to supplement] students' close observation of their expert mentors in education settings, followed by discussions with their mentors about how they negotiate space, time, resources, concepts, and feelings in the real time of classroom practice' (p. 361). The knowledge, skills and dispositions that underpin critical inquiry in ITE programs need to be explicitly and sequentially taught and practised.

Risk 2: Sufficiency of Opportunity to Apply Feedback and Learn to Reflect and Self-monitor

The requirement of a teacher performance assessment to provide evidence of readiness for the profession, that is readiness for independent practice, without direct supervision, also brings into question the place of formative and summative assessment in the teacher education program. It is important to note that 'readiness' as used here does not discount the role of quality graduate mentor programs that have been identified as a key component of graduate retention in the teaching profession (Mayer et al. 2017). What is required of teacher education is the development of reflective practitioners who can independently work in a classroom while being guided towards more sophisticated practice though the mentoring of an experienced colleague.

Of significance to fidelity in the implementation of a teaching performance assessment is consideration of the implications and conditions of formative assessment and summative assessment. We suggest that a TPA, as a summative and culminating assessment, shifts the relationship between formative and summative assessment in a way that is distinctive from assessments in other phases of the ITE program. This brings into consideration what formative feedback is provided to preservice teachers completing a TPA, by whom and when, and how such feedback enables preservice teachers to develop the skills of a reflective practitioner, or, in contrast, *over scaffolds* the production of the TPA to the point where it is invalid as evidence of readiness.

As previously stated, in completing the GTPA, preservice teachers are required to reflect on their practice and demonstrate how this has led to decisions being made or changes in their teaching practice. While formative assessment is a critical feature of quality preparation in both the academic program and the experiences of the preservice teacher during professional placements, we suggest that by the end of an ITE program, it is a reasonable expectation that the preservice teacher would have developed the skills to self-monitor and self-assess their progress, including their teaching performance and in completing the GTPA. Such self-assessment and self-regulatory skills require preservice teachers to appreciate what quality performance looks like, evaluate their performance against this standard and have a range of strategies to draw from to appropriately modify their practice (Sadler 1989). The development of such self-regulatory skills are key attributes of a profession, and apply to a graduate teacher who is about to move into the profession. As mentioned earlier, explicit provision of opportunities for preservice teachers to develop the knowledge, skills and dispositions to self-assess and self-regulate, across a teacher education program, is critical to ensure they are best placed for successful completion of a final summative assessment.

Risk 3: Moderation as a Part of Intelligent Accountability and Efforts to Demonstrate Comparability

Demonstrating comparability of standards across sites is one goal of teaching performance assessments that operate within and across states and territories. This goal needs to be responsive to the political, social and cultural contexts of teacher education occurring in universities working under common national guidelines for higher education institutions, the state teacher regulatory authorities and the local sociocultural contexts in which professional experience is completed. Thus, it is necessary to establish some practices that are common across all sites while accommodating the situated local practices. Without adherence to these matters, it would be difficult to meet accountability requirements and the attribution of fairness, and difficult to ascertain aspects of the assessment or the program that require modification or improvement over time (Century et al. 2010; Ruiz-Primo 2006).

We therefore propose that moderation within universities and across universities is linchpin in national efforts to demonstrate comparability in the use of standards in initial teacher education. At the time of writing, exploratory work is underway to investigate the potential of new technologies in connecting teacher educators across the country to facilitate moderation online. Just as standards alone are insufficient to demonstrate quality, so too TPAs alone fall short of providing a basis for national confidence in the quality of ITE.

A second consideration is the professional development of teacher educators who can recognize elements of quality within localized contexts such that performance does not become performativity where preservice teachers' responses in the form of a TPA become a checklist of skills and competences. Thus, fidelity in the implementation of a TPA requires attention to both system and site validity through the professional development of teacher educators in collective and idiosyncratic ways. While fidelity calls for a common approach across all sites, it also requires rigorous interrogation of how responses to a TPA will look different across varied contexts.

Conclusion: A Culture Shift and an Accompanying Mindset Shift

There can be no doubt that the introduction of teaching performance assessments in Australia represents a momentous culture shift in teacher education. Wyatt-Smith (2017) has referred to it previously as *a throwing of the switch*. As discussed in this chapter, many challenges have already surfaced in relation to the conceptualization, design and fidelity of implementation of the assessment. We have provided a sketch of these in this chapter. Other challenges have included the trialling of the assessment across state and territory jurisdictions, and standard-setting methodologies. These go beyond the confines of this chapter.

Research being undertaken to identify the impact of teaching performance assessments in other countries on the quality of teachers and teaching have produced variable results. For example, Boston College led a review of four systems employed in the USA to evaluate ITE programs. They found that

> across three of the four initiatives (HEA regulations, CAEP accreditation, and NCTQ's reviews), there is thin evidence to support the claims proponents make about how the assumed policy mechanisms will actually operate to improve programs (Cochran-Smith et al. 2016, p. 3).

The fourth initiative, the edTPA, was found to have 'some evidentiary support as a policy initiative' (Cochran-Smith et al. 2016, p. 4) but there were concerns amongst the community of teacher educators that were limiting uptake.

The second key finding from the Boston College review was a call for perspective. Teacher education, and thus teachers, cannot fix the inequity problems of the world; these issues are far more deeply entrenched in other sociocultural factors that also need to be addressed (Cochran-Smith et al. 2016). However, this finding does not omit ITE as an influencing factor. Thus, every effort to enhance teacher practice is worthy of consideration, particularly if it is based on research findings into quality teaching practices and can provide evidence of positive impact. Taking account of these findings, it is important that, as the GTPA is introduced across many Australian universities, a research program is also in place to determine its impact on improving the quality of teachers and teaching. Plans for this vital work is underway in the partnership research between the Institute for Learning Sciences and Teacher Education and allied universities both nationally and internationally. It will include the collection and analysis of completed GTPAs across years to look for performance trends; surveys and interviews to gain the perspectives of preservice teachers, supervising teachers, school leaders, and systemic authorities to ascertain shifts in cultures and mindsets in ITE, and in the longer term, the impact of the GTPA on student learning.

Culture shifts and shifts in mindsets about *proper* teacher education take time. More than this, they require an openness to do the work of ITE differently, to explore new ideas and new ways of working, both within and across institutions, thus bringing together system and site validity. They also involve risk taking. Those involved in teacher education consortia in Australia are engaged in crossing borders between fields of research; teacher educators are working together as collectives, exploring spaces and practices beyond those with which they are most familiar. We believe that it is in the strengthening of relationships among all involved in teacher education that culture and mindset shifts will take place. Evidence from the GTPA Trial indicates a new dialogue is occurring among teacher educators, teachers and preservice teachers, extending to the vital link between teaching and student growth. We are moving across theory, practice and policy in the work of connecting systemic requirements, ITE academic programs and professional experience placements in new ways. In the next phase of this work, it is already clear that the mature application of professional standards and evidence requires cross-institutional moderation practices. It is in this new era that standards and evidence will have the chance to come together and where system and site validity can be seen as interconnected in change processes.

References

Akiba, M. (2017). Editor's introduction: Understanding cross-national differences in globalized teacher reforms. *Educational Researcher, 46*(4), 153–168. https://doi.org/10.3102/0013189X17711908.

Alexander, C. (2016). *Reforming the reform of teacher education: A critical grounded theory of a social approach to change and continuity (Unpublished doctoral dissertation)*. Adelaide, Australia: University of Adelaide.

Australian Government. Department of Education and Training. (2015). *Teacher education ministerial advisory group—Action now: Classroom ready teachers: Australian government response*. Retrieved October 9, 2017 from https://docs.education.gov.au/system/files/doc/other/150212_ag_response_-_final.pdf.

Australian Institute for Teaching and School Leadership [AITSL]. (2011). *Australian professional standards for teachers*. Retrieved May 1, 2017 from https://www.aitsl.edu.au/australian-professional-standards-for-teachers/standards/overview/organisation-of-the-standards.

Australian Institute for Teaching and School Leadership [AITSL]. (2015). *Accreditation of initial teacher education programs in Australia: Standards and procedures*. Retrieved May 30, 2017 from http://www.aitsl.edu.au/docs/default-source/initial-teacher-education-resources/accreditation-of-ite-programs-in-australia.pdf.

Ball, S. J. (2016). Neoliberal education? Confronting the slouching beast. *Policy Futures in Education, 14*(8), 1046–1059. https://doi.org/10.1177/1478210316664259.

Beck, J. (2009). Appropriating professionalism: Restructuring the official knowledge base of England's "modernised" teaching profession. *British Journal of Sociology of Education, 30*(1), 3–14. https://doi.org/10.1080/01425690802514268.

Beyer, L. (2002). The politics of standards and the education of teachers. *Teaching Education, 13*(3), 305–316.

Biesta, G. J. J. (2010). *Good education in an age of measurement: Ethics, politics, democracy*. Boulder, CO: Paradigm Publishers.

Brown, T., Rowley, H., & Smith, K. (2015). *The beginnings of school led teacher training: New challenges for university teacher education*. Manchester Metropolitan University. Retrieved January 5, 2018 from https://e-space.mmu.ac.uk/602385/2/SchoolDirectResearchReport.pdf.

Century, J., Rudnick, M., & Freeman, C. (2010). A framework for measuring fidelity of implementation: A foundation for shared language and accumulation of knowledge. *American Journal of Evaluation, 32*(2), 199–218.

Charters, W. W., & Waples, D. (1929). *The commonwealth teacher-training study*. Chicago, IL: The University of Chicago Press.

Cochran-Smith, M., Piazza, P., & Power, C. (2013). The politics of accountability: Assessing teacher education in the United States. *The Educational Forum, 77*(1), 6–27.

Cochran-Smith, M., Stern, R., Sánchez, J. G., Miller, A., Keefe, E. S., Fernández, M. B., et al. (2016). *Holding teacher preparation accountable: A review of claims and evidence*. Boulder, CO: National Education Policy Center. Retrieved January 16, 2018 from http://nepc.colorado.edu/publication/teacher-prep.

Cowie, B., & Cooper, B. (2016). Exploring the challenge of developing student teacher data literacy. *Assessment in Education: Principles, Policy & Practice, 24*(2), 147–163. https://doi.org/10.1080/0969594X.2016.1225668.

Cowie, M., Taylor, D., & Croxford, L. (2007). 'Tough, intelligent accountability' in Scottish secondary schools and the role of standard tables and charts [STACS]: A critical appraisal. *Scottish Educational Review, 39*(1), 29–50.

Craven, G., Beswick, K., Fleming, J., Fletcher, T., Green, M., Jensen, B., et al. (2014). *Action now: Classroom ready teachers*. Retrieved January 16, 2018 from https://docs.education.gov.au/system/files/doc/other/action_now_classroom_ready_teachers_print.pdf.

Darling-Hammond, L., & Snyder, J. (2000). Authentic assessment of teaching in context. *Teaching and Teacher Education, 16*(5–6), 523–545. https://doi.org/10.1016/S0742-051X(00)00015-9.

Delandshere, G., & Arens, S. A. (2001). Representations of teaching and standards-based reform: Are we closing the debate about teacher education. *Teaching and Teacher Education, 17*(5), 547–566. https://doi.org/10.1016/S0742-051X(01)00013-0.

Duckor, B., Castellano, K., Téllez, K., Wihardini, D., & Wilson, M. (2014). Examining the internal structure evidence for the performance assessment for California teachers. *Journal of Teacher Education, 65*(5), 402–420.

Edwards, F. C. E., & Edwards, R. J. (2017). A story of culture and teaching: The complexity of teacher identity formation. *The Curriculum Journal, 28*(2), 190–211. https://doi.org/10.1080/09585176.2016.1232200.

Ewell, P. T. (2013). *The lumina degree qualifications profile (DQP): Implications for assessment.* Champaign, IL: National Institute for Learning Outcomes Assessment. Retrieved January 16, 2018 from http://www.learningoutcomesassessment.org/documents/EwellDQPop1.pdf.

Flowers, C. (2006). A measure of dispositions for preservice teachers. *Educational and Psychological Measurement, 66*(3), 478–488.

Freebody, P., & Wyatt-Smith, C. (2004). The assessment of literacy: Working the zone between system and site validity. *Journal of Educational Enquiry, 5*(2), 30–49.

Furlong, J. (2015). *Teaching tomorrow's teachers. Options for the future of initial teacher education in Wales.* Retrieved January 16, 2018 from http://gov.wales/docs/dcells/publications/150309-teaching-tomorrows-teachers-final.pdf.

Hamilton, L., Halverson, R., Jackson, S., Mandinach, E., Supovitz, J., & Wayman, J. C. (2009). *Using student achievement data to support instructional decision making* (NCEE 2009–4067). Washington, DC: National Center for Education Evaluation and Regional Assistance, Institute of Education Sciences, U.S. Department of Education. Retrieved October 9, 2017 from https://ies.ed.gov/ncee/wwc/Docs/PracticeGuide/dddm_pg_092909.pdf.

Hattie, J. (2009). *Visible learning: A synthesis of over 88 meta-analyses relating to achievement.* Oxon, England: Routledge.

Hiebert, J., Morris, A. K., Berk, D., & Jansen, A. (2007). Preparing teachers to learn from teaching. *Journal of Teacher Education, 58*(1), 47–61.

Hill, M. F., Ell, F., Grudnoff, L., Haigh, M., Cochran-Smith, M., Chang, W., et al. (2017). Assessment for equity: Learning how to use evidence to scaffold learning and improve teaching. *Assessment in Education: Principles, Policy & Practice, 24*(2), 185–204. https://doi.org/10.1080/0969594X.2016.1253541.

Huston, T. (2016). edTPA, videotape, and occupational identity: A study of pre-service teachers. *Teaching Education, 28*(2), 194–210. https://doi.org/10.1080/10476210.2016.1237482.

Ingvarson, L., & Rowley, G. (2017). Quality assurance in teacher education and outcomes: A study of 17 countries. *Educational Researcher, 46*(4), 177–193. https://doi.org/10.3102/0013189X17711900.

Klenowski, V., & Wyatt-Smith, C. (2014). *Assessment for education: Standards, judgement and moderation.* London, England: Sage.

Korthagen, F., & Vasalos, A. (2005). Levels in reflection: Core reflection as a means to enhance professional growth. *Teachers and Teaching: Theory and Practice, 11*(1), 47–71.

Little, J. W., Gearhart, M., Curry, M., & Kafka, J. (2003). Looking at student work for teacher learning, teacher, community and school reform. *Phi Delta Kappan, 85*(3), 184–192. https://doi.org/10.1177/003172170308500305.

Livingston, K., & Hutchinson, C. (2017). Developing teachers' capacities in assessment through career-long professional learning. *Assessment in Education: Principles, Policy & Practice, 24*(2), 290–307. https://doi.org/10.1080/0969594X.2016.1223016.

Looney, A., Cumming, J., van Der Kleij, F., & Harris, K. (2017). Reconceptualising the role of teachers as assessors: Teacher assessment identity. *Assessment in Education: Principles, Policy & Practice*, 1–26. https://doi.org/10.1080/0969594x.2016.1268090.

Mandinach, E. B., & Gummer, E. S. (2016). What does it mean for teachers to be data literate: Laying out the skills, knowledge, and dispositions. *Teaching and Teacher Education, 60*, 366–376. https://doi.org/10.1016/j.tate.2016.07.011.

Matters, G. (2006). *Australian education review: Using data to support learning in schools: Students, teachers, systems*. Camberwell, Australia: Australian Council for Educational Research.

Mayer D., Dixon, M., Kline, J., Kostogriz, A., Moss, J., Rowan, L., et al. (2017). Employment pathways, mobility and retention of graduate teachers. In D. Mayer, M. Dixon, J. Kline, A. Kostogriz, J. Moss, L. Rowan, et al. (Eds.), *Studying the effectiveness of teacher education: Early career teachers in diverse settings* (pp. 99–119). Singapore: Springer.

Mory, E. H. (2004). Feedback research revisited. In D. H. Jonassen (Ed.), *Handbook of research on educational communications and technology* (2nd ed., pp. 745–784). New Jersey, NJ: Lawrence Erlbaum.

Nayfield, I., Pecheone, R., Whittaker, A., Shear, B. R., & Klesch, H. (2015). *Educative assessment and meaningful support: 2014 edTPA administrative report*. Stanford, CA: Stanford Center for Assessment, Learning and Equity.

Newton, P., & Shaw, S. (2014). *Validity in educational and psychological assessment*. London, England: Sage.

Ord, K., & Nuttall, J. (2016). Bodies of knowledge: The concept of embodiment as an alternative to theory/practice debates in the preparation of teachers. *Teaching and Teacher Education, 60*, 355–362. https://doi.org/10.1016/j.tate.2016.05.019.

Ruiz-Primo, M. (2006). *A multi-method and multi-source approach for studying fidelity of implementation*. Retrieved October 9, 2017 from http://source.ucdenver.edu/cgi/viewcontent.cgi?article=1001&context=research_reports.

Sadler, D. R. (1989). Formative assessment and the design of instructional systems. *Instructional Science, 18*(2), 119–144.

Sadler, D. R. (2010). Fidelity as a precondition for integrity in grading academic achievement. *Assessment & Evaluation in Higher Education, 35*(6), 727–743. https://doi.org/10.1080/02602930902977756.

Shulman, L. S. (2013). Those who understand: Knowledge growth in teaching. *Journal of Education, 193*(3), 1–11.

Sinnema, C., Meyer, F., & Aitken, G. (2017). Capturing the complex, situated, and active nature of teaching through inquiry-oriented standards for teaching. *Journal of Teacher Education, 68*(1), 9–27. https://doi.org/10.1177/0022487116668017.

Smith, K. (2016). Functions of assessment in teacher education. In J. Loughran & M. L. Hamilton (Eds.), *International handbook of teacher education* (Vol. 2, pp. 405–428). Singapore: Springer.

Stobart, G. (2014). *The expert learner: Challenging the myth of ability*. Maidenhead, England: Open University Press.

Stobart, G., & Gipps, C. (2010). Alternative assessment. In P. Peterson, E. Baker, & B. McGraw (Eds.), *International encyclopedia of education* (3rd ed., pp. 202–208). Oxford, England: Elsevier.

Van der Vleuten, C. P. M., Schuwirth, L. W. T., Scheele, F., Driessen, E. W., & Hodges, B. (2010). The assessment of professional competence: Building blocks for theory development. *Best Practice & Research: Clinical Obstetrics & Gynaecology, 24*(6), 703–719. https://doi.org/10.1016/j.bpobgyn.2010.04.001.

Wyatt-Smith, C. (2017, September). *Reforming initial teacher education in Australia: A national consortium approach*. Paper presented at the New International Perspectives on Future Teachers' Professional Competencies Congress, Hamburg, Germany.

Wyatt-Smith, C., Alexander, C., Fishburn, D., & McMahon, P. (2017). Standards of practice to standards of evidence: Developing assessment capable teachers. *Assessment in Education: Principles, Policy & Practice, 24*(2), 250–270. https://doi.org/10.1080/0969594X.2016.1228603.

Wyatt-Smith, C., & Gunn, S. (2009). Towards theorising assessment as critical inquiry. In C. M. Wyatt-Smith & S. Gunn (Eds.), *Educational assessment in the 21st century: Connecting theory and practice* (pp. 83–102). Dordrecht, The Netherlands: Springer.

Wyatt-Smith, C., & Looney, A. (2016). Professional standards and the assessment work of teachers. In L. Hayward & D. Wyse (Eds.), *Handbook on curriculum, pedagogy and assessment* (pp. 805–820). London, England: Routledge.

Lenore Adie is Associate Professor of Teacher Education and Assessment, and a Senior Research Fellow with the Assessment, Evaluation and Student Learning Research concentration in the Institute for Learning Sciences and Teacher Education (ILSTE), Australian Catholic University. Her research focuses on assessment and moderation processes as these contribute to supporting teachers' pedagogical practices and student learning. She has a further interest in the enactment of assessment policy and the validity of assessment processes. Her research has generated new knowledge in the field of assessment focussing on quality in assessment practices and processes, in particular within systems of standard-referenced assessment. This work addresses the alignment of curriculum, assessment and pedagogic practices through the design of assessment tasks and the application of criteria and grading. Lenore has extensive professional experience working in schools as a teacher and within leadership positions, and in teacher education for over 30 years.

Claire Wyatt-Smith is the Director of the Institute for Learning Sciences and Teacher Education (ILSTE) and Professor of Educational Assessment and Evaluation, Australian Catholic University. Claire's research is focused on teaching and evaluative expertise. It examines the role of standards, professional judgement and moderation, as well as the use of data to inform teaching and improve learning. She acts as an advisor to various agencies within Australia and internationally and is currently leading a large-scale Australian study involving a national collective of universities undertaking the Graduate Teacher Performance Assessment and cross-institutional standard-referenced moderation. Recent books include *Assessment for education: Standards, judgement and moderation* (Sage 2014) and *Designing assessment for quality learning* (Springer 2014). In addition to the Series, *Teacher Education, Learning Innovation and Accountability*, she is the Foundation Editor of *The Enabling Power of Assessment Series*.

Part II
Preparing Teachers for Diverse Learners and Contexts

Chapter 9
Analyzing Curriculum Orientations of Kindergarten Curriculum

Barley Mak, Chrysa Keung and Alan Cheung

Background of the Study

Kindergarten education is viewed as the very first stage in children's learning, which is vital for laying the foundation for 'lifelong learning and whole-person development' (Curriculum Development Council 2017, p. 8). The purpose of kindergarten education is to provide children with equitable access to quality early childhood education and care services so that young children can learn happily and grow healthily.

Over the past 30 years, the Hong Kong Government has offered guidelines for improving the quality of kindergarten education. It has offered training and professional support to early childhood teachers. In 2017, the Curriculum Development Council (CDC) of the Education Bureau (formerly known as Curriculum Development Committee) issued the latest *Kindergarten Education Curriculum Guide* (hereafter referred to as the *2017 Guide*), which provides new directions in kindergarten education for endeavoring to nurture children's whole-person development. The theme is 'joyful learning through play, balanced development all the way' (p. 1), with the core values of developing a child-centeredness curriculum and highlighting free play in kindergartens. The new guide also makes comprehensive suggestions on school-based curriculum planning and professional development for early childhood teachers.

Similar kindergarten curriculum reforms have taken place in other countries. In conjunction with educational changes, new curriculum pedagogies or models for kindergarten education have emerged, for example, Developmentally Appropriate Practices (DAP), Reggio Emilia and High Scope. Along with these educational reforms, kindergarten curricula, and practices are becoming more diversified and flexible (Li and Wang 2017). It appears that the objectives of kindergarten education are shifting from a teacher-directed approach to child-centered learning for young

---

B. Mak (✉) · C. Keung · A. Cheung
The Chinese University of Hong Kong, Hong Kong, China
e-mail: barleymak@cuhk.edu.hk

© Springer Nature Singapore Pte Ltd. 2018
C. Wyatt-Smith and L. Adie (eds.), *Innovation and Accountability in Teacher Education*, Teacher Education, Learning Innovation and Accountability,
https://doi.org/10.1007/978-981-13-2026-2_9

children. With regard to such paradigm shifts in the curriculum reforms, teachers from kindergartens are increasingly responsible for making decisions about curriculum content, teaching strategies, and assessment methods.

Research in curriculum studies has revealed that teacher beliefs on curriculum orientations influence their curriculum decision-making, judgements about teaching approaches, and strategies (Cheung 2000b; Ennis 1992; Ennis and Hooper 1988; McNeil 1996). The consistency of the orientations to the curriculum guide is crucial to the effectiveness and sustainability of the curriculum development. It will therefore be seen that, if the teachers agree with the objectives and principles of the kindergarten curriculum as stated in the *2017 Guide*, such as the concept of 'child-centeredness' (p. 9) and balanced development, the relevant pedagogical changes are more likely to be developed. Because the curriculum guide forms a basis for the kindergarten curricula, it is valuable to review the provisional draft[1] of the kindergarten curriculum official document—the *2017 Guide*. This chapter uses curriculum orientations as the analytical tool, which focuses on the recommendations stated in the new guide regarding curriculum intentions, contents, learning activities, and assessment strategies for kindergarten education. Based upon the critical review of these recommendations, this study conceptualizes the major orientations of the kindergarten curriculum. The discussion will be useful for teachers when they formulate kindergarten curricula and corresponding curriculum decisions. Other stakeholders including parents, primary school teachers and members of community could refer to analyses of the study for enhancing their knowledge of kindergarten education.

Kindergarten Curriculum Reforms in Hong Kong

In Hong Kong, kindergartens and kindergarten-cum-child care centers have long been operated either by private enterprises or non-governmental organizations. Kindergarten education refers to the education and care services provided to young children aged from two to six. The official curriculum guides issued by Education Bureau provides a broad set of objectives, guiding principles, learning strategies, and teaching methods on the kindergarten curricula. Kindergartens are encouraged to gradually implement the recommendations set out in the curriculum guides in accordance with their readiness, their level of adoption of the curriculum mode, and their context and needs. Since the 1980s, the Curriculum Development Committee[2] (now known as the Curriculum Development Council) has published six guides on kindergarten curriculum. These guides provide recommendations on kindergarten education policy and curriculum. They offer examples for Hong Kong early childhood teachers. The

---

[1] The official document of the *2017 Guide* had not been released when this chapter was being drafted. As such, this chapter reviews the provisional draft.

[2] The Curriculum Development Committee was first establishment in 1972, re-organized its structure in 1988 and renamed the Curriculum Development Council. Detail can be found in the following webpage http://cd1.edb.hkedcity.net/cd/cdc/en/background.html.

following outlines some significant kindergarten curriculum reforms over the past three decades.

In 1984, the Curriculum Development Committee compiled the first *Guide to the Kindergarten Curriculum*. This Guide responded to the recommendations of the White Paper (Hong Kong Government 1981), which set out general directions for the development of kindergarten teaching and curriculum in Hong Kong. The aim of kindergarten education (as stated in this 1984 *Guide*) was to nurture children's interests in ways that are conducive to their growth. The 1984 *Guide* covered several teaching exemplars in various learning domains, including 'language', 'basic mathematics concepts', 'general studies', 'music', 'artworks', and 'play activities'. The 'spiral curriculum' mode and thematic approach were recommended to be adopted in teaching and learning. Other practical recommendations were included in this guide such as timetabling, school environment, classroom settings, and strategies on recording children's abilities. This first guide provided teaching materials together with suggested activities for the teachers' easy reference.

The 1984 *Guide* was targeted at upper and lower kindergarten classes. It excluded the three-year-old children who were enrolled in nursery classes. The Curriculum Development Committee, in 1987, issued the *Guidelines on Nursery Class Activities*. Considering the developmental characteristics and needs of children who were three years of age, the second guide suggested designing:

> game(s) and activities for young children so as to provide them with routine training and help them to cultivate good habits, to face emotional problems, to develop social skills and to attain a balanced development in both physical and intellectual aspects. (CDC 1993, p. 2)

Between 1993 and 1996, two curriculum guides—the *Guide to the Kindergarten Curriculum* and the *Guide to the Pre-primary Curriculum*—were issued by the CDC. The aim, as stated in the former curriculum guide, was 'to provide children with a balanced development in the moral, intellectual, physical, social and aesthetic aspects and to prepare them to be good citizens' (CDC 1993, p. 1). An integrated approach was advised to be adopted in class. Six learning areas were recommended to be covered in the curriculum: 'emotional and social development'; 'physical play'; 'language development'; 'early mathematical experience'; 'experience in natural science'; and 'creative activities' (CDC 1993, p. 12). In 1996, the *Guide to the Pre-primary Curriculum* pointed out that, 'factual knowledge obtained through stereotypical textbook teaching or rote-learning is only superficial. These teaching methods will only curb the creativity and cognitive thinking of children' (CDC 1996, p. 1). Therefore, the 1996 *Guide* advocated, 'apart from the acquisition of academic knowledge, children should also equip themselves with other life skills, such as self-care skills, communicative skills, social skills, so as to enable them to adapt to society' (CDC 1996, p. 1). The 1996 *Guide* recommended that kindergartens should motivate children's curiosity and thirst for knowledge, as well as providing children with opportunities to express themselves, to be creative, and to enjoy the fun of activities.

Responding to changes in society and education reform in the early 2000s, the CDC subsequently revised the *Guide to the Pre-primary Curriculum* in 2006. This Guide echoed the *Learning for Life, Learning through Life: Reform Proposals for the Education System in Hong Kong* (Education Commission 2000), which set out the following goals of future education for Hong Kong:

> To enable every person to attain all-round development according to his/her own attributes in the domains of ethics, intellect, physique, social skills and aesthetics, so that he/she is capable of life-long learning, critical and exploratory thinking, innovating and adapting to change. (p. 4)

The *2006 Guide* introduced a curriculum framework that placed an emphasis on designing a child-centered, comprehensive and well-balanced curriculum, and adopting play as a learning strategy. The key emphases of the kindergarten curriculum are that, 'pre-primary institutions should provide a diversified learning environment for children to develop their different potentials' (CDC 2006, p. 6). The basic principles of kindergarten education, such as children's development and children's learning, are highlighted (CDC 2006, p. 10).

In 2015, the Committee on Free Kindergarten Education[3] released a report which made recommendations on providing free education for children aged three to six. The report stated that the objective of kindergarten education is to help children become lifelong learners, preparing them to meet the challenges in a globalized and competitive society (Committee on Free Kindergarten Education 2015). The CDC compiled the new guide in 2017 on the basis of the report's recommendations. In 2017, the Education Bureau launched the new *Kindergarten Education Curriculum Guide* and organized a series of briefing sessions for the different stakeholders to enhance their understanding of the up-to-date educational initiatives. This chapter provides a critical review of the *2017 Guide*, in terms of curriculum framework, curriculum planning, learning and teaching, as well as assessment.

The evolution of educational reforms has revealed a shift in the curriculum orientations of kindergarten education over three decades. Each guide spelt out the beliefs on kindergarten education, which were developed based on current societal and educational changes (Fung 2014). With an understanding of the key emphases on guides, the review of the previous curriculum documents reflected that, 'curriculum development is an ongoing process, schools should regularly review the current situation of their curriculum to respond to changes in society, as well as educational trends and new issues' (CDC 2017, p. 58). Fung and Lee (2008) reviewed education reform proposals in Hong Kong from 1986 to 2006, also arguing that 'curriculum planning should be in line with the needs and development of society' (p. 40). In light of contextual changes, kindergartens should continuously review their curriculum content, teaching methods and strategies, and learning outcomes to align with child development.

---

[3] Starting from the 2017/18 school year, free education has been extended to 15 years (covering three years kindergarten, six years primary, and six years secondary education).

Five Orientations to Kindergarten Curriculum

Curriculum orientations are widely discussed in the current literature and are defined as a set of beliefs about the objectives, content, organization, teaching methods, learning activities, and assessment methods (Cheung 2000a; Cheung and Ng 2000; Cheung and Wong 2002). Teachers may have distinct curriculum orientations due to the differences in their cultural backgrounds, experiences, knowledge, and dispositions (Cheung 2000b; Cheung and Ng 2002; Ennis 1992; McNeil 1996). The concept of curriculum orientations may refer to the teachers' overall perceptions and understandings toward the curriculum (i.e., which education goals should be achieved, which teaching methods should be adopted, and how students should learn).

There are diverse opinions from scholars concerning the categorization[4] of curriculum orientations, which are shown in Table 9.1 (Cheung 2000b; Cheung and Wong 2002; Eisner and Vallance 1974; Ennis and Hooper 1988; McNeil 1996; Miller 1983). Eisner and Vallance (1974) suggested five types of curriculum orientations: namely cognitive processes, curriculum as technology, self-actualization or curriculum as consummatory experience, social reconstruction relevance, and academic rationalism. Miller (1983) highlighted seven specific orientations—behavioral, subject/disciplines, social, developmental, cognitive processes, humanistic and transpersonal or holistic. Ennis and Hooper (1988) identified five curriculum orientations—disciplinary mastery, learning process, social reconstruction, self-actualization, and ecological validity. McNeil (1996) believed that there should be four prevailing curriculum conceptions—humanistic, social reconstructionist, technological, and academic.

Cheung and Wong (2002) stated that the previous research on measuring teacher beliefs about curriculum orientations was problematic with regard to providing sufficient reliability and validity on the dataset. They therefore used hierarchical confirmatory factor analysis to identify five curriculum orientations: academic, cognitive process, social reconstruction, humanistic, and technological. Data were collected through the Curriculum Orientation Inventory (COI), with a sample of 648 primary and secondary school teachers in Hong Kong. The results indicated that experienced teachers (with 20 or more years of teaching experience) tended to value the academic orientation more than teachers with less teaching experience. English language teachers tended to be more humanistic than science teachers.

To measure teacher beliefs about curriculum orientations, Jenkins (2009) replicated the work of Cheung and Wong (2002) with a sample of 308 elementary and secondary school teachers in the USA. The modified COI was tested, and it identified six curriculum orientations: namely academic rationalism, social reconstruction, cognitive process, humanistic, behavioral, and eclectic. With regard to the demographic characteristics of the participants, significant differences were found in the value teachers placed on different curriculum orientations according to their gender, the year level they taught, what subject they specialized in, and how long they had been teaching. Men were more likely to place less value on humanistic orienta-

---

[4]This chapter is not intended to identify the best available categorization of curriculum orientations.

Table 9.1 Categorization of curriculum orientations from previous major studies

Studies	Orientations to curriculum
Eisner and Vallance (1974)	Cognitive processes Curriculum as technology Self-actualization or curriculum as consummatory experience Social reconstruction relevance Academic rationalism
Miller (1983)	Behavioral Subject or disciplines Social Developmental Cognitive processes Humanistic Transpersonal or holistic
Ennis and Hooper (1988)	Disciplinary mastery Learning process Social reconstruction Self-actualization Ecological validity
McNeil (1996)	Humanistic Social reconstructionist Technological Academic
Cheung and Wong (2002)	Academic Cognitive process Social reconstruction Humanistic Technological
Jenkins (2009)	Academic rationalism Social reconstruction Cognitive process Humanistic Behavioral Eclectic

tion than women. Elementary school teachers were more likely to place less value on social reconstruction orientation than secondary school teachers. Experienced teachers (with 23 years or more of teaching experience) were more likely to place greater value on behavioral orientation and cognitive process orientation than teachers with less experience. Mathematics and Science group teachers were more likely to be less humanistic and social reconstructive than teachers in other subject groups.

As part of a project on the *Development of Curriculum Leaders for Quality Pre-primary Education*, the center for University and School Partnership (2015) conducted a study to measure the dimensions of Hong Kong kindergarten teachers' beliefs on curriculum orientations. Participants in the study were 717 early childhood educators from 50 pre-primary institutions which included principals, curriculum leaders, head teachers, teachers, and assistant teachers. The instrument was adapted from the COI of Cheung and Wong (2002) to measure teacher beliefs, views, and practices about their curriculum orientations. The results revealed that humanistic orientation places emphasis on designing and organizing curriculum content, highlighting the importance of the environmental setting and self-learning in fostering children's holistic development.

Although research on curriculum orientation is well documented (e.g., Cheung and Wong 2002; Ennis and Hooper 1988; McNeil 1996; Miller 1983), the inventory used to study the dimensions of curriculum orientations is still discipline-specific (e.g., Capel 2016; Cheung and Ng 2000; Jenkins 2009). These studies are limited to the categorizations within primary and secondary education. The characteristics of curriculum orientation in kindergarten education have not yet been fully examined.

In this chapter, we have adopted Cheung and Wong's (2002) five major orientations for our study of the provisional draft of the kindergarten curriculum official document—the *2017 Guide*. The rationale for the categorization selection is based on Cheung and Wong's study conducted in Hong Kong which shares a similar education system and cultural background to those in the present study. The following section provides an overview of the five orientations to the kindergarten curriculum which are used as the analytical tool in this chapter.

Teachers adopting an *Academic Orientation* may consider the content of learning areas as the core of curriculum design. Teachers who adopt this orientation emphasize enhancing children's content knowledge and developing their cognitive learning through studying traditional academic disciplines, such as science and mathematics. The teaching approach is didactic because teachers may rely on textbooks to illustrate or demonstrate the content. The educational objective is to prepare children for learning advanced knowledge, rather than to develop their interests during the learning process. The role of teachers is mainly to transmit factual knowledge to children and to assess children's acquisition of particular knowledge. The children in the class are passive learners who are merely listening to the teachers' talk, practising writing, and memorizing words.

Proponents of a *Cognitive Process Orientation* emphasize the process of inquiry, instead of content knowledge transmission. The purpose of the curriculum is to develop the children's abilities and skills to discover, analyze, and solve problems. Teachers who hold a cognitive process orientation provide children with ample opportunities to participate in this investigation without giving them direct instruction on how to complete it. Teaching is less focused on a content-led approach than on inquiry-based learning. Teachers may ask children to collect and analyze the data in designated missions or tasks. They may set out some questions to guide the children in the inquiry process. Under this orientation, children are required to understand and define problems, as well as formulate feasible ways to solve these problems. They may also need to use their observation and analytical skills. Teachers conduct their assessment through observation of the children's performance in the study areas.

Unlike other curriculum orientations, those who hold a *Social Reconstructionist* orientation address the connections between children's interests and social contexts.

Under this orientation, the purpose of kindergarten education is to increase children's awareness of social needs and issues and to develop their ability to solve social problems. The curriculum emphasizes 'real-life' cases, in which topics are relevant to the children's everyday experiences and concerns. Teachers may set up scenarios and equip children with knowledge about the causes, impacts, and outcomes of social issues. Sometimes, teachers may employ resources from the community when demonstrating cases. Children are provided with more time to discuss and analyze the cases, list the alternatives, and make informed decisions. To assess the children's performance, teachers may observe their ability to interpret societal issues. In a broad sense, teachers who hold this orientation value the importance of empowering children to be responsible learners in kindergarten and to be good citizens in society.

Humanistic Orientation broadens the purpose of education to include the social and emotional aspects of life and happiness. Those who hold this curriculum orientation emphasize the importance of self-actualizing in promoting children's personal well-being. The curriculum's intent is to provide children with learning opportunities to foster personal growth, develop affections, attitudes, and values. With this view, the core value of the curriculum is to make learning fun and rewarding. Teachers may regard the children's self-confidence, personal satisfaction, and their enjoyment in learning as essential parts to assess. This orientation considers that learning is initiated by the children, but is not teacher directed. The curriculum content is decided upon and organized in accordance with the children's interests, needs, and learning patterns. Teachers may use portfolios, self-assessment, and peer feedback as major assessment methods.

Different from other orientations, proponents of *Technological Orientation* do not focus on particular curriculum content. The curriculum decision is reached by logical reasons, which places emphasis on searching for efficient means and procedures to achieve predetermined learning goals. All intended learning objectives are predetermined with teacher instruction before the lessons. The children's learning is determined by a logical sequence with measurable objectives and outcomes. Teachers may rely on using computer-assisted instruction to design learning and teaching activities. The children are expected to be competent users of information technology. Traditional tests such as multiple choice questions, matching, and true/false statements are used to assess the children's performance.

Discussion

Understanding of the curriculum guide is particularly important because it has a far-reaching effect on the teaching and learning process. Four curriculum elements[5]

---

[5] Other than these four aspects related to curriculum, the *2017 Guide* also included sections about 'catering for the learner diversity, 'adaptation to school life and the interface between kindergarten and primary education', 'home-school collaboration and community participation', and 'teachers' professional development' (pp. 3–4).

regarding curriculum framework, curriculum planning, learning and teaching, as well as assessment, form a basis of the discussion in this section. The key characteristics of each orientation in accordance with the above-mentioned curriculum elements are presented in Table 9.2.

Curriculum Framework

To meet future challenges and to respond to an ever-competitive atmosphere, laying the foundation for children's lifelong learning, and whole-person development is the prime concern for early childhood education. The introductory section of the *2017 Guide* states explicitly that the aim of kindergarten education is to foster in 'children a balanced development in the domains of ethics, intellect, physique, social skills and aesthetics, thus achieving the goal of whole-person education' (CDC 2017, p. 7). To ensure the quality of early childhood education, the principles guiding curriculum places great importance on 'fostering children's interest in learning, cultivating positive values and attitudes, as well as strengthening self-confidence and self-care abilities' (CDC 2017, p. 21). Knowledge acquisition in kindergarten education is mainly the development of basic concepts, instead of learning specific subjects. The initiatives in the *2017 Guide* encourage teachers to nurture every child so that they become 'happy, healthy, positive, proactive, inquisitive, communicative, sociable, creative and imaginative' (p. 11).

The curriculum structure set out in the *2017 Guide* has predetermined the importance of promoting whole-person development, which covers all five orientations. The *2017 Guide* puts emphasis on developing school-based curriculum to help children achieve five developmental objectives, namely 'moral development', 'cognitive and language development', 'physical development', 'affective and social development', and 'aesthetic development'. These objectives are achieved through six Key Learning Areas to provide integrated and comprehensive learning experiences which are conducive to the children's learning and development of multiple intelligences. The six Key Learning Areas are 'physical fitness and health', 'language', 'early childhood mathematics', 'nature and living', 'self and society', and 'arts and creativity'. Through school-based curriculum, kindergartens define learning areas, set learning objectives, and formulate teaching principles in accordance with school missions and children's needs (CDC 2017, p. 20).

The development of moral education outlined in the *2017 Guide* reflects the essence of social reconstruction and humanistic orientations. Moral and civic education has been one of the key emphases in the curriculum reforms for primary and secondary education. Moral education was newly included as one of the developmental objectives in kindergarten education. In the *2017 Guide*, it is expected that teachers will cultivate children's abilities to persevere, to care, and to have a sense of responsibility (CDC 2017, p. 24). Such moral development may help children to adapt to societal rules and norms for daily living, and to cultivate positive values and attitudes. The learning outcome is to 'let children … come to an initial understanding

Table 9.2 Key characteristics of curriculum orientations to kindergarten education referring to the recommendations stated in the *2017 Guide*

Curriculum orientations	Key characteristics	Recommendations of the *2017 Guide*
Academic	• Objective is to prepare children for learning advanced knowledge • Enhance children's content knowledge and develop children's cognitive learning through studying traditional academic disciplines • Didactic teaching approach • Rely on textbooks to illustrate or demonstrate the content • Teacher role is to transmit the factual knowledge to children and assess children's acquisition of particular knowledge • Children are passive learners	• Teachers should not stick to any 'standard answer' • Instead of adopting a one-way lecturing form of teaching, teachers should view children as unique individuals and provide them with opportunities in an open communicative setting • Teachers can organize diversified activities such as games, story-telling, role-playing, and experimenting with objects • Standardized criteria should be avoided when assessing children's abilities and performance during their early childhood stage
Cognitive process	• Objective is to develop children's abilities and skills to find out, solve and analyze problems • Emphasize the process of inquiry instead of content knowledge transmission • Inquiry-based teaching approach • Teacher role is to provide children with opportunities to participate in the investigation without direct instruction • Teachers conduct assessments through observation of child performance	• Develop the children's abilities and skills to find out, solve and analyze problems • Teachers are advised to plan lessons to facilitate children to explore freely and construct knowledge • Develop creativity and problem-solving skills, as well as build up the children's self-confidence through play-based learning
Social reconstruction	• Objective is to increase the children's awareness of the social needs and issues and to develop their ability to solve social problems • Emphasize 'real-life' cases in which topics are relevant to the children's everyday experiences and concerns • Teacher role is to set up the scenarios and equip children with knowledge about the cases, impacts, and outcomes of social issues • Teacher may observe the children's ability to interpret societal issues	• Cultivate the children's positive values and attitudes through moral education • Use real-life learning themes which are related to the children's everyday life to arouse their interests • Make good use of community resources to organize suitable activities • Adopt methods based on observation and documenting for analyzing the children's performance in an authentic learning environment

(continued)

9 Analyzing Curriculum Orientations of Kindergarten Curriculum

Table 9.2 (continued)

Curriculum orientations	Key characteristics	Recommendations of the *2017 Guide*
Humanistic	• Objective is to include the social and emotional aspects of life and happiness • Emphasize the importance of self-actualizing in promoting the children's personal well-being • Provide the children with learning opportunities to foster personal growth, develop affections, attitudes, and values • Make learning fun and rewarding • Consider learning as being initiated by children • Teachers may use portfolios, self-assessment and peer feedback as major assessment methods	• Teachers are advised to take into consideration the children's interests and comprehension abilities when deciding the teaching content and learning strategies • Children should be allowed to choose to take part in an activity they are interested in, either on their own or in groups • Enable children to understand the value of individuals, the concept of right and wrong conduct, their own emotions and feelings through moral education • Make learning fun and rewarding • Set up learning portfolios to record and reflect progress as evidence of child development
Technological	• Children's learning is determined by a logical sequence with measurable objectives and outcomes • Using computer-assisted instruction to design learning and teaching activities • Children are expected to be competent in using information technology • Traditional tests are used to assess the children's performance	• Teachers can select electronic devices as a medium for the children's learning • Teachers should avoid over-reliance on prepared learning aids • Rather than traditional tests, information collected from multiple sources to understand the children's learning progress is recommended

of the fact the behaviours can be classified as 'right' or 'wrong', as well as 'good' or 'bad" (CDC 2017, p. 24). The *2017 Guide* states that 'there is no pressing need to discuss with children moral issues which require higher order thinking skills' (CDC 2017, p. 24).

Several cognitive process elements are also considered in the curriculum framework. The learning area of 'nature and living' is one example. Through learning processes of observation, questioning and making assumptions, children are expected to develop curiosity about the environment and the phenomena around them (CDC 2017, p. 46). This guiding principle of the curriculum focuses heavily on cognitive process orientation, which relies on developing the children's abilities and skills to find out, analyze and solve problems. The role of the teacher is to help the children make hypotheses, guess, ask questions, and make records. Teachers are advised to plan lessons to facilitate children to explore freely and construct knowledge. Children are responsible for sharing and discussing in groups or with the whole class. They are viewed as active learners who like to discover new things through, for instance, exploring their surroundings (CDC 2017, p. 47).

Curriculum Planning

The core principle for guiding curriculum planning is adopted in an integrated approach by connecting the six Key Learning Areas through real-life themes. Children's first-hand experience is the foci in the curriculum design. The *2017 Guide* recommends kindergarten teachers use real-life learning themes that are related to children's everyday life to arouse their interests. Examples of real-life themes are schools, families, friends and relatives, food, transportation, community, the four seasons and festivals (CDC 2017, p. 61) These real-life themes may concretely connect the learning goals and the content of various learning areas in a meaningful manner. Children can explore familiar themes related to their daily life, and thereby enable themselves to acquire ample and diverse thematic experiences from integrated activities. The curriculum planning puts more emphasis on a social reconstruction orientation in designing the thematic-based approach.

The development of a children-centered curriculum has long been the key emphasis of kindergarten education in Hong Kong, but it does not place enough focus on how to design a developmentally appropriate curriculum for children. In the *2017 Guide*, teachers are advised to take into consideration the children's interests and comprehension abilities when deciding the teaching content and learning strategies. In the interest corner, for example, children should be allowed 'to choose to take part in an activity they are interested in either on their own or in groups' (CDC 2017, p. 142). In such child-initiated classrooms, children are expected to learn through daily experiences, understand the links between learning and life, and develop an interest in learning (CDC 2017, p. 66). This echoes the humanists' views on the importance of self-actualization in learning. Humanistic orientation believes that providing children with intrinsic rewarding experiences may contribute to their whole-person development.

Further, the curriculum intent of the *2017 Guide* is cognitive process-oriented in a way that encourages children to engage in the process of inquiry. The *2017 Guide* sets up expectations of children to 'be curious, and fond of observing their environment and discerning how things are interrelated' and 'be capable of using the senses of sight, hearing, taste, smell and touch to explore and understand new things of their environment' (CDC 2017, p. 22). It implies that the school-based curriculum emphasizes the importance of fostering in children an interest in learning, an inquisitive mind, as well as an interest in exploration. Kindergartens, in this view, should develop an open and flexible curriculum plan, which provides children with opportunities to discover and inquire, as well as to develop relevant problem-solving skills. Teachers are advised to take up the multiple roles of learning facilitator, motivator and supporter to help children learn and grow (CDC 2017, p. 71).

Learning and Teaching

The most obvious difference between former curriculum guides and the *2017 Guide* is that free play becomes the key learning and teaching strategy. Free exploration in play is an indispensable part of children's growth and development. The CDC (2017) defines that, 'free play is a behavioral activity evoked by the intrinsic motivation of children. It places emphasis on children's autonomy and free participation and children are not limited by the rules or preset goals established by adults' (p. 141). As children grow older they engage in different types of play, namely 'solitary play', 'parallel play', 'associative play', and 'co-operative play' (CDC 2017, p. 73). The *2017 Guide* also delineates that different kinds of play can be classified as 'function play', 'constructive play', 'creative play', and 'imaginative play' (CDC 2017, p. 74). Developing play-based learning may deepen the children's understanding of themselves and the environment, developing creativity and problem-solving skills, as well as building up their self-confidence (CDC 2017, p. 73). In the *2017 Guide*, children should be given enough time to participate in free play. Time for free play should be structured in a lesson period—not less than 30 min for half-day kindergartens and 50 min for full-day kindergartens each day (CDC 2017, p. 75). Teachers should no longer take a dominant role in play activities. In contrast, the children are allowed to arrange play on their own during free play, such as choosing tools, materials, playmates and activity areas as well as formulating the play rules (CDC 2017, p. 141). As such, cognitive process orientation is reflected in the 'play' of learning.

In regard to the curriculum design, child-centeredness is the core value of kindergarten education. Learning and teaching activities are therefore designed to be in line with the learning goals, closely related to the children's life experiences, abilities and interests (CDC 2017, p. 70). Instead of relying on books and teaching packages, teachers can organize diversified activities such as games, story-telling, role-playing, and experimenting with objects. With the advancement of information technology, teachers can select electronic devices as a medium for the children's learning. However, they should avoid over-reliance on prepared learning aids (CDC 2017, p. 76). Teachers are recommended to consider the activity design and whether it is appropriate to use electronic devices as learning tools.

The school, the family, and the community play a pivotal role in kindergarten education. In the *2017 Guide*, there is a new chapter about the mode of home–school collaboration and community participation. Kindergartens are encouraged to explore other learning environments and settings, in order to make good use of community resources to organize suitable activities. This learning approach may foster the children's awareness with respect to the community they are living in (CDC 2017, p. 72). From the social reconstruction perspective, such learning and teaching activities are designed to enrich the children's learning and life experiences. However, the *2017 Guide* has not provided adequate practical recommendations for teachers about how to utilize the community resources in designing learning activities.

The curriculum content related to humanistic orientation is also incorporated in the *2017 Guide*. One of the curriculum goals is to help the children enjoy social life and to possess basic social skills. The *2017 Guide* makes clear that teachers should view children as unique individuals and provide them with opportunities in an open communicative setting, instead of adopting a one-way lecturing form of teaching (CDC 2017, p. 29). The teacher's role has been recognized as important for offering children continuous encouragement and support through use of diverse approaches to learning and teaching. Teachers may foster children's personal development by cultivating the values and attitudes of accepting and respecting others in a pleasurable learning atmosphere (CDC 2017, p. 71).

Assessment

In the learning process, assessment is a significant component of the curriculum. Information obtained through assessment enables kindergartens to review overall curriculum planning and content and to evaluate the implementation experience. Teachers can refer to assessment results to refine the curriculum design and respective strategy (CDC 2017, p. 77). The *2017 Guide* recommends teachers not stick to any 'standard answer' or 'disclose the results' too early (CDC 2017, p. 49). The Guide also clearly states that standardized criteria should be avoided when assessing children's abilities and performance in their early childhood stage (CDC 2017, p. 11). Rather, teachers are encouraged to show recognition and appreciation of children's strengths and efforts. The ultimate goal of assessment is to provide an effective evaluation in reflecting the children's learning progress, thus providing them with positive feedback to help them to improve (CDC 2017, p. 77).

Instead of assessing children's performance by means of dictation and tests, information collected from multiple sources to understand the children's learning progress is recommended. The *2017 Guide* advocates that kindergarten teachers document their observations to analyze children's performance. These observations should be carried out through an authentic learning environment (CDC 2017, p. 78). One way of achieving such analysis is through a portfolio. The guide states that 'a portfolio is a systematic record of children's growth, not an assessment tool' (CDC 2017, p. 82). This recommendation may alter the usual assessment practices, which depend on scientific data to measure children's performance. In contrast, setting up learning portfolios to record and reflect children's progress as evidence of children's development is a continuous process.

Turning to homework, the *2017 Guide* affirms that an appropriate amount of assignments can extend and consolidate children's learning. The Guide asserts that the writing tasks involving academic drilling that teachers assigned to children might have placed unnecessary pressure on children's growth. Rather than academic homework, the *2017 Guide* recommends that teachers set simple learning tasks or arrange for children to do parent–child exercises. To help the children develop good habits and a sense of responsibility, as well as to strengthen the parent–child relationship, kindergartens should encourage children to perform simple learning tasks which are relaxing and fun, for example, reading picture books, collecting objects, and passing on messages (CDC 2017, p. 82). The *2017 Guide* also highlights that children should have sufficient time to enjoy family life after school. The Council suggests that teachers and parents avoid imparting knowledge, placing importance on cultivating attitudes and developing skills instead. This focus on encouraging children's learning, and caring for their needs and interests indicates that the *2017 Guide* advocates kindergarten education be based on a humanistic orientation to children's well-being,

Conclusion and Implications

In reviewing the directions of kindergarten education set out in the *2017 Guide*, all five curriculum orientations are embedded within the curriculum framework. The *2017 Guide* values multiple orientations toward the kindergarten curriculum, which provides a comprehensive curriculum structure of promoting the balanced development of children. Specifically, five developmental objectives (i.e., 'moral development', 'cognitive and language development', 'physical development', 'affective and social development', and 'aesthetic development' [p. 20]) proposed in the *2017 Guide* are components of the kindergarten curricula, which are designed for the construction of knowledge and to provide children with contexts for the development and application of basic skills, values and attitudes. The diversity of curriculum orientations in kindergarten education has underlying implications; however, these are not presented as the dominance of one orientation over others. Instead, the relative contributions of each orientation reflect essential parts of children's development.

Considering all curriculum orientations, social reconstruction and cognitive process emerged as the two major orientations in the current kindergarten curricula. Moral education becomes the core of the kindergarten curricula, recommending kindergartens encourage children to participate in social affairs and to develop their sense of social responsibility. Moral development enables children to understand the value of individuals, the concept of right and wrong, and their own emotions and feelings, etc. In addition, the *2017 Guide* suggests offering more opportunities for children to play, but not to press for the development of academic literacy. This conforms to cognitive process orientation, which places the emphasis on what is learned by children. Instead of teacher-directed instruction, children are encouraged to become actively involved in the play-learning process. Such child-initiated learning looks at the process of engaging in learning rather than the curriculum content. Children's learning capabilities and potential can be developed by inspiring and interesting play activities. Yet the *2017 Guide* provides no recommendation on implementation strategies or on the support for play-based learning in schools. This initiative should be seen as the challenge for teachers to design play-based activities to cater for children's pace of development.

With an increased focus on children's healthy development, a humanistic orientation also places emphasis on designing and organizing the curriculum contents. The children's learning through having a pleasurable and enjoyable environment becomes central to effective learning and teaching. The *2017 Guide* emphasizes pursuing personal development and fostering a good relationship with others. In the classroom, teachers should cultivate a pleasurable learning atmosphere which assists the children to engage in learning. This underlying principle of the function of kindergarten education is extended to children's well-being. That is, kindergarten curriculum should provide each child with intrinsically rewarding personal experiences. Further, the *2017 Guide* recommends that teachers adopt a 'child-centered' approach when designing the curriculum content and learning activities. A flexible and open curriculum framework is developed that allows the children to select their order of learning. The emphasis is placed on the characteristics of children's learning, needs, and emotions in line with their developmental stages.

The *2017 Guide* is viewed as developing kindergarten education curriculum in an integrated, comprehensive, balanced and school-based approach. Under the principle of kindergarten education, an integrated curriculum incorporating different learning areas is proposed. Such modification involves adopting new pedagogical knowledge and skills into curriculum design. Concerning the *2017 Guide*'s expectation that children are the owners of learning, teachers' mindsets and roles are therefore changed from transmitting factual knowledge to facilitating children's knowledge construction on their own (Fung and Lee 2008). This paradigm shift conveys an important message on how to facilitate teachers providing children with appropriate and quality learning opportunities. Teachers' understanding of core curriculum orientations directly affects their curriculum planning and arrangement for learning and teaching. An identical message can be found in the *2017 Guide*, which states that 'teachers' understanding, recognition and commitment to kindergarten are key elements of quality kindergarten education' (CDC 2017, p. 71). Moreover, effective assessment, as stated in the *2017 Guide*, relies on teachers' careful observation and accurate record on children's daily learning. Teachers are thus advised to be capable of observation and recording skills for making good use of assessment, so as to provide feedback for curriculum planning and assure children of their learning performance. The strategies recommended in the *2017 Guide* can be used as teachers' reference for developing curriculum. However, kindergarten teachers may need to adjust or revise their curriculum plan or strategy in accordance with their school conditions in order to achieve the intended objectives. In light of change, teachers' knowledge of strategic learning and teaching approaches would be of value to enhance the professional competence of teachers in mastering the principles in the curriculum framework.

Noting that curriculum decisions on selecting orientations are greatly dependent on contextual factors, implementation only works when teachers have reviewed the relevant educational policies and documents. To ensure the successful implementation of a curriculum, an emerging need is articulated in the *2017 Guide* to facilitate the teachers' understanding and transfer in their curriculum planning. It is important to note that teachers play a critical role in actualizing the recommendations as stated, leading to the success of the implementation. Previous studies have shown that the teachers' attitudes and skills in planning and conducting activities exert a significant influence on the effectiveness of curriculum implementation (Fung and Lee 2008; Jenkins 2009). As such, further study should include the understanding of how teachers internalize the curriculum guide and form their curriculum orientations. In this chapter, there were no substantial discussions on understanding the extent to which kindergarten teachers internalize curriculum orientations on the *2017 Guide*, and how kindergarten teachers respond to the *2017 Guide* and make decisions regarding classroom practices. Future research in this area would lead to understanding the teachers' perceptions and values of curriculum orientations, as well as their implementation experiences in the classroom.

The practical significance of this review is useful for Hong Kong kindergarten teachers in developing and making curriculum decisions. As we mentioned earlier, teacher beliefs about curriculum orientation are the guiding thought for curriculum design. How teachers design various forms of learning activities should be consistently echoed by educational goals and policies. Otherwise, the disconnection between policy and practice may have a profound impact on student learning outcomes (Jenkins 2009). For example, the objective of kindergarten education, as stated in the *2017 Guide*, is to provide children with a diversified learning experience. However, if kindergarten teachers believe that the educational goal is to provide children with essential academic knowledge, their views may impact their concepts of teaching and curriculum design (which are teacher-centered) by arranging learning activities for children such as reading texts, writing words, and counting numbers. Therefore, using curriculum orientations as an analytical tool in this study, kindergarten teachers can understand the requirements of the *2017 Guide*. The recommendations spelt out in the *2017 Guide* can increase teachers' knowledge in deploying particular kinds of curriculum and modes of learning and teaching in the classroom. Teachers can draw on these curriculum orientations to form the basis for setting school-based learning objectives and evaluate their own teaching practices. This, in turn, can facilitate teachers to design and organize learning and teaching activities that meet children's abilities and interests.

References

Capel, S. (2016). Value orientations of student physical education teachers learning to teach on school-based initial teacher education course. *European Physical Education Review, 22*(2), 167–184.

Centre for University and School Partnership. (2015). *A final report on 'Development of curriculum leaders for quality pre-primary education' submitted to Quality Education Fund* (Unpublished manuscript). Centre for University and School Partnership, Faculty of Education, The Chinese University of Hong Kong, Hong Kong.

Cheung, D. (2000a). Analyzing the Hong Kong junior secondary science syllabus using the concept of curriculum orientations. *Educational Research Journal, 15*(1), 69–94.

Cheung, D. (2000b). Measuring teachers' meta-orientations to curriculum: Application of hierarchical confirmatory factor analysis. *The Journal of Experimental Education, 68*(2), 149–165.

Cheung, D., & Ng, P. H. (2000). Science teachers' beliefs about curriculum design. *Research in Science Education, 30*(4), 357–375.

Cheung, D., & Ng, P. H. (2002). Teachers' beliefs about curriculum design: Evidence of a superordinate curriculum meta-orientation construct. *Curriculum and Teaching, 17*, 85–102.

Cheung, D., & Wong, H. (2002). Measuring teacher beliefs about alternative curriculum design. *The Curriculum Journal, 13*(2), 225–248.
Committee on Free Kindergarten Education. (2015). *Children first right start for all. Report of the committee on free kindergarten education*. Hong Kong: Government Printer.
Curriculum Development Committee [CDC]. (1984). *Guide to the kindergarten curriculum* (in Chinese only). Hong Kong: Government Printer.
Curriculum Development Committee [CDC]. (1987). *Guidelines on nursery class activities*. Hong Kong: Government Printer.
Curriculum Development Council [CDC]. (1993). *Guide to the kindergarten curriculum*. Hong Kong: Government Printer
Curriculum Development Council [CDC]. (1996). *Guide to the pre-primary curriculum*. Hong Kong: Government Printer.
Curriculum Development Council [CDC]. (2006). *Guide to the pre-primary curriculum*. Hong Kong: Government Printer.
Curriculum Development Council [CDC]. (2017). *Kindergarten education curriculum guide-Draft*. Hong Kong: Government Printer. Retrieved October 26, 2017 from http://www.edb.gov.hk/attachment/en/curriculum-development/major-level-of-edu/preprimary/KGECG-En-Draft-2017.pdf.
Commission, Education. (2000). *Learning for life, learning through life. Reform proposals for the education system in Hong Kong*. Hong Kong: Government Printer.
Eisner, E. W., & Vallance, E. (1974). Five conceptions of curriculum: Their roots and implications for curriculum planning. In E. W. Eisner & E. Vallance (Eds.), *Conflicting conceptions of curriculum* (pp. 1–18). Berkeley, CA: McCutchan.
Ennis, C. D. (1992). The influence of value orientations in curriculum decision making. *Quest, 44*(3), 317–329.
Ennis, C. D., & Hooper, L. M. (1988). Development of an instrument for assessing educational value orientations. *Journal of Curriculum Studies, 20*(3), 277–280.
Fung, K. H. (2014). The Hong Kong early childhood curriculum reform for the 21st century: A retrospective and prospective analysis. *Educational Journal, 42*(2), 95–112.
Fung, K. H., & Lee, C. K. (2008). A critical review of the early childhood education (ECE) curriculum development in Hong Kong. *Journal of Basic Education, 17*(1), 33–57.
Hong Kong Government (1981). *White paper on primary education and pre-primary services*. Hong Kong: Government Printer. Retrieved October 26, 2017 from http://www.edb.gov.hk/attachment/en/about-edb/publications-stat/major-reports/pried_e.pdf.
Jenkins, S. B. (2009). Measuring teacher beliefs about curriculum orientations using the modified-curriculum orientations inventory. *The Curriculum Journal, 20*(2), 103–120.
Li, H., & Wang, C. X. (2017). International perspectives on early childhood education in the PRC, Hong Kong, Macao and Taiwan. In N. Rao, J. Zhou, & J. Sun (Eds.), *Early childhood education in Chinese societies* (pp. 235–250). Dordrecht, The Netherlands: Springer.
McNeil, J. D. (1996). *Curriculum: A comprehensive introduction* (5th ed.). New York, NY: Harper Collins College.
Miller, J. P. (1983). *The educational spectrum: Orientations to curriculum*. New York, NY: Longman.

Barley Mak is an Associate College Head of the United College at The Chinese University of Hong Kong, formerly an Associate Professor in the Department of Curriculum and Instruction and the founding Director of the Centre for Enhancing English Learning and Teaching. Her main publications and research interests are in language assessment, curriculum evaluation, language teaching methodology and teacher professional development. She has been involved in many large-scale publicly funded studies on these topics and is the author or co-author of many journal articles, book chapters, and technical reports.

Chrysa Keung is currently a Postdoctoral Fellow in the Faculty of Education, Centre for University and School Partnership (CUSP) at The Chinese University of Hong Kong. Her research areas include early childhood education, international assessment of student performance (PISA), parental involvement and sociology of education. She has a further interest in child-centred play pedagogy, kindergarten teachers' beliefs and practices on play-based curriculum, parental perception towards play, and assessment of children's whole-person development. Her work is also concerned with how cultural and social capital determines children's learning, as well as the interplay between structure and agency in shaping children's learning behaviors. She was recently involved in school-based professional support projects related to play-based learning and positive education for early childhood children.

Alan Cheung is currently Chair and Professor in the Department of Educational Administration and Policy, and Director of the Centre for University and School Partnership (CUSP) at The Chinese University of Hong Kong. His research areas include curriculum reform, reading interventions, and research reviews. He has been involved in many large-scale randomized experiments and studies on these topics and is the author or co-author of numerous journal articles, book chapters, and technical reports.

Chapter 10
Engaging with Ambivalence: The Neglect of Early Childhood Teacher Education in Initial Teacher Education Reform in Australia

Joce Nuttall

Introduction

Government reviews of initial teacher education typically have one conspicuous omission: the preparation of teachers for the early childhood education sector. Yet overwhelming evidence from education effectiveness research, early childhood education, psychology, and neuroscience has convinced policy-makers of the critical significance of children's learning in the years before school. How, then, can this absence be explained? This chapter adopts a cultural-historical theoretical perspective on continuity and change in early childhood education in an attempt to explain the neglect of early childhood teacher effectiveness in initial teacher education policy reform.

I begin by touching on the long history of political and policy attempts to address the 'problem' of teacher education in the school sector, followed by an outline of some of the more obvious reasons why early childhood teacher education has 'flown under the radar' of initial teacher education policy for so long. I then argue that these explanations are increasingly contradictory in a time when early childhood education is the subject of intense policy interest for governments and non-government organisations internationally. In the second half of the chapter, I support this argument by noting recent shifts in research and policy directions in early childhood provision. My analysis is drawn primarily from the Australian context, not because the issue of early childhood teacher qualifications is confined to this country but because it is the teacher education context I know best. I conclude by speculating on the future for early childhood initial teacher education in the light of ongoing developments in policy and research.

J. Nuttall (✉)
Institute for Learning Sciences and Teacher Education, Australian Catholic University, Melbourne, Australia
e-mail: Joce.Nuttall@acu.edu.au

© Springer Nature Singapore Pte Ltd. 2018
C. Wyatt-Smith and L. Adie (eds.), *Innovation and Accountability in Teacher Education*, Teacher Education, Learning Innovation and Accountability,
https://doi.org/10.1007/978-981-13-2026-2_10

The chapter is underpinned by a cultural-historical analysis of early childhood education. Cultural-historical theory allows analysis of fields of practice in at least two ways: first, it understands them as continuous and historically accumulating cultural forms; second, it argues that fields of human activity are riven with contradictions that can open up opportunities for development. Cultural-historical theory, therefore, allows for exploration of the highly contradictory nature of early childhood education policy, and its relationship with initial teacher education outlined in this chapter. The central argument of this chapter is that neglect of initial teacher education for early childhood education is an increasingly contradictory policy position in an era when early childhood education is subject to rapidly increasing government investment.

A (Very) Brief History of Reviews of Teacher Education in Australia

Louden, writing in 2008, characterised the 101 reviews of teacher education in Australia from 1979 to 2008 as '101 damnations' (p. 357). Louden (2008) noted:

> This sustained concern reflects the importance of the enterprise of teacher education to the social and economic development of Australia, concerns about declining recruitment standards and the continuing scepticism of practicing teachers about the impact of teacher education. Such concerns are not particular to Australia, but the absence of any significant government intervention [in Australia] is remarkable. (p. 357)

Despite strong bipartisan recommendations in the Australian Government's 2007 review, *Top of the Class* (Australian Government House of Representatives 2007), this position of non-intervention largely remained until 2014 and the release of *Action Now: Classroom Ready Teachers* (Teacher Education Ministerial Advisory Group [TEMAG] 2014). As with earlier reviews, *Action Now* expressed concern about a lack of robust evidence for the impact of teacher education but its political reception has been markedly different. Its recommendations are now being implemented by the Australian Institute for Teaching and School Leadership (AITSL) at a breathtaking pace. Reform strategies include development of a research agenda for initial teacher education, new standards for course accreditation in initial teacher education, literacy and numeracy testing of all pre-service teachers, and development of approaches to assessing graduating teachers against the graduate level of the *Australian Professional Standards for Teaching* (APST).

None of these reforms address initial teacher education for early childhood (prior to school) education. Why has the preparation of early childhood teachers been absent from debates about initial teacher education? The reasons for this are historically complex and of long standing. A useful concept to summarise this situation is that of 'ambivalence', defined by psychologists as the simultaneous experience of positive and negative aspects of a phenomenon, often leading to avoidance or procrastination (Weisbrode 2012). I now outline the origins of ambivalence about teachers and teaching in early childhood education, before returning to my core argument that the era of avoidance and procrastination may soon be at an end.

The Origins of Policy Ambivalence About Early Childhood Education and Care

Cultural-historical analyses of human psychological and practical activity understand social phenomena as contemporary outgrowths of historically accumulating cultural practices; in other words, the origins of the present status of early childhood teaching qualifications are deeply anchored in the past. Scholars such as Brennan (1994) and Ailwood (2007) have traced the historical emergence of early childhood education in Australia to the shifts in household economies and labour relations caused by industrialisation and migration. May (2009) documents how, by the mid-to-late 1800s, concerns about the number of children living in poverty on the streets of industrial Britain and its colonies saw middle- and upper-class women voluntarily establishing day nurseries to care for the children of the working poor. Writing in the US context, Rose (1999) argues that the class distinction central to these arrangements was the origin of public ambivalence about early childhood education that persists today:

> When elite women in Philadelphia created day nurseries for the children of wage-earning mothers in the late nineteenth century, they sought to take children off the streets and to enable mothers to keep their families together. But by defining day care as a charity for women who were driven into the labor force by economic desperation, these philanthropic reformers attached a stigma to day care that it still carries today. (Rose 1999, p. 5)

As middle-class women increasingly found worthwhile occupation working with young children, they were anxious to transcend the movement's history of welfarism. One mechanism for this was the development of formal qualifications for teachers who would work with children to complement the work of mothers in the home, rather than to care for the children of working women. Thus, the middle-class women who would have previously engaged in charity work became the early graduates of the kindergarten teacher training colleges established in Australia and elsewhere in the first decade of the 1900s. As the kindergarten movement grew in strength into the 1930s (Nuttall and Grieshaber 2017), the crèche (childcare) sector drew further into the shadows until the rise of post-World War II employment for women and the 'second wave' of feminist demands in the 1970s.

At the same time, as early childhood education was developing in the late 1800s, Britain and its colonies were engaged in the establishment of compulsory schooling. May (2013) has documented the rise of the infant school across the British Empire (noting that 'infant' in this context refers to children we now consider to be 'kindergarten' age, rather than babies). Like the early kindergartens and crèches, infant schools were staffed by women, who did not enjoy the status of the men who were typically engaged in primary (elementary) schools. When schooling was made compulsory in many Western democracies by the end of the 1800s, mandatory school entry was typically set at six years of age (the age that persists in many countries today), relegating the women who worked in crèches, kindergartens and infant schools to the 'non-compulsory' sector.

This positioning of early childhood education outside the compulsory education sector is the most obvious explanation for why early childhood teacher education has been largely ignored by policy-makers. However, it is not a sufficient explanation in itself. Rather, I argue it is but a symptom of a deeper and enduring ambivalence about the complex relationships between women, their paid and unpaid work, male employment, women's bodies, mothering, infancy, and the private sphere of the home. By taking seriously the idea that early childhood educators should be qualified at the same level as teachers, and their qualifications subject to the same scrutiny, politicians, and policy-makers would be overthrowing deeply patriarchal assumptions about women, young children, and their place in society that can be traced back to ancient Greece (Arendt 2003).

Treating early childhood teaching qualifications on a par with school teaching qualifications also opens up more pragmatic political and economic risks. The most obvious of these is the ongoing campaign for parity of pay and conditions between the early childhood and school sectors. Any reader doubting that such social and economic ambivalence remains in our postmodern, post-feminist times need look no further than the draft report of the Australian Government's Productivity Commission (2014) into the care and education sector. The Commission concluded:

> It is accepted that children are learning and developing very rapidly in their early years; it is also accepted that the quality of children's environment and interactions is important for learning and developing outcomes. What is not supported by the research evidence, and what the Commission does not accept, is that either (or a combination) of these findings necessitates that children require a tertiary qualified educator from birth. This is certainly an option that some parents may wish for and choose, but it should not be a minimum requirement imposed by governments, at considerable cost, on all families and taxpayers, until evidence substantiating the benefits for the additional cost is available. (p. 18)

The response from professionals across fields as diverse as economics, education, and infant mental health was swift and strong (Cheeseman et al. 2015). Their submissions in response to the draft report provided copious research evidence for the positive relationship between teacher qualifications, developmental outcomes for very young children, and economic effectiveness. I turn to this evidence in the second half of this chapter. Yet the requirement to ensure that degree-qualified educators work with all young children remains elusive in Australian early childhood policy. I argue that a deep ambivalence remains at the core of early childhood teacher education policy in Australia: Is it care or education? Should mothers be supported to participate fully in the paid workforce? And is work with young children teaching or caregiving? As Ailwood (2007) argues:

> As a historically philanthropic sector, embedded in maternalistic discourses of a woman's natural mothering instincts, the work of ECEC [early childhood education and care] teachers is deeply undervalued in Australia (Organisation for Economic Co-operation and Development, 2006). This undervaluing is regularly manifest in poor remuneration and working

conditions for many working in formal ECEC settings. There is also evidence that mothers who use institutional childcare for children before school age are still judged in terms of their perceived worthiness as mothers based on the reasons the children are in care, and that early childhood educators continue to identify themselves as undertaking a mothering role. (p. 163)

In the remainder of this chapter, I argue that recent changes in policy and practice mean this ambivalence is becoming increasingly difficult to sustain. I highlight six areas where 'buds' of development (Vygotsky 1978, p. 86) have emerged, signalling the potential for a shift from the paralysis of ambivalence to a period of developmental change, arising from increasingly uncomfortable contradictions within early childhood teacher education. The first, which provides the platform for the five areas that follow, is the recent major growth in public policy investment in early childhood education internationally.

The Growth of Public Policy Investment in Early Childhood Education

The neglect of early childhood initial teacher education by policy-makers is increasingly difficult to comprehend, given the recent rapid growth in policy attention to early childhood education. In cultural-historical terms, this neglect is increasingly contradictory, in that it points to a deep systemic tension within early childhood policy and practice. On the one hand, there is only limited attention to the critical role of teachers in providing high-quality early education, while, on the other hand, early childhood education is a major area of national investment for Australia (Australian Government Productivity Commission 2015).

The Australian Government has historically spent over $5 billion annually on early childhood education. In 2017, this figure was increased by a further $3.5 billion across the three-year period from 1 July 2018. This policy has been largely bipartisan, with successive Australian Governments identifying the need to increase the quality and accessibility of ECE services. As with many governments internationally, this investment is a risk mitigation strategy, anchored in theories of human capital. Human capital theory, which argues that high-quality early childhood education ameliorates the effects of early deprivation (García et al. 2016), measures human flourishing primarily in economic terms. It argues that investment in the early years of life can be shown empirically to reduce the economic burden on governments in later years by increasing the likelihood that children will grow into productive members of society, with minimal interaction with the health, justice, and welfare systems that are the major costs to governments.

Despite *the quality of early childhood services* providing the cornerstone for human capital theory's applicability to early childhood education, the recent policy focus for early childhood education in Australia has instead been on mothers' participation in paid work outside the home. The Australian government, rather than positioning the recent large increase in funding for early childhood education as an investment in early childhood provision, wrapped the increase up in its *Family Assistance Legislation Amendment (Jobs for Families Child Care Package) Bill 2016*. I argue the *Jobs for Families* title reflects, once again, political ambivalence about the relationship between mothers, paid work, and early childhood education. In recent years, policy-makers have been able to deflect serious engagement with contradictory aspects of the early childhood policy process by treating early childhood education as a site of convergence for two forms of human capital development, a position policy-makers have labelled 'dual benefits' (Government of Victoria 2014). First, it increases the likelihood that young children will develop into productive citizens and make few demands on government systems of health and youth justice; human capital theory has particular relevance for children living in vulnerable circumstances, since the economic gains resulting from quality early childhood education are greatest when targeting these children (Heckman 2011). Second, it facilitates the multiple economic benefits of increased workforce participation for many mothers of young children. Early childhood policy in Australia has therefore had to navigate a politically tricky balance between universal provision of services (to support women's workforce participation) and targeting children in vulnerable circumstances (since these children are known to be more likely to mature into a 'burden' on society and the state).

There is a third way in which early childhood education is relevant in human capital debates that is almost never explicitly addressed by the policy process: the development of the early childhood workforce itself. Despite widespread application of human capital theory in relation to post-secondary education and training (Quiggin 1999), public policy investment in early childhood education has included only limited investment in early childhood teachers (e.g. through fee help schemes for diploma-qualified educators completing degrees). This is despite persistent advice from the Organisation for Economic Co-operation and Development (OECD 2012, 2015) that workforce capacity-building is an integral component of early childhood policy formation.

Despite a lack of investment in early childhood teachers, buds of developmental change have erupted within early childhood policy in Australia that are likely to have consequences for initial teacher education in the field. In Engeström's (1999) cultural-historical analysis, these growth buds erupt at the edges of existing systems of activity as a consequence of underlying contradictions and can then be cultivated (or not) for developmental purposes. At least five growth buds have recently emerged in the Australian early childhood education policy and research fields that are now under active cultivation:

1. Increased regulatory requirements for the employment of degree-qualified teachers;
2. Implementation of a mandatory early years learning framework;
3. State-based registration of early childhood teachers;
4. Increased accountability in early childhood provision; and
5. Empirical evidence of the relationship between teacher qualifications and child outcomes.

I now briefly describe each of these five areas in turn, before finally discussing how these policy outgrowths must inevitably lead to greater scrutiny of initial teacher education for early childhood education and care.

Increased Regulatory Requirements for the Employment of Degree-Qualified Teachers

In 2011, the Coalition of Australian Government (COAG)—the joint working group of Australia's six states, two territories, and the Australian (federal) Government—agreed upon Australia's first national law and regulatory framework for early childhood services: the *Education and Care Services National Law Act 2010* and the *Education and Care Services National Regulations 2011*. Previous to this national legislation, Australian states and territories had regulated their own early childhood services. Amongst a number of agreed initiatives within the *Regulations* was the requirement for every early childhood service to employ a degree-qualified teacher, in order to hold a licence to operate. The *Regulations* came into effect in 2013, providing a two-year period during which services not meeting this requirement (principally childcare services) could recruit a qualified teacher or invest in upgrading the qualifications of existing staff. At the same time, 1500 additional university places were made available (on a contestable basis) for diploma-to-degree pathways qualifications in early childhood teacher education.

From 2020, all early childhood services will be required to employ a second suitably qualified staff member. Work is now under way by the national authority responsible for co-ordinating and monitoring implementation of the *National Law* and *Regulations*, the Australian Children's Education and Care Quality Authority (ACECQA), to gauge the readiness of the sector to increase qualified staffing. This is slow progress for those who advocate for lifting the overall qualification base of the profession and reflects the debate (which I return to later in the chapter) about the impact of *level* of qualifications versus *number* of qualified staff.

Implementation of a Mandatory Early Years Learning Framework

The National Law and Regulations were one part of a larger COAG umbrella, the National Quality Framework for Early Childhood Education and Care (Australian Government Department of Education and Training [AGDET] 2016), which also drove the development of Belonging, Being and Becoming—The Early Years Learning Framework for Australia (Department of Education, Employment and Workplace Relations [DEEWR] 2009). This learning framework identifies the principles, practices, and learning outcomes that early childhood services are required to adopt and implement as part of their curriculum provision for young children.

A cornerstone of the framework is the practice of 'intentional teaching', which requires teachers to be educationally purposeful, deliberate, and reflective in their interactions with children as part of their wider practices of curriculum and assessment (Epstein 2015). The *Early Years Learning Framework* reflects international trends that move early childhood educators beyond curriculum anchored in children's self-initiated ('free') play to more pedagogically oriented practices linked to specified learning outcomes. Some early childhood scholars have been critical of this trend because of a perceived 'schoolification' of early childhood curriculum (e.g. Clausen 2015). In the context of this chapter, this policy development reflects scholars who have consistently noted the link between the development of curriculum frameworks and the professional status of the early childhood field (e.g. O'Dwyer and McCormack 2014).

State-Based Registration of Early Childhood Teachers

Australian states and territories have not historically required early childhood teachers to be registered with their local Teacher Regulatory Authority, with the exception of South Australia, which has required early childhood teachers to be registered since 1976. Although there is no requirement for registration under the *National Quality Framework*, some early childhood teacher registration requirements have arisen across Australia, albeit in uneven ways. In Tasmania and the Northern Territory, for example, kindergartens (preschools) are attached to schools, so that early childhood teachers are required to be registered to be employed as a teacher by the school. In Victoria, registration is required for kindergarten teachers, both in preschools and in licensed preschool programs run within long-day childcare programs, but separate registers are maintained for early childhood teachers and teachers in schools. In Queensland, by contrast, early childhood teachers are not currently required to be registered unless this is specified as an employment condition by their employer.

Registration (known as 'accreditation' in New South Wales) requires that teachers continue to be able to demonstrate their capacity to fulfil the *Australian Professional Standards for Teachers* (AITSL 2011), originally designed to govern the registration of teachers in schools. The graduate level of the APST specifies the capacities required of pre-service teachers in order to enter the teaching profession. I argue that, as registration slowly but surely becomes a universal requirement on early childhood teachers in Australia, scrutiny of their pre-service qualifications will only increase.

Increased Accountability in Early Childhood Provision

A third provision of the *National Quality Framework*, in addition to the *Early Years Learning Framework* and the *National Law* and *Regulations*, is an Australia-wide system of early childhood service accreditation. All services are now under regular scrutiny against the *National Quality Standard*, which specifies standards of service provision. Prior to the *National Quality Framework*, only childcare services were accredited (principally for funding purposes) by the National Childcare Accreditation Council. Since 2013, all early childhood services (including family day care programs and outside-school-hours care services) have been subject to assessment ratings that are made available to the public.

The *National Quality Standard* describes seven quality areas, including educational programs and planning (Quality Area 1). Analysis of the first cycle of assessments across all states and territories by ACECQA (2016) suggests that kindergartens (preschools) are most likely to be assessed as 'Exceeding' the *NQS* and family day care schemes are most likely to be assessed as 'Working Towards' the *NQS*. This assessment likely reflects the long history of kindergartens employing degree-qualified teachers, while childcare and family day care services can operate with large teams of staff but only one degree-qualified teacher.

As qualification requirements increase, particularly the requirement for a second qualified staff member in every service from 2020, it will be interesting to note whether average quality assessment ratings also increase. Irrespective of this outcome, my prediction is that analysis of the relationship between teacher qualifications and ratings outcomes will eventually turn policy-makers' attention to the requirements, content, structure, and impact of early childhood teacher education courses.

Empirical Evidence of the Relationship Between Teacher Qualifications and Child Outcomes

A recent Campbell Collaboration report (Manning et al. 2017) provides compelling evidence of the positive link between graduate teacher qualifications and early childhood program quality. The authors' meta-analysis of 48 studies conducted since 1980 (reduced from an original pool of 2023 unique studies) shows statistically significant positive relationships between teacher qualifications and program structure, interactions, activities, language and reasoning, and interactions with parents.

Nevertheless, questions continue to be asked about the impact of teacher qualifications on children's learning outcomes. Blanden et al. (2017) compared the school achievement of over 2 million children aged 5–7 years with the characteristics of childcare services these children attended between 2008 and 2010. Their conclusion was that services with a graduate staff member added only two points (out of a potential score of 117) to achievement indices, with four points added for disadvantaged children. However, the authors acknowledge the extraordinary complexity of the relationship between early education settings and children's later achievement. Indeed, their findings may be less related to qualifications per se than to the difficulty of isolating teacher qualifications from other variables that tend to correlate with higher qualifications, such as better interactions with parents (Manning et al. 2017) and better mentoring of lower-qualified staff (Siraj-Blatchford et al. 2002).

Despite such ongoing debates, the OECD has been unequivocal in its policy advice to governments about this relationship:

> As pointed out by the OECD teachers' review (OECD, 2005), education systems need to invest in intensive teacher education and training if teachers are to deliver high-quality outcomes. This also refers to the ECEC [early childhood education and care] sector (OECD, 2006). Specific knowledge, skills and competencies are expected of ECEC practitioners. There is a general consensus, supported by research, that well educated, well-trained professionals are the key factor in providing high-quality ECEC with the most favourable cognitive and social outcomes for children. Research shows that the behaviour of those who work in ECEC matters and that this is related to their education and training. (OECD 2012, p. 1)

The same OECD Research Brief goes on to argue that governments have been reluctant to fully address teacher qualifications in early childhood education for the reasons of cost noted earlier in this chapter. They also warn governments of the risk inherent in this:

> In spite of the consensus on the importance of well-trained staff, governments often fear the funding consequences of raising staff qualifications. Higher qualifications can be followed by increased wage demands, which, in turn, contribute significantly to the costs of services. Although the evidence is strong that improved training and qualification levels raise the quality of interaction and pedagogy in ECEC services — and similar evidence exists in favour of staff qualifications — governments often choose not to invest in raising qualifications or funding staff training (OECD, 2006). This might seriously affect ECEC quality, and with this, child development outcomes, since staff are not being optimally trained or educated to stimulate early learning and development. (OECD 2012, p. 1)

Conclusion

The five policy and research growth buds described above are united in their implications for early childhood initial teacher education. Each essentially positions teacher qualifications as a proxy for program quality. I predict this proxy will come under increased scrutiny as the sector experiences ongoing cycles of assessment ratings and researchers continue to debate the validity of this proxy.

Their other unifying factor is a reliance on the positivistic assumptions that underpin the research reviewed by Manning et al. (2017). This ontological stance is about to reach its apotheosis in a recent initiative from the OECD, *The International Early Learning and Child Well-being Study* (IELS; OECD 2017a). The study aims to develop a common language and framework for assessment of five-year-olds in order to:

- Provide robust empirical data on children's early learning through a broad scope of domains that comprise cognitive and social and emotional development.
- Identify factors that foster and hinder children's early learning, both at home and in early childhood education programs.
- Provide findings that will allow parents and caregivers to learn about interactions and learning activities that are most conducive to child development.
- Inform early childhood education centres and schools about skill levels of children at this age as well as contextual factors related to them that they could use to make more informed decisions about curriculum and pedagogy.
- Provide researchers and educators in the field of early education with valid and comparable information on children's early learning and characteristics obtained from a range of sources and accompanied by a broad scope of contextual variables. (OECD 2017b, p. 3).

A coalition of over 170 early childhood academics has described the study as a preschool version of the PISA program and criticised its 'decontextualised' approach (Urban and Swadener 2016). New Zealand academics have recently succeeded in ensuring New Zealand does not participate in the study and opposition is mounting in many other countries, including Finland and Ireland. At the time of writing, at least two Australian states have decided to not implement the study. As Moss et al. (2016) argue:

> The IELS and similar testing regimes seek to apply a universal framework to all countries, all pedagogies and all services. This approach rests on the principle that everything can be reduced to a common outcome, standard and measure. What it cannot do is accommodate, let alone welcome, diversity – of paradigm or theory, pedagogy or provision, childhood or culture. The issue raised – and not acknowledged, let alone addressed by the OECD in its documentation – is how an IELS can be applied to such diversity, to places and people who do not share its (implicit) positions, understandings, assumptions and values. (p. 348)

As long as research and policy debates focus on the dual benefits of child outcomes and maternal employment, questions about the effectiveness of early childhood initial teacher education will continue to be sidelined. However, a consequence of implementing the IELS not discussed by these authors is the likelihood its outcomes will be used to question the effectiveness of early childhood teaching practice in Australia, in the way that PISA scores have been used to stimulate debates about 'teacher quality' and, in turn, teacher qualifications.

Scrutiny of early childhood teacher education qualifications in Australia is currently confined to processes of course accreditation by ACECQA, which ensures qualifications meet specified content areas and practicum requirements. I predict this level of oversight will not be able to be maintained once questions start being asked by policy-makers (particularly in Treasury departments) about evidence for the effectiveness of increased qualification requirements. New Zealand and England have already experienced this scrutiny, resulting in a rolling back of resources for early childhood teacher education; New Zealand has also seen a reversal of a previous requirement for early childhood services to be wholly staffed by degree-qualified teachers. These policy reversals reflect questions about whether there is a point at which an early childhood service has *enough* teachers at a graduate level and whether, beyond this, requiring all teachers to be degree-qualified simply adds to the cost of service provision without adding further to children's outcomes.

Although initial teacher education for schools has come under regular review in Australia, the question of whether all teachers in schools should be degree-qualified has not been a topic of debate; indeed, current debates in Australia include whether new teachers for schools should all hold qualifications at the postgraduate level. To argue that school teachers do not need to be qualified would present an unsustainable contradiction for policy-makers because of the accumulated cultural-historical expectation that teachers need to hold a relevant teaching degree (even though this has not always been the case). In looking to historical sources, the early childhood field could learn much from women who worked in the early infant schools of the British Empire and their successful campaign for eventual recognition as teachers.

Contemporary researchers in initial teacher education and early childhood education also have much to contribute to the policy reform process. For example, the recently concluded E4Kids study (Tayler et al. 2016) tracked the relationship between teaching practices and the effectiveness of Australian early childhood programs. The researchers concluded that 'the findings confirm that certain teaching and learning dimensions within a program make a significant difference to children's achievement outcomes, having controlled for other influences such as home learning environment...' (p. 6). Consistent with the OECD's stance, the most significant of these dimensions was 'the *quality of adult-child engagements*' (p. 7, emphasis in original). The researchers also identified that most settings provided a high level of emotional support to children and that services 'providing low levels of Emotional Support were rare' (p. 7). However,

> A significant finding was the level, across service types, of teaching behaviours that encourage or promote learning during play activities: no services were scored in the high range, and 87 per cent of services were rated in the low-quality range for the active level of Instructional Support provided to the children within the play environment. (Tayler et al. 2016, p. 7)

Such findings have important implications for research in early childhood initial teacher education in Australia. In particular, what initial teacher education curricula and pedagogies develop graduates who address both emotion *and* instruction in children's learning? E4Kids has identified the characteristics of early childhood teachers who provide such support to children. Research is now needed to identify how a range of variables in Australian early childhood initial teacher education (e.g. pre-service teacher dispositions, pre-service course content, the organisation of practicum placements, specific pedagogical approaches within initial teacher education, and the impact of the varied contexts in which graduates begin their independent teaching careers) help to develop these highly skilled graduates. Such variables are consistent with those being explored in the compulsory education sector. However, there are distinctive differences in curriculum and pedagogy between schools and early childhood services. The answers to questions about effective teaching in early childhood education may therefore be markedly different (or not) to arguments put forward about effective teaching in schools.

In this chapter, I have argued that recent policy and research moves point to the likelihood of increased scrutiny of initial teacher education for early childhood teachers. I am agnostic about the risks and benefits of such scrutiny. Increased government investment inevitably leads to increased accountability regimes, as evidenced in Australia's early childhood assessment ratings system. Whether the reverse is true—that increased scrutiny of early childhood teachers will lead to increased investment in their development—remains to be seen.

References

Ailwood, J. (2007). Mothers, teachers, maternalism and early childhood education and care: Some historical connections. *Contemporary Issues in Early Childhood, 8*(2), 157–165. https://doi.org/10.1080/0142569950160102.

Arendt, H. (2003). *The portable Hannah Arendt*. P. R. Baehr (Ed.). New York, NY: Penguin Books.

Australian Children's Education and Care Quality Authority [ACECQA]. (2016). *Educational program and practice. An analysis of quality area 1 of the national quality standard*. Sydney, Australia: Author.

Australian Government Department of Education and Training. (2016). *National quality framework for early childhood education and care*. Retrieved August 4, 2017 from https://www.education.gov.au/national-quality-framework-early-childhood-education-and-care.

Australian Government Department of Education and Training. (2017). *Jobs for families child care package*. Retrieved August 4, 2017 from https://www.education.gov.au/jobsforfamilies.

Australian Government House of Representatives. (2007). *Top of the class. Report on the inquiry into teacher education*.
Canberra, Australia: House of Representatives Standing Committee on Education and Vocational Training.

Australian Government Productivity Commission. (2015). *Childcare and early childhood learning*. Canberra, Australia: Author.

Australian Government Productivity Commission. (2014). *Childcare and early childhood learning. Draft report*. Canberra, Australia: Author.

Australian Institute for Teaching and School Leadership [AITSL]. (2011). *Australian professional standards for teachers*. Melbourne, Australia: Education Services Australia.

Blanden, J., Hansen, K., & McNally, S. (2017). *Quality in early years settings and children's school achievement. CEP discussion paper 1468*. London, England: London School of Economics and Political Science Centre for Economic Performance.

Brennan, D. (1994). *The politics of Australian child care: From philanthropy to feminism*. Cambridge, England: Cambridge University Press.

Cheeseman, S., Sumsion, J., & Press, F. (2015). Infants of the productivity agenda: Learning from birth or waiting to learn? *Australasian Journal of Early Childhood, 40*(3), 38–45. https://doi.org/10.1080/14681366.2014.

Clausen, S. B. (2015). Schoolification or early years democracy? A cross-curricular perspective from Denmark and England. *Contemporary Issues in Early Childhood, 16*(4), 355–373. https://doi.org/10.1177/1463949115616327.

Department of Education, Employment and Workplace Relations [DEEWR], & Council of Australian Governments. (2009). Belonging, being & becoming: The early years learning framework for Australia. Retrieved August 27, 2018 from https://www.acecqa.gov.au/sites/default/files/2018-02/belonging_being_and_becoming_the_early_years_learning_framework_for_australia.pdf

Engeström, Y. (1999). Activity theory and individual and social transformation. In Y. Engeström, R. Miettinen, & R.-L. Punamaki (Eds.), *Perspectives on activity theory* (pp. 19–38). Cambridge, England: Cambridge University Press.

Epstein, A. S. (2015). *The intentional teacher: Choosing the best strategies for young children's learning* (Revised ed.). Washington, DC: National Association for the Education of Young Children.

García, J. L., Heckman, J. J., Leaf, D. E., & Prados, M. J. (2016). *The life-cycle benefits of an influential early childhood program. HCEO working paper 2016–035*. Chicago, IL: University of Chicago.

Government of Victoria. (2014). *Productivity Commission inquiry into childcare and early childhood learning. Victorian Government submission*. Melbourne, Australia: Author.

Heckman, J. J. (2011). The economics of inequality. The value of early childhood education. *American Educator, 35*(1), 31–35, 47.

Louden, W. (2008). 101 damnations: The persistence of criticism and the absence of evidence about teacher education in Australia. *Teachers and Teaching, 14*(4), 357–368. https://doi.org/10.1080/13540600802037777.

Manning M., Garvis S., Fleming C., & Wong T. W. G. (2017). The relationship between teacher qualification and the quality of the early childhood care and learning environment. *Campbell Systematic Reviews*, 2017(1). https://doi.org/10.4073/csr.2017.1.

May, H. (2009). *Politics in the playground: The world of early childhood in New Zealand* (Revised ed.). Dunedin, New Zealand: Otago University Press.

May, H. (2013). *The discovery of early childhood* (2nd ed.). Wellington, New Zealand: NZCER Press.

Moss, P., Dahlberg, G., Grieshaber, S., Mantovani, S., May, H., Pence, A., et al. (2016). The Organisation for Economic Co-operation and Development's international early learning study: Opening for debate and contestation. *Contemporary Issues in Early Childhood, 17*(3), 343–351. https://doi.org/10.1177/1463949116661126.

Nuttall, J., & Grieshaber, S. (2017). Early childhood education research and development in Australia. In M. Fleer & B. van Oers (Eds.), *International handbook on early childhood education and development* (Vol. I, pp. 511–530). Dordrecht, Netherlands: Springer.

O'Dwyer, M., & McCormack, M. (2014). *Quality through professionalisation: Local evaluation of the Tallaght national early years access initiative*. Dublin, Ireland: Early Childhood Ireland.

Organisation for Economic Co-operation and Development [OECD]. (2012). *Encouraging quality in early childhood education and care (ECEC). Qualifications, education and professional development matter*. Research brief. Paris, France: OECD Publishing.

Organisation for Economic Co-operation and Development [OECD]. (2015). *Starting strong IV: Monitoring quality in early childhood education and care*. Paris, France: OECD Publishing.

Organisation for Economic Co-operation and Development [OECD]. (2017a). *International early learning and child well-being study (IELS)*. Retrieved August 4, 2017 from http://www.oecd.org/edu/school/international-early-learning-and-child-well-being-study.htm.

Organisation for Economic Co-operation and Development [OECD]. (2017b). *International early learning and child well-being study—The study*. Retrieved August 4, 2017 from http://www.oecd.org/edu/school/the-international-early-learning-and-child-well-being-study-the-study.htm.

Quiggin, J. (1999). Human capital theory and education policy in Australia. *Australian Economic Review, 32*(2), 130–144. https://doi.org/10.1111/1467-8462.00100.

Rose, E. (1999). *A mother's job: The history of day care, 1890–1960*. New York, NY: Oxford University Press.

Siraj-Blatchford, I., Sylva, K., Muttock, S., Gilden, R., & Bell, D. (2002). *Research report no 356. Researching effective pedagogy in the early years*. London, England: Department for Education and Skills.

Tayler, C., Thorpe, K., Nguyen, C., Adams, R., & Ishimine, K. (2016). *The E4Kids study: Assessing the effectiveness of Australian early childhood education and care programs. Overview of findings at 2016*. Melbourne, Australia: Melbourne Graduate School of Education.

Teacher Education Ministerial Advisory Group [TEMAG]. (2014). *Action now: Classroom ready teachers*. Canberra, Australia: Australian Department of Education and Training.

Urban, M., & Swadener, B. B. (2016). *Democratic accountability and contextualised systemic evaluation. A comment on the OECD initiative to launch an international early learning study (IELS)*. Retrieved August 3, 2017 from http://receinternational.org/RECE-comment-on-OECD-ICCPS.html#sthash.5qpO5N3d.dpbs.

Vygotsky, L. S. (1978). Mind in society: The development of higher psychological processes. In M. Cole, V. John-Steiner, S. Scribner, & E. Souberman (Eds.), *Cambridge*. MA: Harvard University Press.

Weisbrode, K. (2012). *On ambivalence: The problems and pleasures of having it both ways*. Cambridge, MA: MIT Press.

Joce Nuttall is Professor and Research Director of the Teacher Education, Quality, and Professional Practice Research Concentration in the Institute for Learning Sciences and Teacher Education at Australian Catholic University. Her research focuses on initial and continuing education, particularly in early years education, and teacher educators' work. Joce's research is principally interventionist in nature, in the critical transformative tradition, and informed by cultural-historical activity theory. Joce is currently President of the Australian Teacher Education Association (2016–2018) and Board Member of the Australian Children's Education and Care Quality Authority. Joce has been a primary school teacher, childcare director, and teacher education academic and researcher for over 30 years.

Chapter 11
Preparing Teachers for Assessment in Schools: The Influence of Teacher Educators

Christopher DeLuca, Andrew Coombs and Ann Sherman

> I have come to the frightening conclusion that I am the decisive element. It is my personal approach that creates the climate…In all situations, it is my response that decides whether a crisis is escalated or de-escalated, a person is humanized or dehumanized. If we treat people as they are, we can make them worse. If we treat people as they ought to be, we help them become what they are capable of becoming. (Haim Ginott 2003)

Introduction

The epigraph above reminds us that teachers hold incredible power in shaping the being and becoming of their students. As educators of pre-service teachers, we often see the effects of the school system on those we teach and hear remnants of that system in their actions and beliefs, their assumptions, and their biases. 'Why don't we just write an exam?' 'It's not fair for one student to get a second chance to re-write a test!' 'What do you mean I can revise it and hand it in again?' They question what is fair, and many have an expectation that they need to treat each of their students in exactly the same manner, even as they learn about diversity and practices of inclusion in their teacher education programs. They slowly begin to understand the difference between equality and equity, but in times of high pressure often resort back to the experiences they had in their own schooling.

C. DeLuca (✉) · A. Coombs
Faculty of Education, Queen's University, Kingston, Canada
e-mail: cdeluca@queensu.ca

A. Sherman
Faculty of Education, University of New Brunswick, Fredericton, Canada

© Springer Nature Singapore Pte Ltd. 2018
C. Wyatt-Smith and L. Adie (eds.), *Innovation and Accountability in Teacher Education*, Teacher Education, Learning Innovation and Accountability,
https://doi.org/10.1007/978-981-13-2026-2_11

It is often said that the problem with school is that we all went there. Most people who have attended school have developed a strong sense of what school should be like. Parents, store clerks, engineers, all seem to have well-established opinions of what schools should teach and how. Pre-service teachers are no different. Lortie (1975) suggests that teacher candidates learn the art of teaching and assessing through years as students in classrooms, many entering with strong views firmly rooted in this period of observation. He suggests this makes unlearning as important as learning, not only because past experiences may not always reflect best practices in their time, but more so because past experiences may not reflect current policies and practices for teaching in today's schools. How do we embrace a program of unlearning in pre-service education and how do we know when this unlearning has happened?

The epigraph above, however, also provokes us to reflect on our power as teacher educators to influence, to sway, to be the decisive authority on what teachers learn and who they become in the classroom. Our priorities become their priorities. Our method of teaching can become models for their pedagogic practice as the medium is often the most dominant of messages (Russell and Loughran 2007). Who we are as teacher educators—our beliefs and understandings about schools, teaching, learning, students, and assessment—and how we respond to teacher candidates' questions, dilemmas, and experiences have immense power to shape future teachers and support their unlearning.

In this chapter, we take a closer look at teacher educators' influence by examining their beliefs and priorities in the area of assessment. In doing so, we aim to consider how teacher educators might be shaping teacher candidates' readiness for classroom assessment and how they might be mediating teacher candidates' classroom experiences. As Brookhart (2016) poignantly argues, a primary influence on teacher candidates' assessment capability involves teacher educators' approaches to assessment: 'teacher candidates' repertoire of effective teaching practices depends on the beliefs about learning and the approach to assessment espoused by the respective teacher educator' (p. 17). Yet despite this potential influence, few scholars have examined teacher educators' approaches to assessment and the direct influence these approaches have on candidates' learning.

Within the current climate of accountability across our schools, studying how teachers are prepared in the area of classroom assessment could not be more important. Across the nation, teachers are repeatedly called through provincial policies to implement assessment-based teaching to support, monitor, and report on student learning in relation to educational standards (DeLuca et al. 2016b; Gotch and French 2014). Research on how teachers develop assessment literacy suggests that they first develop their conceptions of assessment throughout their experiences as students (Lortie 1975; Pajares 1992), then as teacher candidates (Bachor and Baer 2001; Volante and Fazio 2007), and finally as they engage in their professional careers as classroom teachers (Klinger et al. 2012; Newmann et al. 1995). Initially, through an apprenticeship of observation (Lortie 1975), future teachers develop conceptions of assessment purposes, processes, and fairness in their own K–12 education, forming the foundation of their approaches to assessment (Daniels et al. 2014). Within relatively short programs (i.e. typically less than two years in Canada), teacher education programs are intended to support teacher candidates' learning from these initial conceptions of assessment to professionally educated perspectives on how assessment is used in classrooms for accountability purposes and, more importantly, in the service of student learning (DeLuca et al. 2013; Graham 2005).

Initial research into assessment education within pre-service programs has shown potentially positive gains in teacher candidates' learning (e.g., Campbell et al. 2002; DeLuca and Klinger 2010; Mertler and Campbell 2005), with the majority of these studies focused on the value of explicit or direct instruction in assessment concepts. However, when we zoom out and look beyond discrete assessment courses, teacher candidates interact and learn from a variety of teacher educators. Across these learning experiences, teacher candidates receive different, and at times contradictory, messages about assessment. These are based largely on teacher educators' personal priorities and approaches to assessment, their views towards testing and accountability, and their conceptualizations of the relationship between assessment, teaching, and learning. Therefore, to understand fully the preparation of teachers in assessment, we must look at the totality of a teacher candidates' pre-service experience and focus on those with the potential to significantly influence their learning—teacher educators.

Assessment in Canadian Schools and Teacher Education programs

Accountability has become a watchword for educational systems around the world with teachers' capacity to integrate and use assessment to monitor and support student learning as a foundational competency (Popham 2009; Xu and Brown 2016). Popham stresses the importance of teacher assessment capacity, noting that 'educators' inadequate knowledge in these arenas can cripple the quality of education. Assessment literacy is seen as a *sine qua non* for today's competent educator' (p. 4). Across Canada's ten provinces and three territories, all of which have their own governance structure and ministry for education, policies and professional standards require teachers to implement continuous assessments to facilitate, track, and report on student learning in relation to curriculum expectations. Interestingly, despite the jurisdictional nature of education across the nation, there is surprising consistency in commitments to assessment-based teaching within government policies and standards for teaching practice.

The push towards teachers' ongoing use of assessment in Canadian schools is supported by mounting evidence on the influence of assessment-based teaching on student learning and the classroom learning environment (Black and Wiliam 1998; Shepard 2000; Stobart 2008). Specifically, research has pointed to benefits related to improved student achievement (Black and Wiliam 1998; Gardner 2006), metacognitive abilities (Earl 2003), motivation and positive self-perception (Harlen 2006), and instruction (Harrison 2005; Willis 2010). Not only in Canada, but internationally, policy developments towards data-informed teaching, assessment *for* learning, and increased use of large-scale assessments have resulted in the proliferation of mandates directing a multitude of assessment practices within classrooms (Birenbaum et al. 2015; Black and Wiliam 2006). In Canada, teachers have a long-standing tradition of grading and summative assessment with provincial testing occurring at various grades and subjects depending on province (Klinger et al. 2008; Volante and Ben Jaafar 2008). Increasingly, assessment *for* learning (AfL) and formative assessment policies are emerging in an effort to promote ongoing assessment throughout instruction, with nearly all provinces and territories endorsing AfL and/or formative assessment. Across provinces, the terms AfL and formative assessment are used largely interchangeably in educational policies. Specifically, several provincial policies describe current priorities towards classroom assessment by articulating the linkages between assessment *for* (formative), *of*, and *as* learning with provincial curriculum expectations. For example, the Western and Northern Canadian Protocol for Collaboration in Education, which represents Ministries of Education in Western and Northern Canada, published a document in 2006 entitled *Rethinking Classroom Assessment with Purpose in Mind* (Manitoba Education, Citizenship and Youth 2006). The document describes assessment as follows:

> Assessment for learning, assessment as learning, and assessment of learning all serve valuable, and different, purposes. It is not always easy, however, getting the balance right. If we want to enhance learning for all students, the role of assessment for learning and assessment as learning takes on a much higher profile than assessment of learning. (p. 14)

When looking across Canadian policies, we see considerable efforts to translate assessment research into high-level policies, establishing the provisions for a broad spectrum of assessment practices in Canadian schools. Unfortunately, research suggests that teachers are not always prepared for this assessment context. Beginning teachers tend to report low levels of assessment literacy, with gaps in core areas of their classroom assessment practice (Bennett 2011; DeLuca and Klinger 2010; MacLellan 2004; Volante and Fazio 2007). Specifically, the research indicates that beginning teachers are limited in their abilities to interpret assessment data, validly communicate assessment results, and effectively use assessment information to guide instructional decisions (Campbell et al. 2002; Chen 2005; DeLuca and Klinger 2010). Qualitative studies point to similar findings and emphasize gaps in teachers' abilities to apply measurement theory to practical classroom contexts, cautioning that this gap could result in negative and detrimental classroom assessment practices (MacLellan 2004; Volante and Fazio 2007).

Researchers have argued that gaps in teacher candidates' assessment knowledge are attributed to various factors and constraints within teacher education programs. First, temporal constraints limit the ability to cover a broad range of assessment topics and arguably to meaningfully model AfL across long learning periods (DeLuca and Volante 2016; Willis 2010). Second, institutional priorities towards accreditation and accountability, credit coverage and accumulation, and summative assessments can diminish efforts of AfL and assessment as learning practices. This factor reflects how the consequence of accreditation and accountability decisions are often higher stakes for teacher candidates, instructors, and programs (Koretz and Hamilton 2006; Stobart 2008). Finally, assessment has historically been a neglected area of study within pre-service programs, often taught as an embedded topic within curriculum or other education foundation courses (La Marca 2006; Shepard et al. 2005; Taras 2007).

However, given the rise of the accountability movement, increased pressure has been placed on professional teacher education programs around the world to develop assessment-capable teachers (Cochran-Smith et al. 2013; Knight et al. 2012). While pre-service programs throughout Canada and elsewhere have historically had minimal requirements related to explicit assessment courses with graduates generally demonstrating low levels of assessment literacy (Crocker et al. 2008; Greenberg and Walsh 2012; Shepard et al. 2005; Taras 2007), certification agencies are increasingly requiring direct instruction in assessment and evaluation (DeLuca and Bellara 2013; Gambhir et al. 2008). For example, in the recently revised US national-level accreditation standards, promoting teacher candidates' assessment literacy has become a primary focus: 'candidates be presented with multiple and rich course material in their preparation that will enable them to become assessment-literate and data-wise' (p. 21). Similar accreditation policies and recommendations are expressed across countries including Canada, the UK, Europe, Australia, and New Zealand (Cochran-Smith et al. 2013; Smith 2016).

In efforts to develop assessment-capable teachers, pre-service programs use a variety of approaches including explicit, integrated, and blended assessment education models (Crocker et al. 2008; Gambhir et al. 2008; Greenberg and Walsh 2012; Poth 2013). In Canada, the trend towards explicit assessment courses has increased with a greater number of teacher education programs now offering a required or elected course discretely in assessment to teacher candidates compared with those offering strictly an integrated model in which assessment is taught within other education courses (i.e. curriculum, foundations, or professional studies courses). However, research on the effectiveness of these various assessment education models is limited and has yielded variable results. Through their recent review of assessment literacy studies, Xu and Brown (2016) noted that quantitative measures of teacher candidates' assessment skill (or proxy constructs such as confidence or competency) consistently point to some strengths in teacher candidates' skills, yet overwhelmingly highlight significant weaknesses in candidates' readiness for assessing student learning.

Emerging research is beginning to explore the benefits of pre-service teacher education in better supporting teacher learning in assessment. For instance, Cowan (2009) in her study of a New Zealand program found formal assessment courses, coupled explicitly with classroom placements, supported teachers' development of formative assessment concepts, especially when teacher candidate learning across both contexts was shared and connected. Too often, learning from one component of a teacher education program remains isolated from another (e.g., from practicum to coursework, or from one course to another), leaving teacher candidates to connect the dots and build their own conceptual frameworks that bridge their experiences, explain contradictions, or prioritize learning from one context over another (Darling-Hammond 2006). This isolation becomes most problematic when teacher candidates are presented with different conceptions of assessment across their program components. As we know from previous teacher education literature, there is a tendency to either favour knowledge that is learned within the most practical of contexts (i.e. placement experience) or to fall back on previously held assumptions from past experiences of assessment. In either case, teacher candidates may be left with an incomplete picture of assessment that does not reflect contemporary notions of assessment *for*, *of*, and *as* learning. Accordingly, the role of teacher education in assessment should be to provide teacher candidates with an opportunity to critically interrogate their experiences and evolving understandings, using sound assessment theories, principles, and strategies, in order to cultivate a professional stance and practice towards the purposeful use of assessments in relation to student learning. Central to fulfilling this role is teacher educators' capacity to support pre-service teachers within this process, as teacher candidates' learning in assessment ultimately depends significantly on teacher educators' conceptualizations of assessment.

Exploring Teacher Educators' Assessment Priorities

Despite teacher educators' potential influence in shaping educational reform through the education of teacher candidates, there is limited empirical evidence on teacher educators' conceptualizations of assessment. Research on teacher educators is often self-study (Bullock and Christou 2009; Grant and Gillette 2006; Zeichner 2005) or drawn upon the experiences of small numbers of teacher educators or singular programs (Cochran-Smith 2003; Swennen et al. 2008). Furthermore, a significant body of this work has been used to explore teacher educators' articulation of teaching philosophy, pedagogical content knowledge, and other key domains of knowledge (e.g., inclusivity, social justice) (Goodwin 2010; Goodwin and Kosnik 2013; Grant and Gillette 2006), while teacher educators' understandings and assessment priorities have not yet been robustly examined.

In a recent empirical study, we surveyed teacher educators from across Canada to begin to understand their approaches and conceptualizations of assessment. This large-scale study drew on data from 108 Canadian teacher educators representing 28 institutions from nine provinces. In this study, the *Approaches to Classroom Assessment Inventory* (ACAI; DeLuca et al. 2016a) were employed to determine how teacher educators would support teacher candidate learning in relation to five different assessment scenarios. The ACAI is composed of three sections, two sections that relate to aspects of teacher educators' approaches to assessment with a third section focused upon individual and institutional demographics.

In order to contextualize teacher educators' approaches to assessment, the ACAI presented teacher educators with five classroom assessment scenarios. Teacher educators were asked to respond to the scenarios based on how they would encourage their teacher candidates to respond to this scenario. These scenarios include the following:

- Scenario 1: You give your class a paper–pencil summative unit test with accommodations and modifications for identified learners. Sixteen of the 24 students fail. What do you do?
- Scenario 2: You discover that one of your students has plagiarized some of his assignment (i.e. an essay). What do you do?
- Scenario 3: Out of 28 students in your class, you have four identified students on Individual Education Plans (IEPs) (who require accommodations but not modified curriculum) as well as several other unidentified students with differentiated learning needs. You must decide how to accurately measure learning in your class.
- Scenario 4: You are planning a unit for your class. How does assessment shape your planning?
- Scenario 5: A parent of an identified student is concerned about an upcoming standardised test. What do you tell the parent?

For each scenario, teacher educators were presented with four multiple-choice questions, each question corresponded to a different assessment literacy theme. Response options for each question were associated with a different priority area/approach within each assessment literacy theme (see Table 11.1).

Responses were not coded with priority areas; instead, teacher educators saw actions that reflected responses to the scenario that aligned with the priority area. Hence, in responding to the scenarios, teacher educators selected actions that aligned most closely with their most likely response to the scenario. For example, if a student has plagiarized some of his/her assignments (Scenario 2), the teacher might prioritize the action *consistently apply a grade of zero to the plagiarized work*, which would align with a standard approach to Assessment Fairness.

By responding to the ACAI, we were able to understand teacher educators' approach to assessment in relation to four assessment literacy themes: (a) Assessment Purposes, (b) Assessment Processes, (c) Assessment Fairness, and (d) Measurement Theory. The four assessment literacy themes that underpin the ACAI were based on systematic analysis of professional standards in assessment conducted in our previous research (DeLuca et al. 2016a). This multidimensional approach to assessment literacy circumvents many of the issues inherent in previous assessment literacy measures (Gotch and French 2014) and aligns more strongly with current assessment policy in Canada and the USA (i.e. *Growing Success: Assessment, Evaluation, and Reporting in Ontario Schools*, Ministry of Education 2010; *The Classroom Assessment Standards for PreK–12 Teachers*, Klinger et al. 2015; *Rethinking classroom assessment with purpose in mind: Assessment for learning, assessment as learning, and assessment of learning*, Manitoba Education, Citizenship and Youth 2006).

Table 11.1 Assessment literacy themes and associated priority descriptions

Theme	Approach	Description of priority
Assessment Purposes	Assessment of Learning	Uses evidence to summate student learning and assign a grade in relation to student's achievement of learning objectives
	Assessment for Learning	Both teachers' and students' use of evidence to provide feedback on progress towards learning objectives (i.e. inform next steps for learning and instruction). Involves both teacher-directed and student-centred approaches to formative assessment
	Assessment as Learning	Focuses on how the student is learning by providing feedback or experiences that foster students' metacognitive abilities and learning skills (e.g., self-assessment, goal-setting, learning plans). Involves teachers but is primarily student-centred
Assessment Processes	Design	Focuses on the development of reliable assessments and items that measure student learning in relation to learning objectives
	Scoring	Focuses on the adjustment and use of scoring protocols and grading schemes to respond to assessment scenarios
	Communication	Focuses on the interpretation of assessment results and feedback through communication to students and parents
Fairness	Standard[a]	Maintains the equal assessment protocols for all students
	Equitable	Differentiates assessment protocols for formally identified students (i.e. special education or English language learners)
	Personalized	Individualizes learning opportunities and assessments that address each student's unique learning needs and goals
Measurement Theory	Reliability	Works to ensure consistency in results within assessments, across time periods, and between teachers
	Validity	Works to ensure assessment or evaluation measures what it claims to measure and promotes valid interpretations of results
	Balanced	Works to ensure consistency in measuring what an assessment or evaluation intends to measure, and degree to which an assessment or evaluation measures what it claims to measure

[a]The term *'standard'* here refers to consistent use of assessment protocols and not educational standards of performance and achievement

Teacher Educators' Responses to the ACAI

Teacher educators' approaches to each assessment theme were remarkably consistent. Teacher educators' approaches to Assessment Purposes were firmly rooted in a formative assessment priority, with 89% of teacher educators supporting either assessment *for* learning or assessment *as* learning. A summative approach (i.e. assessment *of* learning) was not well supported (11.0%). In regard to the Assessment Processes theme, a focus on the use and scoring of assessment was rarely observed (6.5%), with teacher educators mainly and evenly split between designing assessments (40.3%) and communicating assessment results with students and parents/guardians (53.2%). Teacher educators' perception of what makes a fair assessment varied depending upon the scenario. In Scenario 5, which centred on addressing a parent's concern about an upcoming standardized test, teacher educators responded by describing how appropriate accommodations would be provided according to the identified student's needs (i.e. 69.8% selected an equitable treatment priority). Conversely, in response to Scenario 1 where the majority of a class failed a summative task, most teacher educators (75.7%) responded that they would negotiate a new task or activity with students who failed the initial task, reflecting a differentiated treatment priority. Overall, teacher educators prioritized a differentiated approach more than an equitable approach (59.7% and 30.3%, respectively). Teacher educators prioritized a focus upon assessment validity across all scenarios (50.0%), with the notable exception being Scenario 1. In this scenario, teacher educators overwhelmingly (70.1%) selected re-testing students with replacement questions for items that students consistently answered incorrectly (i.e. assessment reliability priority).

While these descriptive results on the surface suggest a fairly consistent pattern in teacher educators' approaches to assessment (i.e. priorities of formative assessment, design/communication of assessment results, differentiated fairness approach, and validity orientation), when we look closer at the results, this simple picture becomes far more complex. As we know, assessment is a multidimensional, context-dependent activity (Willis et al. 2013) and how a teacher educator understands, instructs, and models an approach under one theme relies upon their approaches to other assessment themes.

Imagine three hypothetical teacher educators, Ms. Watson, Ms. Facey, and Mr. Jones. All three prioritize the instruction, modelling, and explicit teaching of assessment *for* learning practices within their classrooms. However, Ms. Watson prioritizes the designing of assessments with an understanding that a fair approach to assessment is an equitable one; Ms. Facey prioritizes communicating assessment results with students and parents/guardians and believes that a differentiated approach to assessment fairness is best; and Mr. Jones focuses on the use and scoring of assessments and promotes a standard approach to assessment fairness. While all three teachers may indeed be prioritizing assessment *for* learning practices, how teacher candidates in their classrooms experience them is vastly different.

In order to gain a more nuanced understanding of teacher educators' approaches to assessment, and how they might be operationalized in the pre-service classroom, we constructed assessment profiles based on their responses to all ACAI questions. Each teacher educator was assigned to an assessment profile based upon their particular set of priorities across the four assessment themes. For example, all teacher educators who prioritized assessment *for* learning, designing assessment, an equitable approach, and a focus upon assessment validity would be assigned to the same profile. Within our study of 108 teacher educators, 65 distinct assessment profiles were identified. Of these, 49 had unique membership (i.e. 49 teacher educators had assessment profiles that were not shared with any other teacher educator), implying a high degree of variation in the way teacher educators conceptualize assessment.

Interestingly, the assessment profiles of teacher educators responsible for instructing explicit courses in assessment differed in two ways from other teacher educators (i.e. those who teach curriculum or professional studies courses). The first difference was that assessment educators did not indicate any support for a standard approach to assessment fairness. As a standard approach to Assessment Fairness is not well supported by provincial assessment policies (e.g., Government of Quebec 2001; Manitoba Education, Citizenship and Youth 2006; Ministry of Education 2010), this finding suggests a higher degree of alignment between assessment policies and assessment educators.

A second difference was that assessment educators had a more balanced support for the three purposes of assessment (i.e. assessment *of* learning, assessment *for* learning, and assessment *as* learning). Support for an assessment *of* learning approach to assessment purpose amongst other teacher educators was almost nonexistent. Conversely, assessment educators, while still favouring formative assessment, displayed a more balanced approach to the purposes of assessment. While prioritizing one approach does not mean that educators lack an understanding of other approaches, it does suggest teacher candidates are engaging with a limited range of assessment experiences. As classroom teachers are expected to be knowledgeable and capable in all purposes of assessment (i.e. Government of Quebec 2001; Manitoba Education, Citizenship and Youth 2006; Ministry of Education 2010), this unbalanced exposure can become problematic if pre-service teachers' limited exposure to approaches to assessment results in decreased classroom assessment proficiencies. Furthermore, an unbalanced understanding of the approaches to assessment may limit the options, tools, and processes a classroom teacher will need to draw upon at various points throughout their career and in response to systemic priorities such as the growing emphasis on accountability and large-scale assessments.

Despite the need to adhere to provincial assessment polices to ensure program accreditation and teacher certification, approaches to assessment described across these policies are high level (i.e. general) and do not necessarily articulate the nuanced multiple dimensions of classroom assessment theory and practice required for beginning teachers. Consequently, teacher educators are provided with significant autonomy in responding to teacher candidates' assessment dilemmas and facilitating assessment education. As a result, in considering the preparation of teachers in assessment, it appears increasingly important to also consider the preparation of teacher educators in this area. In suggesting this, our aim is not to narrow the range of assessment profiles amongst teacher educators, but rather ensure that teacher educators are able to provide sound arguments for the prioritisation of assessment approaches in relation to contemporary assessment theory and practices.

Discussion

There is little question that assessment is a high priority for many teachers in Canadian schools due in part to the growing accountability mandates throughout the nation as well as current provincial policies that encourage the ongoing use of assessments in teaching and learning. As Hopmann (2008) recognizes, a vast number of sectors (i.e. business, health care, psychology) have encountered increased accountability requirements in recent years with an international movement calling for greater transparency and monitoring of performance at all levels. Education is no different. Interestingly, however, these sectors have conceptualized accountability differently and have responded with alternative models that prioritize assessment processes and outcome evidences in various ways. Across educational systems, we too see variability in how systems have understood and responded to accountability mandates. Some systems have established rigorous large-scale and standardized protocols (international, national, and jurisdictional) that track student learning, while others have put the onus on teacher performance and corresponding evaluations (Stobart 2008). In Canada, provincial systems maintain some degree of systemic tracking and accountability through large-scale tests but the majority of student monitoring is derived from teacher-constructed and administered assessments, with increasing requirements for continuous classroom assessments leading to a body of evidence relating student achievement to educational standards. Drawing on assessments of various forms (e.g., test-based, observational, conversations, visual) and for various functions (i.e. assessment *for, of,* and *as* learning), teachers in Canada maintain a significant responsibility to fulfil accountability mandates in ways that not only demonstrate student learning, but that also facilitate and inform the learning process. In this way, teachers are asked to heed Sahlberg's (2010, p. 53) call for 'intelligent accountability' that 'balance[s] qualitative with quantitative measures and build on mutual accountability, professional responsibility and trust' (p. 53).

Within this context, the primary challenge becomes preparing educators with the capacity and knowledge to take on this professional responsibility. Evidence from previous research has shown us that simply learning the principles of assessment design and developing technical assessment skill does not yield educators who can enact intelligent accountability in their classrooms for there are always gaps in how knowledge is translated into practice, and how assessment knowledge confronts and counters other classroom priorities. Accordingly, emerging from the literature is a growing awareness that assessment literacy is not solely about a teachers' skill and learned knowledge, but also (and perhaps more importantly) about how teachers conceptualize assessment; understand its relationship to teaching context, pedagogy, and learning; negotiate assessment priorities in relation to learning intentions and student diversities; and how a teacher thinks through or unlearns assessment experiences to enable practices that are more congruent with their teaching beliefs and assessment theories (Looney et al. 2017; Willis et al. 2013). If this is the case, learning to assess is a relational process in which teacher candidates must actively integrate their learning from across domains and experiences to cultivate a professional capacity for practising intelligent accountability and assessment in schools. In forming this professional capacity throughout a pre-service program, teacher educators' approaches to and conceptualizations of assessment intersect with teacher candidates' experiences (past and present) to shape and direct their learning in potentially powerful ways (Brookhart 2016).

Through our investigation of teacher educators' approaches to assessment, we came to the realization that, while there are clear core priorities in assessment, there are also complex and vastly different assessment profiles amongst teacher educators. These profiles provide teacher candidates with varying perspectives as they learn about assessment and with different responses and rationalizations to assessment dilemmas. While these differing perspectives are fodder for learning, the challenge is providing teacher candidates with the time and pedagogical space to synthesize, unpack, and negotiate these perspectives alongside assessment theories so that they can develop their own professional stance. While it is our intention to create environments that help pre-service teachers problematize and question schooling in order to slowly shift their thinking of what learning and assessment can be for their future students, in a postgraduate degree program of 20 courses completed in 11–16 months, it is challenging to find the structures that enable candidates to do this work meaningfully. Driving our continued thinking in this area then is the exploration of pedagogical structures that allow teacher candidates and teacher educators to negotiate simultaneously their culturally constructed and contextually situated understandings of assessment in relation to practical and theoretical contexts. To this end, we aim to consider pedagogical structures (e.g., Akkerman and Bakker 2011; Nolan et al. 2011) that would enable the learning of assessment through the sharing of ideas, theories, and practices in relation to teacher candidates' experiences. In this way, teacher candidates will push on the boundaries of their thinking to reconsider what assessment can look like in schools and how it might work in the service of intelligent accountability and enhanced student learning.

Acknowledgments This chapter is dedicated to the late Dr. Ann Sherman who will be remembered for her passion for teacher education and advocacy for the role of assessment for learning in positively shaping the learning experiences of students.

References

Akkerman, S. F., & Bakker, A. (2011). Boundary crossing and boundary objects. *Review of Educational Research, 81*(2), 132–169. https://doi.org/10.3102/0034654311404435.

Bachor, D. G., & Baer, M. R. (2001). An examination of preservice teachers' simulated classroom assessment practices. *Alberta Journal of Educational Research, 47*(3), 244.

Bennett, R. E. (2011). Formative assessment: A critical review. *Assessment in Education: Principles, Policy & Practice, 18*(1), 5–25. https://doi.org/10.1080/0969594X.2010.513678.

Birenbaum, M., DeLuca, C., Earl, L., Heritage, M., Klenowski, V., Looney, A., et al. (2015). International trends in the implementation of assessment: Implications for policy and practice. *Policy Futures in Education, 13*(1), 117–140. https://doi.org/10.1177/1478210314566733.

Black, P., & Wiliam, D. (1998). Assessment and classroom learning. *Assessment in Education: Principles, Policy & Practice, 5*(1), 7–74. https://doi.org/10.1080/0969595980050102.

Black, P., & Wiliam, D. (2006). Developing a theory of formative assessment. In J. Gardner (Ed.), *Assessment and Learning* (pp. 81–100). Los Angeles, CA: Sage.

Brookhart, S. M. (2016). Formative assessment in teacher education. In D. J. Clandinin & J. Husu (Eds.), *The SAGE handbook of research on teacher education* (pp. 927–943). London, England: Sage Publications.

Bullock, S. M., & Christou, T. (2009). Exploring the radical middle between theory and practice: A collaborative self-study of beginning teacher educators. *Studying Teacher Education, 5*(1), 75–88. https://doi.org/10.1080/17425960902830468.

Campbell, C., Murphy, J. A., & Holt, J. K. (2002, October). *Psychometric analysis of an assessment literacy instrument: Applicability to preservice teachers*. Paper Presented at the Annual Meeting of the Mid-Western Educational Research Association, Columbus, OH.

Chen, P. (2005). Teacher candidates' assessment literacy. *Academic Exchange Quarterly, 62*(5), 62–66.

Cochran-Smith, M. (2003). Learning and unlearning: The education of teacher educators. *Teaching and Teacher Education, 19*(1), 5–28. https://doi.org/10.1016/S0742-051X(02)00091-4.

Cochran-Smith, M., Piazza, P., & Power, C. (2013). The politics of accountability: Assessing teacher education in the United States. *The Educational Forum, 77*(1), 6–27.

Cowan, E. M. (2009). Implementing formative assessment: Student teachers' experiences on placements. *Teacher Development, 13*, 71–84. https://doi.org/10.1080/13664530902858519.

Crocker, R. K., Dibbon, D. C., & Raham, H. (2008). *Teacher education in Canada*. Kelowna, BC: Society for the Advancement of Excellence in Education.

Daniels, L. M., Poth, C., Papile, C., & Hutchison, M. (2014). Validating the conceptions of assessment-III scale in Canadian preservice teachers. *Educational Assessment, 19*(2), 139–158.

Darling-Hammond, L. (2006). Constructing 21st-century teacher education. *Journal of Teacher Education, 57*(3), 300–314. https://doi.org/10.1177/0022487105285962.

DeLuca, C., & Bellara, A. (2013). The current state of assessment education: Aligning policy, standards, and teacher education curriculum. *Journal of Teacher Education, 64*(4), 356–372. https://doi.org/10.1177/0022487113488144.

DeLuca, D., Chavez, T., Bellara, A., & Cao, C. (2013). Pedagogies for preservice assessment education: Supporting teacher candidates' assessment literacy development. *The Teacher Educator, 48*(2), 128–142. https://doi.org/10.1080/08878730.2012.760024.

DeLuca, C., & Klinger, D. A. (2010). Assessment literacy development: Identifying gaps in teacher candidates' learning. *Assessment in Education: Principles, Policy & Practice, 17*(4), 419–438. https://doi.org/10.1080/0969594X.2010.516643.

DeLuca, C., LaPointe-McEwan, D., & Luhanga, U. (2016a). Teacher assessment literacy: A review of international standards and measures. *Educational Assessment, Evaluation and Accountability, 28*(3), 251–272. https://doi.org/10.1007/s11092-015-9233-6.

DeLuca, C., LaPointe-McEwan, D., & Luhanga, U. (2016b). Approaches to classroom assessment inventory: A new instrument to support teacher assessment literacy. *Educational Assessment, 21*(4), 248–266. https://doi.org/10.1080/10627197.2016.1236677.

DeLuca, C., & Volante, L. (2016). Assessment for learning in teacher education programs: Navigating the juxtaposition of theory and praxis. *Journal of the International Society for Teacher Education, 20*(1), 19–31.

Earl, L. (2003). *Assessment as learning*. Thousand Oaks, CA: Corwin.

Gambhir, M., Broad, K., Evans, M., & Gaskell, J. (2008). *Characterizing initial teacher education in Canada: Themes and issues*. Toronto, Canada: Ontario Institute for Studies in Education.

Gardner, J. (2006). Assessment for learning: A compelling conceptualization. In J. Gardner (Ed.), *Assessment and learning* (pp. 197–204). Los Angeles, CA: Sage.

Ginott, H. (2003). *Between parent and child: The bestselling classic that revolutionized parent-child communication (Revised and Updated)*. New York, NY: Three Rivers Press.

Goodwin, A. L. (2010). Globalization and the preparation of quality teachers: Rethinking knowledge domains for teaching. *Teaching Education, 21*(1), 19–32. https://doi.org/10.1080/10476210903466901.

Goodwin, A. L., & Kosnik, C. (2013). Quality teacher educators = Quality teachers? Conceptualizing essential domains of knowledge for those who teach teachers. *Teacher Development, 17*(3), 334–346. https://doi.org/10.1080/13664530.2013.813766.

Gotch, C. M., & French, B. F. (2014). A systematic review of assessment literacy measures. *Educational Measurement: Issues and Practice, 33*(2), 14–18. https://doi.org/10.1111/emip.12030.

Government of Quebec. (2001). *Teacher training: Orientations and professional competencies*. Montreal, QC: Government of Quebec.

Graham, P. (2005). Classroom-based assessment: Changing knowledge and practice through preservice teacher education. *Teacher and Teacher Education, 21*, 607–621. https://doi.org/10.1016/j.tate.2005.05.001.

Grant, C. A., & Gillette, M. (2006). A candid talk to teacher educators about effectively preparing teachers who can teach everyone's children. *Journal of Teacher Education, 57*(3), 292–299. https://doi.org/10.1177/0022487105285894.

Greenberg, J., & Walsh, K. (2012). *What teacher preparation programs teach about K–12 assessment: A review*. New York, NY: National Council on Teacher Quality.

Harlen, W. (2006). On the relationship between assessment for formative and summative purposes. In J. Gardner (Ed.), *Assessment and learning* (pp. 87–103). Los Angeles, CA: Sage.

Harrison, C. (2005). Teachers developing assessment for learning: Mapping teacher change. *Teacher Development, 9*(2), 255–263.

Hopmann, S. T. (2008). No child, no school, no state left behind: Schooling in the age of accountability. *Journal of Curriculum Studies, 40*(4), 417–456. https://doi.org/10.1080/00220270801989818.

Klinger, D. A., DeLuca, C., & Miller, T. (2008). The evolving culture of large-scale assessments in Canadian education. *Canadian Journal of Educational Administration and Policy, 76*, 1–34.

Klinger, D. A., McDivitt, P. R., Howard, B. B., Munoz, M. A., Rogers, W. T., & Wylie, E. C. (2015). *The classroom assessment standards for PreK–12 teachers*. (n.p.): Kindle Direct Press.

Klinger, D. A., Volante, L., & DeLuca, C. (2012). Building teacher capacity within the evolving assessment culture in Canadian education. *Policy Futures in Education, 10*(4), 447–460. https://doi.org/10.2304/pfie.2012.10.4.447.

Knight, S. L., Edmondson, J., Lloyd, G. M., Arbaugh, F., Nolan, J., Jr., Whitney, A. E., et al. (2012). Examining the complexity of assessment and accountability in teacher education. *Journal of Teacher Education, 63*(5), 301–303. https://doi.org/10.1177/0022487112460200.

Koretz, D., & Hamilton, L. (2006). Testing for accountability in K–12. In R. L. Brennan (Ed.), *Educational measurement* (4th ed., pp. 531–578). Westport, CT: American Council on Education/Praeger.

La Marca, P. (2006, June). *Assessment literacy: Building capacity for improving student learning*. Paper Presented at the National Conference on Large-Scale Assessment, Council of Chief State School Officers, San Francisco, CA.

Looney, A., Cumming, J., van Der Kleij, F., & Harris, K. (2017). Reconceptualising the role of teachers as assessors: Teacher assessment identity. *Assessment in Education: Principles, Policy & Practice*, 1–26. https://doi.org/10.1080/0969594x.2016.1268090.

Lortie, D. C. (1975). *Schoolteacher*. Chicago, IL: Chicago University Press.

MacIellan, E. (2004). Initial knowledge states about assessment: Novice teachers' conceptualisations. *Teaching and Teacher Education, 20*(5), 523–535.

Manitoba Education, Citizenship and Youth. (2006). *Rethinking classroom assessment with purpose in mind: Assessment for learning, assessment as learning, and assessment of learning*. Retrieved January 10, 2018 from http://www.wncp.ca/media/40539/rethink.pdf.

Mertler, C. A., & Campbell, C. (2005, April). *Measuring teachers' knowledge & application of classroom assessment concepts: Development of the 'Assessment Literacy Inventory'*. Paper Presented at the Annual Meeting of the American Educational Research Association, Montreal, Canada.

Ministry of Education. (2010). *Growing success: Assessment, evaluation, and reporting—Improving student learning*. Toronto, Canada: Queen's Printer for Ontario.

Newmann, F. M., Secada, W. G., & Wehlage, G. (1995). *A guide to authentic instruction and assessment: Vision, standards and scoring*. Madison, WI: Wisconsin Center for Education Research.

Nolen, S. B., Horn, I. S., Ward, C. J., & Childers, S. A. (2011). Novice teacher learning and motivation across contexts: Assessment tools as boundary objects. *Cognition and Instruction, 29*(1), 88–122. https://doi.org/10.1080/07370008.2010.533221.

Pajares, M. F. (1992). Teachers' beliefs and educational research: Cleaning up a messy construct. *Review of educational research, 62*(3), 307–332.

Popham, W. J. (2009). Assessment literacy for teachers: Faddish or fundamental? *Theory into practice, 48*(1), 4–11.

Poth, C. A. (2013). What assessment knowledge and skills do initial teacher education programs address? A Western Canadian perspective. *Alberta Journal of Educational Research, 58*(4), 634–656. Retrieved January 10, 2018 from http://hdl.handle.net/10515/sy5z60cj0.

Russell, T., & Loughran, J. (Eds.). (2007). *Enacting a pedagogy of teacher education: Values, relationships and practices*. New York, NY: Routledge.

Sahlberg, P. (2010). Rethinking accountability in a knowledge society. *Journal of Educational Change, 11*(1), 45–61. https://doi.org/10.1007/s10833-008-9098-2.

Shepard, L. A. (2000). The role of assessment in a learning culture. *Educational Researcher, 29*(7), 4–14.

Shepard, L., Hammerness, K., Darling-Hammond, L., & Rust, F. (2005). Assessment. In L. Darling-Hammond & J. Bransford (Eds.), *Preparing teachers for a changing world: What teachers should learn and be able to do* (pp. 275–326). San Francisco, CA: Jossey-Bass.

Smith, K. (2016). Functions of assessment in teacher education. In J. Loughran & M. L. Hamilton (Eds.), *International handbook of teacher education* (Vol. 2, pp. 405–428). Singapore: Springer.

Stobart, G. (2008). *Testing times: The uses and abuses of assessment*. New York, NY: Routledge.

Swennen, A., Lunenberg, M., & Korthagen, F. (2008). Preach what you teach! Teacher educators and congruent teaching. *Teachers and Teaching, 14*(5–6), 531–542.

Taras, M. (2007). Assessment for learning: Understanding theory to improve practice. *Journal of Further and Higher Education, 31*(4), 363–371.

Volante, L., & Ben Jaafar, S. (2008). Educational assessment in Canada. *Assessment in Education: Principles, Policy & Practice, 15*(2), 201–210.

Volante, L., & Fazio, X. (2007). Exploring teacher candidates' assessment literacy: Implications for teacher education reform and professional development. *Canadian Journal of Education, 30*(3), 749–770.

Willis, J. (2010). Assessment for learning as a participatory pedagogy. *Assessment Matters, 2*, 65–84.

Willis, J., Adie, L., & Klenowski, V. (2013). Conceptualising teachers' assessment literacies in an era of curriculum and assessment reform. *The Australian Educational Researcher, 40*(2), 241–256. https://doi.org/10.1007/s13384-013-0089-9.

Xu, Y., & Brown, G. T. (2016). Teacher assessment literacy in practice: A reconceptualization. *Teaching and Teacher Education, 58,* 149–162. https://doi.org/10.1016/j.tate.2016.05.010.

Zeichner, K. (2005). Becoming a teacher educator: A personal perspective. *Teaching and Teacher Education, 21*(2), 117–124. https://doi.org/10.1016/j.tate.2004.12.001.

Christopher DeLuca is an Associate Professor and Graduate Faculty Member in Classroom Assessment at the Faculty of Education, Queen's University. Dr. DeLuca leads the Classroom Assessment Research Team and is Member of the Queen's Assessment and Evaluation Group. Dr. DeLuca's research examines the complex intersection of curriculum, pedagogy, and assessment as operating within the current context of school accountability and standards-based education. Dr. DeLuca's research centres on how pre-service and in-service teachers learn to engage the complexities of assessing student learning in relation to the evolving accountability culture in today's classrooms. Dr. DeLuca's research has been published in national and international journals. Dr. DeLuca has served as President of the Canadian Educational Researchers' Association and Editor of the Canadian Journal of Education.

Andrew Coombs is a doctoral student in the Assessment and Evaluation Group at the Faculty of Education, Queen's University, Canada. His research is centred on how teacher candidates, K–12 teachers, and teacher educators approach classroom assessment decisions. Currently, he is an Associate Editor of the Canadian Journal for New Scholars in Education. His work has been published in international journals including Teaching and Teacher Education, Assessment in Education: Principles, Policy and Practice.

Ann Sherman was Dean of the Faculty of Education at the University of New Brunswick, Canada. Her areas of research in assessment, early childhood education, science education, and leadership were based on her 13 years as an elementary and secondary school teacher. Dr Sherman was a Committed Member of the International Assessment for Learning Network, hosting the 6th symposium at the University of New Brunswick in 2014. Dr Sherman was deeply committed to promoting assessment as a way to support student learning and teacher practice across classrooms.

Chapter 12
Looking for Synergies to Meet the Challenges of Teacher Education

Bronwen Cowie and Beverley Cooper

Introduction

Internationally, and in New Zealand, questions about the nature of effective teacher education have come to the fore as a consequence of the demands to produce equitable outcomes from an ever more diverse range of learners and an ever more challenging curriculum (Darling-Hammond 2014; Education Council New Zealand/Matatū Aotearoa 2017; UNESCO 2014). Most curricula now include an expectation that students will develop the competencies and capabilities they need for learning and living lifelong and lifewide. This expectation adds to the complex challenges teachers and teacher educators face as learning and knowing are now understood as entangled with becoming and being (Lave and Wenger 1991). In conjunction with these expectations and understandings, policy makers have introduced a range of mechanisms to hold teachers, schools, and teacher educators to account for student learning and achievement (Priestley et al. 2012). These mechanisms can include the specification of standards for either or both of student learning and teacher performance, along with a requirement to provide evidence of impact.

Each of these developments has a range of implications for students, teachers and teacher educators—their agendas, aspirations and practices. For students, curricula have expanded to include their mastery of disciplinary knowledge and understanding of the processes involved in its production (epistemic matters) along with the expectation for learning and living lifelong and lifewide, competencies and capabilities. Teachers are now faced with classes that are characterized by diversity in student cultures, languages and experiences and the expectation that they will support *all* students to succeed. Teacher educators, as university-based practitioners, not only

B. Cowie (✉) · B. Cooper
University of Waikato, Hamilton, New Zealand
e-mail: bronwen.cowie@waikato.ac.nz

need to support teachers to respond to these changes but also to the expectations that come with their university roles. University-based teacher educators are in unique positions of being accountable to students, teachers and teacher accreditation agencies for teacher learning and development that impacts positively for students in the classroom, and of being accountable to their university in terms of research productivity. They also need to ensure student teacher graduates develop the attributes specified in their university graduate profile.

In this chapter, we use New Zealand as a case study to explore some of the convergences that teacher educators might usefully consider across school curriculum goals, university graduate attributes, and teacher performance standards for graduate and practicing teachers, where these have the potential to shape and inform their practice and learning. We begin by elaborating on the landscape of change and then provide two examples of convergence from our own work and that of our colleagues. Then, drawing on our analysis, we scope some of the possibilities for exploiting synergies these shifts can have for initial teacher education and teacher educators.

Mapping the Territory

Over the last 10 or so years, there has been a substantial shift and expansion in expectations for student learning outcomes as specified within school curricula. This expansion has arisen in part from a realisation that mastery of formal conceptual or propositional knowledge alone is no longer a sufficient basis for active participation in today's knowledge society. The expansion also reflects common developments and concerns to do with the nature and growth of knowledge, neoliberal and marketplace agendas, and global social, environmental, economic and equity challenges. As such, it has been led as much by global conglomerates such as the OECD (e.g. the DeSeCo project), UNESCO (Delors et al. 1996; Faure et al. 1972, UNESCO 2014) and the World Bank (2011) as by national-local educational agendas (Care et al. 2017). The United Nations Sustainable Development Goal 4 asserts the need to ensure inclusive and quality education for all, along with the promotion of lifelong learning (United Nations 2016). The *Sustainable Development Goals Report 2016* (United Nations 2016) identifies literacy and numeracy skills as fundamental for further learning throughout the life course and positions these, in combination with skills needed for employment and entrepreneurship, as targets for all children and youth by 2030. However, while competencies such as critical and creative thinking, collaboration and communication are endorsed in vision statements (e.g. Pellegrino and Hilton 2012), they are less frequently embedded in formal national curricula (Care et al. 2016).

At the tertiary level, the authors of 'A New Skills Agenda for Europe' (European Commission 2016) assert that, with the right skills, people are equipped for good-quality jobs and can fulfil their potential as confident and active citizens. In this document, the word 'skill' is used synonymously with 'competence', with competencies construed as generic, highly transferable and relevant to multiple social arenas and work situations. Internationally, graduate attribute profiles include skills such as communication, collaboration and critical thinking making it reasonable to conclude that these attributes are increasingly being used to inform curriculum design in universities around the world (Barrie 2007; Hill et al. 2016). This said, questions about the relative priority given to more generic competencies and disciplinary knowledge are a feature of discussion within both school and undergraduate curricula. This discussion revolves around whether student learning will become more superficial and less powerful, without careful attention to disciplinary forms of inquiry that have been developed over time (O'Connor et al. 2017; Priestley and Sinnema 2014; Young 2008).

Alongside the promotion of more generic, crosscutting or transversal competencies, there has been recognition that multi- and trans-disciplinary approaches are needed to address the complex and 'wicked' problems the world faces. Traditionally, this understanding has been enacted in schools via an integrated curriculum pedagogical approach. The recent curriculum in Finland takes this approach beyond chance, making it compulsory for the schools to organize one multidisciplinary learning module every school year. The document positions 'Integration and dialogue between subjects' as a central aim of the curriculum in the expectation students need to and will come to understand the relationship and interdependencies between different learning areas and be able to combine and apply the knowledge and skills provided by different subjects to form meaningful wholes (Finnish National Agency for Education 2014). These developments recognize that it is important to foster students' ability to recognize and apply knowledge and skill in different contexts, to understand how concepts and topics in different subjects are interlinked, and to recognize the connections and interdependency among the world's phenomena (see also Kress 2000).

These changing expectations for student learning have implications for students', teachers', and teacher educators' learning (Windschilt and Stroupe 2017). They come with the possibility that teachers and teacher educators will need to develop new understandings of the subjects they teach, particularly in relation to familiarity with the methods of inquiry employed, and the distinctive ways competencies such as communication and collaboration manifest in their subject. They may need to learn to teach in ways and for outcomes they do not have direct experience of themselves. This combination of demands suggests that we would be wise to attend to coherence across the system (Cuban 2013).

In this chapter, we explore possible synergies across the demands on students, teachers and teacher educators. We foreground the needs of initial teacher educators because, whilst they are widely seen as 'linchpins in educational reforms' (Cochran-Smith 2003, p. 3), their learning needs have largely gone unacknowledged (Floden et al. 2017; Murray and Male 2005; Murray et al. 2017; Van der Klink et al. 2017). This is surprising given, as Windschilt and Stroupe (2017) point out, the '*greatest demands of knowing and expert practice fall upon teacher educators ...*' (p. 253, italics in the original). In the next section of the chapter, we explore the implications and synergies for student, teacher and teacher educator learning and knowing linked to (i) the need for all citizens to be numerate or have the capacity to employ mathematical thinking across contexts and (ii) the press to develop student lifelong learning capacity and for teachers/teacher educators to engage in ongoing professional learning.

Responding to the Need for Numerate Citizens

In this example, we focus on numeracy or mathematical thinking as a valued student outcome, as embedded across the breadth of teachers' curriculum and professional work, and as a graduate/student teacher learning outcome. Within a knowledge or information society, the challenges of inclusion, equity and informed citizenship raise the need for 'democratic access to powerful mathematical ideas' because these support meaningful participation in work, leisure and political action, locally and globally (Skovsmose and Valero 2002, p. 383). This imperative makes mathematics education a matter of concern in teaching for equity and social justice, all the more so because mathematics can act as a key gatekeeper to educational and economic advancement and reproduce inequity and social stratification (Gutiérrez 2008). This imperative implies that teacher educators seeking to engage beginning teachers with issues of social justice need to attend to the development of their mathematical thinking and to their capacity to develop this in their students (de Freitas 2008).

All school curricula include mathematics as a learning area with some positioning numeracy as a competency that runs across the curriculum (e.g. Australia). The inclusion of mathematics in international testing regimes, such as the OECD Program for International Student Assessment (PISA), the Program for the International Assessment of Adult Competencies (PIAAC) and Trends in International Mathematics and Science Study (TIMSS), is a practical manifestation of the importance attributed to the capacity to use mathematical and statistical thinking by governments worldwide. Important to us, the OECD definition for PISA encompasses the capacity of individuals to recognize the role that mathematical thinking plays in the world and to use mathematical thinking to make well-founded judgments and decisions (OECD 2013). Through this definition, the OECD makes clear the mathematical demands of active citizenship. This definition also supports the need to develop mathematical thinking across the curriculum because it relies on students being able to recognise mathematical thinking in a range of contexts. It becomes important therefore that teachers attend to the mathematical thinking demands and opportunities that emerge when teaching subjects other than mathematics (Bennison 2015; Geiger et al. 2015). This does not mean that all teachers need to be expert teachers of mathematics, rather that they need to be familiar with the inherent numeracy demands of their subject, to be able to recognize a numeracy opportunity when it arises, and have the disposition and pedagogical skill to take advantage of such opportunities (Goos et al. 2014). Seen this way, teacher educators, irrespective of their teaching area, need to be aware of and support student teacher capacity to identify and use mathematical thinking when and where it is appropriate.

Within the wider university context, Galligan (2013) has identified that mathematical skills are necessary in many academic disciplines. She argues that mathematical competence, critical awareness of mathematics, and confidence in the use of mathematical thinking are critical for students to be numerate in the context of their degree. She notes that for students to move beyond incidental development, systematic approaches are needed. Her work thus provides justification for a coherent cross program approach to the development of student teacher mathematical thinking.

Turning to New Zealand initial teacher education as the context for this chapter, we note that New Zealand participates in the three international testing regimes detailed above. Numeracy or mathematical thinking is not named as a competency within the curriculum in New Zealand although it can be viewed as embedded in the competency 'Using language, symbols and texts' (Ministry of Education 2007, p. 12) and can be interpreted as being embedded in most of the seven learning areas (Furness et al. 2017). Mathematics is included along with reading and writing in the National Standards program, which requires schools to report on student achievement against specified standards in school years 1–8 (5–13 year olds). To gain a National Certificate of Educational Achievement (NCEA) at Level 1 usually completed by 15 year olds, 10 of the 80 credits students have earned need to be in 'numeracy'. As well as completion of a Level 3 NCEA certificate, 10 NCEA credits in mathematics are required as an exit qualification for entry to a university degree program. Whilst some countries assess student teachers' mathematics on entry or exit (e.g. England and Australia, respectively), initial teacher education in New Zealand does not have a formal requirement of this kind beyond university entry although some universities do assess their students. This said, the nature, development and implication of primary student teachers' numeracy has been the subject of research by teacher educators (e.g. Hill et al. 2011).

The New Zealand Graduating Teacher Standards state that teachers need to demonstrate proficiency in numeracy 'relevant to their professional role' and that they need the knowledge and skills to systematically and critically engage with evidence to improve learning, teaching and the communication of assessment information (Education Council New Zealand 2015). As background to this, the shift in New Zealand, as elsewhere, to require more formal assessment and reporting of student achievement and progress has increased the need for teacher data literacy, where this encompasses the capacity to make sense of a range of qualitative and quantitative data. As noted elsewhere (Mandinach et al. 2015), this has produced new demands on teacher educators and teacher education programs (see also Cowie and Cooper 2016).

Our recent study into the development of the mathematical thinking and reasoning that teachers need across the breadth of their professional work identified that, initially, neither lecturers nor student teachers appreciated the extent to which mathematical thinking was embedded across the program courses or in teachers' work (Cooper et al. 2017). However, their participation in a number of interviews appeared to raise awareness of both participant groups. In an interview near the end of their year-long course, the eight student teacher focus group participants detailed a range of situations where they had seen mathematical thinking in action in the classroom and around the school. These situations included the different learning areas in the New Zealand curriculum (Ministry of Education 2007), as part of student assessment and reporting, and for classroom management (e.g. grouping, budgeting). Unprompted, they raised that the interview process contributed to their awareness of when and where mathematical thinking was involved (Bailey and Cowie 2017). For the teacher educators, their initial interview and their involvement in the development of a curriculum map assisted them to develop an overview of the place of mathematical thinking in their course and the program. Initially, most lecturers associated mathematical thinking with doing calculations and only through discussion began to consider ideas to do with data representation and analysis, measurement and probability.

Curriculum mapping is a process that has been used elsewhere to understand cross curricula ideas, to embed graduate capabilities across courses and improve program coherence (Kertesz 2015; Spencer et al. 2012). In our case, a mapping template, based on teacher educator initial interviews and analysis of documented course learning outcomes, acted as a boundary object (Akkerman and Bakker 2011) that facilitated later interviews and a deeper understanding of mathematical thinking in their course and across the program. However, as others have found (e.g. Uchiyama and Radin 2009), teacher educators did not consider it was their role to teach mathematical thinking in their already time-pressured courses. Nonetheless, those teacher educators who decided to make the role of mathematical thinking in their courses more explicit reported that this action had value, in part because they were often surprised at what their students did and did not know (Cooper et al. 2017).

As part of the project, we became interested in and explored the link between teacher assessment literacy, data literacy, and teacher mathematical and statistical literacy (Cowie and Cooper 2016). We concluded, as did Mandinach et al. (2015), that initial teacher education has a pivotal role to play in helping to build teacher data literacy but that integrating data use more explicitly into curricula faces a number of challenges, not the least being teacher educator confidence, commitment and knowledge and an already crowded curriculum.

This example illustrates some of the possibilities and challenges in developing cross-curricular understandings and commitments within an initial teacher education program. Teachers are now being expected to teach for competencies that run across the curriculum but research is only beginning to explore what this might mean. There appears to be even less focus on what it might mean for teacher educators to provide their students with a coherent and cumulative experience of learning and teaching competencies across the curriculum.

Responding to the Need to Develop the Capacity for Learning Lifelong

The need to develop student capacity to engage in lifelong learning and teacher capacity for continuous professional learning is the second example of synergy across school curriculum and teacher/teacher educator workplace demands. Compulsory schooling curricula worldwide are endorsing the need for students to develop the capacities and dispositions to learn lifelong and lifewide, with this agenda often linked to student participation in inquiry activities. Teachers and teacher educator capacity and inclination for learning lifelong is seen as essential given that the context in which they work and the context for which they are preparing students/student teachers is subject to ongoing change (European Commission 2013). The curricular argument is that teacher educators as role models need to demonstrate what it means to be professionals who are lifelong learners as a part of promoting similar attitudes in their student teachers (Brandenburg et al. 2016; Loughran and Berry 2005; Lunenberg et al. 2007). In many countries, however, there are no policies in place that support or encourage teacher educator learning and development (Snoek et al. 2011). For university-based teacher educators, who are required to undertake research, self study and/or collaborative practitioner research, there are two avenues that they can use to pursue professional development whilst simultaneously meeting the research demands of universities (Van der Klink et al. 2017). There is clear evidence that this research can improve educators' own practice and inform the practice of others (Cochran-Smith 2005; Loughran 2014; Zeichner 2005).

Teacher educator research can also model to student teachers and teachers in the field the value of collaboration. This can be achieved by sharing research experiences and findings and or by involving student teachers and teachers in research as partners. In our study into the development of student teacher mathematical thinking, discussed above, we collaborated with a small group of students during their year-long program and followed up with them in their first year of teaching. A majority of these students had joined the research because their previous university studies had demonstrated how helpful research can be, 'So if you've got the time, why not volunteer?' The group consensus was that they had continued their involvement across the year because, 'just from coming to the first MARKITE meeting that we had, it really opened my eyes to knowing that there's Maths outside of Maths' (Student focus group, October 2016). They were keen to continue to be part of research projects as beginning teachers. More generally, as Cochran-Smith (2003, p. 7) explains, 'the opportunity to engage in inquiry within a learning community may be a vital part of teachers' and teacher educators' ongoing education'. Research that involves collaboration with peers, and or with teachers who are partners in the process of student teacher education, can draw on and build collective knowledge of effective practice and serve as a way of developing coherence across universities and schools as settings for learning. Research partnerships between teacher educators and teachers as a wider group can also make a significant contribution to our understanding of what serves as effective pedagogy (McNae and Cowie 2017).

Returning to the New Zealand context, student inquiry is a central goal for student learning and learning experiences (Ministry of Education 2007). The curriculum document depicts effective teaching as a cyclic process, whereby teachers inquire into the impact of their teaching on their students over a variety of time scales (Ministry of Education 2007). Initial teacher education accreditation requirements stipulate that courses and programs are research informed (Education Council New Zealand

2017). Typically, some course assignments require student teachers to inquire into the impact of their teaching on student learning and engagement.

Within our faculty, colleagues have researched the implications for their practice of changes in the school curriculum and our initial teacher education curriculum. The first example we present here comes from a group of professional practice, literacy education and mathematics education lecturers who collaborated to undertake practitioner research into the implications for their courses of the 'front end' of the 2007 curriculum (Bailey et al. 2011). The front end includes the vision, values and principles that underpin the curriculum, specifies five 'key competencies' and includes 'essence statements' for each of seven curriculum learning areas. It encapsulates the main changes from the previous national curriculum. In all three cases, a series of research activities were designed to examine student teachers' knowledge of and responses to changes to the 'front end' of the curriculum. In the case of professional practice, student teachers' personal beliefs did not always align with the principles of the *New Zealand Curriculum*. For mathematics, the integration of content knowledge and key competencies in planning proved problematic for some students. Students working with the English learning area statement were challenged by changes in the definition of literacy. Overall, the findings indicated that learning to incorporate aspects of the front end of the document within their teaching is a complex process for student teachers. This project offered significant learning opportunities in that it brought together teacher educators from different fields for in-depth discussion. Moreover, their focus on different aspects of the front end meant that they were able to learn about the overall curriculum structure whilst still working on an aspect of particular interest to them. The authors contended, that like their student teachers, the need to grapple with complex ideas allowed them to deepen their understanding of how to support new forms of learning, forms they might not have experienced themselves.

Research alongside a program change can provide an opportunity for building 'principled practical knowledge' (Bereiter 2014, p. 5). In our context, the Collaborative University School Partnership (CUSP) project, which re-visioned the first-year practicum in our three-year Bachelor of Teaching program, was guided through a developmental evaluation (Patton 2011). For the CUSP program, student teachers were placed in pairs in the same classroom one day a week during the school year culminating with three weeks full time in the same classroom. Data were collected from two cohorts of year one students, their associate teachers and school-based associate lecturers, and the university program lecturers. The first two cohorts of CUSP students were followed through to their final year, when they were asked to reflect on the impact of the CUSP program (Harlow et al. 2014a, b). The developmental evaluation findings were used to make evidence-based adjustments to the program and informed the development of new postgraduate ITE programs (Cooper and Grundoff 2017).

The CUSP developmental evaluation spawned and supported three additional projects. The first was by the team of art, dance, drama and music specialists. They investigated teacher views of the assignments they set for student teachers for working with children (Harlow et al. 2014a, b). In the second project, a lecturer followed a small number of student teachers throughout their three years of study and into their first year as beginning teachers (Cobb and Harlow 2017; Harlow and Cobb 2014). In the third project, a lecturer worked with a whole school staff to review and re-vision their science curriculum. This project emerged from the lecturer's concern about support for the development of student teacher pedagogical content knowledge and the school's desire to enhance their students' science learning (Hume and Furness 2017). Through their research, lecturers in all three projects gained insights that allowed them to enhance their teaching. They each shared and published their findings so the projects supported both their teaching and research roles.

We consider that practitioner research and development evaluation involve a disposition to social inquiry as much as they do a method (Leonard et al. 2016). Collegial and collaborative involvement in research on developments can act as a site of professional learning and contribute to teacher educators' research profile. It can be viewed as a proactive response to accountability demands that also moves our field forward. Others have referred to engagement in systematic and critical inquiry as involving a 'habit of mind' (Livingston et al. 2009, p. 193) or 'inquiry as stance' (Cochran-Smith 2003; Cochran-Smith and Lytle 2009). Cochran-Smith (2003, p. 21) refers to the latter approach as 'an intellectual perspective—a way of questioning, making sense of, and connecting one's day-to-day work with the work of others and to larger social, historical, cultural and political contexts'. According to her, this kind of systematic inquiry contributes to educators' actual practices (local knowledge), as well as to a broader context of the profession (public knowledge) (see also Tack and Vanderlinde 2014).

Reflecting on the Potential of Synergies

Over recent years, there have been a number of changes to school curricula, to the expectations held of university graduates, and to the standards student teachers and teachers are expected to meet. There has also been discussion of linking student achievement to initial teacher education programs though the evaluation of the performance of the students in graduate teachers' classes. For university-based teacher educators, there has been an increased expectation that they will be active as researchers. As separate initiatives, the demands of these various and multiple changes could easily be seen and experienced as overwhelming. In this chapter, we have begun the process of looking for places of intersection and synergy between the new demands on student, teacher and teacher educator learning and knowing. We have drawn on our own research and that of colleagues in our university to illustrate and argue that there are synergies around these expectations. We have used as one example the espoused need for all citizens in a democracy to have an understanding of key mathematical ideas for them to succeed, and to contribute to and enjoy their work, leisure, community and family life. We have also attempted to illustrate the congruence between the expectation that students engage in inquiry, current conceptions of effective teaching as a process of inquiry, and the expectation that teacher educators engage in research as consistent with them inquiring into their practice.

Teacher education programs are complex social ecologies. Teacher educators are expected to address curricular aspirations and expectations which are not well bounded or understood and where what are effective strategies are almost certainly context specific and emergent. Teacher educators need to find a balance between the demands of the school curriculum, teacher accreditation agencies and the requirements of their university employment. Making connections across contexts, ideas and activities is a sophisticated process, one that requires a high level of knowledge and skill. It relies on a habit of mind to make links, which in turn pivots on sensitivity to those occasions where making connections might be productive. We hope we have illustrated that there is merit in teacher educators looking for and exploiting synergies across the curriculum and performance demands currently facing students, teachers and themselves. We think there is value in what Kress (2000) talks about as learning how to see connections.

References

Akkerman, S. F., & Bakker, A. (2011). Boundary crossing and boundary objects. *Review of Educational Research, 81,* 132–169.
Bailey, J., Blakeney-Williams, M., Carss, W., Edwards, F., Hawera, N., & Taylor, M. (2011). Grappling with the complexity of the New Zealand curriculum: Next steps in exploring the NZC in initial teacher education. *Waikato Journal of Education, 16*(3), 125–142. https://doi.org/10.15663/wje.v16i3.40.
Bailey, J., & Cowie, B. (2017). *Developing student teachers' awareness of maths across a teacher's professional work*. Paper presented at the New Zealand Association of Educational Research conference, Hamilton, New Zealand.
Barrie, S. C. (2007). A conceptual framework for the teaching and learning of generic graduate attributes. *Studies in Higher Education, 32,* 439–458.
Bennison, A. (2015). Developing an analytic lens for investigating identity as an embedder-of-numeracy. *Mathematics Education Research Journal, 27,* 1–19. https://doi.org/10.1007/s13394-014-0129-4.
Bereiter, C. (2014). Principled practical knowledge: Not a bridge but a ladder. *Journal of the Learning Sciences, 23*(1), 4–17.
Brandenburg, R. T., McDonough, S., Burke, J., & White, S. J. (2016). Teacher education research and the policy reform agenda. In R. Brandenburg, S. McDonough, J. Burke, & S. White (Eds.), *Teacher education: Innovation, intervention and impact* (pp. 1–14). Singapore: Springer. https://doi.org/10.1007/978-981-10-0785-9.
Care, E., Anderson, K., & Kim, H. (2016). *Visualizing the breadth of skills movement across education systems*. Washington, DC: The Brookings Institution.
Care, E., Kim, H., Anderson, K., & Gustafsson-Wright, E. (2017). *Skills for a changing world: National perspectives and the global movement*. Washington, DC: Brookings Institution.
Cobb, D., & Harlow, A. (2017). Rethinking the associate teacher and pre-service teacher relationships: Powerful possibilities for co-learning partnerships. In R. McNae & B. Cowie (Eds.), *Realizing innovative partnerships in educational research* (pp. 87–95). Rotterdam, The Netherlands: Sense. https://doi.org/10.1007/978-94-6351-062-2_10.

Cochran-Smith, M. (2003). Learning and unlearning: the education of teacher educators. *Teaching and Teacher Education, 19,* 5–28.

Cochran-Smith, M. (2005). Teacher educators as researchers: Multiple perspectives. *Teaching and Teacher Education, 21*(2), 219–225.

Cochran-Smith, M., & Lytle, S. L. (2009). *Inquiry as stance: Practitioner research for the next generation.* New York, NY: Teachers College Press.

Cooper, B., Cowie, B., Furness, J., Peter, M., & Bailey, J. (2017). *Mathematical reasoning and knowledge in initial teacher education (MARKITE).* Wellington, New Zealand: TLRI.

Cooper, B., & Grudnoff, L. (2017) Redesigning authentic collaborative practicum partnerships: Learnings from case studies from two New Zealand universities. In M. Peters, B. Cowie, & I. Menter (Eds.), *A companion to research in teacher education?* (pp. 223–236). Singapore: Springer Nature. https://doi.org/10.1007/978-981-10-4075-7.

Cowie, B., & Cooper, B. (2016). Exploring the challenge of developing student teacher data literacy. *Assessment in Education: Principles, Policy and Practice, 24*(2), 147–163. https://doi.org/10.1080/0969594X.2016.1225668.

Cuban, L. (2013). *Inside the black box of classroom practice: Change without reform in American education.* Cambridge, MA: Harvard Education Press.

Darling-Hammond, L. (2014). Strengthening clinical preparation: The holy grail of teacher education. *Peabody Journal of Education, 89*(4), 547–561. https://doi.org/10.1080/0161956X.2014.939009.

de Freitas, E. (2008). Troubling teacher identity: Preparing mathematics teachers to teach for diversity. *Teaching Education, 19*(1), 43–55.

Delors, J., Al Mufti, I., Amagi, I., Carneiro, R., Chung, F., Geremek, G., et al. (1996). *Learning: The treasure within.* UNESCO, Paris, France.

Education Council New Zealand/Matatū Aotearoa. (2015). Graduating teacher standards: Aotearoa New Zealand. Retrieved August 12, 2017 from http://www.educationcouncil.org.nz/sites/default/files/gts-poster.pdf.

Education Council New Zealand. (2017). Educating teachers for our changing world. Retrieved August 12, 2017 from https://educationcouncil.org.nz/sites/default/files/Proposals%20for%20Initial%20Teacher%20Education.pdf.

European Commission. (2013). *Supporting teacher educators for better learning outcomes.* Brussels, Belgium: European Commission Education and Training.

European Commission. (2016). *A new skills agenda for Europe: Working together to strengthen human capital, employability and competitiveness.* Brussels, Belgium: European Commission. Retrieved August 12, 2017 from https://ec.europa.eu/transparency/regdoc/rep/1/2016/EN/1-2016-381-EN-F1-1.PDF.

Faure, E., Herrera, F., Kaddoura, A-R., Lopes, H., Petrovsky, A. V., Rahnema, M., et al. (1972). *Learning to be: The world of education today and tomorrow.* Paris, France: UNESCO.

Finnish National Agency for Education. (2014). *National core curriculum for basic education 2014.* Helsinki, Finland: Finnish National Board of Education.

Floden, R., Richmond, G., & Andrews, D. (2017). Responding to the challenge of new standards. *Journal of Teacher Education, 68*(3), 236–238. https://doi.org/10.1177/0022487117702380.

Furness, J., Cowie, B., & Cooper, B. (2017). Scoping the meaning of 'critical' in mathematical thinking for initial teacher education. *Policy Futures in Education,* 1–16. https://doi.org/10.1177/1478210317719778.

Galligan, L. (2013). A systematic approach to embedding academic numeracy at university. *Higher Education Research & Development, 32*(5), 734–747. https://doi.org/10.1080/07294360.2013.777037.

Geiger, V., Forgasz, H., & Goos, M. (2015). A critical orientation to numeracy across the curriculum. *ZDM Mathematics Education, 47,* 611–624. https://doi.org/10.1007/s11858-014-0648-1.

Goos, M., Geiger, V., & Dole, S. (2014). Transforming professional practice in numeracy teaching. In Y. Li, E. Silver, & S. Li (Eds.), *Transforming mathematics instruction: Multiple approaches and practices* (pp. 81–102). New York, NY: Springer.

Gutiérrez, K. (2008). Developing a socio-critical literacy in the third space. *Reading Research Quarterly, 43*(2), 148–164.

Harlow, A., & Cobb, D. J. (2014). Planting the seed of teacher identity: Nurturing early growth through a collaborative learning community. *Australian Journal of Teacher Education, 39*(7), 70–88. https://doi.org/10.14221/ajte.2014v39n7.8.

Harlow, A., Cooper, B., & Cowie, B. (2014a). *Collaborative university school partnerships research brief: Hamilton—The first-year practicum experience, 2013.* Retrieved October 20 from http://www.waikato.ac.nz/__data/assets/pdf_file/0008/190655/CUSP-Research-Brief-Y1-Hamilton-2013-01_05_14.pdf.

Harlow, A., Short, C., Waititi, C., Maubach, C., Price, G., Cheesman S, et al. (2014b). *Collaborative university school partnerships research brief: ARTS in CUSP—2013*. Retrieved October 20, 2017 from http://www.waikato.ac.nz/__data/assets/pdf_file/0003/190659/ARTS-in-CUSP-Research-Brief-01_05_14.pdf.

Hill, M., Grudnoff, L., & Ell, F. (2011). Learning to think as an effective mathematics teacher: Teacher educator impacts on curriculum knowledge and learning to teach. *Teachers Curriculum, 12*, 13–22.

Hill, J., Walkington, H., & France, D. (2016). Graduate attributes: Implications for higher education practice and policy. *Journal of Geography in Higher Education, 40*(2), 155–163. https://doi.org/10.1080/03098265.2016.1154932.

Hume, A., & Furness, J. (2017). A school-researcher partnership with pragmatism at its core. In R. McNae, B. Cowie (Eds.), *Realising innovative partnerships in educational research* (pp 135–145). Rotterdam, The Netherlands: Sense. https://doi.org/10.1007/978-94-6351-062-2_10.

Kertesz, J. (2015). U-Map: Beyond curriculum mapping. *Advances in the Scholarship of Teaching and Learning, 2*(1), 16–29.

Kress, G. (2000). "You've just got to learn how to see": Curriculum subjects, young people and schooled engagement with the world. *Linguistics and Education, 11*(4), 401–415. https://doi.org/10.1016/S0898-5898(00)00030-9.

Lave, J., & Wenger, E. (1991). *Situated learning: Legitimate peripheral participation*. Cambridge, England: Cambridge University Press.

Leonard, S., Fitzgerald, R., & Riordan, G. (2016). Using developmental evaluation as a design thinking tool for curriculum innovation in professional higher education. *Journal of Higher Education Research & Development, 35*(2), 309–321. https://doi.org/10.1080/07294360.2015.1087386.

Livingston, K., McCall, J., & Morgado, M. (2009). Teacher educators as researchers. In A. Swennen & M. van der Klink (Eds.), *Becoming a teacher educator: Theory and practice for teacher educators* (pp. 191–204). Amsterdam, The Netherlands: Springer.

Loughran, J. (2014). Professionally developing as a teacher educator. *Journal of Teacher Education, 65*(4), 271–283. https://doi.org/10.1177/0022487114533386.

Loughran, J., & Berry, A. (2005). Modelling by teacher educators. *Teaching and Teacher Education, 21*, 193–203. https://doi.org/10.1016/j.tate.2004.12.005.

Lunenberg, M., Korthagen, F., & Swennen, A. (2007). The teacher educator as a role model. *Teaching and Teacher Education, 23*, 586–601.

Mandinach, E. B., Friedman, J. M., & Gummer, E. S. (2015). How can schools of education help to build educators' capacity to use data? A systemic view of the issue. *Teachers College Record, 117*(4), 1–50.

McNae, R., & Cowie, B. (Eds.). (2017). *Realising innovative partnerships in educational research*. Rotterdam, The Netherlands: Sense Publishers.

Ministry of Education. (2007). *New Zealand curriculum*. Wellington, New Zealand: Ministry of Education.

Murray, J., Lunenberg, M., & Smith, K. (2017). *Educating the educators: Policies and initiatives in European teacher education*. Singapore: Springer. https://doi.org/10.1007/978-981-10-4075-7-44.

Murray, J., & Male, T. (2005). Becoming a teacher educator: Evidence from the field. *Teaching and Teacher Education, 21*(2), 125–142. https://doi.org/10.1016/j.tate.2004.12.006.

O'Connor, K., Yates, L., Woelert, P., & Millar, V. (2017). *Knowledge at the crossroads? Physics and history in the changing world of schools and universities*. Singapore: Springer.

OECD [Organisation for Economic Co-operation and Development]. (2013). *PISA 2012 assessment and analytical framework: Mathematics, reading, science, problem solving and financial literacy*. Paris, France: OECD Publishing. http://dx.doi.org/10.1787/9789264190511-en.

Patton, M. (2011). Developmental Evaluation: Applying complexity concepts to enhance innovation and use. *The Canadian Journal of Program Evaluation, 26*(2), 108–110.

Pellegrino, J., & Hilton, M. (Eds.). (2012). *Education for life and work: Developing transferable knowledge and skills in the 21st century*. Washington, DC: National Academic Press.

Priestley, M., Robinson, S., & Biesta, G. (2012). Teacher agency, performativity and curriculum change: Reinventing the teacher in the Scottish curriculum for excellence? In B. Jeffery & G. Troman (Eds.), *Performativity in UK education: Ethnographic cases of its effects, agency and reconstructions* (pp. 87–108). Painswick, England: Ethnography and Education Publishing.

Priestley, M., & Sinnema, C. (2014). Downgraded curriculum? An analysis of knowledge in new curricula in Scotland and New Zealand. *The Curriculum Journal, 25*(1), 50–75. https://doi.org/10.1080/09585176.2013.872047.

Skovsmose, O., & Valero, P. (2002). Democratic access to powerful mathematical ideas. In L. D. English (Ed.), *Handbook of international research in mathematics education* (pp. 383–407). Mahwah, NJ: Lawrence Erlbaum Associates, Incorporated.

Snoek, M., Swennen, A., & van der Klink, M. (2011). The quality of teacher educators in the European policy debate: Actions and measures to improve the professionalism of teacher educators. *Professional Development in Education, 37*(5), 651–664. https://doi.org/10.1080/19415257.2011.616095.

Spenser, D., Riddle, M., & Knewstubb, B. (2012). Curriculum mapping to embed graduate capabilities. *Higher Education Research & Development, 31*(2), 217–231. https://doi.org/10.1080/07294360.2011.554387.

Tack, H., & Vanderlinde, R. (2014). Teacher educators' professional development: Towards a typology of teacher educators' researcherly disposition. *British Journal of Educational Studies, 62*(3), 297–315.

Uchiyama, K., & Radin, J. (2009). Curriculum mapping in higher education: A vehicle for collaboration. *Innovative Higher Education, 33*(4), 271–280. https://doi.org/10.1007/s10755-008-9078-8.

UNESCO [United Nations Educational, Scientific and Cultural Organization]. (2014). *UNESCO education strategy 2014–2021*. Paris, France: UNESCO. Retrieved January 9, 2018 from http://unesdoc.unesco.org/images/0023/002312/231288e.pdf.

United Nations. (2016). *Transforming our world: The 2030 agenda for sustainable development*. Retrieved January 09, 2018 from https://sustainabledevelopment.un.org/content/documents/21252030%20Agenda%20for%20Sustainable%20Development%20web.pdf.

Van der Klink, M., Kools, Q., Avissar, G., White, S., & Sakata, T. (2017). Professional development of teacher educators: What do they do? Findings from an explorative international study. *Professional Development in Education, 43*(2), 163–178. https://doi.org/10.1080/19415257.2015.1114506.

Windschitl, M., & Stroupe, D. (2017). The three-story challenge: Implications of the next generation science standards for teacher preparation. *Journal of Teacher Education, 68*(3), 251–261. https://doi.org/10.1177/0022487117696278.

World Bank. (2011). *Learning for all: Investing in people's knowledge and skills to promote development*. Washington, DC: Author.

Young, M. (2008). From constructivism to realism in the sociology of the curriculum. *Review of Research in Education, 32,* 1–28. https://doi.org/10.3102/0091732x07308969.

Zeichner, K. (2005). Becoming a teacher educator: A personal perspective. *Teaching and Teacher Education, 21*(2), 117–124.

Bronwen Cowie is Professor and Director of the Wilf Malcolm Institute of Educational Research, the University of Waikato, New Zealand. Bronwen's particular interests are in learning and assessment. Working in partnership with teachers, she has explored the nature of teacher assessment for learning interactions and the influence of teacher understanding of curriculum, of student understandings of a subject domain and of students' diverse funds of knowledge. She has investigated the development of student–teacher assessment capability and of the mathematical and statistical thinking teachers need across the breadth of their professional work. Bronwen has experience with development evaluation and has conducted research to understand teacher and teacher educator implementation of curriculum innovation in school and school–university partnership contexts.

Beverley Cooper is Associate Dean, Teacher Education, the University of Waikato, Hamilton New Zealand. She has extensive professional experience working as a secondary teacher and in teacher education in various leadership roles locally and nationally. Beverley's research is focused on teacher education program development and implementation. Current projects are investigating the development of shared understanding of practicum judgements between school and university, the development of mathematical thinking across an Initial Teacher Education program for a teacher's professional role, and the development of innovative practicum and program collaborative partnerships between the university and schools. She has been involved in a number of large national and international research projects focused on the development of expertise in teacher education programs such as assessment capability, curriculum and innovative practices.

Chapter 13
Enhancing Inclusive Education Through Teacher Education Reforms

Joy Cumming, Megan Tones, Chantelle Day and Elizabeth Heck

Introduction and Context

Equity in education, in the general sense of opportunity for all (Ministerial Council on Education, Employment, Training and Youth Affairs [MCEETYA] 2008), but without specific definition or necessarily justification, is internationally endorsed as a good and desirable policy focus. Education equity policies reflect international human rights conventions and treaties to which many nations are signatory. Equity policies provide rights to all in education (and other life opportunities) free from 'distinction of any kind, such as race, colour, sex, language, religion, political or other opinion, national or social origin, property, birth or other status' (United Nations [UN] 1948)[1].

Such student diversity in classrooms is a major factor impacting on teaching practice in modern classrooms. For example, Fig. 13.1 demonstrates the diversity of students that Australian teachers may encounter in their classroom on a daily basis, with students having potentially multiple characteristics that impact on their learning.

The right to equity and equal opportunity in education free from discrimination is not just policy but embedded internationally in law. The UK *Equality Act* 2010 protects against discrimination in education on a range of characteristics, with the

---

[1] See also, for rights in education, the Convention on the Elimination of All Forms of Racial Discrimination, (UN 1966), the Convention on the Rights of the Child (UN 1989) and the Convention on the Rights of Persons with Disabilities (UN 2007).

Electronic supplementary material The online version of this chapter (https://doi.org/10.1007/978-981-13-2026-2_13) contains supplementary material, which is available to authorized users.

J. Cumming (✉) · M. Tones · C. Day · E. Heck
Institute for Learning Sciences and Teacher Education, Australian Catholic University, Brisbane, Australia
e-mail: Joy.Cumming@acu.edu.au

Fig. 13.1 Diversity of students in Australian schools

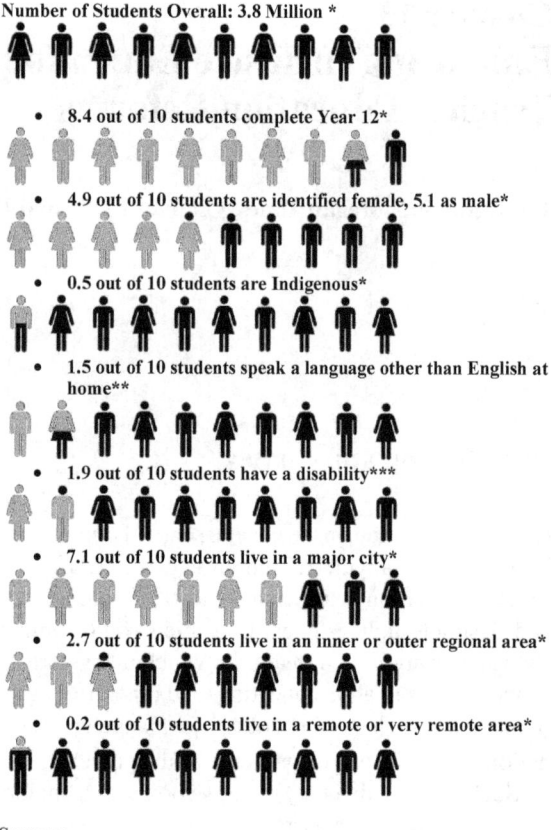

Number of Students Overall: 3.8 Million *

- 8.4 out of 10 students complete Year 12*
- 4.9 out of 10 students are identified female, 5.1 as male*
- 0.5 out of 10 students are Indigenous*
- 1.5 out of 10 students speak a language other than English at home**
- 1.9 out of 10 students have a disability***
- 7.1 out of 10 students live in a major city*
- 2.7 out of 10 students live in an inner or outer regional area*
- 0.2 out of 10 students live in a remote or very remote area*

Sources:
* (Australian Bureau of Statistics [ABS] 2016)
** (Australian Council on Educational Research 2016)
*** (Education Council 2016)

requirement to manage access to, and provision of, education and to make 'reasonable adjustments' as needed [section 85(6)]. Federal anti-discrimination legislation in the United States of America (USA) addresses characteristics such as race, age, gender and disability, with a core basis of individual rights in the US Constitution, and specific legislation addressing discrimination in education, including the well-known US Act introducing standardised accountability testing, the *No Child Left Behind* legislation of 2002, intended to focus attention on learning outcomes for all students including students with disability. Australian anti-discrimination legislation includes Commonwealth anti-discrimination laws addressing specific individual characteristics and omnibus state and territory anti-discrimination laws.

The strongest legal protections in education, accompanied by sanctions for breach, are provided for students with disability (Cumming and Dickson 2007). In Australia, subsidiary legislation implementing the federal *Disability Discrimination Act* 1992 (Cth), the *Disability Standards for Education* 2005 (Cth), requires education providers to provide equity of access for students with disability to education (including curriculum and other programs) on the same basis as other students, with 'reasonable' adjustments to enable such access (Dickson 2006).

Central to conventions, legislation and policies is a common philosophy of commitment to education of all students, with few exceptions, through inclusive education in a 'mainstream school' (see, e.g. Policy Scotland 2015). Statements of values, operationalisation procedures and practices and policies support this commitment (European Agency for Special Needs and Inclusive Education 2017). Worldwide acceptance of inclusive education policy is attributed to the 1994 *Salamanca Statement of Spain* (United Nations Educational, Scientific and Cultural Organisation [UNESCO] 1994). Inclusive education is considered the 'most effective means of combating discriminatory attitudes, creating welcoming communities, building inclusive society and achieving an education for all' (Ackah 2016, p. 39). Universal Design for Learning (UDL) builds on such inclusive education expectations that schools and teachers should and can adapt education provision to meet learning requirements of all students. Based on the architectural universal design principles, UDL envisages flexible design and provision of education programs and facilities in a manner suited to all so that the need for adjustments to a 'mainstream' program (Hehir 2009) is redundant. In practice, such flexibility does not mean that one size should suit all but that multiple approaches to aspects of education are in play to allow sufficient choice to meet the needs of all.

Education equity policies and legislation and inclusive education therefore place high expectations on teachers' repertoire of everyday classroom practices. These expectations are noted in professional standards for teachers, including new graduates, as shown in an overview for six countries in Table 13.1. Teachers are expected to be able to demonstrate a range of teaching approaches to meet individual student needs, whether due to cultural grounds, disadvantage, or to disability or giftedness. Importantly, standards also incorporate ethical statements and values, such as respect, that teachers should hold regarding student diversity.

Legislative and policy attention to inclusive education practices and expectations for teacher practice thus indicate a significant area that should be a critical component in teacher education, both in initial programs and ongoing professional development.

Quality teaching and teacher reform have been a major focus internationally in recent years, with many countries undertaking reviews and presenting reform reports on future directions for teacher education and professional development. Given the significance of teaching to diversity highlighted here, we present in this chapter systematic qualitative analyses of recent teacher education reform reports and other relevant documents to identify the attention that has been paid to inclusive education and teacher preparation.

Caveat We note that this review is situated in education contexts where quality of provision and resources are already high; our sights are set on what could be considered ideal education contexts and quality experiences for all students. Our challenges are minor compared to those encountered in education reforms to achieve equity in many countries, including the need to address student poverty, students in rural and remote areas, sometimes inaccessible, and lack of infrastructure and

Table 13.1 Overview of expectations in teacher professional standards regarding student diversity from six countries

Country	Source	Standards expectations
Australia	Australian Institute for Teaching and School Leadership [AITSL] (2011)	Practice Addresses: • 'Students with diverse linguistic, cultural, religious and socioeconomic backgrounds' (AITSL 2011, pp. 1–2) • Differentiation of teaching 'to meet specific learning needs of students across the full range of abilities' (AITSL 2011, pp. 1–2) • 'Strategies to support full participation of students with disability' (AITSL 2011, pp. 1–2) Values • '…Understanding of and respect for Aboriginal and Torres Strait Islander histories, cultures and languages' (AITSL 2011, p. 4)
Canada	British Columbia Ministry of Education [BCME] (2012)	• 'Educators value and care for all students and act in their best interests' (BCME 2012, p. 4) • 'Educators respect the diversity in their classrooms, schools and communities' (BCME 2012, p. 4) • 'Educators have the knowledge and skills to facilitate learning for all students and know when to seek additional support for their practice' (BCME 2012, p. 4)
	Ontario College of Teachers [OCT] (2017)	Standards of Practice • 'Commitment to Students and Student Learning: [Members] treat students equitably and with respect and are sensitive to factors that influence individual student learning' (OCT 2017) • 'Professional Practice: [Members] use appropriate pedagogy, assessment and evaluation, resources and technology in planning for and responding to the needs of individual students and learning communities' (OCT 2017) Ethical Standards • Emphasise acceptance and fair-mindedness
Ireland	The Teaching Council [TTC] (2012)	Professional Practice • 'Develop teaching, learning and assessment strategies that support differentiated learning in a way that respects the dignity of all pupils/students' (TTC 2012, p. 7) Professional Values and Relationships • 'Acknowledge and respect the uniqueness, individuality and specific needs of pupils/students and promote their holistic development' (TTC 2012, p. 6) • 'Be committed to equality and inclusion and to respecting and accommodating diversity including those differences arising from gender, civil status, family status, sexual orientation, religion, age, disability, race, ethnicity, membership of the Traveller community and socio-economic status, and any further grounds as may be referenced in equality legislation in the future' (TTC 2012, p. 6)

(continued)

13 Enhancing Inclusive Education Through Teacher Education Reforms

Table 13.1 (continued)

Country	Source	Standards expectations
New Zealand	Education Council New Zealand [ECNZ] (2017)	Professional Practice • 'Respecting the diversity of the heritage, language, identity and culture of all learners' (ECNZ 2017, p. 10) • 'Promoting inclusive practices to support the needs and abilities of all learners' (ECNZ 2017, p. 10) • 'Demonstrate high expectations for the learning outcomes of all learners, including for those learners with disabilities or learning support needs' (ECNZ 2017, p.20) • 'Develop an environment where the diversity and uniqueness of all learners are accepted and valued' (ECNZ 2017, p. 20) • 'Critically examine how my own assumptions and beliefs, including cultural beliefs, impact on practice and the achievement of learners with different abilities and needs, backgrounds, genders, identities, languages and cultures' (ECNZ 2017, p. 18)
United Kingdom	Department for Education [DfE] (2011) (applies to trainees as well as teachers)	'Adapt teaching to respond to the strengths and needs of all students: • Know when and how to differentiate appropriately, using approaches which enable pupils to be taught effectively • Have a secure understanding of how a range of factors can inhibit pupils' ability to learn, and how best to overcome these • Demonstrate an awareness of the physical, social and intellectual development of children, and know how to adapt teaching to support pupils' education at different stages of development • Have a clear understanding of the needs of all pupils, including those with special educational needs; those of high ability; those with English as an additional language; those with disabilities; and be able to use and evaluate distinctive teaching approaches to engage and support them' (DfE 2011, pp. 10–12)
USA (model standards)	Council of Chief State School Officers [CCSSO] (2011)	'The teacher uses understanding of individual differences and diverse cultures and communities to ensure inclusive learning environments that enable each learner to meet high standards: • [2(a)] The teacher designs, adapts, and delivers instruction to address each student's diverse learning strengths and needs and creates opportunities for students to demonstrate their learning in different ways • [2(f)] The teacher accesses resources, supports, and specialised assistance and services to meet particular learning differences or needs • [2(g)] The teacher understands students with exceptional needs, including those associated with disabilities and giftedness, and knows how to use strategies and resources to address these needs • [2(m)] The teacher respects learners as individuals with differing personal and family backgrounds and various skills, abilities, perspectives, talents, and interests' (CCSSO 2011, p. 11)

learning materials: the need for 'safe climate-resistant learning environments' (Education Sector Advisory Committee [Samoa] 2013, p. 7); availability of 'water, toilets and electricity' and sufficient classrooms (Department of Basic Education Republic of South Africa 2015, p. 45); and the challenge of language diversity, such as 860 languages in Papua New Guinea, and 'equivalent diversity in culture and traditions' (National Executive Council 2009, p. 4) with a goal to provide early childhood education in the language of the child's community (p. ix). Despite these major concerns, these countries remain committed to basic education plans that address equity for all and teacher education that builds teacher knowledge of inclusive education (see, e.g. VVOB vzw 2015).

The following analyses are therefore based in contexts where, despite frequently voiced teacher concerns regarding physical, human and financial resource support, provision of basic infrastructure and resources to support inclusive education is not the major issue.

Methodology

Data Collection

A critical, narrative-based review of relevant international teacher education reform literature between the dates of 2005 and 2017 was conducted. The methodological design incorporated characteristics included in systematic review methodology (Bearman et al. 2012). Systematised searching strategies, adopting an open approach to the literature, including databases and platforms used to source grey literature, were undertaken. The primary databases and reference sources included: Australian Catholic University's Electronic Library Catalogue, Google and Google Scholar, Commonwealth and State Government Department of Education Web sites and electronic platforms such as Twitter, ResearchGate and Academia. Text and reference lists of initially identified sources were hand-searched to identify additional relevant publications ('snowballing').

To address our basic question regarding the extent to which development of teacher capability in inclusive education has been considered in education reform and other documents, and to acknowledge the vast array of literature available, both inclusion criteria and exclusion criteria were adopted. Three overarching criteria were identified: first, literature targeting existing national and/or international teacher education reform, including review reports, policy, reform initiatives and professional standards, between the years of 2005 and 2017 was included; second, literature targeting existing national and/or international reforms on disability and inclusion in education, between the years of 2005 and 2017, was included; third, literature targeting existing national and international education reform at a broader level, including reports and reviews on national education initiatives (e.g. Norwegian Ministry of Education and Research n.d.), was excluded.

Keywords to identify sources based on these criteria included variations of the following: 'teacher education OR teacher education reforms', 'disability AND inclusion OR inclusive education', 'teacher education AND disability OR inclusion', 'disability AND education reforms AND Australia' and 'international teacher education reform AND diversity OR inclusion OR disability'. The outcome of these searches revealed a total of 15 relevant sources. These sources comprised: five national and international teacher education reform reports (Carter 2015; Craven et al. 2014; Donaldson 2010; Furlong 2015; Sahlberg et al. 2014); two international teacher education and inclusion reviews (Blanton et al. 2014; Darling-Hammond 2010); and eight government and UNESCO inclusive education documents (Cologon 2013; Deloitte Access Economics 2017; Department of Education and Training (DET) Victoria 2016a, b; Ministry of Education 2014, 2017; Collins et al. 2017; UNESCO 2017). An overview of the 15 selected sources is provided in Table 13.2.

Table 13.2 Overview of the selected sources

No.	Author(s) and publication year	Country[a]	Education setting[b]	Specific focus[c]	Coding density[d]
1	Carter (2015)	GB	PE, SE	TE	H
2	Craven et al. (2014)	AU	PE, SE	TE	VH
3	Donaldson (2010)	GB	PE, SE	TE	L
4	Furlong (2015)	GB	PE, SE	TE	VL
5	Sahlberg et al. (2014)	GB	PE, SE	TE	M
6	Blanton et al. (2014)	US	PE, SE	TE	H
7	Darling-Hammond (2010)	US	PE, SE	TE	M
8	Cologen (2013)	AU	PE, SE	IN	VH
9	Deloitte Access Economics (2017)	AU	PE, SE	IN	VH
10a	DET Victoria (2016a)	AU	PE, SE	IN	VH
10b	DET Victoria (2016b)	AU	PE, SE	IN	VH
11	Ministry of Education (2014)	CA	PE, SE	IN	L
12	Ministry of Education (2017)	CA	PE, SE	IN	VH
13	Collins et al. (2017)	CA	PE, SE	IN	VH
14	UNESCO (2017)	*	PE, SE	IN	VH

Note
[a]Country codes: United Kingdom (GB), Australia (AU), United States of America (US), Canada (CA), International (*)
[b]Education setting: primary/elementary education (PE), secondary education/high school (SE)
[c]Specific focus: teacher education (TE), inclusion (IN)
[d]Coding density: very high (VH), high (H), moderate (M), low (L), very low (VL)

Data Analysis

Using NVivo 11 qualitative data analysis software (QSR International 2015), four phases of data analysis were conducted (see e-Appendix 1 for detailed outcomes of each phase). In phase one, the 15 sources were imported into NVivo 11 as 'internal coding sources'. Following importation, word frequency queries and text search queries were conducted using key terms. The initial list of these key terms was collectively formed as part of a group discussion and included commonly cited terms within the lexicon of equity, inclusion and disability, namely inclusion, inclusive, disability, equity, access and participation. These initial key terms were then used to create nodes, or coding groups, and a corresponding node hierarchy (e.g. parent node, first-level child node, second-level child node). This node hierarchy formed the initial coding framework for the remaining phases of data analysis and is illustrated in e-Table 1 (e-Appendix 1). The imported sources were then auto-coded in accordance with these nodes, via text search queries, and aggregated to reveal the total number of key term references for the sources. For example, the results of an initial query revealed that the terms 'Accessibility and Access' were referenced 26 times in six ($n = 6$) documents.

In phase two, auto-coded sources were manually searched, assessed and noted for content relevance (i.e. context). Relevant key terms were then coded in vivo—that is, added to the initial node hierarchy based on terms or phrases used in the analysed texts, e.g. Carers and Care, Parents and Guardians, Justice, and Special Education—or noted and created at a later date. Following the creation of the new nodes and corresponding node hierarchies, additional text search queries were conducted and coded (see e-Table 2, e-Appendix 1) and again manually assessed for content relevance. All contextually inappropriate or irrelevant codes, from the initial and additional assessment processes, were manually deleted (see e-Table 3, e-Appendix 1).

In the third and fourth phases of analysis, the contextually appropriate coded sources were individually examined to assess the level to which equity and diversity were addressed or omitted in relation to teacher preparedness and capability in the teacher education reform documents. For example, while areas of high-density coding suggested sections of potential significance in relation to the focus concepts, areas of low-density coding suggested potentially significant areas of omission. Relevant data from the coded sources were then extracted, analysed and synthesised thematically.

Findings

International Teacher Education Reform Reports

The overall NVivo coding density of key terms in the five reform reports is shown in Fig. 13.2. While a range of characteristics involved in equity policies was included in our search and coding, Fig. 13.2 shows that the predominant reference points, if

Coding Density: Teacher Education Reforms

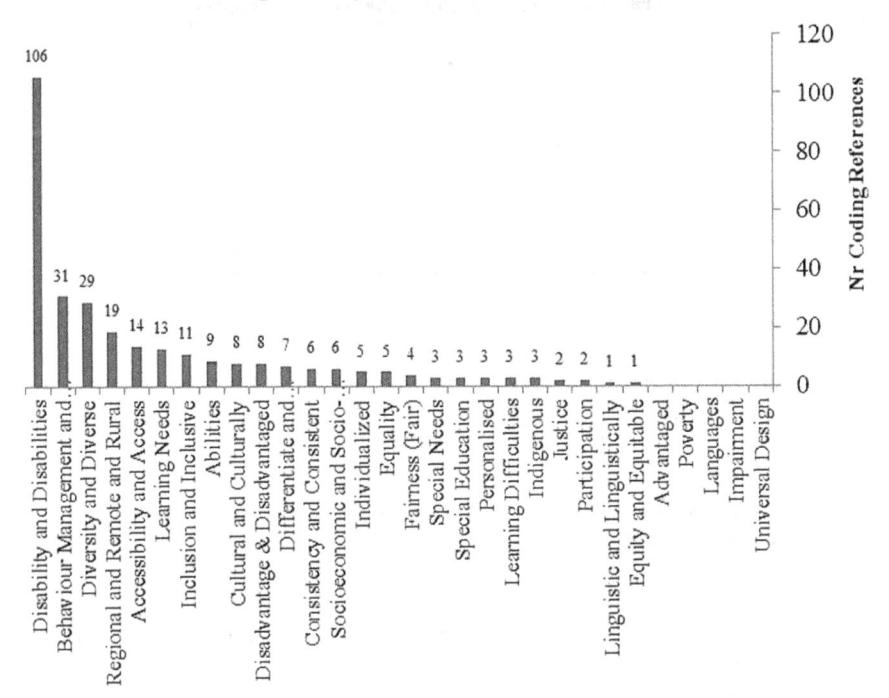

Fig. 13.2 Coding density of identified key terms for the five international teacher education reform reports

Behaviour Management is excluded as this was not a focus of our analyses, were Disability, Diversity, Location, Accessibility and Access, and Learning Needs. Remaining terms received few referents within the reports.

As Fig. 13.3 shows, analyses of the five reform reports revealed high- and low-density coding across the node hierarchy. For instance, while the second-level child node, Disability and Disabilities, accounted for 35% of the coding total ($N = 302$), with more than one-hundred coding references across the reports, these references were primarily derived from two sources—Carter (2015) and Craven et al. (2014)—which accounted for 90% of the coding total ($N = 106$), aligning with the coding density graphic illustrated in Fig. 13.3. As the remaining three sources failed to include these key terms, these findings suggest a potentially low level of consideration throughout those reports.

While closer examinations of the overall teacher education reform data revealed similar findings across the second-level child nodes of the node hierarchy, coding majorities were not always derived from the two dominant sources, Carter (2015) and Craven et al. (2014). For example, while the second-level child node, Diversity and Diverse, accounted for 10% of the coding total with nearly 30 coding references across the reports, 59% of coding for this node was derived from Sahlberg et al.

International Teacher Education Reform Reports

Furlong (2015) — VL
Donaldson (2010) — L
Sahlberg et al. (2014) — M
Carter (2015) — H
Craven et al. (2014) — VH

Coding Density Scale of Inclusion

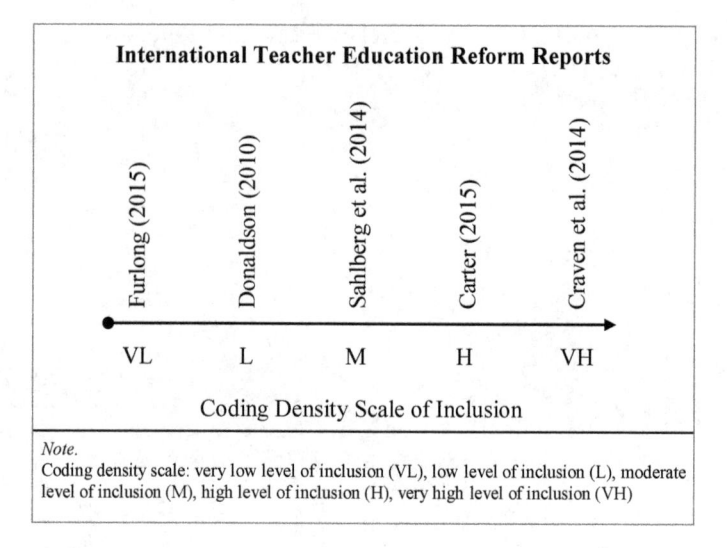

Note.
Coding density scale: very low level of inclusion (VL), low level of inclusion (L), moderate level of inclusion (M), high level of inclusion (H), very high level of inclusion (VH)

Fig. 13.3 An illustration of the relationship between coding density and inclusion in international teacher education reform reports

(2014), reflecting the moderate density coding level for Sahlberg et al., with the remaining 41% stemming from Craven et al. (2014). Thus, while a majority of the coding references across the hierarchy can be attributed to Craven et al. (2014) and Carter (2015), in some cases the remaining sources also contribute to the coding totals, despite their lower coding densities.

Our analyses of the reports, therefore, revealed mixed findings. Craven et al. (2014) and Carter (2015) reviewed initial teacher education in Australia and England (respectively) to inform improvements in teacher preparation and practice. The content analyses revealed several relevant sections of text relating to diversity and inclusion, most of which directly related to the target context of inclusive teacher preparation and practice, with a focus on disability, equity and accountability. Both reports made specific recommendations for inclusive education: 'special educational needs and disabilities should be included in a framework for ITT [initial teacher training] content' (Carter 2015, Recommendation 1g, p. 11); and, for inclusive education to be a 'core requirement of all teachers' (Craven et al. 2014, p. 20), 'higher education providers [should] equip pre-service teachers with … skills to assess the learning needs of all students … [and] effectively engage with parents about the progress of their children' (Recommendation 15–16, p. xiii). Thus, the higher-density coding with respect to inclusive education throughout these reports reflected targeted recognition and promotion of inclusion in terms of culture, linguistics, learning difficulties, disability, abilities, diversity, learning needs, special needs, socio-economic(s), behaviour management, differentiation, parents and carers:

> The diversity of students in Australian classrooms requires teachers to be prepared to engage with students who are culturally and linguistically diverse and have specific learning difficulties or disabilities. Initial teacher education programs must ensure pre-service teachers learn to apply evidence-based theory to their teaching strategies to cater for the distribution of abilities in every classroom. (Craven et al. 2014, pp. 19–20)

and

> It is important that ITT [Initial Teacher Education] recognises that good teaching for SEND [Special Educational Needs and Disabilities] is good teaching for all children. ITT should introduce trainees to the most common issues they will encounter and practical strategies for addressing these. There should be an emphasis on instilling a clear expectation of on-going development. Trainees should be introduced to how to work with a range of colleagues and professionals, as well as parents and carers, to support children with SEND. (Carter 2015, p. 10)

and concerns these were not being met

> The Advisory Group heard concerns that beginning teachers were not adequately equipped to address diverse student learning needs and work with cultural and community complexities. (Craven et al. 2014, p. 20)

By contrast, content analyses of Sahlberg et al.'s (2014) evaluation of the teacher education system in Northern Ireland revealed many instances of text related to diversity and inclusion that applied generally to teacher education and teaching all students, rather than more specific direction to effective preparation of teachers to meet the needs of diverse learners. Therefore, while the evaluation sought to provide recommendations for future advancements in teacher education practice, data analyses revealed moderate density coding throughout the review, suggesting a moderate level of targeted recognition and promotion of inclusion. No specific recommendations were made regarding inclusive education in practice, and hence, no clear guidance on how to achieve this in teacher education programs is provided. Donaldson's (2010) review of teacher education reform and practice in Scotland focused on building the professional capacity of teachers and strengthening the existing teacher education system. Content analyses revealed that while some sections of text related to diversity and inclusion, most of these applied generally to teacher education and/or the wider school cohort. Only one of the Donaldson's 50 recommendations partially relates to inclusive education: '[initial teacher training] should include more substantial experience for all prospective teachers in relating to parents and working with other professionals' (Recommendation 21, p. 92). These findings are illustrated respectively in the following excerpts.

> The UU [University of Ulster] lists among the challenges facing teacher education in Northern Ireland "the needs of a divided society emerging from conflict", and refers to its practice of encouraging students to learn from each other and cross boundaries between their practice schools…in the context of local sectarian divides". …. Stranmillis University College … [shows commitment] to shared education in the … program … with St Mary's University College entitled CREDIT (Classrooms Reimagined: Education in Diversity and Inclusion for Teachers), which "involves teachers working in all phases and sectors to help them to develop skills and confidence in dealing with issues of diversity, inclusion and community cohesion in the classroom and on a whole-school basis". (Sahlberg et al. 2014, pp. 28–29)

and

> All new teachers in Scotland should be aware of the key challenges …, [including] doing more to overcome the effects of disadvantage and deprivation on educational outcomes, and contribute personally to addressing these. In addition to developing their subject and pedagogical knowledge and skills, therefore, all new teachers should be confident in their ability to: address underachievement, including the potential effects of social disadvantage; …address additional support needs (particularly dyslexia and autistic spectrum disorders)… (Donaldson 2010, p. 36)

Finally, data analyses of Furlong's (2015) review of initial teacher training in Wales to raise the quality of existing provisions and identify potential strategies for improvement revealed very few relevant sections of text relating to diversity and inclusion and effectively preparing teachers for the diversity of students. Content analyses revealed very low-density coding throughout the report, suggesting very low levels of targeted recognition and promotion of inclusion. No report recommendations target how inclusive education should be achieved. These findings are illustrated in the following excerpt which relates to the node of individualisation (e.g. second-order child node, 'Individualized').

> If Wales was to achieve the school system that it needs and wants in the future, then … [i]t needs teachers who … are able to take a sharper focus on the needs of individual learners, including helping them in 'learning how to learn'… (Furlong 2015, p. 3)

International Teacher Education and Inclusion Reviews

Analyses of the two international teacher education and inclusion reviews revealed varying findings. Blanton et al.'s (2014) historical review of US teacher education reform initiatives was framed by the assumption that all teachers are responsible for teaching students with disabilities. Content analyses revealed several relevant sections of text relating to diversity and inclusion, most of which related directly to the target context of inclusive teacher preparation and practice, with a focus on disability, equity and accountability. Thus, high-density coding was evident throughout the review, suggesting a high level of targeted recognition and promotion of inclusion. In contrast, content analyses of Darling-Hammond's (2010) review of US teacher education revealed that while several relevant sections of text related to diversity and inclusion, many of these applied generally to teacher education and teaching all students, rather than directly identifying teacher preparation to meet the needs of diverse learners. While her review was framed by the assumption that effective teacher preparation can transform teaching and learning for all students, data analyses revealed moderate density coding throughout the review, suggesting merely a moderate level of targeted recognition and promotion of inclusion.

Government and UNESCO Inclusive Education Documents

Teacher preparation and practice were addressed with significant purpose in the majority of the eight reviewed inclusive education documents from Australia, Canada and UNESCO, which focused predominantly on students with disability. Australian states, Queensland (Deloitte Access Economics 2017) and Victoria (Department of Education and Training [DET] 2016a, b) have undertaken reviews of the state of inclusive and equitable education for these students. The Victorian review, and related state government response, acknowledged that while substantial funding has been available for inclusive education, delivery in practice was flawed. They recommended improved future delivery of effective teacher education in pre-service teacher training and relevant professional development for experienced teachers.

> From September 2016, all registered teachers will have to have either undertaken relevant professional development in the last two years or take it before renewing their registration in September 2017. From 2016, all initial teacher education programs must also include specific learning activities about teaching students with disabilities in order to be accredited by the Victorian Institute of Teaching. (DET 2016b, p. 7)

The review also recommended that teacher capability is further developed through an 'Inclusive Education Workforce Capability Strategy', including 'professional learning opportunities relevant to disability and inclusive education practices at a system, school and classroom level' (DET 2016a, p. 76). Further, the review recommended a feasibility study to establish a Victorian Inclusive Education Institute and collaborate with 'universities and not-for-profit advocacy groups to further advance inclusive education knowledge and skills' (DET 2016a, p. 76).

The Queensland review of students with disability in government schools provided comparable recommendations, with its authors suggesting that the current state of pre-service education in inclusive education was inadequate. The review acknowledged that Queensland, like other school systems internationally, needed to engage more effectively to value student diversity and allow all students to realise their full potential.

> Schools have struggled to value diversity and difference and turn difference into a tool for improving the quality of teaching and learning. Effectively responding to the challenges and opportunities of student differences – and ensuring that education systems and practices support all students engaging with education in a manner that allows them to realise their potential – requires the most careful crafting of policy, programs and practices. (Deloitte Access Economics 2017, p. i)

Developing policy, workforce capability and training was noted as a key finding in the review. A recommendation was for a position to be established to coordinate professional development in inclusive education across state schooling, and engagement of the state department with universities to ensure inclusive education curriculum in teacher training and education.

> Initial teacher education programs are not delivering the curriculum required for school staff to develop these skills – with particular reference drawn to practical education within diverse classrooms and instruction in UDL. (Deloitte Access Economics 2017, p. xvi)

The Queensland review did find 'examples of leading international practice in Queensland state schools' (Deloitte Access Economics 2017, p. iii), which was encouraging.

The third Australian document, an issues paper by Cologon (2013), targeting school principals, teachers, support staff and the wider community, focused principally on policy recommendations for children with disabilities in school settings.

> Bringing about inclusive education requires providing education in disability studies and inclusion as an essential component of teacher education and ongoing professional development for all teachers and all other professionals involved in supporting inclusive education. (p. 35)

Cologon noted in her recommendations that improvement in inclusive teacher education required an attitudinal change in teacher thinking, '[t]eacher education is directly related to teacher attitudes' (p. 32). Cologon emphasised teacher engagement in critical thinking and reflection to enhance teachers' professional knowledge and practice in inclusive education.

Although all three Australian documents emphasised education for all, the Canadian inclusive education review documents, two from Ontario (Ministry of Education [MoE] 2014, 2017) and the third from Newfoundland and Labrador (Collins et al. 2017), were dissimilar in approach and discussion of inclusive and equitable education. Ontario's 2014 document (MoE 2014) primarily took a social justice position and coded highly for the keywords, 'inclusion' and 'equity'. It broadly addressed how teachers, and specifically a school board, are best situated to implement effective inclusive education practice. Professional learning was discussed generally in the setting of proposed implementation guidelines and tabulated as suggested key points. The 2017 Ontario document (MoE 2017), with distinct focus on disability in inclusive and equitable education for all emphasised this thinking as a field that requires its own dedicated expertise. This contrasted with Cologon's Australian perspective that 'perpetuation of the 'special' education paradigm—rather than resulting in inclusive education—further entrenches ableist thinking and practices. Transformation of educational systems, policies and practices is required' (2013, p. 35). The 2017 Ontario document, therefore, demonstrates variations in thinking on inclusive education and disability across countries. Teacher education and training are mentioned briefly in the document under current teacher practice standards and recommendations and discussed loosely throughout.

The Newfoundland and Labrador review (Collins et al. 2017) focused primarily on disability in education, with particular reference to UDL, providing recommendations and an action plan for teacher education and training, '(t)eachers have a profound impact on student learning. Investment in teachers from the beginning of their teacher education programs and throughout their careers is directly related to improved educational outcomes for students' (p. 113). Five recommendations addressed initial and ongoing teacher education to improve proficiency in inclusive education practices, as well as the need for 'a review of the standards for teacher certification to determine the alignment between the requirements for certification, the needs of the school system and initial teacher education programs' (p. 118). These recommendations emphasise the perceived importance of improving future inclusive educational outcomes for all students in the province through more effective teacher preparation and practice.

The final document, UNESCO (2017), focused primarily on equity and inclusion and students with disability as a guide for countries to 'review and evaluate the level of equity and inclusion in existing policies' (p. 47). It addressed strategies for participation, presence and achievement for all learners and ways in which to address students at risk of underachievement, marginalisation and exclusion. Recommendations in regard to teacher preparation for inclusive and equitable education were highlighted as four core values:

1. Valuing learner diversity: Students' differences are viewed as a resource and an asset to education;

2. Supporting all learners: Teachers have high expectations for all learners' achievements;

3. Working with others: Collaboration and teamwork are essential approaches for all teachers; and

4. Continuing personal professional development: Teaching is a learning activity and teachers must accept responsibility for their own lifelong learning.

Embedding these values in teacher education programs can help empower teachers and support them in developing a wider range of responses to learners who experience difficulties in their learning. Being explicit about these values helps to establish the potential of teacher education to be a high-leverage activity in bringing about change. (UNESCO 2017, p. 35)

Discussion and Conclusion

Our content analyses have highlighted the differing extent to which teacher education reform documents and other relevant documents have addressed equity in education and the preparation of teachers to engage in inclusive education practices for all students. They make differing recommendations regarding teacher education programs and the reforms needed.

Preparing teachers to engage effectively with inclusive education in classrooms is not a simple case of content preparation or strategy development. Research on inclusive practice with students with disability has shown that many factors are at play. Teacher effectiveness in inclusive education in mainstream schooling relates to reported feelings of self-efficacy and adequacy of training and support (Avramidis and Norwich 2010; Forlin et al. 2008; Pearce et al. 2010; Shaddock et al. 2009). As Cologon had noted, research shows that teacher attitudes and values impact on teaching practice. Practice is not just the result of knowledge and confidence but incorporates teachers' values, beliefs, emotions and dispositions that create their teaching identity—identity that is not fixed but changes over time according to the external environment (Avramidis and Norwich 2010; Beijaard et al. 2004; Cologon 2013; Day et al. 2006; Looney et al. 2017). Evidence is mixed as to whether teachers become more positive or negative about inclusive education with classroom experience. Research results identify contrasting findings that teachers with less teaching experience have positive attitudes to inclusion and that experience is not significantly related to attitude (Avramidis and Norwich 2010). Other research shows that as teachers gain experience with students with disabilities, their confidence increases (Cologon 2013), although whether this confidence was due to teaching experience or general experience is not clear. Reasons as to whether and how attitudes change have not been investigated.

Attitudes and values also go beyond teachers to include the whole school ethos, with research identifying the significant role that school principals play and should play in establishing an ethos of inclusive education reflecting their own attitudes and beliefs (Avramidis and Norwich 2010; Graham and Scott 2016). Changing attitudes, values and beliefs requires more than encouragement to teachers and teacher education students about values they should hold; commitment requires deeper philosophical understandings than 'positive attitudes' or 'acceptance' (Avramidis and Norwich 2010). Our initial overview of international professional teacher standards had identified that teacher values and affective underpinnings of inclusive education were seen by some regulatory authorities to be as critical as pedagogical knowledge and strategies.

Core to teacher education students' beliefs and values must be the attitudes of teacher educators. While a substantial body of research has investigated teacher attitudes to inclusive education, little research has examined attitudes of teacher educators. Although one study found that teacher educators on average held more positive attitudes towards inclusive education than student teachers or practicing teachers (Casperson 2013), teacher educator values and beliefs regarding inclusive education can be just as varied as those of teachers (Casperson 2013; Lambe 2011). While the role teacher education programs should play in shaping teacher education students' values, morals and beliefs is not an uncontested area (Casperson 2013), it is clear that teacher educators and ITE programs are critical and not neutral in this regard (Casperson 2013; Lambe 2011).

We therefore identify as the *next question for research and practice* in teacher education reforms, the need to address two elements of teacher education provision to enhance inclusive education. First, we would argue that further research is needed to understand teacher educators' attitudes regarding inclusive education and how these impact on teacher education students. We need greater understanding of the emotions, beliefs, values and attitudes of teacher education staff and students to enable implementation of the spirit of inclusive education.

Second, there is a need for further research into the nature of teacher education programs and the best way to enhance inclusive education. Most models of teacher education programs focus on imparting curriculum knowledge and teaching strategies, with few examining the 'balance between the epistemic and moral purposes of teacher education' (Casperson 2013, p. 110). In our qualitative analyses of the teacher education reform documents, even when we found high-density reference to inclusive education and its significance in teacher preparation, the focus was on the need for programs to impart knowledge, 'equipp[ing]' teachers with a 'broad range of skills and strategies' to respond to 'diverse student learning needs' (Craven et al. 2014, p. 20). The expectation is that teacher education students will 'develop' the appropriate attitudes to inclusive education. The reports that aspired to inclusive education and social justice for all took a broader focus, identifying the need for 'commitment to genuine inclusive education at all levels' (Cologon 2013, p. 46), and the crucial role not only teachers play but also other members of the school and general community and policy makers (UNESCO 2017). Opportunities within program constructions to reflect on teacher educator and teacher student values may, therefore, be as critical to create reform as focus on theoretical or practical content (Casperson 2013; Cologon 2013; Graham and Scott 2016). There is therefore a need for further exploration into how inclusive education reforms identified in teacher education reforms can be achieved through teacher education program reforms.

We emphasise once more that the research cited here has tended to focus on students with disabilities. However, there is a gap in our research knowledge about how these findings relate inclusive education to address other factors within our schooling systems that can lead to student disadvantage, such as socio-economic circumstances, homelessness, gender, race, culture and language. The Australian Melbourne Declaration, echoing the general principles of international human rights principles, focuses on equity that provides high-quality education and 'nurtures' the learning of every child within a 'culture of high expectations in schools' (MCEETYA 2008, p. 11). Teacher education programs play a significant role.

References

Ackah, F. (2016). *Implementation of inclusive early childhood education policy and change in Ghana: Four case sites of practice* (Unpublished doctoral thesis). Griffith University, Brisbane, Australia. Retrieved December 19, 2017 from http://librarycatalogue.griffith.edu.au/record=b2357307.
Anti-Discrimination Act 1993 (NT) (Austl.).
Anti-Discrimination Act 1977 (NSW) (Austl.).
Anti-Discrimination Act 1988 (Tas) (Austl.).
Anti-Discrimination Act 1991 (Qld) (Austl.).
Australian Bureau of Statistics [ABS]. (2016). Schools, Australia, 2016. Catalogue no. 4221.0. Retrieved December 19, 2017 from http://www.abs.gov.au/ausstats/abs@.nsf/mf/4221.0.
Australian Council on Educational Research. (2016). *TIMSS 2015: a first look at Australia's results*. Melbourne, Victoria: ACER.
Australian Institute for Teaching and School Leadership [AITSL]. (2011). *National professional standards for teachers*. Retrieved December 19, 2017 from https://www.aitsl.edu.au/teach/standards.
Avramidis, E., & Norwich, B. (2010). Teachers' attitudes towards integration/inclusion: a review of the literature. *European Journal of Special Needs Education, 17*(2), 129–147. https://doi.org/10.1080/08856250210129056.
Bearman, M., Smith, C., Carbone, A., Slade, S., Baik, C., Hughes-Warrington, M., et al. (2012). Systematic review methodology in higher education. *Higher Education Research and Development, 31*(5), 625–640. https://doi.org/10.1080/07294360.2012.702735.
Beijaard, D., Meijer, P. C., & Verloop, N. (2004). Reconsidering research on teachers' professional identity. *Teaching and Teacher Education, 20,* 107–128. https://doi.org/10.1016/j.tate.2003.07.001.

Blanton, L., Pugach, M., Boveda, M. (2014). *Teacher education reform initiatives and special education: Convergence, divergence, and missed opportunities.* Retrieved December 19, 2017 from http://ceedar.education.ufl.edu/wp-content/uploads/2014/09/LS-3_FINAL_09-20-14.pdf.
British Columbia Ministry of Education [BCME]. (2012). *Standards for the education, competence and professional conduct of educators in British Columbia* (4th ed.). Retrieved December 19, 2017 from https://www.bcteacherregulation.ca/documents/AboutUs/Standards/edu_stds.pdf.
Carter, A. (2015). *Carter review of initial teacher training.* Department of Education, London, England. Retrieved December 19, 2017 from https://www.gov.uk/government/uploads/system/uploads/attachment_data/file/399957/Carter_Review.pdf.
Casperson, J. (2013). The valuation of knowledge and normative reflection in teacher qualification. A comparison of teacher educators, novice and experienced teachers. *Teaching and Teacher Education, 30,* 109–119.
Collins, A., Philpott, D., Fushall, M., Wakeham, M., Strong, C., & Tulk-Lane, S. (2017). *Now is the time: The next chapter in education in Newfoundland and Labrador.* Retrieved December 19, 2017 from http://www.ed.gov.nl.ca/edu/task_force/report.pdf.
Cologon, K. (2013).*Inclusion in education: towards equality for students with disability* (Issues paper). Children and Families Research Centre, Institute of Early Childhood, Macquarie University, Sydney, Australia. Retrieved January 10, 2018 from http://apo.org.au/node/36129.
Committee, Education Sector Advisory. (2013). *Samoa education sector plan: Improved focus on training and quality outcomes.* Samoa: Government of Samoa.
Council of Chief State School Officers [CCSSO]. (2011). *InTASC model core teaching standards: a resource for state dialogue.* Retrieved 19 Dec 2017 from http://www.ccsso.org/resource-library/intasc-model-core-teaching-standards.
Craven, G., Beswick, K., Fleming, J., Fletcher, T., Green, M., Jensen, B., et al. (2014). *Action now: classroom ready teachers.* Retrieved December 19, 2017 from https://docs.education.gov.au/system/files/doc/other/action_now_classroom_ready_teachers_print.pdf.
Cumming, J. J., & Dickson, E. A. (2007). Equity in assessment: Discrimination and disability issues from an Australian legal perspective. *Education and the Law, 19*(3), 201–220. https://doi.org/10.1080/09539960701762854.
Darling-Hammond, L. (2010). Teacher education and the American future. *Journal of Teacher Education, 61*(1–2), 35–47. https://doi.org/10.1177/0022487109348024.
Day, C., Kington, A., Stobart, G., & Sammons, P. (2006). The personal and professional selves of teachers: Stable and unstable identities. *British Educational Research Journal, 32,* 601–616. https://doi.org/10.1080/01411920600775316.
Deloitte Access Economics. (2017).*Review of education for students with disability in Queensland state schools.* Department of Education and Training, Brisbane, Australia. Retrieved December 19, 2017 from http://education.qld.gov.au/schools/disability/docs/disability-review-report.pdf.
Department for Education-United Kingdom [DfE]. (2011). *Teachers' standards.* Retrieved December 19, 2017 from https://www.gov.uk/government/publications/teachers-standards.
Department of Basic Education Republic of South Africa. (2015). *Action plan to 2019. Towards the realization of schooling 2030.* Retrieved December 19, 2017 from https://www.education.gov.za/Portals/0/Documents/Publications/Action%20Plan%202019.pdf?ver=2015-11-11-162424-417.
Department of Education and Training Victoria. (2016a). *The education state: review of the program for students with disabilities.* Department of Education and Training, Victoria, Melbourne, Australia. Retrieved December 19, 2017 from http://www.education.vic.gov.au/Documents/about/department/PSD-Review-Report.pdf.
Department of Education and Training Victoria. (2016b). *Inclusive education for all students with disabilities and additional needs: The government's response to the review of the program for students with disabilities.* Department of Education and Training, Victoria, Melbourne, Australia. Retrieved December 19, 2017 from http://www.education.vic.gov.au/Documents/about/department/PSD-Review-Response.pdf
Dickson, E. A. (2006). Disability standards for education and the obligation of reasonable adjustment. *Australia and New Zealand Journal of Law and Education, 11*(2), 23–42.

Disability Discrimination Act 1992 (Cth) (Austl.).
Disability Standards for Education 2005 (Cth) (Austl.).
Discrimination Act 1991 (ACT) (Austl.).
Donaldson, G. (2010). *Teaching Scotland's future: Report of a review of teacher education in Scotland. Edinburgh, Scotland: The Scottish Government*. Retrieved December 19, 2017 from http://www.gov.scot/Resource/Doc/337626/0110852.pdf.
Education Council. (2016). *Nationally consistent collection of data: School students with disability: 2016 emergent data on students in Australian schools receiving adjustments for disability*. Retrieved January 9, 2018 from http://www.educationcouncil.edu.au/site/DefaultSite/filesystem/documents/Reports%20and%20publications/ED17-0046%20SCH%20NCCD%20Report%202017_ACC.PDF.
Education Council New Zealand [ECNZ]. (2017). *Our code. Our standards. Code of professional responsibility and standards for the teaching profession*. Retrieved December 19, 2017 from https://www.educationcouncil.org.nz/content/our-code-our-standards.
Equal Opportunity Act 1984 (SA) (Austl.).
Equal Opportunity Act 1984 (WA) (Austl.).
Equal Opportunity Act 2010 (Vic) (Austl.).
Equality Act 2010 (UK) s. 85.6.
European Agency for Special Needs and Inclusive Education. (2017). *The Agency's position on inclusive education systems*. Retrieved December 19, 2017 from https://www.european-agency.org/about-us/who-we-are/position-on-inclusive-education-systems.
Forlin, C., Keen, M., & Barrett, E. (2008). The concerns of mainstream teachers: Coping with inclusivity in an Australian context. *International Journal of Disability, Development and Education, 55*(3), 251–264.
Furlong, J. (2015). *Teaching tomorrow's teachers. Options for the future of initial teacher education in Wales (Report to Huw Lewis, Minister for Education and Skills)*. Oxford University, Oxford, England. Retrieved December 19, 2017 from http://gov.wales/topics/educationandskills/publications/wagreviews/teaching-tomorrows-teachers/?lang=en.
Graham, L., & Scott, W. (2016). *Teacher preparation for inclusive education: Initial teacher education and in-service professional development*. Report prepared for the Victorian Department of Education and Training. Melbourne Graduate School of Education, Melbourne, Australia. Retrieved December 19, 2017 from http://www.deafeducation.vic.edu.au/Documents/NewsEvents/LitRevIncTe.pdf.
Hehir, T. (2009). Policy foundations of universal design for learning. In D. T. Gordon, J. W. Gravel, & L. A. Schifter (Eds.), *A policy reader in universal design for learning* (pp. 35–45). Cambridge, MA: Harvard Education Press.
Lambe, J. (2011). Pre-service education and attitudes towards inclusion: The role of the teacher educator within a permeated teaching model. *International Journal of Inclusive Education, 15*, 975–999. https://doi.org/10.1080/13603110903490705.
Long, B. (2015). *An estimate of the economic effects of the implementation of the National Disability Insurance Scheme*. The Centre for Applied Disability Research, Sydney, Australia. Retrieved December 19, 2017 from http://www.cadr.org.au/images/Publications_Files/ndis_economic_benefits%20main%20(1).pdf.
Looney, A., Cumming, J., van der Kleij, F., & Harris, K. (2017). Reconceptualising the role of teachers as assessors: teacher assessment identity. *Assessment in Education: Principles, Policy & Practice*. https://doi.org/10.1080/0969594X.2016.1268090.
Ministerial Council on Education, Employment, Training and Youth Affairs [MCEETYA]. (2008). *Melbourne declaration on educational goals for young Australians*. Retrieved December 19, 2017 from http://www.scseec.edu.au/site/DefaultSite/filesystem/documents/Reports%20and%20publications/Publications/National%20goals%20for%20schooling/National_Declaration_on_the_Educational_Goals_for_Young_Australians.pdf.

Ministry of Education. (2014). *Equity and inclusive education in Ontario schools*. Author, Ontario, Canada. Retrieved January 10, 2018 from http://www.edu.gov.on.ca/eng/policyfunding/inclusiveguide.pdf.

Ministry of Education. (2017). *Special education in Ontario: Kindergarten to grade 12: Policy and resource guide (Draft)*. Author, Ontario, Canada. Retrieved December 19, 2017 from http://www.edu.gov.on.ca/eng/document/policy/os/onschools_2017e.pdf.

National Executive Council. (2009). *Achieving universal education for a better future: Universal basic education plan 2010–2019*. Waigani, Papua New Guinea: Papua New Guinea Department of Education.

Norwegian Ministry of Education and Research. (n.d.) *Education: From kindergarten to adult education*. Retrieved December 19, 2017 from https://www.udir.no/Upload/Brosjyrer/5/Education_in_Norway.pdf?epslanguage=no.

Ontario College of Teachers [OCT]. (2017). *Professional standards*. Retrieved December 19, 2017 from http://www.oct.ca/public/professional-standards.

Pearce, M., Campbell-Evans, G., & Gray, J. (2010). Capacity to be inclusive: Secondary teachers' perspective. *Special Education Perspectives, 19*(1), 15–27.

Policy Scotland. (2015). *Policy implementation in inclusive education*. Retrieved December 19, 2017 from http://policyscotland.gla.ac.uk/policy-implementation-in-inclusive-education/.

QSR International. (2015). *NVivo qualitative data analysis software* (Version 11).

Sahlberg, P., Broadfoot, P., Coolahan, J., Furlong, J., & Kirk, G. (2014). *Aspiring to excellence: Final report of the international review panel on the structure of initial teacher education in Northern Ireland* (Report to the Minister for Employment and Learning). Department for Employment and Learning, Belfast, Ireland. Retrieved December 19, 2017 from http://dera.ioe.ac.uk/20454/1/aspiring-to-excellence-review-panel-final-report.pdf.

Shaddock, A., MacDonald, N., Hook, J., Giorcelli, L., & Arthur-Kelly, M. (2009). *Disability, diversity and tides that lift all boats: Review of special education in the ACT*. Chiswick, Australia: Service Initiatives Pty Ltd.

The Teaching Council [TTC]. (2012). *Code of professional conduct for teachers* (2nd ed.). The teaching council: Maynooth, Ireland. Retrieved January 11, 2018 from http://www.teachingcouncil.ie/en/Publications/Fitness-to-Teach/Code-of-Professional-Conduct-for-Teachers.pdf.

United Nations [UN] General Assembly. (1948). *Universal declaration of human rights*. Retrieved December 19, 2017 from http://www.ohchr.org/EN/UDHR/Documents/UDHR_Translations/eng.pdf.

United Nations [UN] General Assembly. (1966). *International convention on the elimination of all forms of racial discrimination*. Retrieved January 10, 2017 from https://treaties.un.org/doc/Publication/MTDSG/Volume%20I/Chapter%20IV/IV-2.en.pdf.

United Nations [UN] General Assembly. (1989). *Convention on the rights of the child*. Retrieved January 10, 2017 from http://www.unhcr.org/refworld/docid/3ae6b38f0.html.

United Nations [UN] General Assembly. (2007). *Convention on the rights of persons with disabilities*. New York, NY: United Nations.

United Nations Educational, Scientific and Cultural Organisation [UNESCO]. (1994). The Salamanca statement and framework for action on special needs education. Retrieved December 19, 2017 from http://www.unesco.org/education/pdf/SALAMA_E.PDF.

United Nations Educational, Scientific and Cultural Organization [UNESCO]. (2017). *A guide for ensuring inclusion and equity in education*. UNESCO, Paris, France. Retrieved December 19, 2017 from http://unesdoc.unesco.org/images/0024/002482/248254e.pdf.

VVOB vzw. (2015). *South Africa—Improving inclusive teaching in primary schools*. Retrieved December 19, 2017 from http://www.vvob.be/vvob/en/programmes/south-africa-teaching-and-learning-inclusive-education.

Joy Cumming is Professor and Research Director of Assessment, Evaluation and Student Learning in the Institute for Learning Sciences and Teacher Education (ILSTE), Australian Catholic University. She is a former secondary school English and mathematics teacher. Her major research focuses are educational assessment and accountability. She is leading a major Australian Research Council Discovery Project on working with teachers to provide adjustments in summative assessments for students with disability in mainstream subjects.

Megan Tones is a Researcher with the Assessment, Evaluation and Student Learning Research concentration in the Institute for Learning Sciences and Teacher Education (ILSTE), Australian Catholic University. Her focus is on quantitative methodology, and she has contributed to a range of education projects on Indigenous and disability inclusive education, and workplace learning. Within the health domain, her projects have focused on mental health, occupational injuries, quality of life and rare diseases. During her 13-year research career, she has co-authored over 30 publications in the fields of lifespan development psychology, workplace education, health and quality of life.

Chantelle Day is Research Assistant to the Assessment, Evaluation and Student Learning Research concentration at the Institute for Learning Sciences and Teacher Education (ILSTE), Australian Catholic University. Her doctoral research explored the educational experiences and support needs of young adult carers in Australian higher education. With undergraduate and postgraduate degrees in Psychology and Education, her areas of expertise include higher education, student affairs, student experience and engagement, sociology of education, equity and inclusive education, social and education policy, and educational psychology.

Elizabeth Heck has a background in secondary media education, short filmmaking and community media practice. She is a Research Assistant with the Assessment, Evaluation and Student Learning Research concentration in the Institute for Learning Sciences and Teacher Education (ILSTE), Australian Catholic University. Elizabeth completed her Ph.D. in social learning in community media, arts and cultural organisations in 2016 and has an interest in amplifying marginalised voices through storytelling and community media education. She has been the administration officer for the Australian Teachers of Media (Qld) for the past 7 years and is actively involved in this field. Her current role with the ILSTE includes research into inclusive education and assessment practices, further contributing to her research interests in both student and community learning.

Chapter 14
Is Quality Initial Teacher Education Where the Music Stops? Conceptualizing the Becoming of a Teacher: Lessons from the Field

Anna E. Du Plessis

Introduction

Initial teacher education (ITE)—the foundation of a teacher's future—is expected to be supported by a graduated program of well-tailored, challenging pedagogical knowledge and skill development designed to continuously improve teaching practices. Preparing prospective teachers for the profession is a process of constructing and internalizing new knowledge and skills while changing views and beliefs. In this chapter, graduate teachers are defined as first-year teachers, and beginning teachers are defined as teachers in their first 5 years of teaching.

Frequent criticism of teacher education as the agent that effectively prepares prospective teachers to be innovators and mediators of educational change (Saud and Johnston 2006) makes it not only necessary to look at ITE, but to move to the teaching space *beyond* ITE. Saud and Johnston (2006) summarize key issues, such as the development of field-based and integrated curriculum for pre-service teachers while keeping close collaboration with schools, cross-cultural influences and specific contexts in mind. This is justified by the strong link that is supposed to exist between ITE and the expectations for quality graduates entering the workplace.

It is, however, necessary to take a close look at what happens to graduates once they enter the workforce. Kelchtermans (2009) claims that a teaching career is 'one's learning process "on the job"' (p. 29). *On the job* learning means that teachers appreciate the significance of moment-by-moment decisions (Schoenfeld 2014) to inform education as '...indispensable in strengthening the bonds that hold communities and societies together' (United Nations Educational, Scientific and Cultural Organization [UNESCO] 2013, p. 12). Decisions taken in the classroom context affect not only students' learning but also their perceptions of the learning process they share with

---

A. E. Du Plessis (✉)
Institute for Learning Sciences and Teacher Education, Australian Catholic University, Brisbane, Australia
e-mail: Anna.DuPlessis@acu.edu.au

others beyond the classroom, which includes parents and the wider school community. Grant and McKinley (2011) state that practices and relations are at the core of the art of teaching and that knowledge of teaching is produced 'in the process of interaction' (p. 378). This chapter focuses on becoming and being a teacher beyond the ITE phase.

The Teaching and Learning International Survey (TALIS) report 2013 states that school principals, reporting on resource issues, rate the shortages of qualified and/or well-performing teachers at 47.8% (Freeman et al. 2014; OECD 2014). This emphasizes that the music does not stop with ITE itself and that context-specific professional learning and development have to address teachers' professional needs. The TALIS report also raises the following questions: (1) Why is ITE unable to adequately prepare pre-service teachers? (2) Is ITE doing a good enough job?, and (3) Is there a lack of workforce planning?

Being a teacher involves specific beliefs: significantly, 92.9% of teachers in Australia report a belief that their role is to facilitate students' own learning (Freeman et al. 2014). The process of becoming a teacher starts with intrinsic, altruistic or extrinsic motivation (Gore et al. 2015). This research further shows that people choose to become teachers because of a high intrinsic motivation. It also shows that they are motivated by their passion for and love of the teaching profession, as well as by their interest, skills development, satisfaction and the sense of accomplishment they expect to get.

Butt et al. (2010) and Curtis (2012) stress that prospective teachers aspire to have just such a meaningful engagement with the subjects they teach. The logical reasoning would then be that ITE will tap into and focus on the intrinsic motivation of prospective teachers or pre-service teachers and the desire of prospective teachers to engage with specific subject areas, fields or year levels. Research (Du Plessis 2014, 2017) shows that teachers often find themselves in challenging teaching positions for which they are not fully prepared or qualified, leaving them to critically question their teaching ability and capacity.

An experienced lead teacher (F1) suggests that graduate or beginning teachers in these positions should 'get extra training', and questions ITE program designs. This teacher voiced concerns about ITE, 'Maybe it is the degrees that are failing more so than the schools picking their staff …' This concern highlights an issue that is clarified by Shulman (2006), who points out that within specific education departments, teachers' content knowledge, curriculum expectations and content standards impact stakeholders' view about teacher quality.

I argue in this chapter that the capacity and teaching quality of beginning teachers are challenged when they experience a disconnection with one or more of the specific subjects they are assigned to teach. The self-efficacy, self-esteem and confidence of beginning teachers are impacted by their experiences when they struggle to teach subjects for which they are not suitably qualified. My argument focuses on the alignment between ITE, pre-service teachers' intrinsic motivation, their utilization in the workplace and fit-for-context professional support available to beginning teachers, graduates or pre-service teachers. With this alignment, the expectation that pre-service teachers will enter the workplace 'with a professional platform from which to develop as high-quality teachers' (Australian Institute for Teaching and School Leadership 2011, p. 2) then becomes a reasonable argument.

Teacher education plays an important role in the improvement of teaching and learning (Plecki et al. 2012). Concerns about the classroom-readiness of pre-service teachers (The Teacher Education Ministerial Advisory Group [TEMAG] Report, Craven et al. 2014; Australian Broadcasting Corporation [ABC News] 2016) turn the focus on the quality of ITE. I emphasize a concern that ITE is accountable for instilling in graduate teachers a sound theoretical awareness that forms the foundation for a smooth and problem-free transition into teaching practice. I further question how closely ITE is connected to the realities that prospective teachers face, once they enter the workforce.

In agreement with Mills (2013), I am aware that teacher education is considered 'largely unsuccessful' in preparing teachers to work with 'difference productively' (Mills 2013, p. 52). A beginning teacher (A3) shares her awareness of professional skill differences between herself and a more confident colleague: 'She knows where to focus, she's specialized, and she has a broader knowledge. I am constantly unsure. Am I on the right track? I can't fully invest …' It is a major concern, shown in research (Du Plessis 2014), that beginning teachers are prone to develop dispositions and perceptions that colleagues are 'good' teachers while they struggle and experience frustrations. If these frustrations are not acted upon, they might develop into causes of attrition.

This teacher's statement validates the claim that ITE, by itself, is not enough or might not efficiently address the needs that develop in the workplace and that it needs careful restructuring. ITE should be the beginning of a lifelong learning adventure for teachers. ITE is just the encouraging first step into a lifelong learning and development process. The question emerges: Is this clearly and explicitly understood by pre-service teachers and educational stakeholders?

This chapter offers the reader messages from the field, based on empirical data, to underscore the impact of ITE on graduate teachers' readiness for the profession and beyond. It has further implications for pre-service teachers' capacity to fulfil the expectations (Kent 2000) that schools have of them. The importance of pre-service teachers' readiness for the profession is summarized by McKinsey and Company's (2007) report and Feiman-Nemser's (2001) analysis: that the quality of an education system cannot exceed the quality of its teachers. The chapter reflects on these key questions:

- What is the perception (by the general public and within the profession) of the teaching quality of beginning teachers?
- What is the expected evidence of quality teaching for graduate teachers?
- How are the teaching capacities and abilities of graduate teachers developed and supported during their first years of teaching?

ITE and the Consciousness of the Everydayness of Teaching

The preparation offered during ITE is carried into the workplace, and the professional support offered to beginning teachers is as important as the encouraging role ITE plays in developing graduate teachers. However, ITE by itself cannot be adequate in the training and education of teachers; it is the *intentional-in-context* professional learning that is the follow-through-action needed to retain beginning teachers in the profession. Reid (2011) highlights a pressing concern around the theoretical base of teacher education and what is referred to as *practice theory*, in broad terms. She further highlights that practice 'broadly refers to the epistemological tradition that concerns itself with "how things get done" in everyday life' (Reid 2011, p. 8). Kemmis (2009) defines practice as 'always embodied (and situated)—it is what particular people do, in a particular place and time, and it contributes to the formation of their identities' (p. 23). This supports the overarching benefit of close collaboration between schools and universities. I argue that the goals and the objectives of quality ITE—to offer well-prepared and well-qualified graduate teachers to the workforce—cannot be effectively executed without a sound knowledge and understanding of classroom realities and school context.

Darling-Hammond (2006) underlines the need for collaboration among schools, higher education institutes and the wider school community to address concerns about the quality of ITE. Furthermore, the TEMAG report, (Craven et al. 2014) claims that valuable information about 'pre-service teachers entering the workforce is lacking'. This report underlines concerns about the 'effectiveness of initial teacher education' and ongoing professional support (p. xii). The literature suggests that ITE programs connect pre-service teachers' pre-existing principles, beliefs and expectations about what it is to be a teacher (Harfitt 2015). Therefore, this chapter takes a closer look at empirical evidence about what becoming a teacher really means for graduate teachers.

'Becoming a teacher' mainly involves constructing a professional identity. Graduate teachers' professional identity development is often underpinned by their personal experiences while at school, in the course of their own educational experiences and contexts. Research (Queensland College of Teachers [QCT] 2017) shows that a large number of prospective teachers choose teaching because of their own teachers' examples. The TEMAG report (Craven et al. 2014) states clearly that the ITE programs higher education providers offer should set pre-service teachers up for success. The phrase 'set up for success' strongly indicates that the 'music does not stop with ITE'—there is an expectation that ITE is just the beginning of the learning and development process for teachers.

Feelings of uncertainty and under-preparedness influence knowledge construction and effective learning approaches. These have implications for teacher and parent trust relationships and confidence in teachers, while trust relationships between parents and teachers support students' learning. A secondary school beginning teacher (A3) found it difficult to manage a subject in its totality that involved curriculum management, planning, teaching and the design of assessment activities. This teacher's professional knowledge and capacity to develop control over the subject and the teaching of it caused difficulties: 'I can't convey information I know nothing about. I asked a colleague to do certain areas. For me it is just a piece of work we need to read through'.

Thus, ITE needs to be presented as the gateway to further professional learning and development. Again, I stress that teacher education must not stop with ITE, because what happens in the classroom and the school impacts ITE program design and development. Many seem oblivious to the significant role and responsibility that the ITE program takes in preparing a strong, high-quality and stable workforce. ITE has a role not only in preparing pre-service teachers to learn how learning happens and how classroom and student evidence inform teaching, but also in the development of teachers with the capacity to prepare themselves and their learners for life beyond the walls of the classroom. This cannot happen if teacher educators and ITE program designs do not move beyond the tertiary classroom.

The transnational empirical data offered in this chapter were gathered from two very different education systems and serve as national cases to provide new information connected to graduate teachers' lived experiences, about which the current literature is vague. The rationale for transnational research lies in the broad context it provides for the deeper understanding of specific concerns (Smith 2005), such as ongoing targeted professional support beyond ITE.

The Theoretical and Methodological Approach that Underpins the Discussion

Theoretical Underpinnings

Englander (2014) suggests that a phenomenological attitude supports empathy and interpersonal understanding. These skills are vital in classrooms, and they direct the learning, teaching and assessment culture, and classroom climate (Masters 2013). Englander (2014) argues that this attitude needs to be explored in ITE programs.

The investigation (Du Plessis 2014) that informs this chapter has a strong social constructivist discourse to develop an in-depth understanding of the lifeworld of beginning teachers and how they experience their capacity to link the theory and practice of teaching. The epistemological realization of 'being' prepared for the workforce has implications for beginning teachers' professional identity, self-esteem and confidence to explore, take risks and experiment with teaching practices.

While it is impossible to have someone else's primary experience (Englander 2014), this chapter offers a look into the lived experiences of graduate teachers and beginning teachers within their first five years of teaching, with accounts of graduate and beginning teachers' lifeworlds, professional identities and perceptions about their fitting in within the workforce. Dall'Alba and Barnacle (2005) point out embodied knowing as a unification of the experience and the person.

A Vygotskian socio-constructivist consideration supports the notion of teachers as *the knowledgeable others* (Vygotsky 1978). A graduate teacher's identity as the knowledgeable other involves the confidence to adapt teaching practices to the diverse needs of students. However, confidence to adapt can only develop from a sound knowledge and theoretical foundation built during ITE. Developing an innovative theoretical frame to emphasize context, to underline consciousness and to develop deeper understanding (the C-CUD theoretical frame, Du Plessis 2018, forthcoming), in the habitus of teacher learning and development, involves a combination of the work of three theorists, Gadamer (1975, 1976), Vygotsky (1978) and Van Manen (1990).

First, developing a deeper understanding of what becoming and being a teacher mean for beginning teachers is supported by asking 'What is there to understand?', based on Gadamer's (1976) claim that self-understanding develops in the process of 'being'—in this case, being a graduate teacher entering the workforce with the skills and knowledge ITE provided. Second, the theoretical framework focuses on the question, 'Why is it important to understand?', grounded in Vygotsky's (1978) social constructivist theory, underlining the role of a graduate teacher as a knowledgeable other guiding effective learning. Third, the theoretical question 'Where does knowing develop, and how?' establishes the concern of knowing, and Van Manen's theory (1990) of knowing through understanding of lived experiences stimulates embodied knowing, where the context is part of knowing.

This theoretical framework offers a foundation for investigating the fundamental concerns of quality ITE through a lens that links improvement strategies to the field. Graduate teachers' lived experiences are accentuated, as are their feelings of 'belongingness' (Gadamer 1975, p. 416) in a specific school or classroom context, subject or year level, and provide valuable information and new knowledge to use in the reassessment and restrategizing or development of ITE.

Methodological Processes

The first phase in this investigation involved a four-phase analytic approach employed by Alhamdan et al. (2014). Relying on content analysis, tentative codes were developed from the literature which include categories such as ITE, beginning teacher identities, professional knowledge, professional skills, quality teaching practices, assessment preparedness, pre-service teachers and workplace experiences. The literature data set includes 122 peer-reviewed papers, reports, policy documents and reviews. The most relevant publications were compiled in a table, with extracts from abstracts and citations, designed to keep a record of key statements linked to the research questions and to identify key phrases as their answers. In certain cases, statements were used verbatim from publications (with page numbers) to explain expectations about ITE.

The second phase included discussions and collaborations directed by the three main research questions presented at the end of the introduction section. This phase involved semi-structured, one-on-one interviews, classroom observations, staffroom observations, field notes and informal discussions with graduates, beginning and experienced teachers, school leaders and parents, who comprised 48 participants in seven schools (primary and secondary schools). The semi-structured, one-on-one interviews (certain participants were interviewed twice) were conducted in 60-min sessions, transcribed in full and coded according to the categories and patterns of discussion derived from the literature searches. In some cases, interviews were followed up by classroom observations. The interpretive analyses of real-life experiences from the field allow readers to step into the classroom space while maintaining an awareness of the expectations for quality ITE.

Messages from the Field: Empirical Data Supporting and Clarifying the *Link*

The data reveal the link between lived experiences from the field and the development of beginning teachers' identities as knowledgeable and valid agents, responsible for effectively guiding, transforming, enhancing and directing teaching and learning. The areas of professional learning and development include professional engagement of teacher educators, leaders and teachers through inquiry and knowledge building, knowledge, awareness and practices connecting pedagogy and control in the classroom. This gradual empowerment of graduate and beginning teachers involves a process of learning new knowledge from the field. Schieman and Plickert (2008) note that knowledge is power in the sense that it develops the confidence, preparedness and self-assurance to act in a manner that underlines authority in a specific field and context.

The need to recognize what works and where to go from here was mirrored two decades ago by Kennedy (as cited in Cochran-Smith et al. in press, p. 8) in the following paragraph:

> Primarily quantitative research on teacher education, intended to inform policy and policy makers, was often more familiar to sceptics and critics of teacher education, including economists and policy analysts, than to teacher educators themselves.

Cochran-Smith and Stern (2014) emphasized the benefit of knowing the field and using empirical evidence from the field for teacher educators, teaching and the preparation of teachers.

Transitioning from ITE to a Culture of Sustained Professional Learning in School Contexts

Encouragement underpins professional learning as a lifelong attribute for quality development (Du Plessis 2018, forthcoming). The improvement of education for teachers that will result in the improvement in the quality of teachers begins with strategies that include professional learning and professional development. Preparing teachers for the workforce needs to involve collaboration, and it needs to engage various educational institutions, governments, teacher educators, school leaders and teachers who provide the actual experiences inside classrooms.

Graduate teachers assigned to challenging positions often question their ability to teach. A parent (B2) shares disquiet about a beginning teacher's capacity to stimulate student achievement by offering in-depth feedback on tasks: 'If concepts do not get tied down, students will struggle in the future. It is fundamental, the basis. Because the next step follows on from the previous content and so it continues …'

A classroom context develops a specific teaching and learning climate that can greatly affect the outcomes of students. Bourdieu and Passeron (1994) suggest that the specific atmosphere and manner in which information is conveyed affect the construction of knowledge. The impact of restricted professional knowledge and skills is described by a teacher (D1):

> Relations with children, understanding where the kids are at socially, emotionally, physically—they don't have that knowledge and that base that allow you to make qualified judgments as to say we need to extend this child or we need to then remediate this child or there are these outside factors that influence this individual …

Significantly, Johnson (2011) notes that covering the curriculum is not the same as meeting the students' needs while carefully guiding them to construct new knowledge. Noble and Henderson (2008) stress that vital transition periods often involve forming new identities and new discourses.

Noble and Henderson (2008) further emphasize that reliable partnerships and relationships are solutions to the transformation of teacher preparations and ITE. An Australian education department director (3) shares this observation: 'They [universities] don't think about what the needs of the employers are. We could be a lot more strategic about who gets placement into universities so that a lot of that angst doesn't arise with young grads'. Graduate and beginning teachers who are not confident about their readiness to enter the workplace, school context or classroom find it hard to collaborate and develop trust relationships.

Parent's confidence in teachers and the school, as well as professional trust relationships, links to students' positive approaches to the teaching and learning environment. Misinterpretation of the curriculum influences students' learning and effective teaching. A parent (A6) comments on a graduate teacher's struggles: 'She can't distinguish between the important and less important information, what the major outcomes are or what they are supposed to be. She just doesn't know'.

The level of preparedness of graduate and beginning teachers further influences these teachers' sustained professional learning. Mentors influence not only the transition into the workplace, but also graduate teachers' professional identity and attitudes about professional learning and development. Smith (2012) links the development of professional knowledge and skills to pre-service teachers' progress, but also emphasizes that it stimulates 'professional and community confidence in the quality of institution programs' (p. 45).

ITE Preparing Candidates for Connected Pedagogy, Knowledge and Influence

The TEMAG report (Craven et al. 2014) states that the first few years in the classroom are critical for developing quality teaching practices. During these years, graduate and beginning teachers develop connected pedagogy, knowledge and influence. A beginning teacher's (D7) protest 'I don't know what I don't know...' underlines the uncertainty these teachers experience about their professional identity. Significantly, Noble and Henderson (2008) stress the value of professional identity development in pre-service teachers and beyond.

An experienced lead teacher (F1) explains how the professional identity of beginning teachers influences their students: 'It is sort of like a web; it is all entwined to that person [beginning teacher], then feeds out to children'. Hirsch (2006) claims that a teacher's lack of content knowledge affects the quality of teaching and causes serious deficiencies in students' learning.

Misinterpretations of curriculum guidelines are a concern. A specialist teacher (C2) discusses her experience with a beginner teacher's knowledge of a specific curriculum: 'I was surprised. We were talking about how we are going to teach something. I witnessed things—I sometimes thought [laugh], are we really reading the same curriculum document? It was very different'.

Classroom observations show that graduate and beginning teachers' confidence, preparedness, professional knowledge and ability to manage specific classroom contexts are matters for alarm (Du Plessis 2014). A beginning teacher (D1) shares a fundamental concern about the implications that under-preparedness—in professional experience, knowledge and skills—has for adjustments to teaching to accommodate specific learning needs of students: 'I need to change this subject but you just do what you know and what you know is insufficient. Add to that the fact that you go without any knowledge or prior experience'.

Developing graduate and beginning teachers for their role as the knowledgeable other in classrooms entails skill improvement and preparedness to identify specific learning needs. This is, or should be, an ITE accountability. Darling-Hammond (2006) defined ITE accountability as programs that offer 'sophisticated knowledge of teaching' while preparing prospective teachers 'to practice effectively in the classroom but also to take into account the "bigger picture" of schools and schooling' (p. 122). A second-year beginning teacher (A2) shares an observation: 'It was hard in the beginning. After teaching the subjects for more than one year, I realized the level of work I used to offer was not good enough to challenge strong students ... I have adjusted it now'.

Transforming Teaching Practices Begins with ITE and Continues Beyond: A Never-Ending Cycle

A lack of professional knowledge shows up in the level of confidence that graduate and beginning teachers have in adjusting to and exploring new teaching practices. A parent of an aspiring student, previously in the classroom of a beginning teacher who lacked the necessary professional knowledge and skills, shared specific dispositions:

> My daughter's expression was *she sucked at English*; I was rather surprised—I've changed schools—I notice now she's getting very high marks in her English because she's a very intelligent girl who can articulate well. The only thing I can put that down to was the way she was being taught or what she's being taught.

Loughran (2010) points out that students' experiences of learning are directly connected to the pedagogical content knowledge of the teacher. The question arises, 'How available is support where it is most needed?'—a question that prompts me to repeat my initial concerns about the adequacy of ITE to continue supporting teachers once they are in the workplace. A beginning teacher (A2) explains: 'In the beginning I just taught the lesson, told them to write the questions down and to answer them and I checked the answers. Now, I have started to discuss the work more …'. Planners of ITE would do well to explore the possibilities for providing additional support and development, once their students move into the teaching workplace.

Becoming a Teacher … and Remaining in the Profession!

The link between theory and practice and the relationships among higher education institutes, schools, teacher standards (e.g. Australian Institute for Teaching and School Leadership [AITSL] 2011, 2015) and improved student learning should be emphasized in quality improvement strategies. Two main elements illustrate the challenges in achieving quality ITE:

1. The careful guidance that pre-service teachers need to receive about becoming a teacher and
2. The realistic preparation to deal with classroom and school contexts that pose extreme challenges in order to keep graduate teachers in the profession.

Developing and maintaining enthusiasm for the classroom as a workplace involves an alignment between pre-service teachers' professional skills and the identity they have developed as beginning teachers (Craven et al. 2014). Reflecting on what becoming a teacher really means involves regarding teaching as more than a profession; it is a profession, life calling and lifestyle (Gore et al. 2015; Wyatt-Smith et al. 2017). The TEMAG report (Craven et al. 2014) underlines the value of a connectedness between higher education institutions and the workplace. Pre-service teachers' preparedness for the demands of a classroom must be linked to quality professional knowledge and skill capacity, as well as to the readiness of pre-service teachers to align teaching practices, learning and assessment evidence to improve quality education (Darling-Hammond 2006).

An expectation, echoed in the literature, is that higher education institutions and the teaching profession must work together to reform and integrate the ITE system (Craven et al. 2014). Cochran-Smith and the Boston College Evidence Team (2009) claim that developing strategies of evidence and inquiry in ITE can transform and revitalize teacher education. Dialogue, co-operation and collaboration between higher education institutions and partnerships in the workplace would support a clearer understanding of needs.

The quality of graduate teachers' professional knowledge and skills, together with their developed emotional skills and capacity to cope with the demands of the workplace, will support them through the challenges they will face in the workplace. Expectations for beginning teachers are to demonstrate a capacity aligned with the desired teacher standards (e.g. Finland, Australia, USA, Sweden, Brazil, South Africa, South Korea and the Netherlands). The effective link between what ITE programs offer and what is expected, according to teacher standards (e.g. AITSL 2011, 2015), validates the preparedness of pre-service teachers. The focus should be on the classroom and the ability of the graduate teacher to confidently function as the knowledgeable other in the teaching and learning environment (Vygotsky 1978).

A research study conducted in the USA (Evans and Tribble 1986) shows major inconsistencies in existing perceptions of teaching problems between pre-service teachers and beginning teachers. Pre-service teachers are primarily concerned about subject knowledge and dealing with learning problems, while beginning teachers are mostly concerned about identifying and assessing their students' work, and their relations with parents. Does this underline the disconnection between the field and the habitus of becoming a teacher, or is it a progression of learning; that is, once content is internalized, can the focus turn back to the students where it was always supposed to be? The TEMAG report (Craven et al. 2014) highlights considerable public unease about the quality of ITE. This report also emphasizes that theory and practice in ITE are inseparable when equipping teachers for classroom practices. However, this also means noticing the concerns that beginning teachers experience in the classrooms. A transnational focus on this chapter highlights the role of the classroom teacher as the knowledgeable other (Vygotsky, 1978), irrespective of the context in which teachers carry out their role as teacher. This also demonstrates the global expectations regarding beginning teachers' professional knowledge and skills (Harfitt 2015).

The literature further points out the impact of ITE on pre-service teachers' capacity to effectively manage and accommodate diversity in classrooms. Pre-service teachers' preparedness to fill expected roles is under question. Reviews state, 'Teacher employers are dissatisfied with the classroom-readiness' of graduate or beginning teachers (Craven et al. 2014, p. 30). ITE is expected to improve pre-service teachers' capabilities and readiness to provide quality teaching and learning to all the students in their classroom. The capacity to accommodate and manage increasing diversity in the classroom involves able, well-prepared, well-informed and confident teachers to carefully assess their students' learning and developmental needs and act upon this assessment with suitable teaching practices. Maxwell (2002) places teachers at the centre of quality assessment processes, with their assessment skills and preparedness to judge their students' work being influential factors for their teaching practices.

An experienced teacher explains a concern about the ability of beginning teachers to provide feedback, especially if they are assigned to a complex and challenging teaching position during their first years of teaching: 'They don't have the experience to be able to give feedback to the parents effectively; their knowledge doesn't allow them to give answers'.

'Access to schooling is not enough on its own: education needs to be of good quality so that children actually learn' (UNESCO 2013, p. 4). The active engagement of pre-service teachers in real classroom contexts and with students' actual learning needs richly informs the process of becoming a teacher. The expectation that tertiary institutions will improve and provide quality ITE is linked to the expectation that improvement of quality teaching will impact students' academic achievement (Hattie 2009). Recently published outcomes of student achievements and results by the Program for International Student Assessment (PISA) of the Organisation for Economic Co-operation and Development (OECD 2016) serve as a wake-up call for various countries. For example, in 2000, out of a total number of 41 countries, Australia ranked sixth for maths, eighth for science and fourth for reading. A troubling backwards slide during 2012 to nineteenth for maths, sixteenth for science and thirteenth for reading, out of 65 countries, signalled underlying problems (Ricci 2015).

Expectations and concerns about strategies to increase the performance of students are of the same importance in both developed and developing countries. Currently, pilot PISA studies are underway in Zambia and Ecuador. Although in-depth studies about quality teacher preparation and quality teaching in developing countries acknowledge contextual complexity, great concerns exist about the quality of education and teaching. Concerns are embedded in the results from annual national assessments (OECD 2016) revealing problems in mathematics and literacy performance, as both Bloch (2014) and the OECD (2013) specified that students in Grade 4 scored an average of 37%, while those in Grade 5 scored 33% in the 2013 PISA results.

The downwards tendency in students' performance results stimulates an urgency to improve and transform education, with an emphasis on teacher education. At this point, referring to Australia, authors of the TEMAG report (Craven et al. 2014) state 'that quality of teachers must begin when they are first prepared for the profession' (p. 7) and present the expectation that 'higher education providers and schools work together' (p. 33).

A principal shares this observation: 'This young teacher is in the class but has no idea what is going on—it is where the trouble starts!' It turns the focus on the quality of ITE programs, as well as the placement and employment conditions of graduate and beginning teachers.

I argue that ITE is only the starting point of *becoming a teacher*, but it is the most influential step towards success in the classroom. ITE covers academic development within specific fields, but it has a major responsibility to move towards guiding pre-service teachers to a deeper knowing and a context-conscious understanding that help teachers to develop the critical inquiry abilities of themselves and their students (read C-CUD theory, Du Plessis 2018, forthcoming).

The ability to notice and the consciousness of the lived experiences of graduate teachers expose professional identity uncertainties, confidence issues and reservations about the quality they uphold as teachers. A hermeneutic theoretical framework supports a context-conscious understanding of teachers' growing, learning and development (Du Plessis 2018, forthcoming), while it stimulates an exploration of the individuals' truths as part of the holistic understanding of what an improvement in ITE really means. The lived experiences of graduate teachers are linked to their professional knowledge and skills, their dispositions and their confidence in their assigned positions.

A Consideration of Counter Positions and Arguments

It can be argued that it is the responsibility of ITE to implement specific programs to develop the professional identities of pre-service teachers—before they move into the workplace. However, the development of beginning teachers' professional identity is influenced by their confidence and skills when applying critical inquiry approaches to inform their teaching (Beijaard et al. 2004). This statement calls to mind Otto et al.'s (1979) theory that beginning teachers find it difficult to make subjects meaningful because a graduate or beginning teacher's professional identity influences his or her effectiveness in a classroom.

Implications for Action

Noble and Henderson (2008) stress that ITE which prepares pre-service teachers to work across educational contexts entails an 'awareness of the demands on beginning teachers in relation to personal and professional skill development' (p. 47). Such awareness needs the involvement of school leaders. The Connectedness, Awareness, Needs Analysis, Negotiation, Action and Support (CANNAS) school leadership model (Du Plessis 2017) provides educational leaders with guidelines to employ strategies of these essential elements. Lingard et al. (2003) discussed productive classroom pedagogics while highlighting a 'connectedness with a difference'. I argue that productive classrooms are greatly impacted by school leaders' connectedness, which means being in the space. By being in the space, they notice, become aware of and are conscious of the realities inside classrooms. This is followed by an in-depth need analysis linking what was noticed or what they became aware of, to 'the person that matters', the teachers and students. This is the phase in which leaders develop and construct views and perceptions and restructure new information.

It is, however, important that school leaders accommodate the need of teachers to engage in negotiation with them. Teachers need to have professional discussions with their leaders; they need trust relationships to be built. The value of these negotiations greatly impacts their decisions to stay in the profession. Thus, professional trust relationships impact retention and turnover rates of beginning teachers.

Interactions and discussions inform what is the most suitable and appropriate action needed in a specific context. School leaders' 'duty of care' involves improving the quality teaching and learning with targeted professional support, which should be intentional, fit-for-context support—this is the phase that builds our workforce and teaching culture.

The Next Essential Questions to be Dealt with

Strategies must be developed to ensure that graduate and beginning teachers develop healthy approaches in order to foster feelings of belonging. Connolly et al. (2012) recognize that quality dialogue and collaboration with colleagues develop reassurance, familiarity and confidence with teaching standards and student evidence assessment procedures. ITE needs to be closely connected to the workplace to offer workplace-orientated programs. Notably, the TEMAG report (Craven et al. 2014) recommends that higher education institutions deliver 'evidence-based content focused on the depth of subject knowledge and pedagogical approaches' in their ITE programs to enable pre-service teachers to foster students' learning (p. xv). The essential questions then are: (1) How do ITE program designs accommodate and address the needs that are voiced by beginning teachers? (2) How do stakeholders develop a platform for teachers' voices to be heard?, and (3) How can a space be developed where truths from the field and evidence of lived experiences add value to ITE's transformation and improvement strategies?

Conclusion

Context influences both a teacher's capacity to offer quality teaching and his or her success in constructing learning environments that fully support students' learning, achievement and outcomes. Complex employment conditions affect new teachers' preparedness and confidence. This means that the 'music does not stop with ITE' and that the goal of teacher quality is the responsibility of all education stakeholders, especially those involved beyond ITE. The challenge for education leaders who seek to improve the quality of ITE that prospective teachers currently receive is to understand, broadly, how ITE impacts graduate teachers' coping strategies during their first placements.

The author further offers an in-depth investigation of the targeted professional support that is needed to uphold and further the work that has been done during ITE in another book in this series. Misperceptions about the implications of graduate teachers' placements in complex teaching positions, such as the out-of-field phenomenon, that is, teaching subject areas or year levels for which they are not suitably qualified, and what this means for perceptions about the quality of ITE programs offered, are major concerns. These concerns accentuate that professional learning and development beyond ITE should not be underestimated. ITE prepares graduate teachers with specific content knowledge and pedagogical content knowledge.

Of serious concern is the common view among educational leaders that allocating graduate teachers to any available post is acceptable. Specific community and school contexts often create circumstances that force teachers to critically reflect on, rethink and reassess their abilities, competencies and beliefs in relation to the quality of teaching they provide. Operative pedagogical content knowledge in the classroom involves understanding the need for knowledge for practice, in practice and of practice (Cochran-Smith and Lytle 1999).

References

ABC News, Australian Broadcast Corporation. (2016). *Australian teacher shortage fears as student numbers soar*. Retrieved June 20, 2017 from http://www.abc.net.au/news/2016-01-18/fears-of-looming-teacher-shortage-as-student-population-soars/7096102.

Alhamdan, B., Al-Saadi, K., Baroutsis, B., Du Plessis, A., Hamid, O., & Honan, E. (2014). Media representation of teachers across five countries. *Comparative Education, 59*(4), 490–505. https://doi.org/10.1080/03050068.2013.853476.

Australian Institute for Teaching and School Leadership [AITSL]. (2015). *Accreditation of initial teacher education programmes in Australia: Standards and procedures*. Retrieved 27 Sept 2017 from https://www.aitsl.edu.au/docs/default-source/initial-teacher-education-resources/accreditation-of-ite-programs-in-australia.pdf.

Australian Institute for Teaching and School Leadership [AITSL]. (2011). *Australian professional standards for teachers*. Retrieved September 26, 2017 from https://www.aitsl.edu.au/docs/default-source/general/australian_professional_standard_for_teachers_final.pdf?sfvrsn=399ae83c_2.

Beijaard, D., Meijer, P., & Verloop, N. (2004). Reconsidering research on teachers' professional identity. *Teaching Teacher Education, 20*(2), 107–128.

Bloch, G. (2014). PISA education tests under fire, but they could help developing countries boost competitiveness. *The Conversation*. Retrieved June 15, 2017 from http://theconversation.com/pisa-education-tests-under-fire-but-they-could-help-developing-countries-boost-competitiveness-26654.

Bourdieu, P., & Passeron, J. (1994). Introduction: Language and relationships to language in the teaching situation. In Bourdieu, P., Passeron, J., & De Saint Martin, M. (Eds.), *Academic discourse: Linguistic misunderstanding and professorial power*, pp. 1–34 (R. Teese, Trans.). Cambridge, England: Policy Press.

Butt, G., MacKenzie, L., & Manning, R. (2010). Influences on British South Asian women's choice of teaching as a career: "You're either a career person or a family person; teaching kind of fits in the middle". *Educational Review, 62*(1), 69–83. https://doi.org/10.1080/00131910903519769.

Cochran-Smith, M., & Boston College Evidence Team. (2009). Re-culturing teacher education: Inquiry, evidence and action. *Journal of Teacher Education, 60*(5):458–468.

Cochran-Smith, M., & Lytle, S. (1999). Relationships of knowledge and practice: Teacher learning communities. *Review of Research Education, 24*(1), 249–305. https://doi.org/10.3102/0091732x024001249.

Cochran-Smith, M., & Stern, R. (2014). Imagining schools as centres for inquiry. In L. Reynolds (Ed.), *Imagine it better: Visions of what schools might be* (pp. 85–96). Portsmouth, NH: Heinemann Books.

Cochran-Smith, M., Villegas, A. M., Abrams, L., Chavez Moreno, L., Mills, T., & Stern, R. (In press). Research on teacher preparation: charting the landscape of a sprawling field. In D. Gitomer & C. Bell (Eds.), *Handbook of research on teaching* (5th ed.). Washington, DC: AERA.

Connolly, S., Klenowski, V., & Wyatt-Smith, C. (2012). Moderation and consistency of teacher judgement: Teachers' views. *British Education Research Journal, 38*(4), 593–614. https://doi.org/10.1080/01411926.2011.569006.

Craven, G., Beswick, K., Fleming, J., Fletcher, T., Green, M., & Jensen, B., et al. (2014). *Action now: Classroom ready teachers*. Retrieved May 9, 2018 from https://docs.education.gov.au/system/files/doc/other/action_now_classroom_ready_teachers_accessible.pdf.

Curtis, C. (2012). Why do they choose to teach—and why do they leave? A study of middle school and high school mathematics teachers. *Education, 132*(4), 779–788.

Dall'Alba, G., Barnacle, R. (2005). Embodied knowing in online environments. *Educational Philosphy Theory 37*(5):719–744. https://doi.org/10.1111/j.1469-5812.2005.00153.x.

Darling-Hammond, L. (2006). Assessing teacher education: The usefulness of multiple measures for assessing program outcomes. *Journal of Teacher Education, 57*(2), 120–138. https://doi.org/10.1177/0022487105283796.

Du Plessis, A. (2014). *Understanding the out-of-field teaching experience* (Unpublished doctoral thesis). University of Queensland, Brisbane, Australia.

Du Plessis, A. (2017). *Out-of-field teaching practices: What educational leaders need to know*. Amsterdam, The Netherlands: Sense Publishers.

Du Plessis A (2018, forthcoming). Teaching workforce complexities: Moving beyond initial teacher education. Focus on targeted professional support, learning and development: Building a strong teaching workforce. Springer, Singapore.

Englander, M. (2014). Empathy training from a phenomenological perspective. *Journal Phenomenological Psychology, 45*(1), 5–26. https://doi.org/10.1163/15691624-12341266.

Evans, E., & Tribble, M. (1986). Perceived teaching problems, self-efficacy, and commitment to teaching among pre-service teachers. *Journal of Education Research, 80*(2), 81–85. https://doi.org/10.1080/00220671.1986.10885728.

Feiman-Nemser, S. (2001). From preparation to practice: Designing a continuum to strengthen and sustain teaching. *Teacher College Record, 103*(6), 1013–1055.

Freeman, C., O'Malley, K., Eveleigh, F. (2014). *Australian teachers and the learning environment: An analysis of teacher response to TALIS 2013*. Final report. Australian Council for Educational Research, Melbourne, Australia.

Gadamer, H. (1975). *Truth and method* (2nd ed.) (J. C. B. Mohr, Trans.). New York, NY: The Seabury Press.

Gadamer, H. (1976). *Philosophical hermeneutics* (D. Linge, 2008, Trans.). Berkeley, CA: University of California Press.

Gore, J., Smith, M., Holmes, K., & Fray, L. (2015). *Investigating the factors that influence the choice of teaching as a first career: A report commissioned by the Queensland College of Teachers*. Brisbane, Australia: Queensland College of Teachers.

Grant, B., & McKinley, E. (2011). Colouring the pedagogy of doctoral supervision: Considering supervisor, student and knowledge through the lens of indigeneity. *Innovations in Education and Teaching International, 48*(4), 377–386. https://doi.org/10.1080/14703297.2011.617087.

Harfitt, G. (2015). From attrition to retention: A narrative inquiry of why beginning teachers leave and then rejoin the profession. *Asia-Pacific J Teacher Asia-Pacific Journal of Teacher EducationEduc, 43*(1), 22–35. https://doi.org/10.1080/1359866X.2014.932333.

Hattie, J. (2009). *Visible learning: A synthesis of over 800 meta-analyses relating to achievement*. London, England: Routledge.

Hirsch, E., Jr. (2006). *The knowledge deficit: Closing the shocking gap for American children*. New York, NY: Houghton Mifflin Company.

Johnson, L. (2011). *Teaching outside the box: How to grab your students by their brains.* San Francisco, CA: Jossey-Bass.

Kelchtermans, G. (2009). Career stories as gateway to understanding teacher development. In: Bayer, M., Brinkkjær, U., Plauborg, H., & Rolls, S. (Eds.), *Teachers' career trajectories and work lives*, pp. 29–47. https://doi.org/10.1007/978-90-481-2358-2.

Kemmis, S. (2009). Understanding professional practice: A synoptic framework. In B. Green (Eds.), *Understanding and researching professional practice* (pp. 19–38). Rotterdam, The Netherlands: Sense.

Kent, S. (2000). Problems of beginning teachers: Comparing graduates of bachelor's and master's level teacher preparation s. *The Teacher Educator, 35*(4), 83–96. https://doi.org/10.1080/08878730009555239.

Lingard, B., Hayes, D., Mills, M., Christie, P. (2003). *Leading learning: Making hope practical in schools.* Philadelphia, PA: Open University Press. Retrieved September 26, 2017 from http://www.mheducation.com.au/9780335210114-aus-leading-learning-making-hope-practical-in-schools.

Loughran, J. (2010). *What expert teachers do: Enhancing professional knowledge for classroom practice.* Australia: Allen & Unwin, Crow's Nest.

Masters, G. (2013). Towards a growth mindset in assessment. *Practically Primary, 19*(2), 4–7.

Maxwell, G. (2002). *Are core learning outcomes standards?*. Brisbane, Australia: Queensland School Curriculum Council.

McKinsey & Company. (2007). *How the world's best-performing school systems come out on top.* Retrieved May 10, 2018 from https://www.mckinsey.com/industries/social-sector/our-insights/how-the-worlds-best-performing-school-systems-come-out-on-top.

Mills, C. (2013). A Bourdieuian analysis of teachers' changing dispositions towards social justice: The limitations of practicum placements in pre-service teacher education. *Asia-Pacific Journal of Teacher Education, 41*(1), 41–54. https://doi.org/10.1080/1359866X.2012.753985.

Noble, K., & Henderson, R. (2008). Engaging with images and stories: Using a learning approach to develop agency of beginning "at risk" pre-service teachers. *Australian Journal of Teacher Education 33*(1):46–61. http://dx.doi.org/10.14221/ajte.2008v33n1.4.

Organisation for Economic Cooperation and Development [OECD]. (2014). *TALIS 2013 results: An international perspective on teaching and learning.* http://dx.doi.org/10.1787/9789264196261-en.

Organisation for Economic Cooperation and Development [OECD]. (2013). *Education at a glance 2013. OECD indicators.* Retrieved September 27, 2017 from http://www.oecd.org/edu/eag2013%20(eng)–FINAL%2020%20June%202013.pdf.

Organisation for Economic Cooperation and Development [OECD]. (2016). *for international students assessment (PISA) 2015 results in focus.* Retrieved September 24, 2017 from http://www.oecd.org/pisa/pisa-2015-results-in-focus.pdf.

Otto, E., Gasson, I., & Jordan, E. (1979). Perceived problems of beginning teachers. *South Pacific Journal of Teacher Education, 1*(1–2), 28–33. https://doi.org/10.1080/0311213790070105.

Plecki, M., Elfers, A., & Nakamura, Y. (2012). Using evidence for teacher education program improvement and accountability: An illustrative case of the role of value-added measures. *Journal of Teacher Education, 63*(5), 318–334. https://doi.org/10.1177/0022487112447110.

Queensland College of Teachers. (2012). *An investigation of best practice in evidence-based assessment within pre-service teacher education s and other professions.* Queensland College of Teachers, Brisbane, Australia. Retrieved May 19, 2017 from https://www.qct.edu.au/PDF/PSU/BestPracticeEvidenceBasedAsessmentPre-serviceReacherEds.PDF.

Reid, J. (2011). A practice turn for teacher education? *Asia-Pacific Journal of Teacher Education, 39*(4), 293–310. https://doi.org/10.1080/1359866X.2011.614688.

Ricci, C. (2015). *OECD education rankings show Australia slipping, Asian countries in the lead. The Sydney Morning Herald, National.* Retrieved June 7, 2017 from http://www.smh.com.au/national/education/oecd-education-rankings-show-australia-slipping-asian-countries-in-the-lead-20150525-gh94eu.html.

Saud, U., & Johnston, M. (2006). Cross-cultural influences on teacher education reform: Reflections on implementing the integrated curriculum in Indonesia. *Journal of Teacher Education, 32*(1), 3–20. https://doi.org/10.1080/02607470500510894.

Schieman, S., & Plickert, G. (2008). How knowledge is power: education and the sense of control. *Social Forces, 87*(1), 153–183. https://doi.org/10.1353/sof.0.0065.

Schoenfeld, A. (2014). What makes for powerful classrooms, and how can we support teachers in creating them? A story of research and practice, productively intertwined. *Educational Researcher, 43*(8), 404–412. https://doi.org/10.3102/0013189X1455445.

Shulman, L. (2006). Mission impossible: The exasperating mentee. In J. Shulman & M. Sato (Eds.), *Mentoring teachers toward excellence: Supporting and developing highly qualified teachers* (pp. 177–196). San Francisco, CA: Jossey-Bass.

Smith, C. (2012). Why should we bother with assessment moderation? *Nurs Educ Today, 32*(2012), 45–48. https://doi.org/10.1016/j.nedt.2011.10.010.

Smith, M. (2005). Power in place/places of power: Contextualizing transnational research. *City and Society, 17*(1), 5–34. https://doi.org/10.1525/city.2005.17.1.5.

United Nations Educational, Scientific and Cultural Organization [UNESCO]. (2013). *Education transforms lives*. Education for all global monitoring report. Paris, France: UNESCO.

Van Manen, M. (1990). *Researching lived experience: Human science for an action sensitive pedagogy*. New York, NY: The State University of New York Press.

Vygotsky, L. (1978). *Mind in society: the development of higher psychological processes*. Cambridge, MA: Harvard University Press.

Wyatt-Smith, C., Du Plessis, A., Wang, J., Hand, K., Alexander, C., & Colbert, P. (2017). *Why choose teaching: A matter of choice: evidence from the field. Report*. Brisbane, Australia: Queensland College of Teachers.

Anna Elizabeth Du Plessis Ph.D. completed her studies at the University of Queensland and is currently a Research Fellow at the Institute for Learning Sciences and Teacher Education (ILSTE). She has 26 years of teaching experience in different countries of which 8 years were in school leadership. Her research projects investigated the implications out-of-field teaching has for professional development, school leadership and classroom pedagogies. She has a specific interest in beginning teachers' well-being, their working environment, and her current research explores beginning teacher workforce planning.

Part III
Partnerships and Professional Cultures

Chapter 15
Early Career Teachers' Perceptions of Initial Teacher Education

Alex Kostogriz

> *Perception is not a science of the world, it is not even an act, a deliberate taking up of a position; it is the background from which all acts stand out, and is presupposed by them.*
>
> Merleau-Ponty 1962, p. xi

Introduction

To study the effectiveness of initial teacher education (ITE) is to court criticism from the outset. What counts as effective teacher preparation? Who makes these judgments and what evidence is used in assessing the utility of teacher education? These questions can be answered in different ways, depending on purposes of posing the question of effectiveness. For instance, in the current context of teacher education reforms in Australia and elsewhere, the effectiveness of teacher education can be judged either prospectively or retrospectively. Prospective judgment entails pre-service teachers' ability to demonstrate 'classroom readiness' and their impact on student learning (Teacher Education Ministerial Advisory Group 2014). Retrospective judgment refers to how beginning teachers perceive the impact of their teacher education programs on their preparedness for professional life, specifically their everyday work in diverse schools (Mayer et al. 2017). These two perspectives differ in their epistemological positions, paradigms of inquiry, and units of analysis. The former is firmly situated within the political context of raising ITE accountability, and the latter is located within the lifeworlds of beginning teachers. In addressing

---

A. Kostogriz (✉)
Monash University, Clayton, Australia
e-mail: alexander.kostogriz@monash.edu

© Springer Nature Singapore Pte Ltd. 2018
C. Wyatt-Smith and L. Adie (eds.), *Innovation and Accountability in Teacher Education*, Teacher Education, Learning Innovation and Accountability,
https://doi.org/10.1007/978-981-13-2026-2_15

the question of ITE effectiveness, both perspectives draw on professional standards for graduate teachers but use them in different ways.

The standards in Australia refer to the three domains of teachers' work—professional knowledge, practice, and engagement—and provide descriptors for evaluating teacher performance across these domains and different stages of their career, from graduate to lead teacher. According to the Australian Institute for Teaching and School Leadership (AITSL), professional standards 'present a common understanding and language' for the profession, teacher educators, bureaucrats, and the public to debate the quality of ITE and teaching practices in schools and, for teachers, 'to recognise their current and developing capabilities, professional aspirations and achievements' (AITSL 2011, p. 2). Therefore, standards play a dual role as a mechanism of teacher accountability and a representation of teacher effectiveness. Standards for graduate teachers are used in this dual role, too, to evaluate the effectiveness of ITE programs and to determine developmental needs of pre-service and novice teachers.

From the accountability perspective, standards for graduate teachers in Australia are currently used in the ITE accreditation process for compliance purposes, as well as in culminating teacher performance assessment (TPA) for evaluating their capabilities to plan, teach, assess, and reflect on their practices, and to impact on student learning. The assessment of graduate teacher performance against the standards becomes a proxy for their classroom readiness. From the representational perspective, standards are used to mediate graduate teacher self-reflection on preparedness for work as well as on the effectiveness of ITE programs in building their capabilities. In this representational function, the standards provide a set of unitary understandings of what counts as effective teaching, knowledge, and engagement. Because these understandings have been abstracted from the actual doings and sayings of teachers across various contexts, they function as common and idealized representations of professionally valued actions to be demonstrated in everyday work.

This chapter argues that in studying the graduate teachers' perceptions of ITE effectiveness—how well they feel prepared for work—and of their own effectiveness as novice teachers—how effective they function as teachers—the standards provide only a general orientation. They do not and cannot capture the richness and complexity of experiences. For beginning teachers, the standards inevitably turn out to be impersonal statements, representing an 'objective' view of teaching practice and professional knowledge that reduces their lived experiences to knowable and controllable indicators of one's effectiveness and preparedness. The challenge is therefore to look below, or beyond, the language of standards to see how one's sense of 'effectiveness' emerges as an achievement that is situated in the lived experiences of work where the very meaning of 'being effective' is not set in stone and where the 'being prepared' depends on a variety of conditions that both afford and constrain the functioning of teachers. While standardization of professional practice relies on a unitary sense of experience, the everyday experience of teachers is a succession of singularities—day-to-day experiences that are alive, pulsating with emotions and complex relationships, as well as deeply corporeal, fractured, and effervescent. In the lifeworlds of teachers, the question of one's preparedness and effectiveness is, therefore, an existential one in a professional sense, when they make decisions about whether to stay in the profession or to leave, rather than just a matter of their performance and accountability.

One can already see how problematic it might be to make judgments about the effectiveness and preparedness of beginning teachers by using approaches that do not recognize the particularities of teachers' lived experiences. Hence, any attempt to map the contours of beginning teachers' work against the standards immediately throws open the doors to a set of critical questions: Why have you not included…? Why have you not considered…? But what about…? Such questions usually signal the insistence of teachers' everyday life and, in turn, of the recognition of situated practices and experiences in making judgments. But where can these two worlds meet if there is a certain relation of identity between the abstract discourse of standards (i.e., the transcendental) and the particular experiences of teachers (i.e., the immanent)? How do the abstract representations enter the inexhaustible and always unfinalizable work of teachers? This chapter reports on a research project that has attempted to address this complexity through its mixed-method, longitudinal design that included both large-scale surveys and case studies of beginning teacher experiences in diverse settings. Studying the effectiveness of preparing 'classroom ready' teachers does not have to be pursued in the name of ascertaining means and averages of their preparedness or teaching productivity. Rather, it can be understood through the realm of everyday work in which teachers' understandings, doings, and relatings (Kemmis et al. 2014) are actively constructed and in which their own perceptions, as well as those of others, provide a 'surplus of vision' in making sense of the capabilities and practices of beginning teachers.

Studying Teacher Perceptions

Teacher perceptions of various educational issues, others, and themselves have been extensively researched (Cochran-Smith et al. 2008; Gitomer and Bell 2016; Klieme and Vieluf 2009). Indeed, one can say that 'perception' is one of the key words in both quantitative and qualitative educational research and this presents an issue of how 'perception' and the 'perceiving subject' are understood (Doyon and Breyer 2015; Jordan 1998; Matthen 2015). Perception, from a phenomenological perceptive, is neither a mode of apprehending reality by the knowing subject nor an exclusive domain of consciousness. Rather, perception is identical to our embodied presence in the world—'I am all that I see, I am an intersubjective field, not despite my body and historical situation, but, on the contrary, by being this body and this situation, and through them, all the rest' (Merleau-Ponty 1962/2002, p. 525). Our embodiment brings to the fore the primacy of perceptions in our experience of the world or, to put it differently, the experience of perception *is* our 'bodily' presence at the moment when things, truths, values, and so on appear to us as part of our being-in-the-world (Heidegger 1962/2008). This embodied presence is the moment when our reflection is born and, therefore, a perception is already charged with a meaning-making potential. But it is not a meaning that is constructed by a subject that perceives the world as an object. Rather, it is revealed for us practically in a certain horizon. As Merleau-Ponty (1964, p. 12) argues, 'we experience a perception and its horizon "in action" [*pratiquement*] rather than by "posing" them or explicitly "knowing" them.'

Studying the Effectiveness of Teacher Education (SETE) project (Mayer et al. 2017) focused on perceptions of beginning teachers 'in action,' by looking, first, at how the teachers perceived their effectiveness in the context of their workplaces and, second, backward-mapping these perceptions to their perceptions of ITE programs. In addressing these two main areas of inquiry, we approached 'perception' as the background of beginning teachers' experiences in the lifeworlds of preparation and work. These two lifeworlds constituted a field of perceptions in which teachers assigned meanings of their preparedness and effectiveness to their actions (e.g., what it meant to be prepared and effective by them and others in particular contexts of work). In this regard, a teacher perception can be understood as 'a reference to a whole which can be grasped, in principle, only through certain of its parts or aspects' (Merleau-Ponty 1962/2002, p. 16). The professional standards, used by us for designing survey and interview questions, were useful for grasping the whole as an ideal or idealized unity of teaching practices. This unity of parts (e.g., the domains of knowledge, practice and engagement and standards within these domains) was distilled from the collective experience of the profession, providing a language for interpretation. Yet, the perceptual consciousness of beginning teachers was beyond this language because it was a consciousness of particular experiences and events that were 'infused with secret life' (Merleau-Ponty 1962/2002, p. 44). In this lies the paradoxical nature of studying perceptions of teachers' preparedness for work and their effectiveness in diverse contexts. Teacher perceptions of preparedness and effectiveness are situated in diverse contexts and are open to a horizon of multiple perspectival views. At the same time, these perceptions blend with one another according to common patterns of teacher education and work experiences. The language of standards plays an important role here in mediating the link between the particular and the common and between the mundane and the ideal.

According to Merleau-Ponty (1964, p. 16), the paradox of perception lies in the simultaneity of immanence and transcendence. In our case, immanence is because beginning teachers, in their particularity, come to know practices through their unique and developing perceptual experience of them. Transcendence is because knowing one's particular experience is related to the experiences of others who perform similar teaching practices and received similar teacher education due to the standardization and regulation of ITE. Perceptions of preparedness and effectiveness therefore appear as the paradoxical phenomenon which renders them accessible to all as abstract essences of professional learning and practice. In this regard, graduate teachers could convey how they perceived the features of different programs through their current experiences of teaching in schools in a way that resembled Husserl's 'synthesis of transition.' That is, their ITE experiences and teaching experiences in schools constituted in this research design a unity of two fields of perception—preparation and work—in which the utility of ITE was deduced, as it were, from their immediate experiences of work. The no longer immediate and visible to our research team experiences were given to us as visible from another standpoint—from a standpoint of the teachers' present field of perception. Thus, the effectiveness of teacher preparation was presented to us as a synthesis of transitional experiences from 'there and then' to 'here and now' in the process of professional becoming in space and time. To study 'effectiveness' would be then to study perceptions of 'essences' of professional learning and practice that become 'visible' in the immediate experience of becoming a teacher. It is here that the immediate provides a vantage point of perceiving the utility of professional education, opening up a spatial-temporal horizon for linking the distant and the proximate.

From a phenomenological perspective, a spatial dimension of professional becoming has to do with joining together the experiences of professional learning at university and the experiences of teaching in school. This is not merely an association of perspectives on these experiences but rather a passage from one (there, far-off) to another (here, close-up). Although work experiences in schools (here) form an anchoring point of perceiving the effectiveness of teacher education (there), the world of practice cannot be seen as 'more true' or real if we understand professional becoming—a passage from there to here—as a transition across two commensurate spaces and, in turn, as a locus of truth. As Merleau-Ponty (1968, p. 22) argues, 'the close, the far-off, the horizon in their indescribable contrast form a system, and it is their relationship within the total field that is the perceptual truth.'

Equally, a temporal dimension of professional becoming has to do with joining together past and future. The time of perceiving the utility of teacher education is both retrospective and prospective in that teachers' experiences of professional education precede its appearance as an 'object' of reflection in a present moment—the object always precedes itself, and, at the same time, it discovers new possibilities in the future. Thus, the transitional synthesis of perception is based on the unfolding of time—an historical orientation across 'double horizon of past and future' (cf. Merleau-Ponty 1962/2002, p. 278). In the process of synthesis, the object of perception evades its final interpretation because it appears to the embodied subject through the medium of time and 'because time slips away as fast as it catches up with itself' (Merleau-Ponty 1962/2002, p. 279). In the unfolding of time, the perceiving subject is not an autonomous one but is the subject that is, as it were, unified with an object. 'There is no related object without relation and without subject, no unity without unification, but every synthesis is both exploded and rebuilt by time which, with one and the same process, calls it into question and confirms it because it produces a new present which retains the past' (Merleau-Ponty 1962/2002, p. 280).

The spatial-temporal synthesis of transition (from the 'here and now' to the 'there and then') in perceptions of one's preparedness through effectiveness poses, moreover, a question of memory. From a phenomenological perspective, the problem of memory in perception arises in relation to the problem of perceptual consciousness (Merleau-Ponty 1962/2002, p. 25). For instance, beginning teachers do not perceive their effectiveness in the lifeworld of teaching just as it appears to them at this moment, but their capacity to apprehend this would involve the 'modification' of relations between preparation and practices in understanding their actions here and now. By being a part of the lifeworld, they see the world (here and now) as self-evident but, in doing so, their former experiences become present to them 'in the form of horizon' which they can reopen in an act of remembering (Merleau-Ponty 1962/2002, p. 27). This horizon becomes then part of perceptual consciousness in which remembering the past provides a 'present atmosphere and significance' for them and for others to perceive the lifeworld and to form a true idea of it. Because I am of the world, 'I would not know that I possess a true idea if my memory did not enable me to relate what is now evident with what was evident a moment ago, and, through the medium of words, correlate my evidence with that of others' (Merleau-Ponty 1962/2002, p. 46). In the experience of perception, memory is not detachable from us and neither are we detachable from experiences of, and relations with, the world and others.

In sum, to study the perceptions of teachers means recognizing their experiences of perceptions as embodied in space and time, inhabiting them. In the transitional synthesis of perceptions across time and space, the memory of the experienced and what one remembers and forgets have a distinctive profile. Memory, however, is not about reconstructing the past. Rather, it is to be found at the intersection of remembering and forgetting or on the edges of memorial boundaries. The key in understanding an experience of perception is 'the field of presence' (Merleau-Ponty 1962/2002, p. 26). This field is the primary experience in which 'here and now' and 'there and then' make their appearance unalloyed and in which the whole lifeworld manifests itself. In the field of presence, memory, for instance, can operatively reopen past, embodied experiences of beginning teachers, motivating their present actions. The sedimentation of the past can create various expectations that may or may not be always possible to realize in their present circumstances. Hence, the synthesis of transition is experienced as either a continuation or breakdown of links between teacher preparation and practice. Teachers' perceptions of their preparedness for work need to be understood 'in the field of presence' and, more specifically, in conditions of their employment and work.

Transition from Initial Teacher Education into the Workforce

The research design of the SETE project included three main sources of data—a desktop mapping of teacher education programs to identify the field of ITE perception in terms of the length, structure, and delivery of the programs; surveys of graduate teachers and principals to explore how they perceive the effectiveness and preparedness of beginning teachers; and qualitative case studies to develop a sense of the lifeworld of beginning teachers. There were four rounds of surveys of 2010 and 2011 graduate teachers and up to five case study visits to 30 selected schools in Victoria and Queensland, Australia. Case studies were conducted throughout the duration of the study and informed a review of questions in subsequent surveys. The longitudinal aspect of the research design was influenced by an understanding of transition from ITE into the workforce as a process of professional becoming in which perceptions are dynamic, embedded in diverse school contexts and embodied (e.g., the emotional labor of beginning teachers). This approach has enabled us to decenter the perceptions of ITE by graduate teachers. That is, unlike in various course satisfaction surveys, graduate teachers in our project were invited to talk about and reflect upon their present experiences in workplaces and link them to their ITE experiences (see for more information, Mayer et al. 2017). Our goal was to reanimate the perceptions of ITE by graduate teachers in the context of their workplaces and to identify characteristics of various programs thought by them to be effective. This working of the past against the present resulted in a picture of diverse and complex relations in which perceptions of ITE experiences became connected to local circumstances as well as to employment destinations and pathways.

In the context of their employment, the majority of graduate teachers perceived themselves as effective and prepared across all of the nine key areas of teachers' work (AITSL 2011) that were used in the surveys and examined in case studies. These areas included teaching culturally, linguistically, and socioeconomically diverse learners; design and implementation of the curriculum; pedagogy; assessment and the provision of feedback and reporting on student learning; classroom management; collegiality; professional engagement with parents/carers and the community; professional ethics; and engagement with ongoing professional learning. Equally, school principals perceived the novice teachers as prepared and more effective than the teachers perceived themselves. These perceptions were embedded in practices of diverse schools, representing the geographic, sociocultural, and socioeconomic specificity of schools in Australia. In our study, however, the secondary school sector was somewhat overrepresented compared to the proportion of these schools across the country. Also, the majority of schools (65%) were in metropolitan cities, while eight percent of participants' schools were in towns with a population of less than 500. Given this diversity, case studies, in particular, highlighted that teacher perceptions of effectiveness and preparedness were context specific and related to challenges that they faced due to the location, size, and demographic composition of schools and, in turn, to teaching expectations and responsibilities, access to professional learning opportunities and mentoring, general school culture, workplace/staffroom politics, and so on (Kline and Walker-Gibbs 2015).

In terms of effectiveness as beginning teachers, the graduate teachers perceived themselves as more effective in the areas of professional ethics and engagement with ongoing professional learning but less effective in teaching culturally, linguistically, and socioeconomically diverse learners; design and implementation of the curriculum; pedagogy; and assessment and the provision of feedback and reporting on student learning. The perceptions of areas in which the graduate teachers felt less effective were firmly located in their classroom work with students. For example, when asked about key challenges faced in their first years of teaching, the graduate teachers and their principals both identified classroom management and catering for diverse learners as the most challenging, although teachers perceived these areas as more of a challenge for themselves than principals thought were a challenge for them. Teachers perceived assessment and reporting and planning as far greater challenges than principals thought they were, while principals viewed pedagogy as a far greater challenge for new teachers than the teachers themselves saw it. In addition, the case studies data highlighted that negotiating relationships with other staff members and with school leadership were areas of challenge, impacting the sense of effectiveness as beginning teachers.

In terms of preparedness for work, graduate teachers had a positive perception of their teacher education programs. A more detailed analysis of perceptions (see Kline and Walker-Gibbs 2015) showed that ITE programs enabled teachers to develop capabilities for working in a variety of schools. In particular, they remembered high-quality academic staff that provided meaningful links between theory and practice in their units and opportunities for practical application of professional knowledge in assessment tasks and collaborative activities in classes and tutorials, as well as during school practicum experiences. This enabled them to build a sense of cohesion between various components of the teacher education curriculum, including their application during professional experience in schools. Graduate teachers felt particularly well-prepared in such areas as pedagogy, professional ethics, and engagement with ongoing professional learning. However, they felt less well-prepared in classroom management; professional engagement with parents/carers and the community; assessment and the provision of feedback and reporting on student learning; and teaching culturally, linguistically, and socioeconomically diverse learners.

The sense of preparedness in these areas reflected challenges of transitioning into workplaces, such as establishing relations with students and parents/carers, responding to diversity in their classrooms and assessing student learning outcomes to maximize teaching and learning. Hence, reflecting on the content and characteristics of ITE programs, graduate teachers tended to focus on their perceived and situated in practice needs. Consequently, they suggested a number of improvements in teacher preparation courses. These included providing more, and earlier in the course, opportunities for professional experience in schools and more focus on managing student behavior, how to respond to diversity in the classroom and to use assessment to inform teaching. At the same time, both graduate teachers and their principals recognized that 'preparation' is a continuing process of learning to teach. The analysis of principals' additional comments in surveys showed that the majority of the principals perceived 'preparedness' as an ongoing process, rather than a fixed outcome of teacher education (Rowan et al. 2015), and as something that continued well into the first two-three years of initial employment. The following quote captures this general perception:

> I don't think any graduate teacher is truly ready for the rigor of teaching for the first time. Much of this is based around learning over the first two years of their work life and it is a maturing process for most graduates. Provided there is good support from the school in a leadership capacity and a collegiality perspective, graduate teachers become better equipped for the needs of the first couple of years of school. (Principal, Round 2)

Many principals had put support and mentorship structures in place to make the transition process as productive as possible and to extend opportunities for beginning teachers to learn the 'craft' through their immersion into the 'real' world of teaching. In this regard, most of the principals perceived their beginning teachers as generally prepared for work and 'assessed' their general preparedness as a foundation on which teachers can build their professionalism. This perspective on 'preparedness' by school principals supports a transitional view of becoming a teacher. That is, one's sense of preparedness evolves through a transitional synthesis of perceptions across time and space and is related to developing a sense of effectiveness in teaching. The transitional synthesis of perspectives toward preparedness requires therefore a close attention to teachers' experiences of physical transitions to workplaces such as their employment pathways.

Our study provided a quantitative descriptive picture of the employment pathways of beginning teachers and their links to education backgrounds. Specifically, the data allowed us to identify what types of programs contributed to better employment opportunities and initial teaching experiences in diverse settings. For example, graduates of bachelors' degrees were more likely to be employed in full-time permanent positions. Graduates of graduate diploma degrees were less likely to be full-time permanent and more likely to be part-time permanent or casual. In the first three years of employment, graduate teachers were more likely to move to full-time or part-time permanent positions and less likely to be employed on a casual basis. Employment was identified as one of the key influences on the graduate teacher perceptions of preparedness and effectiveness; those who were employed on an ongoing, permanent basis felt that they were better prepared and more effective in comparison with those in casual or contract positions. Many teachers who participated in case studies had either contract positions or worked in casual relief teaching roles in their first two years. These early career teachers often were reluctant to discuss their challenges and/or seek assistance from their colleagues or school leadership, fearing to be perceived as not capable enough and hence reducing their chance of renewing contracts or getting permanent employment. Moreover, if graduates were employed casually, they had little opportunity for sustained classroom practice that would enable their learning and for accessing professional development and mentoring in the schools in which they provided relief teaching.

Workplace conditions impacted on the teachers' perceptions of preparedness and effectiveness, too. Early experiences in the teaching workforce are a critical period. It is during this time that perceptions of one's self as a teacher and of the profession are formed and continue to shape the subsequent years of teaching. Workplace conditions are therefore a crucial factor in shaping beginning teachers' perceptions and in their decision-making to stay in the profession or to leave. The responses to open-ended questions in the graduate teacher surveys provided a rich data source for understanding more about obstacles to securing a teaching position, reasons for not seeking employment as a teacher, as well as about the role of induction and support in schools. For instance, 20% of teachers in their first year of teaching wanted to change their conditions of employment. This included issues ranging from industrial concerns (e.g., low pay for long hours of work, workplace bullying), to professional practice challenges (e.g., lack of professional agency, misrecognition of their strengths and capabilities, lack of collegiality and mentoring), to dissatisfaction with administration (e.g., perceived inadequacies of school leadership). The following comment from one of the beginning teachers serves to sum up the major issues highlighted in the comments of our final survey:

> It saddens me that a culture has developed that puts pressure on teachers to do many hours of unpaid overtime and use personal funds to buy equipment for school. Performance reviews contribute to an attitude of suspicion that teachers are not working hard enough. More contracts also contribute to a lack of stability in the living circumstances of an early career teacher. In my third year of teaching I am still unable to apply for a mortgage because I am officially on a contract ending in 9 months' time. Nothing other than a complete overhaul of the system and a campaign to improve attitudes from a government-led position, will achieve this. I'm not holding out hope. (Graduate Teacher, Round 4 Survey)

From this analysis, one can see how graduate teachers' perceptions of ITE are situated in the present moment of practices and in conditions in which they find themselves. This is not just about remembering what had happened in the past but rather perceiving the utility of past experiences as these appear here and now—in the 'field of presence.' It is in this particular moment of their becoming that the past acquires a practical sense. But it is also here that teachers' employment status and workplace conditions appear to have the greatest bearing on their perceptions of preparedness and effectiveness. This is not to say that graduate teachers were not critical of their teacher education courses. On the contrary, their criticism has provided a basis for teacher educators' reflexivity and orientation to building those capabilities that would enable the transition of graduate teachers into diverse schools and into the teaching profession, more broadly.

Therefore, a transitional perspective on learning to teach developed in the SETE project implies a stronger relationship between teacher education programs and schools to construct their own questions and then begin to develop courses of action that are relevant to their contexts and, in turn, to the preparation of new teachers. The transitional perspective on learning to teach can open up, therefore, a space of possibility where teacher educators and teachers can move beyond their boundaries and into the 'third space'—'one where learning teaching and/or doing teaching is not situated at one point in time with one side of the 'partnership' (in university), and then at another point in another partnership space (in school), and then somewhere in between after graduation and during early employment where the graduates themselves are left to make sense of and negotiate the context and their learning, often with little support' (Mayer et al. 2017, p. 130). In thinking about an opportunity of the third space, teacher educators and the profession may attend to the transitional synthesis of perceptions by beginning teachers who have already experienced the transgression of boundaries, firsthand.

Concluding Remarks

Concerns with the quality of initial teacher preparation increasingly dominate the political landscape in Australia and elsewhere, leading to large-scale reforms and regulation of teacher education. In this context, it is critical to question teacher education policy that is based on mistrust, 'moral panics,' or stories of perceived failure. Articulating a response requires not only courage but also research with which policy-makers would be prepared to engage (Rowan et al. 2015). The SETE project provided a large-scale evidence base 'to inform teacher education policy and accountability mechanisms that regularly drive political agendas and anecdotal claims of teacher education's (in)effectiveness' (Mayer et al. 2017, p. 1). The project generated a set of rich findings that revealed the state of teacher education and beginning teachers' work in Australia through the analysis of perceptions and experiences of beginning teachers and principals. In doing so, the project team sought to make sense of teacher education effectiveness through its longitudinal, mixed methods, iterative research design, and the involvement in the study of approximately 5000 beginning teachers and 1000 principals.

One outcome emerging from this project is a transitional perspective on teacher preparation. This perspective has wide-ranging implications for understanding teacher education. First, the experience of beginning teachers' perceptions showed that it is problematic to think about teacher education as an end point of professional readiness and hence make judgments about the effectiveness of teacher education on this basis. Learning to teach extends beyond university-based experiences to school contexts where workplace conditions can support or constrain ongoing professional learning. Second, a transition from university to school is not a cumulative experience of moving progressively from a stage of survival and discovery to a stage of experimentation and consolidation, and, finally, to a stage of mastery and stabilization (Feiman-Nemser and Remillard 1996). Rather, transition should be understood as an ongoing and open-ended participation in a cultural-historical milieu of schooling—a situation where teachers' professional capabilities come into being in their concrete co-participation and engagement with others and where their professional becoming cannot be severed from cultures and histories of schools. Lastly, the transitional perspective on the professional learning of beginning teachers calls for stronger relationships between teacher educators and the profession. Starting with our situations and shared accountability for teacher education, we can illuminate a transitional space for graduate teachers beyond our perceived boundaries and, in doing so, prompt them to have a keen awareness of their capabilities and responsibility for the shaping of education futures in contexts into which they enter.

Acknowledgements The *Studying the Effectiveness of Teacher Education* project was supported by a strong partnership involving the Victorian Institute of Teaching (VIT), the Queensland College of Teachers (QCT), the Victorian Department of Education and Early Childhood Development (DEECD, now the Department of Education and Training), the Queensland Department of Education Training and Employment (QDETE), Deakin University's School of Education in Victoria, and Griffith University's School of Education and Professional Studies in Queensland. This research was supported under Australian Research Council's Linkage Projects funding scheme (project LP110100003). The views expressed herein are those of the author and are not necessarily those of the other members of the research team, the Australian Research Council or the Industry Partners. The project team consisted of Diane Mayer (Victoria University/Sydney University), Brenton Doecke (Deakin University), Mary Dixon (Deakin University), Alex Kostogriz (Monash University), Andrea Allard (Deakin University), Simone White (Queensland University of Technology), Bernadette Walker-Gibbs (Deakin University), Leonie Rowan (Griffith University), Jodie Kline (Deakin University), Julianne Moss (Deakin University), and Phillipa Hodder (Deakin University).

References

Australian Institute for Teaching and School Leadership. (2011). *Australian professional standards for teachers*. Retrieved January 11, 2018 from https://www.aitsl.edu.au/docs/default-source/general/australian-professional-standards-for-teachers-20171006.pdf?sfvrsn=399ae83c_12.

Cochran-Smith, M., Feiman-Nemser, S., & McIntyre, D. (Eds.). (2008). *Handbook of research on teacher education: Enduring questions in changing contexts* (3rd ed.). New York, NY: Routledge.

Doyon, M., & Breyer, T. (Eds.). (2015). *Normativity in perception*. London, England: Palgrave Macmillan.

Feiman-Nemser, S., & Remillard, J. (1996). Perspectives on learning to teach. In F. Murray (Ed.), *A knowledge base for teacher educators* (pp. 63–91). San Francisco, CA: Jossey-Bass.

Gitomer, D., & Bell., C. (Eds.). (2016). *Handbook of research on teaching* (5th ed.). https://doi.org/10.3102/978-0-935302-48-6.

Heidegger, M. (1962/2008). *Being and time*. Malden, MA: Blackwell Publishing.

Jordan, J. (1998). *System theories and a priori aspects of perception*. Burlington, NJ: Elsevier Science.

Kemmis, S., Wilkinson, J., Edwards-Groves, C., Hardy, I., Grootenboer, P., & Bristol, L. (2014). *Changing practices, changing education*. Singapore: Springer.

Klieme, E. & Vieluf, S. (2009). Teaching practices, teachers' beliefs and attitudes. In Indicators and Analysis Division of the OECD Directorate for Education (Eds.), *Creating effective teaching and learning environments: First results from TALIS* (pp. 87–124). Paris, France: OECD Publishing.

Kline, J., & Walker-Gibbs, B. (2015). Graduate teacher preparation for rural schools in Victoria and Queensland. *Australian Journal of Teacher Education, 40*(3), 68–88. https://doi.org/10.14221/ajte.2014v40n3.5.

Matthen, M. (Ed.). (2015). *The Oxford handbook of philosophy of perception*. Oxford, England: Oxford University Press.

Mayer, D., Dixon, M., Kline, J., Kostogriz, A., Moss, J., Rowan, L., et al. (2017). *Studying the effectiveness of teacher education: Early career teachers in diverse settings*. Singapore: Springer.

Merleau-Ponty, M. (1968). *The visible and the invisible*. Evanston, IL: Northwestern University Press.

Merleau-Ponty, M. (1964). *The primacy of perception*. Evanston, IL: Northwestern University Press.

Merleau-Ponty, M. (1962/2002). *Phenomenology of perception*. London, England: Routledge.

Rowan, L., Mayer, D., Kline, J., Kostogriz, A., & Walker-Gibbs, B. (2015). Investigating the effectiveness of teacher education for early career teachers in diverse settings: The longitudinal research we have to have. *The Australian Educational Researcher, 42*(3), 273–298. https://doi.org/10.1007/s13384-014-0163-y.

Teacher Education Ministerial Advisory Group [TEMAG]. (2014). *Action now: Classroom ready teachers*. Canberra, Australia: Department of Education and Training.

Alex Kostogriz is Professor in Languages and TESOL Education at the Faculty of Education, Monash University. He has previously held leadership positions at Deakin University and Australian Catholic University. Alex's research is based on sociocultural approaches to learning and teaching and centers on two overarching goals. The first is to understand the conditions by which students' involvement in various classroom practices is shaped, and how such involvement affects both what is learned and how it is learned. The second is to use this understanding to help create effective classroom communities of learners and inform teaching practices. Alex's current research projects focus on the professional practice and ethics of language teachers, teacher education and experiences of beginning teachers.

Chapter 16
Revisiting the Teaching Practicum: Effecting Innovation or Entrenching the Status Quo? Reflections from an ITE Program in South Africa

Anil Kanjee

Introduction

The Minimum Requirements for Teacher Education Qualifications policy (DHET 2015), popularly known as MRTEQ, specifies key principles and requirements for the development of teacher education programs in South Africa. The primary purpose of the policy, according to Rousseau (2014), is to align teacher education qualifications to the Higher Education Qualifications Framework (HEQF) to promote closer links between theory and practice, to encourage active knowledge and to motivate applied knowledge sensitive to context. While the policy does not prescribe specific pedagogies, theories, and structures that education providers need to adhere to (Sayed and Carrim in press), it does list key exit outcomes that highlight the different domains of knowledge required for students to graduate. Regarding the teaching practicum (also referred to teaching practice or student teaching), the policy specifies that 'students should spend a minimum of 20 weeks and a maximum of 32 weeks in formally supervised and assessed school-based practices over the four-year duration of the degree. In any given year, a maximum of 12 such weeks could be spent in schools, and at least three of these should be consecutive' (DHET 2015, p. 23). However, while the successful completion of the teaching practicum comprises a critical component of Initial Teacher Education (ITE) programs across all South Africa universities, the structure, duration, criteria for completion, supervision, feedback as well as the assessment of students vary substantially (Deacon 2016; Reddy et al. 2008; Rusznyak and Bertram 2015).

In their review of how the practicum in ITE programs are implemented across nine historically advantaged institutions in South Africa, Reddy et al. (2008) highlight a number of discrepancies and similarities, which include the following: (a) in all institutions supervisors were allocated to assess students using specific guidelines,

A. Kanjee (✉)
Tshwane University of Technology, Pretoria, South Africa
e-mail: KanjeeA@tut.ac.za

© Springer Nature Singapore Pte Ltd. 2018
C. Wyatt-Smith and L. Adie (eds.), *Innovation and Accountability in Teacher Education*, Teacher Education, Learning Innovation and Accountability, https://doi.org/10.1007/978-981-13-2026-2_16

usually in the form of rubrics, and were required to provide written reports of the assessment as well as to provide written and oral feedback to students; (b) most institutions require students to complete a practice teaching journal or portfolio, which was also used to award the final grade, while in all cases school mentors were required to report on students' performance; (c) the use of reflection and self-assessment by student teachers for improving their own practices was encouraged in some institutions; and (d) there are wide variations in who assessed students during the practicum. In most institutions, the assessments were conducted by all staff teaching in the program; some institutions only involved staff who specialize in specific phases or subjects, while other institutions hired external temporary or part-time staff during this period.

In his review of five ITE programs, Deacon (2016) found that the cumulative length of teaching practice reported varied significantly, from 10 to 35 weeks, over the duration of the different programs. Regarding the quality of the time spent during their teaching practicum, Deacon (2016) notes that approximately 20% of students reported teaching for less than an hour a day during the final year teaching practicum while most students also reported that they spent little, if any, time observing and learning from experienced teachers. Deacon (2016) also notes that only one institution indicated that most of its students on teaching practice were being assessed by specialists in the subjects they were teaching while he found substantial differences in the nature and type of feedback that student teachers received across different ITE programs. Regarding the instruments used to assess students, Deacon (2016) notes that the integrated conception of teaching that was in the teaching practice assessment instruments used by all programs studied 'was often counteracted by a tendency for discrete marks to be awarded for each assessment category or criterion, thus creating the impression that teaching consists more of a set of separate routines than an interrelated whole' (p. 13). Furthermore, Deacon (2016) reports that 'the assessment instruments' indicators of competence were insufficiently explicit and lacked the detail needed to provide adequate formative and motivational feedback to students' (p. 13).

Investigating student teachers' experiences in Malawi, Mtika (2011) found that the interaction with their mentors contributed significantly to the professional development of trainee teachers, and that those trainee teachers who received appropriate support from formally identified mentors tended to have a stronger commitment to teaching. However, Mtika (2011) also reports on difficulties encountered by some trainee teachers, including the complexity of conducting learner-centered lessons, which the author ascribes to the inability of students to master college course work. Another challenge, noted by Mtika (2011), regards the practice of requiring student teachers to take on the responsibility and workload of a 'mentor' teacher despite their not having the qualifications or the experience to function as teachers. Similarly, in their study of third-year students in South Africa, Marais and Meier (2004) found that many student teachers reported having full teaching loads during their practicum, effectively serving as substitute teachers for their mentors. However, the authors also found that the most positive teaching practicum experience reported by many students was the support received from their mentor teachers.

In their study on how one teacher training institution in South Africa undertakes student assessments during the teaching practicum, Sedumedi and Mundalamo (2012) report that most students were assessed by staff who did not possess the requisite content and/or pedagogical knowledge required for the lesson being assessed. The authors found that the 'non-specialist assessors' were unable to provide relevant feedback to students while students 'assessed by those educators who were subject specialists benefited immensely, because they also went back and reflected on how they could improve their own subject matter knowledge and how they could deliver such knowledge' (p. 86). Sedumedi and Mundalamo (2012) also found no evidence of self-assessment or reflective practice among student teachers and attribute this to lack of any space for self-reflection in the teacher practice journals.

Several challenges highlighted by Deacon (2016), Mtika (2011), Reddy et al. (2008), Marais and Meier (2004), and Sedumedi and Mundalamo (2012) also impact on the ITE program offered by the School of Education at the Tshwane University of Technology (TUT). As part of the School's initiative to address these challenges, several new programs have been offered, current courses and modules revised and key changes effected to the teaching practicum. This chapter reports on the results of an evaluation conducted to obtain information on the extent to which students' practical knowledge and skills gained during their teaching practicum were aligned to the theoretical knowledge and practical skills gained during the Foundation Phase course. Specifically, the primary aim was to determine the impact of the changes effected to the Professional Studies theory and teaching practicum components offered to Foundation Phase students.

Framework for Developing Effective Teaching Practicum Experiences

The teaching practicum, or clinical experience, is regarded as one of the most critical components of any ITE program for successfully preparing students to enter the world of teaching (Clemans et al. 2017; Darling-Hammond 2006; Sayed and Carrim in press). The Ontario Teachers' Federation (2013) regards the practicum as the most valuable part of their teacher preparation experience as it constitutes essential, experiential learning where theory and practice come together, and through which teacher candidates hone their teaching knowledge, skills and abilities, and come to understand the complexity of the life of the teacher, and the critical issues they expect to encounter in classrooms and schools. Similarly, the MRTEQ policy (DHET 2011) calls for the implementation of teacher education programs that: (i) 'describes clear, specific requirements for the development of learning programs, as well as guidelines regarding practical and work-integrated learning (WIL) structures' (p. 8) and (ii) 'brings the importance of inter-connections between different types of knowledge and practices into the foreground, as well as the ability of teachers to draw reflexively from integrated and applied knowledge, so as to work flexibly and effectively in a variety of contexts' (p. 9).

However, the construct of 'teaching practicum' is a contested one between traditional conceptualization and alternative models of the 'teaching practice' (Clemans et al. 2017, p 715). For Clemans et al. (2017), traditional models of ITE programs are distinguished by 'the series of discrete and disjointed course work units that are broken up by practice teaching opportunities in schools—with the practicum typically being more highly valued by students of teaching—creating a fragmented view of knowledge; a view that yet again plays out through notions of the theory-practice divide' (p. 715). Darling-Hammond (2006) notes that traditional models of ITE programs 'often had students taking batches of front-loaded course work in isolation from practice and then adding a short dollop of student teaching to the end of the program—often in classrooms that did not model the practices that had previously been described in abstraction' (p. 307). Similarly, Sayed and Carrim (in press) note that the teaching practicum in current ITE programs in South Africa is often treated as marginal and disconnected from other ITE courses. These authors argue in favor of developing effective and relevant ITE programs that integrate theoretical-based knowledge gained in university classrooms with practice-based knowledge gained in schools. Within this context, providing students with an opportunity to undertake relevant and effective teaching practice is critical for developing successful teachers.

Sayed and Carrim (in press) argue that the teaching practicum should become the core of any ITE program and should serve as the bridge for integrating theory and practice (see Fig. 16.1). The authors note that while frameworks about teacher knowledge and learning 'helps to understand the conceptual framing of ITE programs, in the end it is how this translates into respective program designs that determine their usefulness' (p. 12). Sayed and Carrim (in press) propose various interrelated knowledge sets within ITE programs to emphasize the key issues and challenges for developing quality teachers and improving quality teaching:

1. Specialist, specific, and general knowledge that is internal to a subject/discipline, and which encompasses specialist as well as general pedagogic knowledge that cut across learning domains (e.g., classroom management).
2. Knowledge that is external to a subject or discipline, and which encompasses curricula knowledge, knowledge about context, and knowledge about the aims and purposes of education.
3. Knowledge that encompasses 'the technical skills and the value dispositions teachers need to establish and promote a social justice agenda within education, and positions teachers as knowing, purposive, and active agents working toward the broad goals of transforming society and forging a more inclusive and equitable future for learners' (Sayed and Carrim in press, p. 10).

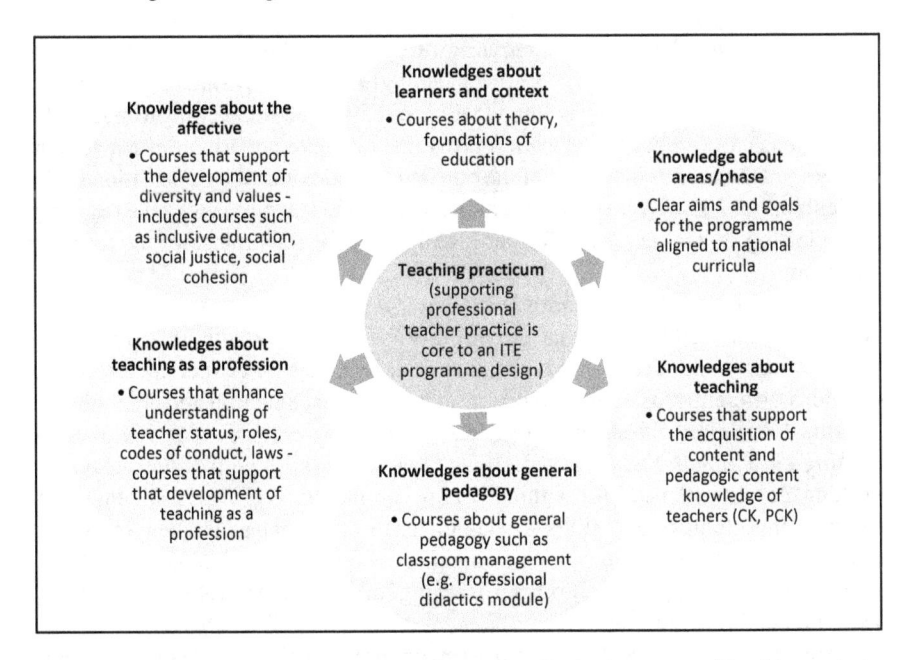

Fig. 16.1 A programmatic approach to ITE (Sayed and Carrim in press, p. 20, with permission from Yusuf Sayed)

Framework for Developing Effective Teacher Education Programs

While Sayed and Carrim (in press) provide a useful framework for centralizing the teaching practicum within the overall ITE program, no details are provided on the development and implementation of ITE programs. For this aspect, the seven principles proposed by Korthagen et al. (2006) were used to guide the restructuring of the ITE program to be responsive to the expectation, needs and practices of student teachers enrolled at the TUT.

First, *learning about teaching involves continuously conflicting and competing demands*. The authors note that learning to teach is a complex activity that occurs in the context of competing demands and argue for ITE programs to support student teachers to recognize and deal with these complexities by promoting 'collaboration in learning and teaching, collaboration of peers and collaboration of teacher educators and student teachers' (Korthagen et al. 2006, p. 1027).

Second, *learning about teaching requires a review of knowledge as a subject to be created rather than as a created subject*. Korthagen et al. (2006) note that student teachers do not only learn from formal courses but also from their own experiences and thus argue for teacher education programs to provide opportunities to create and reflect on their experiences as individuals or groups, so as to create their own professional knowledge of teaching.

Third, *learning about teaching requires a shift in focus from the curriculum to the learner*. Korthagen et al. (2006) note that meaningful learning by student teachers can only occur when their learning is embedded in the experience of learning to teach. The authors thus call for teacher education programs to create opportunities for student teachers to 'experience the doing of the curriculum more than the information of the curriculum' (p. 1030) by involving them in planning the teaching, doing the teaching, and reflecting on that teaching; further highlighting the importance of the teaching practicum.

Fourth, *learning about teaching is enhanced through (student) teacher research*. Korthagen et al. (2006) note that providing student teachers with opportunities to research their own practice can serve as a catalyst to see and experience teaching situations differently, as well as to better understand that situation and act within it.

Fifth, *learning about teaching requires an emphasis on those learning to teach working closely with their peers*. Korthagen et al. (2006) note that the process of working closely with peers (or within learning communities) provides student teachers with opportunities and skills to support each other, enhances their individual competence for reflection, develops their expertise on how to guide their own learners in schools to support each other's learning, and develops lifelong practices of peer or community learning.

Sixth, *learning about teaching requires meaningful relationships between schools, universities, and student teachers.* Korthagen et al. (2006) note cooperation between universities and schools can only be meaningful for supporting student teacher learning if teacher educators 'understand the many intricate ways in which *teaching itself* is similar to and different from teaching about teaching' (p. 1034). Thus, the authors argue that 'teacher educators also require a practical understanding of the impact of practice on theory and of theory on practice' (p. 1034).

Seventh, *learning about teaching is enhanced when the teaching and learning approaches advocated in the program are modeled by the teacher educators in their own practice*. Korthagen et al. (2006) note that contradictions exist between theory and practice partly due to the inability of teacher educators to model practices that they advocate. To address this challenge, the authors argue that teacher educators must make their pedagogical reasoning for their practice clear, explicit, and understandable so that student teachers can 'see into their teachers' thinking about teaching so that they can access the ideas and feelings associated with taking risks and learning about teaching in meaningful ways' (p. 1037).

Revising the Teaching Practicum

The opportunity for restructuring the program to address the theory–practice divide arose with the introduction of the B.Ed. Foundation Phase program in 2013. Both the preparation of students for the practicum (theory) and the teaching practicum (practical) are offered in the Professional Studies course (PDF). This course became the focal point for restructuring the new Foundation Phase program. However, the nature and type of revisions effected were constrained by a number of accreditation stipulations for the Program. These include (i) the minimum number of credits required for graduation, (ii) the minimum number of weeks for the teaching practicum, and (iii) the specific courses approved for each year of study.

Two key shortcomings were identified from an internal review conducted to determine the extent to which the B.Ed. Foundation Phase program was aligned to the MRTEQ policy requirements (DHET 2011). First, the requirement that all ITE programs should highlight 'the inter-connections between different types of knowledge and practices as well as develop the ability of teachers to draw reflexively from integrated and applied knowledge' (DHET 2011, p. 7). Second, the requirement that all ITE programs prepare students to function as scholars, researchers, lifelong learners, and effective assessors. Respectively, these were stipulated in the Policy (DHET 2011) as:

> The educator will achieve ongoing personal, academic, occupational and professional growth, through pursuing reflective study and research in their field, in broader professional and educational matters, and in other related fields. (p. 52)

> The educator will understand that assessment is an essential feature of the teaching and learning process and know how to integrate it into this process. The educator will have an understanding of the purposes, methods and effects of assessment and be able to provide helpful feedback to learners. The educator will design and manage both formative and summative assessments in ways that are appropriate to the level and purpose of the learning and meet the requirements of accrediting bodies. The educator will keep detailed and diagnostic records of assessment. The educator will understand how to interpret and use assessment results to feed into processes for the improvement of learning programmes. (p. 53)

In addressing these shortcomings, several key changes were affected. First, the course content was updated, most significant of which was the introduction of an integrated module for improving teachers' use of assessment for improving learning and teaching (Kanjee and Mthembu 2015). As noted in Table 16.1, the Assessment for Learning (AfL) module comprised a set of units presented as two sections focussing on summative and formative assessment respectively. To facilitate students' development, and consolidation, of the essential theoretical knowledge and practical skills to effectively use assessment in schools, the units were introduced consecutively from Year 2 onwards.

Second, the teaching approach applied, as well as the underlying philosophy advocated, in the course across the different years was streamlined. Reflective teaching (Korthagen and Wubbels 1995; Pollard 2008) was adopted as the basis for supporting students to develop and consolidate relevant knowledge and skills at the university, as well as during their teaching practicum. Reflective practices were integrated into the program by: including activities during all lectures that required students to reflect on their knowledge and practices individually and in groups; providing students with opportunities to demonstrate, review and reflect on the application of practical skills during lectures; establishing student professional learning communities for students to support each other in reviewing and completing assigned tasks, during, and after class; and including reflection exercises in the course materials provided to students.

Table 16.1 Assessment for learning units and year introduced

Summative assessment	Formative assessment	Year introduced
Unit 1: Review of curriculum and assessment policy statements: Identifying learning objectives, targets, and progression		Year 2
Unit SA2: Defining purpose of testing, identifying instruments, and use of results Unit SA3: Developing summative instruments Table of specification Item writing/selection	Unit FA2: Clarifying and sharing learning intentions and success criteria Unit FA3: Managing effective classroom discussions and activities to elicit evidence of learning	
Unit SA4: Compilation and administration Development of the rubric/memo Unit SA5: Reviewing, grading, and analysis Recording and reporting of results	Unit FA4: Providing feedback that moves learners forward	Year 3
Unit SA6: Formative use of results to improve learning	Unit FA5: Activating learners as learning resources for each other (peer assessment) Unit FA6: Activating learners as owners of their own learning (self-assessment)	Year 4
Unit 7: Using assessment data to improve teaching		

Third, given the absence of any relevant text, learning material, in the form of a student portfolio, was developed to: (i) address the reality that English, the language of learning and teaching at the university, was the second language of all students; (ii) present relevant theory on assessment and include practical exemplars where possible, that account for the specification of the national curriculum policy as well as the learning and teaching context of South African schools; (iii) sequence and pace the course content in a manner that would allow students to develop and consolidate new theoretical concepts and practical skills learnt; (iv) incorporate theory and practical tasks as well as reflection activities for students to complete, either during or after class, and to provide an avenue for recording discussions and outcomes of student professional learning community meetings; and (v) align the course content, activities, and assignments to the teaching practicum, especially in Years 2 and 3 when the practicum takes place in the middle of the academic year. An unintended consequence of using these portfolios was the greater accountability it engendered among students to complete their work, as any incomplete activities in the portfolios were immediately obvious to both students and lecturers.

Fourth, the course content was better aligned to facilitate students' development and consolidation of relevant theoretical knowledge and practical skills from Year 2 onwards, as well as to ensure that students were better prepared for the teaching practicum in Years 2, 3, and 4, and the completion of the teaching practicum project in Year 4. Specifically, these changes focused the central role of teacher pedagogy on developing specific practical knowledge and skills to better prepare students to function effectively within the realities that impact on learning and teaching across South African schools.

Fifth, two key changes were effected to the schedule for Year 4 students. First, two classes were added after the teaching practicum, breaking away from the traditional practice where students only returned to campus to write examinations. These extra classes provided an opportunity for students to reflect on and share their teaching practicum experiences with their peers and teacher educator, as well as to provide recommendations for improving the course. In addition, students also used these two weeks to convene professional learning community meetings with peers, most often for discussing, reviewing, and revising their teaching practicum project. The recommendations of the 2014 class to provide a clearer structure for the practicum project resulted in the revision of the 2015 project. Similarly, the 2015 students' recommendation that the lesson plans and reflection exercises for the project be incorporated into the teaching practicum journal resulted in the revision of the 2016 teaching practicum journal. Second, 'catch-up classes' were included into the course schedule to accommodate the inevitable student strikes. Over the last few years, these 'catch-up classes' have proved extremely valuable for both students and lecturers. However, this change did not help in 2016, when violent and destructive student strikes disrupted all university activities during and after the teaching practicum, and thus no additional classes were held.

Sixth, improving the theoretical knowledge and practical skills of lecturers to ensure that lecturers presenting the PDF course can apply and model AfL strategies and techniques during lectures. In practice, this required all lecturers to (i) participate in AfL capacity development workshops that covered all aspects of the AfL module noted in Table 16.1; (ii) establish a professional learning community to share experiences and address challenges regarding the presentation of the PDF course; (iii) work with teachers in local schools to present lessons where their newly acquired knowledge and skills could be implemented in real-life classroom contexts; and (iv) actively participate in the development, review and revision of materials used in the course. In this way, all students in the PDF course were exposed to both the theory and practice regarding the effective use of assessment in the classroom. For example, for the class on learning intentions and success criteria, lecturers used learning intentions and success criteria to introduce the lesson while simultaneously providing the theoretical rationale and using specific formative assessment techniques, e.g., name sticks or pair-and-share, to engage students in the lesson.

Seventh, introducing a teaching practicum project that served dual purposes for awarding a grade for the PDF theory component as well as supporting students' engagement with the theory covered in the course during the practicum. Specifically, students were required to (i) undertake two action research activities for obtaining evidence on the effectiveness of specific strategies and techniques; (ii) plan and prepare for lessons; (iii) apply available, and/or develop their own, tools and templates as well as collect evidence on the application of relevant strategies, techniques, and materials used in the classroom; and (iv) record and reflect on their classroom activities over the duration of the practicum. For example, for one research activity, students collected data to compare learners' knowledge of the lesson purpose across different lessons introduced with or without learning intentions.

Eight, key changes were effected to improve the assessment of students during the teaching practicum, including (i) ensuring students are assessed by lecturers with both the requisite content and pedagogical knowledge and experience. While all lecturers trained in the use of AfL were allocated to assess Foundation Phase students, a small number of students were still assessed by 'non-specialist assessors' due to the large number of students, as well as logistics of accessing schools; (ii) revising the classroom observation protocols that require lecturers to begin their school visits with a discussion and reflection on key successes and challenges experienced by the student, to identify specific aspects that students require assistance with, and to provide specific feedback that allows students to move learning forward, i.e., identifying key areas of success as well as providing specific suggestions for improving one or two key areas of their practice (Wiliam 2011); (iii) revising the observation schedules to focus on pedagogical practices that foreground key assessment for learning strategies and techniques. In addition, these schedules were also discussed with students before the practicum and copies were included in the teaching practice journal.

While the changes effected were continuously monitored, reviewed and even revised where possible, a comprehensive evaluation could only be conducted after the first cohort of students completed all three years of the revised course. Fortuitously, the opportunity for such an evaluation was provided with the invitation from the Centre for International Teacher Education for the School of Education to participate in a national project tracking student teachers' experiences during and after their ITE programs. For TUT, an additional purpose for participating was to determine the extent to which the revised PDF course contributed to enhancing students' teaching knowledge and the extent to which the teaching practicum was aligned to the theoretical knowledge and practical skills gained during the course.

Methodology

Data for this chapter was obtained from a larger study involving four ITE programs offered in South Africa. Questionnaires were administered to a sample of final (fourth) year students while several focus group interviews were also conducted with the same cohort (see Table 16.2). All data was collected by researchers based at the Centre for International Teacher Education, after students completed the teaching practicum.

Table 16.2 Sample of students responding to the questionnaire and participating in interviews

Institution and language	Questionnaire	Interviewed
ITE Program 1—English	64	12
ITE Program 2—Afrikaans	87	8
ITE Program 3—English	58	13
ITE program TUT—English	34	11
Total	243	54

An overwhelming majority of the students sampled were female (96%), with 87% falling in the 21–25-year-old age category. All participants at the TUT classified themselves as 'Black' while the composition of participants from the three other ITE programs comprised 67% 'White', 28% 'Colored', 3% 'Black', 1% 'Indian', and 1% of the data was missing. The number of participants that reported having the same home language as the language of teaching used in their B.Ed. program varied across the four ITE programs: Program 1—76%, Program 2—97%, Program 3—33%, and TUT—0%.

The questionnaire sought information on students' general experiences during the teaching practicum regarding the knowledge and skills they acquired when teaching mathematics and languages; their interaction with school and university staff, including their mentors; as well as their views about the value of their specific academic programs in preparing them to function as effective teachers. The focus group interviews further explored participants' views regarding the teaching practicum, their academic program as well as their feelings, strengths, and doubts about their level of preparedness in entering the teaching profession.

Descriptive statistics were used to analyze the quantitative data while thematic analysis was used to categorize the main findings of the focus group interviews. Additional chi-square analysis was also conducted to determine differences in response patterns between participants' from TUT and the other ITE programs.

Results and Discussion

The results presented in this section are based on participant responses obtained from the questionnaire and focus group interviews regarding their experiences of the teaching practicum. To provide a reference against which to understand experiences of TUT students, the data was aggregated to reflect the responses of participants from TUT as well as the combined responses of participants from the other ITE programs.

Student Experiences During the Practicum

As reported in Table 16.3, the majority of participants across the ITE programs reported that their lecturers adequately prepared them for the teaching practicum, that they found the lesson plans provided by their respective institutions useful during their practicum period, and that the completion of the portfolios served as a valuable opportunity to reflect on their development as a teacher. Significantly more TUT participants responded affirmatively to these questions. Regarding the feedback practices of their lecturers, the majority of respondents across all the ITE programs reported that the process was useful and that they were also able to provide feedback to their lecturers. Similarly, most respondents across all ITE programs indicated that they were provided with useful feedback after the teaching practicum and that they were also able to provide feedback on their experiences after the teaching practicum. However, approximately 15% of TUT respondents and 19% of respondents from the other ITE programs reported that the number of visits from lecturers was not sufficient.

During the interviews, TUT participants also highlighted specific challenges encountered regarding their level of preparedness to deal with issues of inclusiveness and language of learning in schools, as noted below:

> When I arrived in the classroom I see that I really need a skill to teach in an inclusive classroom. For me it was not even, it was half a chapter and most of the time they were telling me the definitions and everything but not the inside of inclusive education to say when you teach inclusive education this is what you have to concentrate on, what we should do. Yes, I did know the definitions and everything but implementing the definitions for me it was limiting. (Focus group 2, TUT student 1)

Being prepared to teach learners in their home language was also highlighted as a critical challenge, with all TUT participants interviewed arguing for the B.Ed. program to include classes on how to teach in the different home languages that they expect to encounter in schools, as noted in the interview comments below:

> Interviewee 1: It's rare where you would find Ma'am (*lecturer name*) will be saying teach, present in SiSwati, Setswana or Sepedi. They use their own language but it's rare. Most of the time they teach in English and it hits us when we go back to school especially when it comes to terminology.
>
> Interviewee 3: Especially in the foundation phase, especially for us. They must teach me how to teach those learners with Sepedi.
>
> Interviewee 2: Because even for me I did Sepedi but I cannot teach in Sepedi. I cannot unless my learners will be failing.

Similarly, TUT participants also highlighted the challenges faced when assessed by lecturers that are not familiar with the language of learning and teaching used during the lesson:

> Interviewee 1: And another thing I think the lecturers also have a problem because for example let's talk about (*name of school*) where I was doing my teaching practice, the LOLT (language of learning and teaching) is Setswana. When he came in I thought I was going to impress him, prepared a lesson on 3D shapes mathematics. Only to find that he couldn't....

Table 16.3 Participant responses regarding the practicum assessment and feedback

Question	ITE program	Strongly disagree (%)	Disagree (%)	Agree (%)	Strongly agree (%)	chi sq	p
(a) My lecturers prepared me for teaching practice	Combined	0.5	6.7	77.5	13.9	30.394	0.000*
	TUT			44.1	52.9		
(b) The lesson design we were given for teaching practice by lecturers was useful	Combined	3.3	12.9	62.7	20.1	11.658	0.020*
	TUT		5.9	47.1	44.1		
(c) Completing the portfolio was a valuable opportunity to reflect on my development as a teacher	Combined	1.9	13.9	67.5	16.3	21.384	0.000*
	TUT		2.9	47.1	50.0		
(d) The number of visits from lecturers/evaluators was sufficient	Combined	2.9	16.3	63.2	16.7	9.248	0.055
	TUT	5.9	8.8	47.1	35.3		
(e) Feedback I received after formal lesson evaluations was useful	Combined	1.4	14.8	54.5	27.3	7.908	0.095
	TUT		8.8	44.1	38.2		
(f) I was able to give feedback to my lecturers/evaluators after lesson evaluations	Combined	3.8	16.7	63.6	14.4	3.488	0.480
	TUT	5.9	5.9	70.6	17.6		
(g) Feedback I received after teaching practice was useful	Combined	1.9	12.4	71.8	13.4	4.893	0.298
	TUT	2.9	5.9	64.7	26.5		
(h) I was able to give feedback to my lecturers about my experiences of teaching practice	Combined	1.4	10.0	64.1	23.0	4.395	0.355
	TUT		5.9	70.6	17.6		

*Differences significant at the 0.05 level

Interviewee 3: (Interrupts) a single word

Interviewee 1: A single word. Yes. The AfL approach was good, the lesson plan was good. Everything was good but the language. He was able to see - media is there, yes, interaction is there even though he had some concerns but totally he didn't hear anything hence he said when I come back can you please prepare something in English.

Support Received During the Practicum

While most participants across all ITE programs reported that their lecturers were helpful, significantly more participants from the other programs indicated 'Not at all' or 'Somewhat helpful,' while significantly more TUT participants indicated 'Very helpful' (see Table 16.4). This finding could be indicative of the positive impact of the changes regarding only assigning Foundation Phase lecturers to assess Foundation Phase students, improved preparedness of TUT lecturers, and revised instruments used to assess students.

Similar response rates were noted between participants from TUT and the other three programs regarding the extent to which fellow students, learners they taught, teacher mentors, and other teachers in the schools were considered as helpful to them during their teaching practicum. A key aspect highlighted in this set of responses is that only 53% of the participants reported that their mentors were 'Very helpful.' Given the critical role that mentors play in supporting student teachers' development of practical knowledge and skills, this result is concerning though not unexpected. Mtika (2011) and Marais and Meier (2004) reported that relationships between students and teaching mentors are not always ideal and vary significantly across and within schools. Similarly, in their review of how student teachers develop their assessment knowledge and skills, Hill and Eyers (2016) found that while some mentors supported their students by modeling a range of assessment practices as well as providing opportunities for students to implement their new knowledge and skills, similar support was not forthcoming from all mentors. Possible reasons noted for such discrepancy vary widely and include mentor teachers' training and understanding regarding their role in supporting student teachers, their subject matter knowledge and experience in teaching, the assessment knowledge and practices of mentor teachers, the accountability contexts impacting on schools, as well as the nature of the relationship between students and mentors (Hill and Eyers 2016; Koh 2011; Marais and Meier 2004; Mtika 2011; Nichols and Harris 2016).

Similarly, TUT participants interviewed conveyed a range of experiences regarding their relationship with their mentors, as noted in their comments below:

> With my mentor, I had support from my mentor. It's just that in the previous year she wasn't in the Foundation Phase so most of the things she actually learnt from me. So yeah, she didn't have a problem, she didn't mind asking me because she knows I have some kind of experience with the Foundation Phase.' (Year 4, TUT Foundation Phase student 1)
>
> Yeah like she's supportive and I think she is too much supportive to me because she never told me that I'm wrong. She was like a mother to me and she has huge experience. She did

Table 16.4 Participant responses regarding support received during the practicum

Question	ITE program	Not at all (%)	Somewhat helpful (%)	Helpful (%)	Very helpful (%)	Not applicable (%)	chi sq	p
(a) Lecturers	Combined	3.3	16.7	42.6	35.9	0.5	15.194	0.010*
	TUT		2.9	26.5	67.6			
(b) Fellow students	Combined	1.9	9.6	33.0	49.3	4.3	7.113	0.212
	TUT	8.8	8.8	38.2	41.2			
(c) Learners	Combined	1.0	7.2	52.2	36.4	1.9	4.035	0.544
	TUT		8.8	38.2	50.0			
(d) Mentors	Combined	1.0	10.5	33.5	53.6	0.5	4.990	0.417
	TUT		11.8	29.4	52.9			
(e) Other teachers	Combined	2.4	14.4	36.4	41.6	3.8	7.643	0.177
	TUT	2.9	14.7	20.6	55.9			

*Differences significant the at the 0.05 level

many things like, that woman, she can teach, actually she teaches everything, I learnt many things. (Year 4, TUT Foundation Phase student 2)

What I can say about my mentor is that she was very supportive, but she wanted me not to ask anyone like when I have a problem, in everything, just ask me, you're assigned to me so don't go anywhere else. (Year 4, TUT Foundation Phase student 3)

Assessment Knowledge and Skills Gained During Language and Mathematics Lessons

The one area where significant differences were detected across all but one response between participants from TUT and the other ITE programs pertains to the development of assessment knowledge and skills. This finding was not surprising given that TUT is the only participating program to offer a comprehensive assessment module (Kanjee et al. 2016). As noted in Tables 16.5 and 16.6, a relatively high percentage of participants from the other ITE programs (between 21 and 33%) reported that they did not gain any knowledge and skills regarding the development of tests, assignments and memoranda, as well as the reporting and use of assessment results. Given that many ITE programs provide some coursework in assessment, most of which focuses on measurement and testing (Kanjee et al. 2016), and the strong emphasis on testing within the curriculum and assessment policies (DBE 2011) within South African schools (Kanjee and Sayed 2013), this result was unexpected. However, Hill and Eyers (2016) note that developing assessment knowledge and skills of student teachers is an extremely complex process that is affected by many factors, and acknowledge that currently, limited information is available on teaching, learning and assessment in the context of developing nations.

Significant differences in response rates were noted for the development of peer and self-assessment knowledge and skills, with approximately one-fifth of respondents from other ITE programs indicating 'Not at all.' Contradicting the finding regarding the use of assessment results, approximately 56% of respondents from other ITE programs indicated 'To a large extent' and 'Completely' regarding the provision of effective feedback during lessons. A possible explanation for this could be students' misunderstanding of the term 'effective feedback.' In his study on teachers' written feedback practices, Kanjee (in press) found that most teachers consider ticks, crosses and short one or two word motivational comments as 'effective feedback,' and expect their students to respond to this 'feedback' by working harder, being motivated or improving their work. The one area where responses of all participants were similar pertains to their knowledge and skills gained in asking higher thinking questions, with the majority responding affirmatively.

The positive experiences of students in the B.Ed. program and the assessment module, in particular, are aptly summed up by the following response:

I can say since from 2013 like, in the first year I experienced like it was somehow difficult, so I had to think otherwise and then as time goes on, I became used to the learners and I enjoyed it. So now I can't go backwards, its forward forever, because like with these techniques and

Table 16.5 Participant perceptions regarding their language assessment knowledge and skills gained

Question	ITE program	Not at all (%)	To some extent (%)	To a large extent (%)	Completely (%)	chi sq	p
(a) I learnt to develop assessments (e.g., tests, assignments, etc.)	Combined	24.4	41.1	26.3	6.7	27.980	0.000*
	TUT		20.6	52.9	23.5		
(b) I learnt to develop assessment memoranda	Combined	30.1	39.2	24.9	4.3	43.407	0.000*
	TUT		23.5	41.2	32.4		
(c) I learnt to use assessment results	Combined	26.8	37.8	28.2	5.7	31.697	0.000*
	TUT		23.5	44.1	29.4		
(d) I learnt to report assessment results	Combined	35.4	37.3	21.1	4.8	42.659	0.000*
	TUT	2.9	23.5	35.3	32.4		
(e) I learnt to provide effective feedback during lessons	Combined	6.7	35.4	45.0	11.5	17.754	0.001*
	TUT		14.7	47.1	35.3		
(f) I learnt to ask higher order thinking questions	Combined	2.4	15.8	57.4	22.0	4.873	0.301
	TUT		26.5	41.2	29.4		
(g) I learnt to train learners to conduct peer assessment	Combined	23.9	39.2	29.7	5.3	26.248	0.000*
	TUT		29.4	41.2	26.5		
(h) I learnt to train learners to conduct self-assessment	Combined	22.5	39.7	30.6	4.8	26.964	0.000*
	TUT	2.9	23.5	44.1	26.5		

*Differences significant at the 0.05 level

Table 16.6 Participant perceptions regarding their mathematics assessment knowledge and skills gained

Question	ITE program	Not at all (%)	To some extent (%)	To a large extent (%)	Completely (%)	chi sq	p
(a) I learnt to develop assessments (e.g., tests, assignments, etc.)	Combined	24.9	37.3	29.7	5.3	33.266	0.000*
	TUT		20.6	44.1	29.4		
(b) I learnt to develop assessment memoranda	Combined	28.7	40.2	22.0	6.2	32.542	0.000*
	TUT		20.6	50.0	23.5		
(c) I learnt to use assessment results	Combined	24.4	38.3	28.7	5.7	31.343	0.000*
	TUT		17.6	50.0	26.5		
(d) I learnt to report assessment results	Combined	32.5	34.0	23.9	6.7	34.297	0.000*
	TUT	2.9	17.6	41.2	32.4		
(e) I learnt to provide effective feedback during lessons	Combined	8.1	33.0	42.1	13.9	23.424	0.000*
	TUT		5.9	47.1	41.2		
(f) I learnt to ask higher order thinking questions	Combined	3.3	19.6	49.8	23.9	2.722	0.605
	TUT		17.6	44.1	32.4		
(g) I learnt to train learners to conduct peer assessment	Combined	20.6	35.9	31.1	9.6	17.612	0.001*
	TUT		23.5	44.1	26.5		
(h) I learnt to train learners to conduct self-assessment	Combined	21.1	35.4	31.1	9.6	17.756	0.001*
	TUT		29.4	35.3	29.4		

*Differences significant at the 0.05 level

strategies, they have equipped us here in TUT, they work well with us and the learners. So, like the sharing of learning intentions, I explained learners they really enjoy learning when they know the reason why they need to learn that and how they're going to achieve that, so its success criteria and learning intentions. So, it makes teaching easier and more fun. (Year 4, TUT Foundation Phase student 1)

However, some TUT participants did struggle with the application of assessment in the classroom as noted in the following response:

I would be knowing, for an example look on the reflection side to say what is [it] that I haven't done right, what is it that I can change, which strategies … which learning area you see. Because the strategies that we're using they are totally different especially I think for me now I'm still struggling with the questioning side of the AfL approach, to say I'm not used to questions where I'd be giving learner's statement and they have to make choices whether is it correct or not. (Year 4, TUT Foundation Phase student 1)

Conclusion

Given that the teaching practicum serves as the bridge between theory and practice and is the site for integration of knowledge obtained in any ITE program, this chapter sought to determine the extent to which the revised Professional Studies theory and teaching practicum components enhanced student teachers' knowledge and skills for teaching in South African classrooms. Using the framework proposed by Korthagen et al. (2006), several changes were effected to the content offered in the Professional Studies course, the teaching approach applied, the development of relevant materials that addressed specific needs of the students, the extension of the course schedule, the improvement of lecturers' pedagogical knowledge and skills, as well as the assessment of students during their practicum. Data was obtained from surveys and interviews conducted by an external team of researchers undertaking a larger sector study involving students from four ITE programs in South Africa. However, a key source of data, obtained from students' verbal and written reflections of their teaching practicum in previous years, was unavailable due to the unusually violent strikes that affected the university after students completed their teaching practicum.

Evidence from the study suggests that the changes to the PDF course had a positive impact on students' knowledge and skills, and its application during the practicum. Significantly more TUT students reported that they were prepared for the teaching practicum, that the lesson plans and journal received were useful, and that their lecturers were helpful in improving their practicum experience. The majority of participants across the different ITE programs reported that their teacher mentors were helpful/very helpful during the practicum. With regard to the assessment knowledge and skills gained during the practicum, participants from TUT were especially positive about both the formative and summative sections of the course, while approximately a quarter to a third of participants from the other ITE programs reported no gains in knowledge and skills regarding the development of tests, memoranda, the reporting and use of test results, as well as the use of peer and self-assessments.

Several challenges experienced by TUT participants were also noted during the interviews. These pertained mainly to their level of preparedness to address issues of inclusivity and deal with the challenge of the different languages of learning and teaching at schools, with a clear call being made for revision to the B.Ed. program to better prepare students to address these issues in the classroom. In addition, these participants also raised an issue regarding the limitation of lecturers who can only understand English and thus are not able to effectively assess lessons presented in any of the other languages of learning and teaching in schools. Notwithstanding the positive experiences reported by TUT participants, and the value of the PDF course in enhancing their theoretical knowledge and practical skills; further, research is required to determine the extent to which the newly acquired knowledge and skills of students, especially with regard to assessment, can and/or will impact on their classroom practices as they begin their teaching careers, and the impact of these practices in addressing the specific learning needs of all learners.

References

Clemans, A., Loughran, J., & O'Connor, J. (2017). University coursework and school experience: The challenge to amalgamate learning. In I. Menter, M. A. Peters, & B. Cowie (Eds.), *A companion to research in teacher education* (pp. 713–724). Singapore: Springer.

Darling-Hammond, L. (2006). Constructing 21st-century teacher education. *Journal of Teacher Education, 57*(3), 300–314.

DBE. (2011). *National protocol for assessment grades R–12*. Pretoria, South Africa: Department of Education.

Deacon, R. (2016). *The initial teacher education research project: Final report.* Johannesburg, South Africa: JET Education Services.

DHET. (2011). *Policy on the minimum requirements for teacher education qualifications*. Pretoria, South Africa: Department of Higher Education and Training.

DHET. (2015). *Revised policy on the minimum requirements for teacher education qualifications*. Pretoria, South Africa: Department of Higher Education and Training.

Hill, M. F., & Eyers, G. F. (2016). Moving from student to teacher: Changing perspectives about assessment through teacher education. In G. T. Brown & L. R. Harris (Eds.), *Handbook of human and social conditions in assessment* (pp. 57–76). New York, NY: Routledge.

Kanjee, A. (in press). Teacher feedback practices and expectations: Reflections from South African schools. In A. A. Lipnevich & J. K. Smith (Eds.), *The Cambridge handbook of instructional feedback*. Cambridge, England: Cambridge University Press.

Kanjee, A., McAuliffe, S., Ramsaroop, S., & Van Staden, S. (2016, October). *Developing student teachers' assessment knowledge and skills: Overview of ITE programmes in South African universities*. Symposium Conducted at the Annual Meeting of the South African Education Research Association, Cape Town, South Africa.

Kanjee, A., & Mthembu, J. (2015). Assessment literacy of foundation phase teachers: An exploratory study. *South African Journal of Childhood Education, 5*(1), 142–168.

Kanjee, A., & Sayed, Y. (2013). Assessment policy in post-apartheid South Africa: Challenges for improving education quality and learning. *Assessment in Education: Principles, Policy & Practice, 20*(4), 442–469.

Koh, K. H. (2011). Improving teachers' assessment literacy through professional development. *Teaching Education, 22*, 255–276.

Korthagen, F. A., & Wubbels, T. (1995). Characteristics of reflective practitioners: Towards an operationalization of the concept of reflection. *Teachers and Teaching, 1*(1), 51–72.

Korthagen, F. A. J., Loughran, J. J., & Russell, T. (2006). Developing fundamental principles for teacher education programs and practices. *Teaching and Teacher Education, 22,* 1020–1041.

Marais, P., & Meier, C. (2004). Hear our voices: Student teachers' experiences during practical teaching. *Africa Education Review, 1*(2), 220–233.

Mtika, P. (2011). Trainee teachers' experiences of teaching practicum: Issues, challenges, and new possibilities. *Africa Education Review, 8*(3), 551–567.

Nichols, S. L., & Harris, L. R. (2016). Accountability assessment's effects on teachers and schools. In G. Brown & L. R. Harris (Eds.), *Handbook of human and social conditions in assessment* (pp. 40–56). New York, NY: Routledge.

Ontario Teachers' Federation. (2013). *Enhancing the practical experience of teachers: Constructing the clinical experiences of teacher candidates in Ontario.* Retrieved June 10, 2017 from https://www.otffeo.on.ca/en/wp-content/uploads/sites/2/2013/11/Enhancing-the-Practical-Experience-of-Teachers.pdf.

Pollard, A. (2008). *Reflective teaching: Evidence-informed professional practice.* London, England: Continuum.

Reddy, C., Menkveld, H., & Bitzer, E. (2008). The practicum in pre-service teacher education: A survey of institutional practices. *Southern African Review of Education, 14*(1–2), 143–163.

Rousseau, N. (2014). Integrating different forms of knowledge in the teaching qualification Diploma in Grade R Teaching. *South African Journal of Childhood Education, 4*(1), 167–186.

Rusznyak, L., & Bertram, C. (2015). Knowledge and judgement for assessing student teaching: A cross-institutional analysis of teaching practicum assessment instruments. *Journal of Education, 60,* 31–61.

Sayed, Y., & Carrim, N. (in press). Initial teacher education in and for the 21st century. In Y. Sayed, N. Carrim, A. Badroodien, M. Singh & Z. McDonald (Eds.), *Becoming a teacher in post-apartheid South Africa: Initial teacher education* (pp. 1–32). Stellenbosch, South Africa: SUN Media.

Sedumedi, T. D. T., & Mundalamo, F. J. (2012). Understanding field assessment of pre-service teachers on school practicum. *Africa Education Review, 9*(sup1), S73–S90. https://doi.org/10.10 80/18146627.2012.755247.

Wiliam, D. (2011). *Embedded formative assessment.* Bloomington, IN: Solution Tree Press.

Anil Kanjee is a Research Professor and coordinator of the Postgraduate and Research Program in the School of Education, University of Technology. He also serves as a Research Fellow at the Oxford University Centre for Educational Assessment, and the Centre for International Teacher Education at the Cape Peninsula University of Technology. His research focuses on addressing the challenge of equity and quality in education, paying particular attention to teacher professional development, learning and learner voice in schools, and the use of assessment and measurement to improve learning and teaching. He has worked as a technical advisor to education ministries in Africa, Asia, and the Middle East as well as to national and international organizations (i.e., UNESCO, UNICEF, World Bank). His current research focuses on enhancing the use of assessment to improve learning and teaching; learners, learning and learner voice in schools; developing effective models of teacher professional development; monitoring and evaluation of education systems, programs and projects.

Chapter 17
School-Based Work in Initial Teacher Education: Responding to Policy in Practice

Bernadette Ní Áingléis and Anne Looney

Introduction

The high calibre of the teaching profession in Ireland[1] is well documented over the years by both national and international experts (Coolahan 1981, 2003; Department of Education and Skills (DES) 2012; Kelly and Hegarty 2017; Organisation for Economic Co-operation and Development (OCED) 1991). In a similar vein, teachers in Ireland have long enjoyed an extraordinarily high level of professional autonomy (Organisation for Economic Co-operation and Development (OCED) 1991) and a 'strong social prestige unlike in most other countries in Europe' (Department of Education and Skills (DES) 2012, p. 5). Entry to initial teacher education (ITE) programs is highly competitive, particularly for undergraduate and graduate primary teacher education courses (Hyland 2012; Darmody and Smyth 2016; Teaching Council 2011b). It is, therefore, partially understandable why attrition rates are almost negligible in Ireland and have remained so over the decades (Hyland 2012).

In the past year, teacher supply has become an issue in Ireland, as teachers graduating from teacher education programs have accepted lucrative offers from education systems across the globe, as an alternative to domestic salaries still suppressed post-financial crisis and extremely high accommodation costs in urban areas. The shortage of graduates in science, technology, mathematics and languages has been impacting both industry and ITE. A further challenge in both primary and post-primary sectors is that restrictions on permanent recruitment remain in place, giving rise to uncertainty and the absence of a tenure track. Workforce planning is relatively underdeveloped for the teaching profession (Department of Education and Skills & The Teaching Council 2015), although now being addressed in the light of contemporary

---

[1] In this chapter, Ireland should be understood as the Republic of Ireland unless otherwise stated.

B. Ní Áingléis (✉) · A. Looney
Dublin City University Institute of Education, Dublin, Ireland
e-mail: bernadette.niaingleis@dcu.ie

© Springer Nature Singapore Pte Ltd. 2018
C. Wyatt-Smith and L. Adie (eds.), *Innovation and Accountability in Teacher Education*, Teacher Education, Learning Innovation and Accountability,
https://doi.org/10.1007/978-981-13-2026-2_17

challenges. Of particular significance in the Irish context is that any teacher shortages are not associated with a lack of candidates for ITE or a lack of interest in the teaching profession, but with a set of circumstances beyond the profession (Ó Ruairc 2017).

What has remained constant through the financial crisis, and in this early phase of recovery, is the nature and extent of goodwill and volunteerism in schools that have provided an indigenous zeitgeist for 'partnership' between higher education institutions (HEIs) and schools in teacher education. This is particularly evident in both induction (Killeavy and Murphy 2006) and ITE programs (The Standing Conference on Teacher Education North and South [SCoTENS] 2004). Following the reconceptualisation of ITE programs (Teaching Council 2011a, b) and the issuing of *Guidelines for School Placement* (Teaching Council 2013), there is a discernible move from the informal, ad hoc participation of schools in the school-based components of ITE, to much more structured arrangements within a partnership paradigm (Teaching Council 2013). This move has given rise to heated debate (albeit on different grounds) between teacher unions and HEIs (Irish National Teachers Organisation [INTO] 2017), within schools (Chambers and Armour 2012; O'Grady 2017), and among teacher educators (Harford and O'Doherty 2016).

The debate has undoubtedly opened up discussion on competing discourses in schools and universities around pedagogies, partnership, knowledge and knowing. The broader influences of global economics on teacher education and Ireland's competitiveness (Mooney Simmie et al. 2016) have also been part of this partnership-in-ITE debate, particularly as teachers' salaries were cut during the financial crisis. The very nature of collaboration, including how 'partnership' is conceptualised and bounded, has emerged as a significant vulnerability in sustaining school–university partnerships (SUPs) (Ní Áingléis 2008). In that context, the fragility of goodwill as a basis for professional learning has been exposed in other jurisdictions (Furlong et al. 2000; McLaughlin et al. 2006). This finding has relevance to the Irish context, given how 'partnership' has been problematised by stakeholders (e.g. The Teaching Council, the Department of Education and Skills, schools and teacher education institutions) in recent years.

This chapter will explore the history of school–university partnerships in ITE in Ireland, specifically in the context of the school-based work undertaken by ITE students. A trajectory of key policy documents will be drawn on, in addition to examining some broader national and international contextual influences. At national level, the role of the Teaching Council and the Inspectorate, as key teacher education stakeholders, will be examined in the context of new structured roles for schools in ITE and increased school-based time for student teachers. The *Guidelines for School Placement* (Teaching Council 2013) will receive particular attention in terms of their underpinning conceptualisation and representation of the proposed partnership between schools and HEIs. This discussion will be followed by a focus on discerning a sense of how stakeholders in SUPs in Ireland are responding to these changes; some voices 'from the field' are shared. Some of the tensions within partnership work in ITE will feature throughout the discussion, and the chapter will close with directions for future development.

From a conceptual viewpoint, the chapter is influenced by social constructivism and the situated learning frameworks proffered by Vygotsky (1978) and Engeström (2001). The writing is strongly influenced by Lave and Wenger (1991) around communities of practice, boundary-crossing and boundary-brokers (Edwards and Mutton 2007; Wenger 1998). Meaningful expansive learning (Engeström 2001) is understood to be social, 'a process that takes place in a participative framework, not in an individual mind' (Lave and Wenger 1991, 14). From our perspective, it is an orientation that acknowledges two key non-negotiables in ITE: firstly, the 'unforgiving complexity of teaching' (Cochran-Smith 2006, p. 12), and secondly, the 'contestability of knowledge' (Furlong 2012, p. 62).

History of School–University Partnerships in ITE in Ireland

Globally, various typologies of SUPs in ITE can be identified. HEI-led models of partnership where schools and universities have clearly defined boundaries, roles and responsibilities exhibit no real sharing of dialogue or critique around repertoires of knowledge (Benton 1990; Edwards et al. 2002; Furlong et al. 2000; Holmes Group 1986, 1990). In the more collaborative model, 'teachers are seen as having an equally legitimate but perhaps different body of professional knowledge from those in higher education' (Furlong et al. 2000, p. 80). There is, therefore, a complementarity of skills and expertise drawn on in the partnership processes and activities. The radical move towards exclusively school-based routes into teaching is now firmly embedded in the ITE landscape in England (Carter 2015; Elmore 2006; Tickle 2000), and in the USA (Goodlad 1990). The move has resulted in little or no role in ITE for the universities. It has led to the belief that the core theoretical base to ITE has been brutally devalued in the process (Gilroy 1992) and a clear 'harbinger for the return to the simplistic perspective that teaching is a set of skills to students and content' (Lambert and Totterdell 1995, p. 14). There have also been very successful school–university collaborations where the focus has been more on the learning potential of all partners. In these collaborations, there is a strong sense of shared responsibility and mutual engagement in the partnership activities, and a shared repertoire of expertise and language, and relationships underpinned by mutuality of trust and reciprocity (Kruger et al. 2009; McLaughlin et al. 2006).

In Ireland, the nature of partnership between schools and universities in the practicum has traditionally been categorised as a work placement or a host model, the school providing the placement setting and the university providing the student teacher (Conway et al. 2009). To a large extent, prior to 2013, 'partnership' in ITE in the Irish context connoted the logistical arrangements by which HEIs related to schools and vice versa based entirely on a spirit of goodwill and volunteerism within schools to offer placements (The Standing Conference on Teacher Education North and South [SCoTENS] 2004). Assessment of students' progress was the sole remit of HEIs, and school-based mentoring by teachers was largely ad hoc, unstructured and more along the lines of 'informal support and guidance' (Young et al.

2015, p. 27). Schools are not *required* to provide placements for student teachers, although most do. However, a root-and-branch review of ITE (primary and post-primary) that commenced in 1999 (the first such review of ITE since the foundation of the State in 1922) heralded a new era for ITE and an enhanced role for schools in the practicum. Two reports followed and were intended to drive reform in ITE; at primary level, the seminal Kellaghan Report (Government of Ireland 2002a), *Preparing Teachers for the Twenty-first Century*, recommended substantial increases to the amount of school-based work on ITE programs, lengthening ITE programs to allow for increased emphases on reflective practice in which student conceptualisations of teaching would be explored. Critically, schools and teachers were to have 'greater and more formal involvement in teaching practice' (Government of Ireland 2002a, p. 161). The Byrne Report (Government of Ireland 2002b), in its review of ITE at post-primary level, confirmed the latter stance.

However, both reports were thin on the detail of 'the why' and 'the how' of more structured participation of schools in the practicum; they were strong on the aspiration that 'a redesign of teaching practice should result in a greater and more formal role for schools and teachers working in partnership with colleges' (Government of Ireland 2002a, p. 161). The review of ITE at post-primary level echoed the recommendations of the Kellaghan Report, but went further in proposing that teachers provide mentoring to students during the practicum (Government of Ireland 2002b). In line with the aspirational nature of the Kellaghan Report, there was no discussion on conceptualisations of mentoring or their underpinning knowledge discourses. Recommendations of both reports remained dormant until the mid-2000s. What was especially significant about both reviews (and regrettably so in our view) is that they seemed to have disregarded a raft of earlier important policy positions developed through 'partnership' fora across the continuum of teacher education, alongside some groundbreaking education legislation and 'a background of twelve years of unprecedented appraisal, analysis and formulation of educational policy' (Coolahan 2003, p. vi). The discontinuity within policy may help to explain the loss of momentum and political will that followed both reviews; the reviews 'were allowed to slip from the public consciousness' (Coolahan 2007, p. 20) with no public debate on the reconceptionalisation of ITE or on the recommendations, most notably those around formalising the role of schools in the practicum elements of ITE.

By the end of the decade, however, global influences had re-ignited the debate. Disappointing 2009 performances of Irish 15-year-olds in literacy and numeracy in PISA (Organisation for Economic Co-operation and Development [OECD] 2010; Hislop 2011), coupled with previous evidence of low levels of achievement in literacy and numeracy of pupils in socio-economic deprived areas (Department of Education and Science 2005a), gave rise to concerns about the quality and relevance of ITE and a justification for radical reform. A 'perfect storm' (Conway and Murphy 2013) was brewing. Preceding PISA, two key reports from the Department of Education and Science directly relevant to teacher education cited poor standards in literacy and numeracy, namely *Beginning to Teach* (2005b) and *Learning to Teach* (2006). The latter report (based on a statistically small sample of final year student teachers) was highly critical of the professional competences of student teachers and claimed that one-third of new entrants to the profession were below par. The report caused outrage in ITE and teacher union circles (Healy 2007; Irish National Teachers' Organisation [INTO] 2007). Absent from both reports were discussions on the concept of teacher-as-learner and any reference to professional knowledge frames and their alignment with pedagogies. Significantly, the final chapter in *Learning to Teach* dealt entirely with promoting the value of school-based work in and the need for more systematic involvement of schools in the practicum (Department of Education and Science 2006).

However, it was not until the launch of the draft Literacy and Numeracy Strategy (Department of Education and Skills 2010) that the promise of both the Kellaghan Report (Government of Ireland 2002a) and the Byrne Report (Government of Ireland 2002b) would be realised, albeit in a rather surprising policy context. The period of ITE was to be extended from three years to four years for undergraduates and from one year to two years for graduates. In all programs, emphasis was to be placed on literacy and numeracy, assessment, reflective and inclusive practices, and doubling the amount of school-based time. Here, structured roles were envisaged for schools. The Teaching Council, in its statutory remit for the accreditation of ITE programs, elaborated in detail on the requirements for new ITE programs in two key policy documents: one on the teacher education continuum and the other on new program criteria for ITE providers (2011a, b). Calls were made for 'new and innovative school placement models' using a 'partnership approach, whereby HEIs and schools actively collaborate in the organisation of the school placement' to include co-operating teachers involved in the key processes of 'mentoring, supervision and constructive feedback' (Teaching Council 2011b, p. 15). While the continuum policy document (Teaching Council 2011a) stated that 'all recognised schools would be expected to host a student on placement', there was no reference to this expectation in the guidelines for ITE providers (Teaching Council 2011b).

To the present day, the status quo position remains: recognised schools in Ireland are not required to offer placements to HEIs but there is an expectation to do so. This is very much in line with the values of the profession as articulated in the *Code of Professional Conduct for Teachers* (Teaching Council 2016) and notions of a learning profession underpinned by professional autonomy that is guarded closely by Irish teachers (Ó Ruairc 2013, 2014, 2016). Embedded within the Code under the standard referencing professional collegiality and collaboration is an explicit requirement that teachers 'work with teaching colleagues and student teachers in the interests of sharing, developing and supporting good practice and maintaining the highest quality of educational experiences for pupils/students' (Teaching Council 2016, p. 8). However, there is no reference in this instance to working with HEIs, arguably a lost opportunity to stitch in a strong call for HEI–school collaborations in ITE. An emphasis on the key role of schools was clearly the uppermost priority reflecting European policy directions in teacher education (European Commission 2007a, b, c, 2010).

The publication of *Teachers Matter* (Organisation for Economic Co-operation and Development [OECD] 2005), followed by the EU Commission's policy statement on teacher competence (European Commission 2005), copper-fastened for the Teaching

Council the centrality of the profession's involvement in ITE and specifically in the practicum elements. The *Guidelines for School Placement* (Teaching Council 2013) developed this policy line further in their articulation of a broad outline of roles and responsibilities for all stakeholders in the practicum including principals (head teachers), co-operating teachers (host teachers), student teachers and HEIs. However, fundamental issues such as the preparation of teachers for their new structured roles, the broader continuing professional development (CPD) requirements of all stakeholders and the resource implications for HEIs were not adequately articulated in the *Guidelines* (Irish National Teachers Organisation [INTO] 2017). Ireland's fragile financial health following the global financial crisis led to a general nervousness in government towards any commitment for additional funding in any but the most front line public services. ITE did not fall into that category.

Others argue that the *Guidelines* lack articulation of the 'fundamental principles of partnership' such as how to build school–university communication processes that would enable joint strategic planning and implementation of placement and a sense of 'shared ownership' (Harford and O'Doherty 2016, p. 47). The latter authors suggest, against the backdrop of greater demands being placed on schools, 'that capacity and 'good will' within the system are now under threat' (2016, p. 44).

However, it should be noted that the *Guidelines* evolved through a strong consultative and collaborative forum over a period of two years involving a full range of ITE stakeholders including teacher educators, teacher unions, teachers, school management and central government. The *Guidelines* are simply '*Guidelines*' and were never intended to be prescriptive or exhaustive. They are also subject to review with research commissioned by the Council informing the next iteration of the *Guidelines* (Teaching Council forthcoming). Critically, the *Guidelines* were never envisaged as a stand-alone policy statement on school–HEI partnerships but rather to be read in light of core professional values which include professional collaboration and collegiality (Teaching Council 2016) and 'shared professional responsibility' (Ó Ruairc 2014, p. 2). The *Guidelines* are described as an addendum to the Council's accreditation criteria for ITE programs (Teaching Council 2011b). Given the broader policy in which they are set, the *Guidelines* are very much in line with the spirit of 'democratic professionalism' (Day and Sachs 2004, p. 7). They are also very much in line with the notion of a community of practice; mutual engagement by schools and HEIs in the practicum; and the sharing of professional repertoires across HEI-school boundaries.

It is the spirit of partnership rather than the latter that is all important, and the language of learning was judiciously selected for the *Guidelines* to reflect that orientation. What is clear, however, in the *Guidelines* and in a catalogue of preceding policy statements is the elevation of the status and expertise of teachers in ITE and particularly in the practicum where they are assigned key roles in the observation of student teachers, in providing feedback and in supporting critical reflection. Ireland's 2013 EU Presidency Conference, dedicated entirely to the question of 'Who is the Teacher Educator?', strongly confirmed that position. Teachers are now viewed as 'teachers of teachers' (Ó Ruairc 2013, p. 10). Further confirmation appears in the *Code of Professional Conduct for Teachers* and in its explicit standards. Teachers are 'members of professional learning communities' with 'a role for the profession in supporting student teachers and newly qualified teachers' (Teaching Council 2016, p. 4).

In all but the assessment of student teachers, the blurring of school–HEI boundaries in the practicum is evident. A strong and long-standing desire by the profession not to have a formal role in the assessment processes (Ievers et al. 2013; Ní Áingléis 2009; O'Grady 2017) leaves HEIs with full responsibility and control of this important professional learning space. Failure to recognise the opportunities for mutual professional learning in collaboration in assessment on the practicum and to share joint responsibility for agreed competence outcomes, arguably, dilutes the potential of 'partnership' in ITE in Ireland. We would argue that it is a missed opportunity for the profession. It is an opportunity that would move partnership from a limited 'connective' conceptualisation to a much higher 'generative', if not 'transformative', level underpinned by relationships of mutual trust (Jones et al. 2016, p. 116). The Sahlberg review of ITE structures in Ireland has captured it well: 'Ideal partnerships involve shared responsibility between the school and the university for the assessment of student competence' (Department of Education and Skills [DES] 2012, p. 22). Such reluctance on the part of the Irish teaching profession to engage in evaluative judgement is not confined to student teachers on placement. Debates are ongoing about the role of the mentor teacher in supporting newly qualified teachers in their first year of teaching. A shift away from a practice where the evaluation of teachers was previously undertaken by the Inspectorate, to the practice of school-led evaluation, met some strong resistance from within the teaching profession and from some school leaders. A revised scheme, now referred to as a non-evaluative professional induction process, is currently being introduced which, although avoiding the disputed issue of assessment, includes the formation of professional support teams in schools for newly qualified teachers (Teaching Council 2017). Of note, the HEIs involved in ITE are not included in these support teams, and there is no explicit connection made between the professional support teams for newly qualified teachers and support for student teachers on placement. Although this program of induction is called 'Droichead', which is the Gaelic word for 'bridge' and is intended to signal the 'crossing' from ITE into the teaching profession, the national roll-out appears to lack systemic connection with ITE and represents, in our view, a missed opportunity to strengthen schools as sites of professional learning for those becoming and new teachers. Despite this missed opportunity at national level, there is evidence that schools and HEIs are developing innovative partnerships where shared dialogue and learning are driving the processes and the structures to enable a sense of 'partnership'. Some research from the field presented below provides insights into how schools and HEIs are interpreting the *Placement Guidelines* (Teaching Council 2013).

Irish Research from the Field

Research by O'Grady (2017) considers the experiences of school principals and co-operating teachers at post-primary in the implementation of the *Guidelines on School Placement*. The study sought to investigate the perspectives of school-based stakeholders at post-primary level concerning (a) recent changes to school placement, within the broader context of emerging SUPs and (b) the formalisation of their responsibilities vis-à-vis ITE.

While additional administrative work associated with new placement procedures is a source of irksome frustration for principals, it is not the 'procedures and paperwork' (Furlong et al. 2000, p. 43) per se that exercises principals and co-operating teachers but rather poor communication processes around placement between HEIs and schools, and within schools. Where HEI–school communication is clear and mutually respectful, relationships are stronger, and dialogue around learning is more likely to feature in school-based interactions than might otherwise have been the case. These dialogic spaces seem to sit on the role boundaries of schools and HEIs and were found by O'Grady (2017) to be mutually rewarding for all parties. It would seem also that where time to dialogue with co-operating teachers was prioritised by HEI staff and where the school leadership valued teacher learning, the conditions for learning were ripe for professional conversations around the deprivatisation of knowledge (Kruse et al. 1995). It is precisely this socially situated commitment to dialogic inquiry that is pivotal in an HEI–school partnership claiming to be a learning community and even more pivotal in light of changing roles and responsibilities. Similarly, research by Conway and Murphy (2013) found that teachers sought more opportunities for 'collegial conversation' with HEIs around learning and teaching; this would include 'review and critique, and reflection between the school and university partners' as a way of dealing with challenges in teaching and building repertoires of best practice (Conway and Murphy 2013, p. 69). The role of the HEIs in ITE in Ireland is, therefore, being perceived as scaffolding reflexive professional conversations and co-creating with teachers, images of the possible in teaching and learning. It is through professional conversations in socially situated settings (e.g. in the school) that a shared vocabulary for talking about teaching and learning is built that in turn generates a kind of interactional excitement; the excitement helps build a sense of mutuality of relational trust and provides a strong basis for ethical relationships in HEI–school partnerships (O'Grady 2017). It is also a strong basis for mutual engagement in a community of practice built around supporting teachers on the practicum.

Case studies in O'Grady (2017) reveal that schools generally perceive changes to placement as positive; there is a sense of 'growing into' more structured 'partnership' with HEIs, but readiness-for-partnership is situated, school-specific and culture-related. Perhaps the gap is closing between the discourse of partnership and the reality of reform (Harford and O'Doherty 2016). However, while co-operating teachers were generally aware of the extended duration of placements, they were not fully aware of what was expected of them as co-operating teachers or where the emphases should lie in their mentoring work with student teachers. The link between mentoring and teacher learning was not entirely clear (O'Grady 2017). This finding is not particular to Ireland (Furlong et al. 2000). For example, general and emotional support dominated the mentoring practices in the Modes of Teacher Education (MOTE) project (Furlong et al. 2000) in England where teachers were more akin to 'local guides' (Feiman-Nemser and Parker 1993, p. 716) rather than facilitators of dialogue and inquiry (Furlong et al. 2000). Not having a shared language to talk about learning and teaching may account for the fact that school-based mentoring has been found to deal largely with the technicalities of teaching as opposed to inquiry-based conversations (Edwards et al. 2002). Accordingly, in the absence of professional development, co-operating teachers in O'Grady's (2017) research relied on their own unchecked assumptions about knowledge, learning and teaching in their work with student teachers; the problem relating to 'apprenticeship of observation' is well documented (Lortie 1975). Furthermore, across the profession (primary and post-primary), the un-met professional development needs of co-operating teachers around mentoring, curriculum pedagogies and reflective practices is emerging as a key tension and a challenge in partnership (Irish National Teachers Organisation [INTO] 2017). In various contexts, it is student teachers who are creatively and courageously mediating these boundary spaces (Ní Áingléis et al. 2012).

Student Teachers and the Practicum

The Sahlberg review of structures in ITE in Ireland has emphasised the importance of a culture of research in teacher education in which student teachers would be actively involved in 'researching their practice, reflecting on it and improving their teaching accordingly' (Department of Education and Skills (DES) 2012, p. 21). Within the practicum, and as part of the reconceptualised placement experience, student teachers in Ireland are now engaging in collaborative research projects with teachers on a wide range of topics over the course of extended school-based experiences. Research by the Teaching Council (forthcoming) presents some examples of collaborative research inquiries by students and teachers in placement settings on such themes as innovative pupil assessment, exploring digital literacies across the primary curriculum, developing drama methodologies in special educational needs settings, and evaluation tools for use on the practicum. The latter research details how student research projects are generating significant teacher talk and curiosity within placement settings around new methodologies and emerging thinking and theories underpinning developments in how people learn. Rather than being viewed as passive learners or as mere 'guests bearing gifts' (Edwards 1997, p. 27), increasingly, student teachers on extended placements are being perceived as valuable resources for the continuing professional development of teachers (Martin 2011). Student teachers are, therefore, becoming important boundary 'objects' (Engeström 2001, p. 134) in school–university partnerships that are enabling learning cultures within schools in which teachers and student teachers learn together.

There are indications also of teachers, student teachers and HEIs engaging in joint school-based research activities. These new collaborative spaces located at the boundaries of roles seem to be providing dynamic and meaningful opportunities for those involved to co-create new understandings of knowledge, learning and teaching. We would argue that the situated transformation of existing knowledge, thinking and behaviour in a shared learning context (as is the practicum) is the fundamental goal not only of a critical constructivist stance (Wang and Odell 2002) but also of HEI–school partnerships. Unless partnership has value and impact for those involved, it would seem to us to be a hollow endeavour. As McLaughlin et al. (2006, p. 182) assert:

> if educational research does not lead to educational practice that is in some sense better – more thoughtful, more just, more effective, more rewarding for pupils or teachers – then there is not much point to it.

Partnership Oriented Towards Teacher Professional Development

It is notable also that one of the most effective collaborations between an HEI and schools in Ireland had learning (as opposed to teaching) as its fulcrum; learning of school-based staff, HEI staff and student teachers (Martin 2011). The *Teacher Professional Development Partnership with Schools* project involved teachers, HEI staff and student teachers co-designing and collaboratively implementing school-wide learning and teaching experiences. Co-planning, co-teaching and structured mentoring of student teachers were integrated; there were opportunities for students, teachers and HEI staff to observe and be observed while teaching in a range of different classrooms in the placement setting. Critically, the opportunities to reflect on new learnings in social spaces each week, sometimes in the school and other times in the HEI, were very significant in terms of teachers, student teachers and HEI tutors making sense of their learnings through the process of sharing. This is, in our view, the essence of dialogic, impactful 'practical theorising' (Hagger and McIntyre 2006, p. 58). For some student teachers, the Wednesday evenings (shared learning time with other students, teachers and HEI tutors) enabled them to tease out some of the pedagogical puzzles in practice including 'bumpy moments' (Romano 2006, p. 974) in safe, scaffolded spaces beyond the classroom. This included making sense of the immediacy, multidimensionality and intensity of school life in ways that were supportive and learning-oriented for the students on placement, as evidenced in some of their comments (Ní Áingléis 2008, p. 102):

> It was just a chance for us all to sit back and chat and discuss the ups and downs of learning and teaching and it was a great way of hearing how other students were getting on….I got to discuss the yard duty today- what an experience! Fights, arguments, children looking to go to the toilet, children falling etc. Extremely dynamic.
>
> I thought the Wednesday evenings were really good, particularly that I could talk to others who had a multi-grade class for placement. Just discussing the methods of teachings, how you were getting on. We had an opportunity to reflect together.

> The parents are hyper-involved (in my placement school). It's terrifying but they're lovely…just because I've never been in a school where they were so involved.

As part of the mentoring project, teachers, HEI staff and student teachers developed a set of mentoring materials including an aide-memoire to assist in classroom observation work, a frame for recording observations and for providing verbal and written feedback. The materials were piloted, reviewed and improved upon over numerous cycles; the manner in which the HEI–school partnership developed these mentoring resources, including tools for evaluation of student competence, contributed to the lifting up of learning for all in the placement setting (Martin 2011). It is a powerful example of transformational relational agency and the capacity-building powers residing in collaborative partnerships (Edwards 2017). It is also an exemplar of the contribution of an HEI–school collaboration to building researching partnership cultures in the process (Martin 2011). The very act of collaborating in developing the mentoring materials (that might be understood as a boundary object in Engeströmian terms) in the partnership activity became the focal point of the energies of the HEI, student teachers and the school; a much more enhanced form of knowing and knowledge grew out of the collaboration (Ní Áingléis et al. 2012). Student teachers were key boundary-brokers in this new knowledge creation and in the interrogation of the old. The potential of student teachers to contribute to building strong sustainable partnerships continues to be explored in the particular HEI. The development of an Advisory Board for placements across the continuum and their related partnerships is a case in point.

Advisory Board for Placements and Related Partnerships

The HEI offers a suite of professional programs with placement components. The Advisory Board for Placements and Related Partnerships currently comprises one external stakeholder from each of the placement sectors (early years, primary, post-primary and further education and training), a student voice (the Vice-President of the Students Union whose remit is placement and education), two critical friends with expertise in the area of partnerships, policy and practice, and two HEI tutors. In our view, an important element of developing strong partnerships underpinning placements is the active and ongoing participation of key stakeholders in policy development, implementation and renewal. The Advisory Board brings diversity in perspective, knowledge, expertise and experience in advising the HEI on matters relating to placement and related partnerships. The advisory functions are designed to inform the work of the university Education Faculty in implementing the vision and key objectives set out in the strategic plan for placements and partnerships. The Advisory Board is, therefore, an important partnership structure in informing the HEI of challenges being experienced in placement settings and making suggestions to the HEI as to how these challenges might best be addressed. It also helps to identify collectively various opportunities for sustaining existing relationships with placement settings and for developing new relationships with new stakeholders in placement work and related research. Critically, the Advisory Board receives ongoing feedback from the university's Education Faculty on how their advisory work has influenced thinking and the implementation of the Faculty's strategy for placements and related partnerships. The dialogic communication processes are transparent within the university; Faculty Board receives the minutes of Advisory Board meetings. These processes are founded on relationships of mutual trust and respect on the Advisory Board and between the Advisory Board and the Faculty; openness to learning is a key driver throughout. Given that the HEI in question is undergoing significant structural change at the time of writing, the Advisory Board also fulfils the important role of affirming best efforts and practices of the HEI in the area of placements and related partnerships. As Fullan (1999, p. 38) reminds us, 'the true value of collaborative cultures is that they simultaneously encourage passion and provide emotional support as people work through the rollercoaster of change'.

The development of a suite of professional development seminars by the same HEI in response to expressed needs of placement schools deserves commentary in terms of how the HEI-led initiative has contributed to sustaining engagement by schools in the practicum. The seminars are held over a number of evenings on topics requested by schools, for example, digital learning, assessment and evaluation, group work methodologies. The seminars are offered to schools that provide placements and mentoring to students of the HEI; the seminars are highly valued by participants in addition to the university certification of attendance. The seminars provide real learning and listening opportunities for the HEI while at the same time building and sustaining professional relationships with teachers and placement schools. They provide, therefore, the context for growing professionality (Hargreaves 2000) and a knowledge landscape rooted in community and inquiry.

Directions for Development

The set of circumstances that has given rise to unprecedented challenges in teacher supply in Ireland, discussed in the opening section of this chapter, may well prove to be the catalyst for some significant developments in placement partnerships between HEIs and schools. At a practical level, any additional places created on ITE courses will generate increased demand for schools to host students on placement. Securing placement for students on ITE courses is already challenging; any additional demand is likely to lead to a change from an *expectation* that schools and teachers support student teachers to a *requirement* to do so. Such a change will inevitably give rise to debate around the nature and dynamics of the partnership. Incentives such as the professional development program discussed above or engagement in formal university structures are unlikely to entice previously non-engaged schools and teachers into meaningful partnerships. Ireland remains committed, thus far at least, to university-based and university-led ITE (Department of Education and Skills (DES) 2012), so the partnerships will always be more university–school, than school–university, despite this latter label being in general use. Students will continue to spend most of their period of preparation in an HEI, and the funding for that preparation will continue to be provided—by the student or the public purse—to the HEI.

The requirement for all schools to become involved in partnerships will lead to a number of immediate debates. The first will be about funding. As discussed, neither schools nor teachers receive any financial incentive or reward to support student teachers. However, neither do they engage in the evaluation or assessment of student teachers. In the case of teachers, there is a strong professional imperative to be involved in the education of new entrants to the profession. This work is generally seen as one of the defining characteristics of a profession, and to date, when financial incentives have been discussed, they have generally been sought for the schools rather than the individual teachers involved. One principal in O'Grady's (2017) research summarised the current tensions succinctly:

> We are struggling to find enough classes for students to teach and enough co-operating teachers to work with the students. We are inundated with cv's, emails and calls from student teachers looking for placements. I think it is very unfair on students that the colleges take the fees over two years but do not put in place a proper system of organising teaching placements. Also, it has become quite clear that the school's role in this arrangement is being taken for granted by the colleges. The work done by the schools in working with the student and helping them through their course is not recognised or rewarded at all. (p. 15)

An interesting slant on the debate about funding for schools in the partnership is whether any funding should be channelled through the HEI, thus making a structural formal link between the school and the HEI (or multiple institutions as is often the case in Ireland), or directly from government (bearing in mind that Ireland is a largely centralised system). The former merits some consideration in that links might have further benefits in research and system innovation, in student progression to higher education, in affording opportunities for those working in teacher education to encounter the 'unforgiving complexity of teaching' (Cochran-Smith 2006, p. 12), and for those doing that complex job to spend some time in an HEI setting or accessing HEI courses.

The second debate will relate to school inspection and evaluation. The current criteria for school self-evaluation frameworks *Looking At Our School* (Department of Education and Skills (DES) 2016a) makes no reference to supporting student teachers on placement. In fact, placement is not mentioned at all in any of the indicators for teaching or for leadership. To us, this seems an obvious gap in signalling that SUPs are important for the education system more broadly and that effective partnerships play a key role in the overall quality and improvement of the education system. If all schools are required to participate in placement partnerships, then such participation should be integral to the quality of the school.

The third set of debates about the future of SUPs arises from developments within the higher education sector in Ireland. The government's *Action Plan for Education 2016–2019* (Department of Education and Skills [DES] 2016b) includes a target of increasing the number of work placements for students pursuing undergraduate degrees by 25%. This growth of placement as part of a quality student experience in an increasing number of higher and further education programs and the rise of university–enterprise and university–community partnerships, adds new voices about and new perspectives on SUPs. They also afford intriguing possibilities for student teachers to have placement experiences beyond schools. In our own institution, we are piloting an internship for student science teachers in the technology practice of one of the major international consulting companies so that they can in turn bring that experience to their teaching in the future. Now in its second year, with a planned expansion to other kinds of industries, the program is challenging traditional conceptualisations of placement in ITE in Ireland and beyond, drawing heavily on theories of teaching as social innovation (Cedarquist and Goluke 2016) and placement as an opportunity to tackle real-world problems. These new placements afford opportunities for student teachers to cross new boundaries (Edwards and Mutton 2007). They also provide important spaces for expansive learning (Engeström 2001). The traditional closed triad of teacher, student and HEI faculty in school placement has already been challenged by new emphases on research, and on collaboration in teacher education and in the teaching profession. The latest challenge to the traditional model comes from new conceptualisations of placement in universities and possibilities for encountering new communities of practice (Wenger 1998). We welcome the challenge and the opportunity it affords to widen the debate, and the experience of those working and learning in ITE in Ireland.

References

Benton, P. (Ed.). (1990). *The Oxford internship scheme: Integration and partnership in initial teacher education*. London, England: Calouste Gulbenkian Foundation.

Carter, A. (2015). *Carter review of initial teacher training [ITT]*. Retrieved December 2, 2017 from https://www.gov.uk/government/uploads/system/uploads/attachment_data/file/399957/Carter_Review.pdf.

Cedarquist, A., & Goluke, U. (2016). Teaching with scenarios: A social innovation to foster learning and social change in times of great uncertainty. *European Journal of Futures Research, 4*(17). https://doi.org/10.1007/s40309-016-0105-1.

Chambers, F., & Armour, K. (2012). School-university partnerships and physical education teacher education student learning: A fruitful division of labour? *European Physical Education Review, 18*(2), 159–181.

Cochran-Smith, M. (2006). *Policy, practice, and politics in teacher education: Editorials from the Journal of Teacher Education*. Thousand Oaks, CA: Corwin Press.

Conway, P. F., & Murphy, R. (2013). A rising tide meets a perfect storm: New accountabilities in teaching and teacher education in Ireland. *Irish Educational Studies, 32*(1), 11–36. https://doi.org/10.1080/03323315.2013.773227.

Conway, P. F., Murphy, R., Rath, A., & Hall, K. (2009). *Learning to teach and its implications for the continuum of teacher education: A nine country cross-national study*. Maynooth, Ireland: The Teaching Council.

Coolahan, J. (1981). *Irish education: Its history and structure*. Dublin, Ireland: Institute of Public Administration.

Coolahan, J. (2003). *Attracting, developing and retaining effective teachers: Country background report for Ireland*. Dublin, Ireland: Stationery Office.

Coolahan, J. (2007). *A review paper on thinking and policies relating to teacher education in Ireland*. Maynooth, Ireland: The Teaching Council.

Darmody, M., & Smyth, E. (2016). *Entry to programmes of initial teacher education*. Dublin, Ireland: The Economic and Social Research Institute.

Day, C., & Sachs, J. (Eds.). (2004). *International handbook on the continuing professional development of teachers*. Berkshire, England: Open University Press.

Department of Education and Science [DES]. (2005a). *Literacy and numeracy in disadvantaged schools: Challenges for teachers and learners*. An evaluation by the Inspectorate of the Department of Education and Science. Dublin, Ireland: The Inspectorate.

Department of Education and Science [DES]. (2005b). *Beginning to teach. Newly qualified teachers in Irish primary schools*. Dublin, Ireland: The Inspectorate.

Department of Education and Science [DES]. (2006). *Learning to teach. Students on teaching practice in Irish primary schools*. Dublin, Ireland: The Inspectorate.

Department of Education and Skills [DES]. (2010). *Better literacy and numeracy for children and young people: A draft national plan to improve literacy and numeracy in schools*. Dublin, Ireland: Author. Retrieved August 18, 2017 from http://www.education.ie/en/schools-colleges/information/literacy-and-numeracy/better-literacy-and-numeracy-for-children-and-young-people-A-draft-national-plan-to-improve-literacy-and-numeracy-in-schools-november-2010-.pdf

Department of Education and Skills [DES]. (2012). *Report of the international review panel on the structure of initial teacher education provision in Ireland: Review conducted on behalf of the Department of Education and Skills (Sahlberg Report)*. Retrieved December 2, 2017 from https://www.education.ie/en/Press-Events/Press-Releases/2012-Press-Releases/Report-of-the-International-Review-Panel-on-the-Structure-of-Initial-Teacher-Education-Provision-in-Ireland.pdf

Department of Education and Skills [DES]. (2016a). *Looking at our school 2016: A quality framework for post-primary schools*. Retrieved July 20, 2017 from https://www.education.ie/en/Schools-Colleges/Services/Quality-Assurance/SSE-Primary-and-Post-Primary/School-Self-Evaluation.htm

Department of Education and Skills [DES]. (2016b). *Action plan for Education 2016–2019: Strategy statement*. Dublin, Ireland: Author.

Department of Education and Skills & The Teaching Council. (2015). *Striking the balance. Teacher supply in Ireland: Technical working group report*. Dublin, Ireland: Authors.

Edwards, A. (1997). Guests bearing gifts: The position of student teachers in primary school classrooms. *British Educational Research Journal, 23*(1), 27–37.

Edwards, A. (Ed.). (2017). *Working relationally in and across practices: A cultural-historical approach to collaboration*. Cambridge, England: Cambridge University Press.

Edwards, A., Gilroy, P., & Hartley, D. (2002). *Rethinking teacher education. Collaborative responses to uncertainty*. London, England: RoutledgeFalmer.

Edwards, A., & Mutton, T. (2007). Looking forward: Rethinking professional learning through partnership arrangements in initial teacher education. *Oxford Review of Education, 33*(4), 503–519.

Elmore, R. F. (2006). *School reform from the inside out. Policy, practice and performance*. Cambridge, MA: Harvard Education Press.

Engeström, Y. (2001). Expansive learning at work. *Journal of Education and Work, 14*(1), 133–156.

European Commission. (2005). *Common European principles for teacher competences and qualifications*. Retrieved August 5, 2017 from http://www.pef.uni-lj.si/bologna/dokumenti/eu-common-principles.pdf

European Commission (2007a). *Relationships between teacher education institutions and schools. Report of a peer learning activity*. Retrieved May 9, 2017 from http://archive.atee1.org/uploads/EUpolicies/pla_relations_tei_and_schools.pdf

European Commission (2007b). *Communication from the Commission to the Council and the European Parliament: Improving the quality of teacher education*. Retrieved May 10, 2017 from http://eur-lex.europa.eu/legal-content/EN/TXT/?uri=CELEX%3A52007DC0392

European Commission. (2007c). *Conclusions of the Council and of the representatives of the Governments of the Member States, meeting within the Council, on improving the quality of teacher education*. Retrieved May 10, 2017 from http://eur-lex.europa.eu/legal-content/EN/ALL/?uri=CELEX:42007X1212%2801%29.

European Commission. (2010). *Improving teacher quality: The EU agenda*. Retrieved May 15, 2017 from http://www.mv.helsinki.fi/home/hmniemi/EN_Improve_Teacher_Quality_eu_agenda_04_2010_EN.pdf.

Feiman-Nemser, S., & Parker, M. B. (1993). Mentoring in context: A comparison of two U.S. programs for beginning teachers. *International Journal of Educational Research, 19,* 699–718.

Fullan, M. (1999). *Change forces: The sequel*. London, England: Falmer Press.

Furlong, J. (2012). The universities and teacher education: Where are we now and where should we be? In F. Waldron, J. Smith, M. Fitzpatrick & T. Dooley (Eds.), *Re-imagining initial teacher education. Perspectives on transformation* (pp. 54–73). Dublin, Ireland: Liffey Press.

Furlong, J., Barton, L., Miles, S., Whiting, C., & Whitty, G. (2000). *Teacher education in transition: Re-forming professionalism?*. Buckingham, England: Open University Press.

Gilroy, P. (1992). The political rape of initial teacher training in England and Wales: A JET rebuttal. *Journal of Education for Teaching, 18,* 5–22.

Goodlad, J. (1990). *Teachers for our nation's schools*. San Francisco, CA: Jossey-Bass.

Government of Ireland. (2002a). *Preparing teachers for the 21st century: Report of the working group on primary preservice teacher education (Kellaghan Report)*. Dublin, Ireland: The Stationery Office.

Government of Ireland. (2002b). *Report of the advisory group on post-primary teacher education (Byrne Report)*. Dublin, Ireland: The Stationery Office.

Hagger, H., & McIntyre, D. (2006). *Learning teaching from teachers. Realizing the potential of school-based teacher education*. Maidenhead, England: OU Press.

Harford, J., & O'Doherty, T. (2016). The discourse of partnership and the reality of reform: Interrogating the recent reform agenda at initial teacher education and induction levels in Ireland. *Centre for Educational Policy Studies Journal, 6*(3), 37–58.

Hargreaves, A. (2000). Four ages of professionalism and professional learning. *Teachers and Teaching, 6*(2), 151–182. https://doi.org/10.1080/713698714.

Healy, A. (2007, February 21). Teacher training needs practical focus. *Irish Times*, 7.

Hislop, H. (2011, September). *Teacher education and Ireland's national strategy to improve literacy and numeracy*. Paper Presented at SCoTENS Annual Conference, Cavan, Ireland. Retrieved January 15, 2018 from http://scotens.org/docs/2011-Hislop-speech.pdf.

Holmes Group. (1986). *Tomorrow's teachers: A report of the Holmes Group*. East Lansing, MI: Author.

Holmes Group. (1990). *Tomorrow's schools: Principles for the design of professional development schools*. East Lansing, MI: Author.

Hyland, A. (2012). *A review of the structure of initial teacher education provision in Ireland: Background paper for the international review team*. Dublin, Ireland: Higher Education Authority.

Ievers, M., Wylie, K., Gray, C., Ní Áingléis, B., & Cummins, B. (2013). The role of the university tutor in school-based work in primary schools in Northern Ireland and the Republic of Ireland. *European Journal of Teacher Education, 36*(2), 183–199. https://doi.org/10.1080/02619768.2012.687718.

Irish National Teachers Organisation [INTO]. (2017). *Joint INTO-Mary Immaculate College Limerick seminar: Colleges of education/initial teacher education providers and schools, school placement: Experiences, challenges and possibilities*. Dublin, Ireland: Author.

Irish National Teachers' Organisation [INTO]. (2007). *Response to learning to teach report* (Press release). Dublin, Ireland: Author.

Jones, M., Hobbs, L., Kenny, J., Campbell, C., Chittleborough, G., Gilbert, A., et al. (2016). Successful university-school partnerships: An interpretive framework to inform partnership practice. *Teaching and Teacher Education, 60,* 108–120. https://doi.org/10.1016/j.tate.2016.08.006.

Kelly, J., & Hegarty, S. (Eds.). (2017). *Schools and schooling, 1650–2000. New perspectives on the history of education. The eight Seamus Heaney lectures*. Dublin, Ireland: Four Courts Press.

Killeavy, M., & Murphy, R. (2006). *National pilot project on teacher induction: Report on phase 1 and phase 2, 2002–2005*. Dublin, Ireland: Department of Education and Science.

Kruger, T., Davies, A. C., Eckersley, B., Newell, F., & Cherednichenko, B. (2009). *Effective and sustainable university-school partnerships: Beyond determined efforts by inspired individuals*. Canberra, Australia: Teaching Australia.

Kruse, S. D., Louis, K. S., & Bryk, A. S. (1995). An emerging framework for analysing school-based professional community. In K. S. Louis, S. D. Kruse & Associates (Eds.), *Professionalism and community: Perspectives on reforming urban schools* (pp. 23–44). Thousand Oaks, CA: Corwin.

Lambert, D., & Totterdell, M. (1995). Crossing academic communities: Clarifying the conceptual landscape in initial teacher training. In D. Blake, V. Hanley, M. Jennings, & M. Lloyd (Eds.), *Researching school-based teacher education* (pp. 13–25). Hants, England: Avebury.

Lave, J., & Wenger, E. (1991). *Situated learning: Legitimate peripheral participation*. Cambridge: Cambridge University Press.

Lortie, D. C. (1975). *Schoolteacher: A sociological study*. Chicago, IL: University of Chicago Press.

Martin, M. (2011). *Teacher professional development partnership with schools project evaluation report*. Dublin, Ireland: DCU St Patrick's Campus.

McLaughlin, C., Black-Hawkins, K., Brindley, S., McIntyre, D., & Taber, K. S. (2006). *Researching schools: Stories from a schools-university partnership for educational research*. Oxon, England: Routledge.

Mooney Simmie, G., Moles, J., & O'Grady, E. (2016). Good teaching as a messy narrative of change within a policy ensemble of networks, superstructures and flows. *Critical Studies in Education*, 1–18. https://doi.org/10.1080/17508487.2016.1219960.

Ní Áingléis, B. (2008). *An exploration of the development of partnership in learning to teach in the Republic of Ireland* (Unpublished doctoral dissertation). Manchester Metropolitan University, Manchester, England.

Ní Áingléis, B. (2009). Learning to teach in collaboration with schools. *Oideas, 54*, 82–101.

Ní Áingléis, B., Murphy, P., & Ruane, B. (2012). Student teacher voice and school placement: What we can learn if we listen. In F. Waldron, J. Smith, M. Fitzpatrick, & T. Dooley (Eds.), *Re-imagining initial teacher education: Perspectives on transformation* (pp. 307–328). Dublin, Ireland: The Liffey Press.

Ó Ruairc, T. (2013). *The role of the teaching council in ensuring quality of teaching in schools*. Paper Presented at the Annual Conference of the Inspectorate, Dublin, Ireland. Retrieved July 19, 2017 from http://www.teachingcouncil.ie/en/_fileupload/teacher-education/presentations/presentation-to-inspectorate-22-march-2013-final.pdf.

Ó Ruairc, T. (2014). Opening remarks to school placement seminar, Athlone, Ireland. Retrieved July 12, 2017 from http://www.teachingcouncil.ie/en/Publications/Promoting-Teaching/education-papers/opening-remarks-to-school-placement-seminar-may-2014.pdf.

Ó Ruairc, T. (2016). *Teaching Council announces significant changes in induction for new teachers* (Press release). Retrieved August 4, 2017 from http://www.teachingcouncil.ie/en/News-Events/Latest-News/Teaching-Council-announces-significant-changes-in-induction-for-new-teachers.html.

Ó Ruairc, T. (2017, September 26). Tackling teacher supply is complex—But we are making progress. *The Irish Times*. Retrieved August 2, 2017 from https://www.irishtimes.com/news/education/tackling-teacher-supply-is-complex-but-we-are-making-progress-1.3234303.

O'Grady, S. (2017). *Policy, practice and partnership: An exploration of the perspectives of post-primary school-based teacher educators in relation to school placement* (Unpublished doctoral dissertation). Dublin City University, Dublin, Ireland.

Organisation for Economic Co-operation and Development [OECD]. (1991). *The OECD review of national policies for education: Ireland*. Paris, France: Author.

Organisation for Economic Co-operation and Development [OECD]. (2005). *Teachers matter: Attracting, retaining and developing effective teachers*. Paris, France: Author.

Organisation for Economic Co-operation and Development [OECD]. (2010). *Information note: Irish students' performance in PISA 2009*. Retrieved August 17, 2017 from http://www.oecd.org/pisa/pisaproducts/46971917.pdf.

Romano, M. E. (2006). 'Bumpy moments' in teaching: Reflections from practising teachers. *Teaching and Teacher Education, 22*(8), 973–985.

The Standing Conference on Teacher Education North and South [SCoTENS]. (2004). *Annual report*. Armagh, Ireland: Centre for Cross Border Studies.

Teaching Council. (2011a). *Policy on the continuum of teacher education*. Maynooth, Ireland: Author.

Teaching Council. (2011b). *Initial teacher education: Criteria and guidelines for programme providers*. Maynooth, Ireland: Author.

Teaching Council. (2013). *Guidelines on school placement* (1st ed.). Maynooth, Ireland: Author.

Teaching Council. (2016). *The code of professional conduct for teachers* (2nd ed. Updated). Maynooth, Ireland: Author.

Teaching Council. (2017). *Droichead*. Retrieved August 28, 2017 from http://www.teachingcouncil.ie/en/Teacher-Education/Droichead/.

Tickle, L. (2000). *Teacher induction: The way ahead*. Buckingham, England: Open University Press.

Vygotsky, L. S. (1978). *Mind in society: The development of the higher psychological processes*. Cambridge, MA: Harvard University Press.

Wang, J., & Odell, S. J. (2002). Mentored learning to teach according to standards-based reform: A critical review. *Review of Educational Research, 72*(3), 481–546.

Wenger, E. (1998). *Communities of practice: Learning, meaning and identity*. Cambridge, England: Cambridge University Press.

Young, A., O'Neill, A., & Mooney Simmie, G. (2015). Partnership in learning between university and school: Evidence from a researcher-in-residence. *Irish Educational Studies, 34*(1), 25–42.

Bernadette Ní Áingléis is Associate Dean for Placements and Related Partnerships at the Dublin City University Institute of Education. She has held Directorship of School Placement (2000–2016) and the National Induction Programme for Teachers-Primary Strand (2000–2002). Her professional career includes a broad range of teaching, research and continuing professional development experiences at all levels of the continuum of teacher education. As a former primary teacher, principal teacher (gaelscoil/Irish medium setting), curriculum designer and member of the Inspectorate (primary), Bernadette has a particular research interest in school–university partnerships and placements and specifically in paradigms of mentoring, learning to teach, student voice and collaborative inquiry in teacher professional development. Her recent research in the area of professional accountability straddles the interface of law, justice and society.

Anne Looney took up the post of inaugural Executive Dean of Dublin City University's new Institute of Education in 2017. From 2001 until 2016, she was the CEO of the National Council for Curriculum and Assessment, the agency responsible for curriculum and assessment for early years, primary and post-primary education in Ireland. A former teacher, she completed her doctoral studies at the Institute of Education in University College London. In 2014/2015, she was Professorial Research Fellow at the Institute for Learning Sciences and Teacher Education, based at Australian Catholic University in Brisbane. Her current research interests include assessment policy and practice, curriculum, teacher identity and professional standards for teachers and teaching. She has also published on religious, moral and civic education, and education policy. She has conducted reviews for the OECD on school quality and assessment systems.

Chapter 18
Designing for Integration in Initial Teacher Education Curricula: The Hong Kong Postgraduate Diploma in Education

Susan Margaret Bridges, Stephen Andrews, Amy Bik May Tsui, Carol Chan Kwai-kuen, Dan Wang, Tammy Yim Lin Kwan, Joseph Wai Ip Lam, Gary James Harfitt, Cheri Chan, Wing-Wah Law, Maurice Man Wai Cheng, Pui-sze Yeung, Wai Ming Cheung and Rhoda Kuan Yun Wang

Introduction

The ontological debate of the relationship between theory and practice has been a perennial one in initial teacher education (ITE). Many university teacher educators have faced criticisms from student teachers that the theoretical, academic content of their degrees was the least helpful in preparing them for classroom teaching, with 'foundation' and 'teaching methods' courses seen as fragmented components of their learning experience (Ure 2009; Orland-Barak and Yinon 2007). In a special issue for the *Educational Researcher*, Akiba (2017) noted a renewed focus on teacher quality over the past two decades and identified the need to situate local efforts for improvement in the context of what she refers to as 'global dynamics' (p. 153). A comparison of the USA and Japanese perspectives on improvement for in-service teachers drew a distinction between 'teachers' and 'teaching' in setting the focus of change for teacher improvement and improved student learning with 'teaching' linked to 'system improvement' as in, for example, the Japanese Lesson Study approach (Hiebert and Stigler 2017). In re-designing the Postgraduate Diploma in Education (PGDE) at the University of Hong Kong, our stance was to focus on system improvement to fundamentally reconceptualize 'teaching' within our postgraduate teacher education program. Our extensive reform process (July 2013–July 2016) included iterative consultations at the system levels of:

- Reform Working Group
- Program Committee
- Faculty
- Student Body
- Partnership Schools (early childhood, primary and secondary) across Hong Kong
- Professional Bodies
- University

Our PGDE reform team began with a set of guiding questions, then conducted an international audit of trends and best practices, along with an ongoing review of the literature. We then entered into cycles of developing, piloting, and refining for each new component of the PGDE. After the first year of implementation in the 2016–2017 academic year, PGDE program applications increased 28%. In what follows, we outline the impetus for change and the directions taken.

Background

From our review of the international higher education landscape and ITE curricula, we identified three distinct trends: the competency movement; constructivist-oriented, inquiry-based curriculum designs; and evidence-based approaches. These are outlined briefly below as background to the landscape of our self-initiated reform.

The Competency Movement

The competency-based movement in higher education, that has gained currency in professional fields such as medical education, is one trend influencing ITE (see ten Cate and Billett 2014). Competency-oriented curricula draw on a craft-based (Menter 2013), apprenticeship approach focusing on pre-defined, skills-based competencies with knowledge situated in terms of application to practice. In ITE, England's introduction of school-based training models (Ellis 2010; Griffiths 2007) was viewed as focusing on classroom practice rather than on university components (Hodson et al. 2012) while Scotland's Donaldson Report (Donaldson 2010) was also seen to be driving this approach (Hulme 2013). Criticisms of the craft-based model in ITE indicate that it may, indeed, re-inforce student perceptions of a practice–theory divide (Smith and Hodson 2010). In identifying domains of teaching (professional knowledge, practice, and engagement), the *National Professional Standards for Teachers* (AITSL 2011) and their associated quality frameworks sought to address the Australian demand for 'classroom ready' teachers (Teacher Education Ministerial Advisory Group 2014). While predominantly focused on practice, these efforts highlight the general desire to capture the full gamut of that which constitutes teacher expertise (Shulman 1986, 1987, 2015). In considering these trends, a concern for our ITE reform in Hong Kong was that a focus on competencies alone may not be sufficient for developing the teachers of tomorrow.

Inquiry-Based Curriculum Designs

A second trend in ITE curriculum designs has been constructivist-oriented, adopting inquiry-based approaches drawing on problem-based learning (PBL) models of cycles of inquiry (Hmelo-Silver 2000; Pedaste et al. 2015) which can be conceived at the levels of curriculum philosophy, design and instructional approach (Lu et al. 2014) to support integration of theory and practice. PBL-influenced models are found in Canada (Filipenko and Naslund 2016) and Scotland (Hulme 2013; Patrick and McPhee 2014). De Simone (2008) viewed PBL as advantageous in blending theory with practice, as well as supporting evidence-based approaches to instructional design. Tang et al. (2012) saw opportunities for PBL in developing professional 'habits of mind' within the theory–practice nexus to inform practice in an evidence-based profession. Likewise, Barrett (2013) posited that problem-based designs in higher education can support the bridging between education and work and address development of threshold concepts. Across professional disciplines, however, problem-based approaches are more likely to be introduced at the course-level (Kwan 2008; Mishan 2011; Reynolds and Hancock 2010) with less frequent instantiations of whole-curriculum PBL designs (see Bridges et al. 2016). A challenge for the redesign of the PGDE was to explore how to expand the theory–practice integration potential of PBL at a holistic level.

Evidence-Based Approaches

A third, concurrent ITE reform trend has been the influence of evidence-based approaches. In Australia (Melbourne) and Scotland (Glasgow), ITE curricula have drawn upon the 'medical metaphor' to distinguish a recent 'paradigm for teacher preparation learning which has at its centre the 'translation' and application of theory and research in the sites of practice' (McLean Davies et al. 2015, p. 515). Similarly, the Finnish 'research-based' approach to teacher education since the 2000s has adopted the goal of educating 'pedagogically thinking teachers who can combine research findings about teaching with the profession's practical challenges' (Tirri 2014, p. 603). The challenge of addressing research-informed or 'evidence-based' practice became an additional focus for the PGDE reform team's design considerations. In what follows, we outline our conceptual design for the remodelling of our government-funded one-year postgraduate ITE program at the University of Hong

Kong, the Postgraduate Diploma in Education (PGDE). The revised PGDE was carefully devised over three years of meticulous, curriculum development arising from a self-initiated reform.

Re-Designing the PGDE

While recognising and acknowledging the philosophical and pragmatic drivers for the practice-oriented trends in ITE noted above, our PGDE reform team sought to devise a completely new, original model based on our University's core principles of curriculum design that underpinned the new four-year undergraduate reform (structure, continuity, coherence of experience) within an outcomes-based curriculum framework (Tsui 2012, 2016). Our PGDE reform team also acknowledged the importance of competencies currently required, and in development, by local professional bodies (Advisory Committee on Teacher Education and Qualifications 2003; Committee on Professional Development of Teachers and Principals 2015). Our starting point, however, was for the faculty to reach a shared vision for a teacher education graduate at the University of Hong Kong (HKU) as encapsulated in our PGDE's 'Concept of Teacher' (see Fig. 18.1). As part of the process of system-wide change, this vision statement was reviewed and revised in consultation with all key stakeholders. It became central to our philosophy as both a recurring motif guiding development and also embedded within the learning design.

In taking a developmental approach, the PGDE design has foregrounded teaching practice with an experiential learning thread running at the *vertical level* of the curriculum design of the program. This includes weekly 'School Experience' (SE) across the academic year and two dedicated 'blocks' for the experiential learning (EL) course in Semester 1 (six weeks) and the professional practicum (PP) in Semester 2 (eight weeks). In taking an epistemological stance on curriculum integration, we recognized the fluid and dynamic nature of disciplinary knowledge (Scott 2014; Hmelo-Silver et al. in press). However, we also recognized that the teaching of school disciplines is central in student teacher identity formation. With the exception of the experiential learning (EL) course block, theoretical and practical components were organized in school disciplinary student groupings but with the curricular goal of integration (see Fig. 18.2).

In adopting a constructivist-inspired curriculum model, our goal was to move beyond essentialist, behaviourist approaches to teaching 'skills' toward an ideal that drew on Shulman's (1987) early vision of 'teaching as comprehension and reasoning, as transformation and reflection' (p. 13). At the *horizontal level* of the integrated design, we drew upon the notion of twin cycles of inquiry anchored to weekly school visits (see Fig. 18.3). Guided by the problem-based model (Hmelo-Silver 2000), the educational inquiry cycle supports acquisition, application, and integration of theories related to learning and the social context of schooling. Guided by the learning study model (Pang and Lo 2012), collaborative lesson inquiry (CLI) supports devel-

18 Designing for Integration in Initial Teacher Education: Hong Kong

A PASSIONATE & CARING FACILITATOR
A passionate, caring facilitator of learning devoted to embracing diversity and bringing out the best in ALL students

A FORWARD THINKING, ETHICAL & REFLECTIVE PRACTITIONER
A forward thinking, ethical and reflective practitioner who integrates theory with practice for student learning

AN ADAPTIVE, CREATIVE, CRITICAL THINKER & LEADER
An adaptive, creative and critical thinker and potential curriculum leader

CONCEPT OF A TEACHER

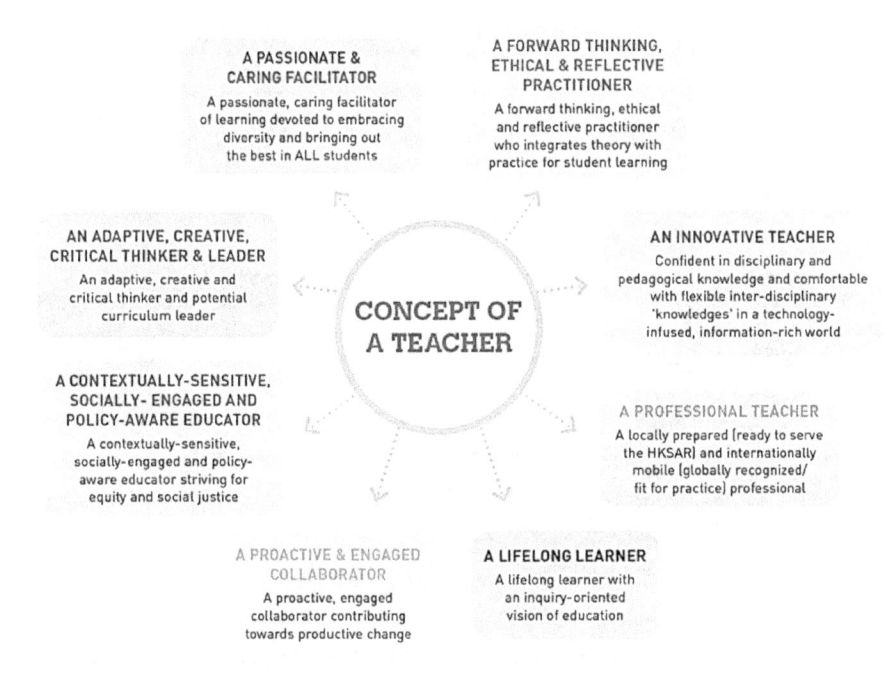

AN INNOVATIVE TEACHER
Confident in disciplinary and pedagogical knowledge and comfortable with flexible inter-disciplinary 'knowledges' in a technology-infused, information-rich world

A CONTEXTUALLY-SENSITIVE, SOCIALLY- ENGAGED AND POLICY-AWARE EDUCATOR
A contextually-sensitive, socially-engaged and policy-aware educator striving for equity and social justice

A PROFESSIONAL TEACHER
A locally prepared (ready to serve the HKSAR) and internationally mobile (globally recognized/ fit for practice) professional

A PROACTIVE & ENGAGED COLLABORATOR
A proactive, engaged collaborator contributing towards productive change

A LIFELONG LEARNER
A lifelong learner with an inquiry-oriented vision of education

Fig. 18.1 Concept of a teacher

PEDAGOGICAL CONTENT KNOWLEDGE
Methods
Collaborative Lesson Inquiry for School Experience (SE)*

INTEGRATED INQUIRY
Inquiry-based sessions
School Forums (principals & teachers)
School Experience (SE)*

HOLISTIC INTEGRATION OF THEORY & PRACTICE

REFLECTIVE PRACTICE
School Experience (SE)*
(linked to Integrated Inquiry & Collaborative Lesson Inquiry)

EXPERIENTIAL LEARNING (METHODS)
Experiential Module (included Language Immersion) (6 weeks)
Professional Practicum (8 weeks)*

*Learning sites related to schools

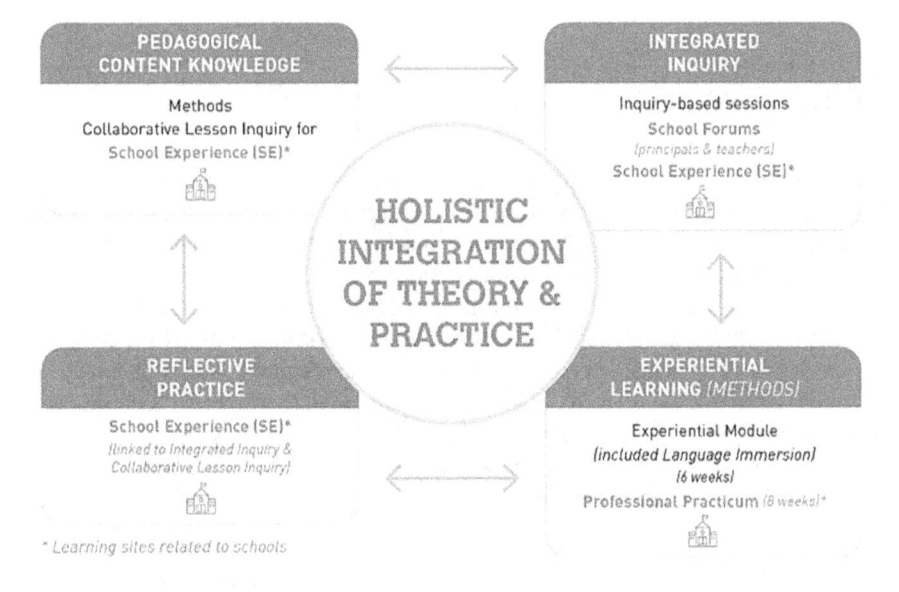

Fig. 18.2 PGDE integration

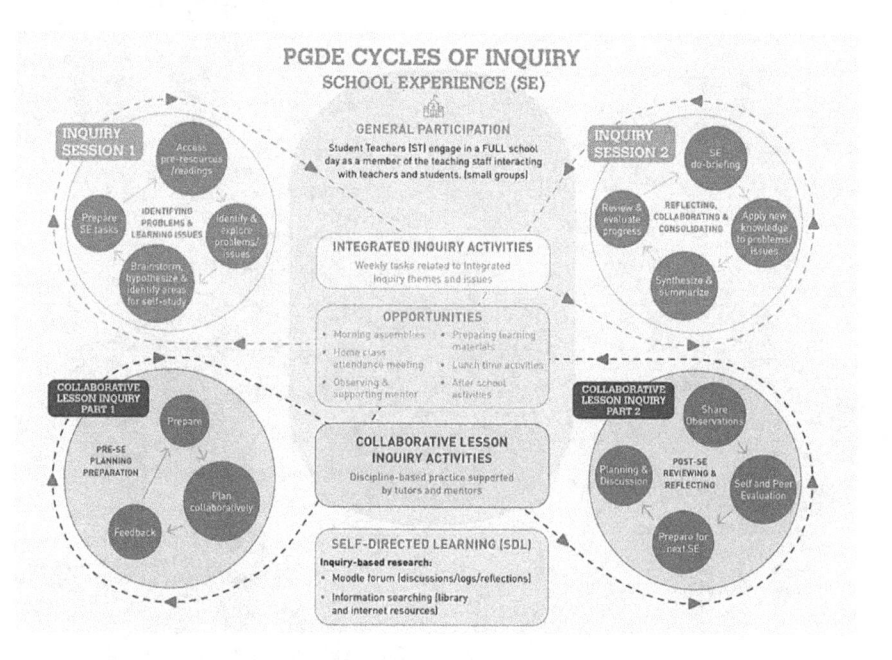

Fig. 18.3 Inquiry-based weekly cycles

opment of teaching practice. Theoretically, both cycles of inquiry draw on authentic, situated notions of learning so that student teachers may generate, apply, synthesize, and reflect upon the planned knowledge, skill and dispositional outcomes.

PGDE Curriculum Components

Educational Inquiry (EI) Aligned with the university educational aims, and the PGDE reform framework of our 'Concept of Teacher,' the EI course is designed to support the professional growth of student teachers in the face of changing education and global contexts. Teachers of the twenty-first century need to be inquirers and learners tackling novel problems; they need to develop conceptual and pedagogical content knowledge about teaching and learning, understanding about the developmental needs of students, appreciation of diversity and equity, and critical analysis of social issues of education. As professionals, they need to use *theory* to guide their action and reflect on their *practice* to sharpen their understanding. In what follows, we discuss the course design in supporting student teachers integrating theory and practice as inquiring learners and teachers.

Integration through a Thematic Approach The EI course develops integrated themes on educational studies emphasizing practice-based understanding. The course includes four inquiry themes with 16 topics, also reflecting a developmental pathway of teacher learning including: (1) aims of education, curriculum and teacher knowledge; (2) classroom and learning processes; (3) equity and diversity and catering for special needs; and (4) social context of education. We aim to provide an integrated framework to help student teachers think about education; different themes unfold gradually with their developing, practice-based understanding grounded in educational theories.

Integration through School Experience One key feature in developing practice-based understanding is school experience (SE): Student teachers are attached to schools one day each week for full-time students. During SE, student teachers engage in inquiry into different themes of teaching, learning, and schooling, to develop practical understanding of theoretical concepts. Specifically, each cycle includes two sessions: in session one, guided by inquiry activities; they discuss key ideas, and in mid-week, they attend SE, where they observe classroom teaching and conduct inquiry to find out how theories discussed may be enacted; consider possible critical incidents, and how school teachers deal with complexities and emerging problems. In developing their inquiry, they share their new learning with peers via Moodle and collectively reflect on their experience in session two. These cycles are linked in an iterative, recursive design so students develop deeper experiences over the year. This approach is considered further in a later subsection on SE.

Integration through Co-Teaching of Theory and Methods Course Contemporary research has shown that deep learning takes place in rich domains and situated contexts (Sawyer 2014); student teachers' understanding needs to be contextualized. An innovative component is the design of 'co-teaching' that provides opportunities for inquiry into theory and practice in the context of their Methods course/disciplinary subject areas. For several key topics, teacher educators who used to teach what has been referred to as 'educational foundation' courses and those who used to teach methodology courses are paired for co-planning and co-teaching the EI course: The inquiry tasks and materials are enriched using examples from the school subject areas. For example, student teachers do not just learn the theories of motivation; they examine the 'what' and the 'how' of motivating students to learn English (or Mathematics etc.). Social issues of inequity are examined as students consider why and how they choose lesson materials. When students share their SE work, both co-teachers provide their perspectives to help students reflect and integrate their understanding from principles, methods and practice. Correspondingly, in collaborative lesson inquiry classes, co-planning and co-teaching are conducted by this pair of teachers to help student teachers use the theories they learn in planning their units and lessons. This approach is considered further in a later subsection on CLI. Such boundary-crossing work is important for the professional growth of not only student teachers but also teacher educators.

Integration through Inquiry and Technology-Enhanced Learning Integrating theory and practice involves student teachers engaging in deep learning and collaborative inquiry. The course adopts a constructivist, inquiry-based approach, with student teachers working on cases, problems, and issues linking to principles and practice.

Typically before class, student teachers conduct focused readings and employ the stated principles to analyse issues and problems. During class, they work collaboratively in inquiry groups using realia and cases to examine the theories in context. As noted above, they continue their inquiry in SE, and synthesize their understanding by sharing their collective inquiry and reflection both in class and online. A key feature is the use of Moodle-based computer-supported collaborative learning. The learning management system, Moodle, is used more than just as a portal for course materials and assignments; we design the discussion forums using learning sciences principles (Chan and van Aalst 2006; Fishman et al. 2014) so students work with each other collaboratively to support their inquiry-oriented, theory–practice integration. Integration through thematic approach, SE, co-teaching, and collaborative inquiry are intertwined components of educational inquiry. Continuing our course design work and experimentation will help improve the bridging between theory and practice in ITE.

School Experience A starting point for re-design was to anchor our program around classroom experience in Hong Kong schools. The inquiry cycles in Fig. 18.3 illustrate the centrality of the weekly 'School Experience' (SE) component to the new PGDE. By placing our full-time student teachers in schools for one day per week as early as possible in the program, this new vertical element enables our student teachers to synergise the learning that takes place on campus and in schools; developing practical understanding of authentic events in relation to theoretical concepts. It also ensures horizontal integration of the theoretical and practical aspects of teacher education from the earliest point of the PGDE program.

Holistic Perspectives SE has been conceptualized as a different learning experience from the eight-week school placement known locally as the *Professional Practicum (PP)*. While the practicum focuses on the attachment to a major school discipline and the development of pedagogical expertise within a designated school subject curriculum, the goal of SE, by contrast, is to develop a holistic understanding of school culture and life both inside and outside the classroom and to integrate broader educational theories with practice (see Fig. 18.1). It is our assumption that our PGDE student teachers are relatively inexperienced to begin with in handling educational and pedagogical issues in schools. Hence, they are required to conduct weekly thematic, inquiry-based and subject-based learning tasks and to immerse themselves in different aspects of the lives of schools and school teachers. In doing so, they learn to become not just a subject teacher but also an all-rounded school teacher as well. With such rich and diverse experiences from the SE, as well as a more balanced and ongoing integration between theory and practice, SE aims for student teachers to have more pragmatic and fruitful learning opportunities to share and debrief each week upon returning to campus.

The regular one-day per week SE and the eight weeks of PP provide opportunities for our student teachers to learn and gain support from the schools, the principals, the school experience coordinators (SECs), the subject teacher advisors (STAs), and, of course, the university tutors. To ensure SE could run smoothly during the first year of implementation and to ensure schools that offer SE placements could indeed provide the kind of support required by SE, invitations for SE placements and specific SE briefings were only sent to schools that showed interest and commitment in 2015–2016. This recruitment strategy was successful and crucial in securing excellent SE placements for our students during the first year of implementation in 2016–2017.

In planning for the second year of implementation, a different strategy was adopted. Introductions and invitations for SE placements were sent to all primary and secondary schools during the second round of recruitment exercise. Interested schools were briefed on the rationale and requirements of SE in an invitation package and video. Feedback from schools and students is generally positive, and as of June 2017, placement offers already exceeded requirements. Ongoing review and stakeholder engagement for this new initiative will continue to refine School Experience to ensure its intended goals are fully met.

Collaborative Lesson Inquiry (CLI): Revisiting Pedagogical Content Knowledge (PCK) In considering classroom readiness, CLI was designed to take a systems-level approach to address the somewhat slippery concept of pedagogical content knowledge (PCK) (Shulman 1987) and to embed this as a distinctive feature within an overarching curriculum design in ITE rather than at subject level. Originally, PCK was conceived as:

> the blending of content and pedagogy into an understanding of how particular topics, problems, or issues are organized, represented, and adapted to the diverse interests and abilities of learners, and presented for instruction. Pedagogical content knowledge is the category most likely to distinguish the understanding of the content specialist from that of the pedagogue. (Shulman 1987, p. 8)

However, there seems to be little consensus on PCK in practice and it is sometimes confused with generic pedagogical knowledge, which is interpreted as 'knowing how to teach' (Hattie 2009). Other critics have indicated that 'the construct itself has not yet positively impacted the valuing of teachers' professional knowledge and practice' (van Driel and Berry 2010, p. 656). Pedagogical content knowledge is undoubtedly neither (domain specific) content knowledge nor (domain independent) generic pedagogical knowledge, but rather it is 'a form of teachers' professional knowledge, which refers to a transformation of subject-matter knowledge so that it can be used effectively and flexibly in the communication process between teachers and learners during classroom practice' (Henze and van Driel 2015, pp. 120–121). According to Shulman (1987), the transformation of teachers' understanding, performance skills, or desired attitudes or values into pedagogical representations and actions is the key to successful implementation of pedagogical content knowledge. In moving forward with reform, we returned to Shulman's vision of transformation and developed CLI as a separate course component linked to the cycle of inquiry (see Fig. 18.3).

Previously, educational theories and discipline-based, subject knowledge aligned to Hong Kong's Key Learning Areas (KLAs) (methods courses) were taught as two separate strands in the PGDE program with minimal interplay between the two, both in terms of design and university classroom practice. The problem with this lack of alignment was that students perceived the two strands as separate entities rather than as two sides of the same coin. CLI, therefore, aims to adopt the spirit of PCK to blend 'content and pedagogy,' thereby facilitating the integration of educational theories and subject knowledge. It is designed to help student teachers to understand the connections between the school subject discipline which they will teach and the theoretical knowledge acquired in the EI course so as to integrate these principles when planning tasks and lessons for their classroom practice. Another new feature introduced through the design of CLI is the co-planning and co-teaching of 50% of the course by methods and educational inquiry tutors. The purpose of the collaboration is to ensure shared understanding of course outcomes and program goals as well as to facilitate authentic integration.

The cycle of inquiry for CLI (Fig. 18.3) takes a distinctly practice-based focus by adopting the concept of collaborative lesson planning. Based on the input from Methods and Educational Inquiry teachers, student teachers are required to design learning activities on a particular topic of subject teaching as learning outcomes of each lesson. They are then expected to find opportunities to implement the learning activities in their SE, in either a 15-minute mini-teaching activity or a full 40-minute formal class. When student teachers return after SE, they are expected to share their experience and/or reflect on their implementation.

The co-planning and co-teaching of CLI enable students to consider teaching the same subject topic from different perspectives. Experiencing differences in the same topic from two distinctive perspectives is the necessary condition of learning in the blending of content knowledge and pedagogical knowledge which constitutes 'pedagogical content knowledge' (Marton 2015). From our frequent experience-sharing faculty development sessions, it has become evident that co-teaching has enriched collaborating teacher educators' understanding of both strands—methods and experiential learning.

Experiential Learning While school-based experience during School Experience and the traditional Professional Practicum was central to our approach to 'classroom readiness,' our PGDE reform team took a broader view of the student teacher experience to embed experiential learning (EL) as a compulsory component for both full-time and part-time students. At the university-level, EL, a newly introduced element in the new undergraduate curriculum, addresses the six educational aims that underpin all HKU curricula. Four of these particularly underpin the EL projects on offer for student teachers: 'tackling novel situations and ill-defined problems', 'intercultural understanding and global citizenship', 'communication and collaboration' and 'leadership and advocacy for the improvement of the human condition'. Through the provision of a mandatory EL block of six weeks, it is hoped that students' learning processes will contribute to the development and actualization of the underlying 'Concept of a Teacher' (see Fig. 18.1).

Partly driven by these concepts and the calls to reconsider traditional models of teacher education (Darling-Hammond 2006a, b; Zeichner 2010; Harfitt and Chan 2017), both professional practicum and community-based EL programs have been aligned as a mandatory component of all undergraduate and postgraduate ITE programs. The compulsory nature of EL in our teacher preparation programs indicates the importance that we attach to enabling future teachers to gain a deeper understanding of the complexities of the issues that the world is confronted through engaging in real world projects, thereby developing values which are central to our *Concept of a Teacher* (for the US perspective, see also Darling-Hammond 2012). While learning activities like service-learning and workplace internships (in contexts other than schools) are commonplace in teacher education institutions, too often student teachers' learning in the wider world is treated as voluntary, and therefore peripheral rather than central.

Since 2015 and the establishment of a permanent EL team in the Faculty, we have forged links with more than thirty community partners including some powerful global advocates of social justice and education. These include: World Vision (HK), UNICEF (HK), OXFAM (HK), World Wildlife Fund or WWF (HK), Asia's largest local marine theme park (HK Ocean Park), HK Science and Technology Park (HKSTP), and a range of Social Services groups, as well as local schools promoting an 'alternative' education (which contrasts with the examination-oriented local curriculum that dominates the local school system). Through this raft of community-based EL programs, we aim to integrate academic knowledge and facilitate student teachers' development of personal and social competency, and cultivation of core values of a fair and just society, thereby complementing the traditional teacher education curriculum that too often focuses on academic knowledge and pedagogy at the cost of key competencies that promote personal and social skills and core societal values. Through these community partnerships, we are addressing what Zeichner (2010, 2013) has called the 'third space' in teacher education by taking students' learning outside of the two traditional bastions of learning, namely the university classroom and the practicum school placement.

Student educators, under the supervision of local and regional non-governmental organizations (NGOs), work in interdisciplinary teams to initiate service tasks closely linked to education and their ongoing role as educators. An illustration may help to contextualize the learning processes we are keen to foster in our programs. For instance, some of our student teachers completed their EL at a science and technology NGO working alongside community partners to design, conduct and revise science, technology, engineering and mathematics (STEM) workshops aimed at local primary and secondary school students who visit the park as extracurricular school activities. Other student teachers worked at an NGO promoting child rights and were responsible for devising mobile workshops presented to thousands of secondary students across multiple schools that visually depicted the interconnectedness between countries on child rights. Another group of student teachers spent their EL block working at a local marine theme park to collaborate with team members from the park's Education Unit to devise a pop-up narration aimed at delivering powerful, interactive messages about conservation themes and endangered species to park visitors (HK visitors as well as many from mainland China and overseas). By actively engaging in such situational learning in a way that is completely new to them, our student educators are in a better position to construct new knowledge by connecting to their prior knowledge.

Through this boundary crossing between our university and the local community, we believe we are better able to facilitate the development of transformative educators who are equipped with technical skills necessary for the classroom as well as crucial moral and ethical attributes. We have seen at first-hand how our student teachers are better able to critically examine educational practices from a more sociocultural perspective (e.g., causes of social injustice and inequity) as a result of participating in these mandatory EL projects. In sum, this leads to the type of adaptive expertise that successful teachers demonstrate (Darling-Hammond 2006a).

Programmatic Assessment

Following the Hong Kong outcomes-based approach, PGDE assessments were designed to support curriculum integration. This proved challenging as achieving vertical and horizontal integration of assessments requires extensive planning (Bridges et al. 2016). The PGDE reform team devised a program-level assessment plan including integrated tasks that are co-assessed by both the educational theory and methods (subject-discipline) teaching staff. A program-level assessment item in the form of a culminating, capstone event and hurdle requirement for program completion supports integration through critical reflection and self-assessment of individual and group progress toward the PGDE vision, our 'Concept of a Teacher'.

Implications and Next Steps

In the model described briefly above, we have elaborated on how an inquiry-based design involving boundary crossing of teacher educators was employed to address the central reform goal of integration of theory and practice in a one-year ITE program. While recognising concerns raised elsewhere such as in the US's inaugural report for the National Council on Teaching Quality (Greenberg et al. 2013) which focuses on candidate quality on admission; Common Core Standards; the effect of the 'reading wars' on teaching strategies; and poor screening and/or partnering with mentor-teachers, as introduced above, the re-design of the PGDE was motivated by ontological concerns in preparing the next-generation's workforce. The challenges of staff and stakeholder engagement were not insurmountable, although they do indicate the enormous lead-in time required if instituting fundamental change from curriculum planning to enactment. For future development, refinement and quality assurance (Ingvarson and Rowley 2017), the PGDE reform team acknowledges the imperative for ongoing evaluation of the new curriculum model for its impact on ITE in Hong Kong.

References

Australian Institute for Teaching and School Leadership [AITSL]. (2011). *National professional standards for teachers*. Retrieved from http://www.teacherstandards.aitsl.edu.au/.
Advisory Committee on Teacher Education and Qualifications. (2003). *Towards a learning profession*. Hong Kong: Printing Department.
Akiba, M. (2017). Editor's introduction: Understanding cross-national differences in globalized teacher reforms. *Educational Researcher, 46*(4), 153–168. https://doi.org/10.3102/0013189X17711908.
Barrett, T. (2013). Learning about the problem in problem-based learning (PBL) by listening to students' talk in tutorials: A critical discourse analysis study. *Journal of Further and Higher Education, 37*(4), 519–535.
Bridges, S. M., Yiu, C. K. Y., & Botelho, M. G. (2016). Design considerations for an integrated, problem-based curriculum. *Medical Science Educator, 26*(3), 365–373.
Chan, C. K. K., & van Aalst, J. (2006). Teacher development through computer-supported knowledge building: Experience from Hong Kong and Canadian teachers. *Teaching Education, 17*(1), 7–26.
Committee on Professional Development of Teachers and Principals. (2015). *Odyssey to excellence: Progress report*. Hong Kong: Government Logistics Department.
Darling-Hammond, L. (2006a). *Powerful teacher education*. San Francisco, CA: Jossey-Bass.
Darling-Hammond, L. (2006b). Constructing 21st-century teacher education. *Journal of Teacher Education, 57*(3), 300–314.
Darling-Hammond, L. (2012). *Creating a comprehensive system for evaluating and supporting effective teaching*. Stanford, CA: Stanford Centre for Opportunity Policy. in Education.
De Simone, C. (2008). Problem-based learning: A framework for prospective teachers' pedagogical problem solving. *Teacher Development, 12*(3), 179–191. https://doi.org/10.1080/13664530802259206.
Donaldson, G. (2010). *Teaching Scotland's future: Report of a review of teacher education in Scotland*. Edinburgh, Scotland: The Scottish Government.
Ellis, V. (2010). Impoverishing experience: The problem of teacher education in England. *Journal of Education for Teaching: International Research and Pedagogy, 36*(1), 105–120. https://doi.org/10.1080/02607470903462230.
Filipenko, M., & Naslund, J. (2016). *Problem-based learning in teacher education*. Cham, Switzerland: Springer International Publishing. https://doi.org/10.1007/978-3-319-02003-7.
Fishman, B., Davis, B., & Chan, C. K. K. (2014). Learning sciences perspectives on teacher learning research. In R. K. Sawyer (Ed.), *Cambridge handbook of learning sciences* (2nd ed., pp. 707–725). New York, NY: Cambridge University Press.
Greenberg, J., McKee, A., & Walsh, K. (2013). *Teacher prep review: A review of the nation's teacher preparation programs*. New York, NY: National Council on Teacher Quality. Retrieved January 08, 2018 from https://eric.ed.gov/?id=ED543515.
Griffiths, V. (2007). Experiences of training on an employment-based route into teaching in England. *Journal of In-Service Education, 33*(1), 107–123.
Hattie, J. (2009). *Visible learning: A synthesis of over 800 meta-analyses relating to achievement*. New York, NY: Routledge.
Henze, I., & van Driel, J. H. (2015). Toward a more comprehensive way to capture PCK in its complexity. In A. Berry, P. Friedrichsen, & J. Loughran (Eds.), *Re-examining pedagogical content knowledge in science education* (pp. 120–134). New York, NY: Routledge.
Harfitt, G. J., & Chan, C. (2017). Constructivist learning theories in teacher education programmes: A pedagogical perspective. In D. J. Clandinin & J. Husu (Eds.), *International handbook of research on teacher education* (pp. 545–560). London, England: Sage Publications.
Hiebert, J., & Stigler, J. W. (2017). Teaching versus teachers as a lever for change: Comparing a Japanese and a U.S. perspective on improving instruction. *Educational Researcher, 46*(4), 169–176. https://doi.org/10.3102/0013189X17711899.

Hmelo-Silver, C. E. (2000). Knowledge recycling: Crisscrossing the landscape of educational psychology in a problem-based learning course for preservice teachers. *Journal on Excellence in College Teaching, 11,* 41–56.

Hmelo-Silver, C. E., Bridges, S. M., & McKeown, J. (in press). Facilitating problem-based learning. In N. Dabbagh, M. Moallem & W. Hung (Eds.), *Wiley handbook of problem-based learning.* Medford, MA: Wiley.

Hodson, E., Smith, K., & Brown, T. (2012). Reasserting theory in professionally based initial teacher education. *Teachers and Teaching, 18*(2), 181–195. https://doi.org/10.1080/13540602.2 012.632269.

Hulme, M. (2013). Enquiry-based professional learning across the career course: Developments in Scotland. In C. McLaughlin (Ed.), *Teachers learning: Professional development and education* (pp. 70–92). Cambridge, England: Cambridge University Press.

Ingvarson, L., & Rowley, G. (2017). Quality assurance in teacher education and outcomes: A study of 17 countries. *Educational Researcher, 46*(4), 177–193. https://doi.org/10.3102/0013189X177 11900.

Kwan, T. Y. L. (2008). Student-teachers' evaluation on the use of different modes of problem-based learning in teacher education. *Asia-Pacific Journal of Teacher Education, 36*(4), 323–343. https://doi.org/10.1080/13598660802375933.

Lu, J., Bridges, S. M, & Hmelo-Silver, C. (2014). Problem-based learning. In R. Keith Sawyer (Eds.), *The Cambridge handbook of the learning sciences* (2nd ed., pp. 298–318). Cambridge, England: Cambridge University Press.

Marton, F. (2015). *Necessary conditions of learning.* New York, NY: Routledge.

McLean Davies, L., Dickson, B., Rickards, F., Dinham, S., Conroy, J., & Davis, R. (2015). Teaching as a clinical profession: Translational practices in initial teacher education—An international perspective. *Journal of Education for Teaching, 41*(5), 514–528. https://doi.org/10.1080/026074 76.2015.1105537.

Menter, I. (2013). From interesting times to critical times? Teacher education and educational research in England. *Research in Teacher Education. 3*(1), 38–40. http://hdl.handle.net/10552/ 1961.

Mishan, F. M. (2011). Whose learning is it anyway? Problem-based learning in language teacher development. *Innovation in Language Learning and Teaching, 5*(3), 253–272. https://doi.org/1 0.1080/17501229.2010.548558.

Orland-Barak, L., & Yinon, H. (2007). When theory meets practice: What student teachers learn from guided reflection on their classroom discourse. *Teaching and Teacher Education, 23,* 957–969. https://doi.org/10.1016/j.tate.2006.06.005.

Pang, M. F., & Lo, M. L. (2012). Learning study: Helping teachers to use theory, develop professionally, and produce new knowledge to be shared. *Instructional Science, 40,* 589–606. https://doi.org/10.1007/s11251-011-9191-4.

Pedaste, M., Mäeots, M., Siiman, L. A., de Jong, T., van Riesen, S. A. N., Kamp, E. T., et al. (2015). Phases of inquiry-based learning: Definitions and the inquiry cycle. *Educational Research Review, 14,* 47–61. https://doi.org/10.1016/j.edurev.2015.02.003.

Patrick, F., & McPhee, A. (2014). Evaluating the use of problem-based learning in a new initial teacher education degree. *TEAN Journal, 6*(2), 3–12. Retrieved January 08, 2018 from http://19 4.81.189.19/ojs/index.php/TEAN/article/viewFile/190/306.

Reynolds, J. M., & Hancock, D. R. (2010). Problem-based learning in a higher education environmental biotechnology course. *Innovations in Education and Teaching International, 47*(2), 175–186. https://doi.org/10.1080/14703291003718919.

Sawyer, R. K. (2014). *The Cambridge handbook of the learning sciences* (2nd ed.). Cambridge, England: Cambridge University Press.

Scott, D. (2014). Knowledge and the curriculum. *The Curriculum Journal, 25*(1), 14–28. https://doi.org/10.1080/09585176.2013.876367.

Shulman, L. S. (1986). Those who understand: Knowledge growth in teaching. *Educational Researcher, 15*(2), 4–14.

Shulman, L. S. (1987). Knowledge and teaching: Foundations of the new reform. *Harvard Educational Review, 57*(1), 1–23.

Shulman, L. S. (2015). PCK: Its genesis and exodus. In A. Berry, P. Friedrichsen, & J. Loughran (Eds.), *Re-examining pedagogical content knowledge in science education* (pp. 3–13). New York, NY: Routledge.

Tang, S. Y. F., Wong, A. K. Y., & Cheng, M. M. H. (2012). Professional learning in initial teacher education: Vision in the constructivist conception of teaching and learning. *Journal of Education for Teaching, 38*(4), 435–451. https://doi.org/10.1080/02607476.2012.688549.

Teacher Education Ministerial Advisory Group (2014). *Action now: Classroom ready teachers*. Retrieved January 08, 2018 from https://docs.education.gov.au/system/files/doc/other/action_now_classroom_ready_teachers_accessible.pdf.

ten Cate, O., & Billett, S. (2014). Competency-based medical education: Origins, perspectives and potentialities. *Medical Education, 48,* 325–332. https://doi.org/10.1111/medu.12355.

Tirri, K. (2014). The last 40 years in Finnish teacher education. *Journal of Education for Teaching, 40*(5), 600–609. https://doi.org/10.1080/02607476.2014.956545.

Tsui, A. B. M. (2012). Transforming student learning: Undergraduate curriculum reform at The University of Hong Kong. In P. Blackmore & C. Kandiko (Eds.), *Strategic curriculum change: Global trends in universities* (pp. 62–72). London, England: Routledge.

Tsui, A. B. M. (2016). Leading transitions: The case of undergraduate education reform at HKU. In S. Marshall (Ed.), *A handbook on leaders in higher education: Transforming teaching and learning* (pp. 129–131). New York, NY: Routledge.

Ure, C. (2009). *Practicum partnerships: Exploring models of practicum organisation in teacher education for a standards-based profession*. Strawberry Hills, Australia: Australian Learning and Teaching Council.

van Driel, J. H. Y., & Berry, A. (2010). Pedagogical content knowledge. In P. Peterson, E. Bake, & B. McGaw (Eds.), *International encyclopaedia of education* (Vol. 7., 3rd ed., pp. 656–661). Oxford, England: Elsevier Science.

Zeichner, K. (2010). Rethinking the connection between campus courses and field experiences in college and university based teacher education. *Journal of Teacher Education, 61*(1–2), 1–11. https://doi.org/10.1177/0022487109347671.

Zeichner, K. (2013). Two visions of teaching and teacher education for the twenty-first century. In X. Zhu & K. Zeichner (Eds.), *Preparing teachers for the 21st century* (pp. 3–19). Berlin, Germany: Springer-Verlag. https://doi.org/10.1007/978-3-642-36970-4_1.

Susan Margaret Bridges is currently Associate Professor and Assistant Dean (Curriculum Innovation) with the Faculty of Education and the Centre for the Enhancement of Teaching and Learning (CETL), Honorary Associate Professor with the LKS Faculty of Medicine, and Adjunct Professor with the Australian Catholic University. She is an award-winning teacher and researcher with a focus on curriculum re-design and staff development projects in higher education. She is particularly interested in integrated curriculum designs and inquiry-based learning and how educational technologies can support and enhance these. Her locally and internationally funded research explores the 'how' of effective pedagogy and communication through interactional and ethnographic approaches. She has published numerous international journal articles and book chapters and is the co-editor of the 2016 Springer book *Educational Technologies in Medical and Health Sciences Education*. She is a member of the Editorial Board for the *Interdisciplinary Journal of Problem-based Learning*.

Stephen Andrews is currently Honorary Professor of English Language Education at the Faculty of Education, the University of Hong Kong (HKU), and Visiting Professorial Fellow at the University of New South Wales, Sydney. He worked at HKU from 1990 to 2017 and was Dean of Education from 2010 to 2017, having previously been Associate Dean (Learning and Teaching) and Head of the Language and Literature Division. Before coming to Hong Kong, he was Head of the TEFL Unit at Cambridge ESOL. He has also worked at the University of Reading, as well as in Thailand, Sudan, Egypt, Mexico, Switzerland, Germany and France. His research and publications mainly concern second language education, particularly the language awareness of L2 teachers, and the impact of assessment on teaching and learning. He has published numerous international journal articles and book chapters, and he is the author of the 2007 Cambridge University Press book Teacher Language Awareness.

Amy Bik May Tsui is Professor Emerita in the Faculty of Education at the University of Hong Kong (HKU). She was Chair Professor of Language and Education in the Faculty of Education, HKU from 1997 to 2017. From 2007 to 2014, she was Pro-Vice-Chancellor and Vice-President (Teaching and Learning) at HKU during which she led the historical reform of undergraduate education at HKU. She has published nine books and over 100 articles on classroom discourse, conversational analysis, language policy, and teacher development. She has presented over 80 keynotes in international conferences in Asia, UK, USA, Europe, Australia, South Africa, and Mexico, and has served on the editorial and advisory boards of over 25 international refereed journals. She has been providing professional and community service locally and internationally throughout her academic career, including serving on government advisory committees, University Councils and advisory boards, and is currently a member of the Board of Governors of the International Baccalaureate. She was awarded an Honorary Doctoral degree in Education by the University of Edinburgh, UK in 2015.

Carol Chan Kwai-kuen is currently is Professor at the Faculty of Education, University of Hong Kong. Her research area is in how people learn, and she specializes in learning, cognition and instruction, computer-supported knowledge building and Chinese learners. Her research is widely recognized by Hong Kong and overseas academic institutions. She is Associate Editor of International Journal of Computer-Supported Collaborative Learning (ijCSCL), Editorial Board member of the Journal of the Learning Sciences, and co-edits the International Handbook of Collaborative Learning. Her papers are published in top research journals including American Educational Research Journal, Journal of the Learning Sciences, Computers and Education and ijCSCL. With her team, she has won several international research awards and she is also a recipient of University Teaching Award and Faculty Outstanding Research Supervisor Award.

Dan Wang is Associate Professor at the Faculty of Education in the University of Hong Kong. She is trained in the discipline of Sociology of Education. Her research focuses on educational inequality and social justice issues in China with special interests on the rural–urban divide, class reproduction, and teachers' work. Her research exposes the social, institutional and organizational causes for educational inequalities between rural and urban schools in China. She criticizes the dominant ideology that treats education primarily as a channel for social mobility and promotes the notion of teaching and learning as collective endeavors for equity and social justice. She is the author of the book *The Demoralization of Teachers: Crisis in a Rural School in China*. Her current work explores ways to empower rural teachers to make curricular and pedagogical changes for sustainable development in the countryside.

Tammy Yim Lin Kwan has retired but is currently Honorary Associate Professor of the Faculty of Education, the University of Hong Kong. Dr. Kwan taught social, geographical and environmental education at Queensland University of Technology from 1992 to 1997 before returning to the University of Hong Kong in 1998 as Associate Professor focusing on Geographical Education and Teacher Professional Development. She was PGDE program director (2005–2007) and was partnership director for initial teacher education from 2007 to 2010. She was appointed Assistant Dean (School-University Partnerships) from November 2010 till June 2017 on her retirement. Dr. Kwan works closely with schools and has a strong commitment to encouraging teachers to become critically reflective professionals to achieve professional development and personal growth as mentors. Dr. Kwan obtained twice the Faculty Knowledge Exchange award in 2009 and 2013 based on her partnership collaboration with teachers and principals in schools. She also got the university outstanding teacher title in 2013.

Joseph Wai Ip Lam is Associate Professor in Faculty of Education at the University of Hong Kong, where he teaches postgraduate courses in pedagogy for teaching Chinese, reading, discourse analysis, and critical discussion. He has taught Chinese language at secondary level in Hong Kong. He is also currently Director of Centre for Advancement of Chinese Language Education and Research (CACLER). His primary research interests focus on network analysis on Chinese language structure, reading, culturally and linguistically diverse students in Chinese language education in Hong Kong, and argumentation in discussion. He is author of more than 80 scholarly articles, chapters, monographs, and books on Chinese language education. His many current research projects include Supporting for Ethnic Minority Students in Local Kindergartens for Effective Learning of Chinese and Progress in International Reading Literacy Study (PIRLS).

Gary James Harfitt is Associate Professor and Associate Dean for Learning and Teaching in the Faculty of Education, the University of Hong Kong. He also heads the experiential learning team in the Faculty. He has lived and worked in Hong Kong for almost 30 years and has extensive professional experience working in schools as an English teacher, department head and then in teacher education. His research interests include the benefits of experiential learning on the process of becoming a teacher, class size reduction, early career teacher experiences connected to teacher attrition as well as good practices in the use of literature and language arts in English classrooms.

Cheri Chan is an Assistant Professor in the Faculty of Education, the University of Hong Kong. She teaches a wide range of courses for the Faculty's undergraduate and postgraduate teacher education programs. Cheri began her career as an English language teacher in 1999 and has taught students across all levels at different schools before she joined the University in 2006. As a teacher educator, Cheri has supported many teachers in the Hong Kong community through different school-university partnership projects. Cheri is interested in teacher education research. In particular, her studies draw on critical social theories to understand the complexities of how language teachers learn together as professionals. Her areas of research include teacher mentoring, collaboration in education and language teacher identities.

Wing-Wah Law is a Professor at the University of Hong Kong, Faculty of Education. His research contributes to the understanding of the interplay between globalisation and localization on education and development in various areas (including educational policy, citizenship and citizenship education, educational and curriculum reforms, culture and leadership, and music education and social change); his work serves as a bridge for the exchange and development of educational research between China and the world. Law's publications have appeared in international journals such as the Cambridge Journal of Education, Comparative Education, the Comparative Education Review, Compare, the International Journal of Educational Development, the International Journal of Music Education, the Journal of Curriculum Studies, and Teachers College Record. He served as an associate editor of the International Journal of Educational Development (2013–2016) and a member of the Comparative Education Review's Advisory Board (2012–2017).

Maurice Man Wai Cheng (Ph.D. (KCL)) is a Senior Lecturer in the Division of Mathematics and Science Education, Faculty of Education, the University of Hong Kong. He served as the Program Director of the Postgraduate Diploma in Education (PGDE) and steered the making of the curriculum of B.Ed/B.Sc science education professional courses in the faculty. His research interest is students' learning of science, particularly on their visual learning of chemical ideas. He has a strong interest in making use of visual representations such as drawings and diagrams in facilitating students' learning. Also, he serves as a Co-National Research Coordinator (Co-NRC) of

Hong Kong in 2019 TIMSS study. He works closely with school teachers and curriculum planners in Education Bureau of the Hong Kong Government.

Pui-sze Yeung is an Associate Professor in the Faculty of Education at the University of Hong Kong. Her research focuses on Chinese developmental dyslexia, Chinese reading comprehension and written composition development, and intervention for supporting struggling writers.

Wai Ming Cheung is an Associate Professor at the Faculty of Education, the University of Hong Kong. She used to be the Program Director of the Postgraduate Diploma of Education in 2013–16. Her research interests include creativity, phenomenography, learning study, teacher professional development, Chinese writing skill, reading literacy, word acquisition, gifted education, and bilingual education. She has extensive experience in working with teachers to develop school-based curriculum.

Rhoda Kuan Yun Wang is a Lecturer with the Division of Learning, Development and Diversity in the University of Hong Kong. Coming from a background of Psychology, her teaching areas are related to child development and learning, focusing on early childhood, and psychology of classroom learning. Her research also focuses on early child development and learning. She has a particular interest in the development of executive functioning of young children as this topic contribute to the understanding of a key factor that affects children's learning, and in supporting teachers to develop appropriate pedagogical practices. Rhoda has diverse teaching experience in kindergarten, primary and secondary schools, and in teacher education.

Chapter 19
Teacher Education in a Crucible of Change

Ian Menter

Introduction

One of the messages that comes over very clearly from the chapters in this book is that teacher education across the world is the focus of much change. Those of us working in teacher education experience continuing upheaval, challenges and opportunities. It is indeed like working in the bowl of a crucible where everything is in a state of flux, and new ingredients are being added all the time. In this final chapter, I explore some of the underlying causes of these experiences and consider some of their implications. Initially, we examine the global context that gives rise to the processes of change and explore the links between globalisation and nationhood. Working then from my own experience of the UK I offer a more detailed account of how change has been manifested here, in order to provide an example of the impacts such turbulence can have. The last major section then returns to the wider field and offers an account of the key indicators of change in teacher education systems, wherever they may be.

The Global Context

Sahlberg's evocative coining of the term 'The GERM'—the Global Education Reform Movement—catches superbly the almost epidemiological way in which aspects of educational policy have swept around the world over recent years (Sahlberg 2010). He identifies standardisation and accountability mechanisms as among the key elements of the GERM. Nowhere within education systems are these two features more evident than within teacher education.

I. Menter (✉)
Department of Education, University of Oxford, Oxford, UK
e-mail: ian.menter@education.ox.ac.uk

© Springer Nature Singapore Pte Ltd. 2018
C. Wyatt-Smith and L. Adie (eds.), *Innovation and Accountability in Teacher Education*, Teacher Education, Learning Innovation and Accountability,
https://doi.org/10.1007/978-981-13-2026-2_19

Globalisation has certainly affected many other features of education, not least curriculum and assessment where there has been an almost universal introduction of greater prescription and rigour, with a significant emphasis on literacy and numeracy. These emphases derive very directly from the ways in which the 'knowledge economy' has become increasingly central to the thinking of politicians and policymakers. Knowledge itself has become a form of capital which nations seek to develop in order to prosper in the new global networks that have dominated commerce and enterprise in the later parts of the twentieth and into the twenty-first centuries.

The particular focus on teachers, teaching and teacher education may be seen as a logical extension of these wider concerns. If the international achievement measures such as PISA and PIRLS show that a particular nation is 'falling behind' in the results achieved by students, then the obvious conclusion to draw is that if there were better teaching, then those results might improve. Little thought is given—at least by those in power—to whether the measures are particularly meaningful in the first place. The league tables that emerge from these studies are accepted by media and politicians around the world and are published widely, so that populations in most countries share in the delight or disappointment that follows.

Thus, if it is important to improve the quality of teaching (in terms of outcomes such as these), then the next step is to think about the teachers themselves, who they are, how they are prepared for their work and how they are then provided with ongoing support. In other words, the recruitment and selection of teachers, their pre-service education and their continuing professional development all become crucial elements of educational policy. Simply speaking, this is the mechanism through which teacher education has become, in the words of Cochran-Smith and Fries (2008), a 'policy problem' in most countries around the world.

The idea that nations and their education systems have a fundamental interconnection is not a new one. The formation and development of nation states in the modern age are very much tied in with the values and orientations of their schools and schooling as Green (1990, 1997) has so effectively shown, through examining the historical cases of England, the USA and France. Adopting a more empirical approach, Alexander (2000) has shown the nature of the relationship between nations, culture and pedagogy in seven particular national settings. If these relationships have been a feature of the development of public education systems during the twentieth century, then we can now argue that in the wake of the globalising forces described above, much the same can now be said about nations and teacher education.

It is because of the urge to create distinctive national developments, rather than simple emulation or 'copying' of successful policies in one country that each nation tends to develop their own 'version' of a policy, even if transnational similarities can be detected, as Rizvi and Lingard (2010) demonstrate. This is the process that they dub 'vernacular globalisation'. One simple example would be the transmogrification of the scheme called Teach for America in the USA into Teach First in England and Wales (see Teachforall.org).

However, in all of these developments we find that usually the political quest is not only for improved effectiveness of teacher education and teaching. Invariably there is also a popular political call for improved social justice in and through education.

In many countries, this is enunciated through aspirations to 'close the achievement gap' between the highest and lowest achieving pupils, with the lowest achievers often being predominantly from economically poorer families. Sometimes, these differentials in achievement are linked also to ethnicity and gender, as well as to disability. The struggle for social justice thus meets the quest for effectiveness in teacher education systems around the world.

A final general observation to be made that also arises from the intensity of political interest in teacher education is that we frequently see the reshaping of the management, control and organisation of teacher education. This may lead to new forms of governance, with governments establishing new agencies to accredit teacher education programs or new bodies to regulate teaching qualifications. Of course, these new forms of governance are not unique to teacher education, and they have emerged in many spheres of social policy and may be seen as a feature of the neoliberal disposition of much contemporary public governance (Clarke and Newman 1997).

The UK Experience

In England and the wider UK, we can see many of the features that have been outlined above being played out in the reform and restructuring of teacher education. Indeed, the case of the UK, most notably in the particular case of England, provides a good illustration of a government's 'possessiveness' of teacher education policy and its links with national identity.

We may note at the outset that there are four education jurisdictions in the UK, and they each have a distinctive approach to teacher education. This distinctiveness has been very explicit since the devolution of a number of powers to national governments in Scotland, Wales and Northern Ireland at the end of the last century. However, education policy in Scotland (including teacher education) has always been very different from the other parts of the UK as can be seen from historical accounts (Paterson 2003). The particular case of teacher education has been examined in some detail by a research collective known as The Teacher Education Group (2016), who came to the conclusion that England had become very much an outlier within the UK during the early part of the current century.

Significant reviews of teacher education were carried out in the three smaller jurisdictions and sought to improve and in some cases rationalise provision in each of them. In all three cases, the contribution of universities was seen as crucial to the continuing development of the teaching profession through initial teacher education. Even though there was a concern in all countries to ensure that teachers were fully prepared to 'hit the ground running', or to be 'classroom ready' as the Australian Teacher Education Ministerial Advisory Group (TEMAG) report would put it (Craven et al. 2014), it was assumed that the intellectual challenges of becoming a teacher were such that all trainees should have access to research and to higher education as a part of their preparation.

In England, on the other hand, there had been a steady undermining of this university contribution which can be traced back to right wing pamphleteering in the 1970s and was echoed and amplified by many politicians (mainly but not exclusively those in the Conservative Party) over subsequent decades. This process came to a critical head in 2010 when the coalition government, with Michael Gove as Secretary of State for Education, issued a White Paper with the title *The Importance of Teaching* (Department for Education [DfE] 2010), which explicitly advocated an apprenticeship approach to pre-service teacher education and sought to put schools in the lead rather than universities. There had been a major growth in school-led schemes such as the 'SCITT' (School Centred Initial Teacher Training) prior to this and also considerable development of 'employment-based routes', including the Graduate Teacher Program and Teach First.

Indeed, Teach First, founded in 2002, with the backing of the McKinsey Corporation among others, is a fascinating symbol of how thinking about teacher education in England has been reshaped in this century. It was introduced as a means of attracting the brightest and best from elite universities into teaching in some of the most challenging schools in urban settings (Wigdortz 2012). However, it is not designed as a preparation for a longterm career in teaching. It is designed as a leadership program, with the first year being a training year and the second year working as a qualified teacher. After that trainees are free (and some would say encouraged) to leave teaching, albeit with this experience added to their CV, and to enter their real chosen profession, usually involving working towards a leadership role in a corporation of some sort. Teach First has been resisted in Scotland so far, although a version has been started in Wales. The resistance in Scotland may be seen as partly ideological. Teach First's elitist emphasis on the best graduates working in the most challenging schools does not fit well with the more strongly established social democratic philosophy which prevails north of Hadrian's Wall.

So it is in England that we now have one of the most diverse and complex sets of arrangements for teacher education imaginable. Indeed a major study which has been trying to make sense of this pattern of provision, led from Bath Spa University, has found it very difficult to make sense of the publicly available data in such a way that what is happening on the ground is actually comprehensible (Whiting et al. 2018; Sorensen forthcoming)

It was the great anxiety about the potential impact of the school-led reforms on education research in England that was a major factor behind the setting up of a major enquiry into teacher education and research by the British Educational Research Association (BERA), working with the Royal Society for the Arts, Manufacture and Commerce (RSA) late in 2012. The enquiry gathered evidence from across the UK and commissioned a number of research reviews before publishing a final report in 2014 (BERA/RSA 2014).

The report found that there was a clear association between successful education systems and an enquiry oriented approach in teaching. It argued for all teacher education to be approached along these lines and for ensuring that all teachers would be 'research literate', meaning that they should have access to and an ability to make sense of the best educational research but also that they should themselves be equipped with skills of enquiry, enabling them to work collaboratively with others and with those in universities to improve their practice. The ideas in the report do appear to have some influence on the profession and even on the policy process. When a head teacher, Sir Andrew Carter, was commissioned to undertake a review of initial teacher training in England in 2015 the report which emerged did make some reference to the BERA/RSA report and also advocated teaching becoming a much more 'evidence-based' profession than it had been hitherto (Carter 2015). However, the report also demonstrated many of the tensions and contradictions that had been inherent in English government policy throughout the recent past (Mutton et al. 2017).

Three universities in England have withdrawn their provision of teacher education during this period, mainly in response to the uncertainty created by the continuing change in policy, especially concerning the allocation of funded places. Those universities that remain find themselves now outnumbered considerably by school-led providers and are having to work in much more responsive ways in order to ensure they recruit trainees and can find schools in which to place them for their professional experience (Murray and Mutton 2016).

Making Sense of Teacher Education Around the World

Following the work carried out by BERA and the RSA, some colleagues in Australia decided to undertake a similar project. Three organisations—the Australian Teacher Education Association, the Australian Association for Educational Research and the Australian Council of Deans of Education—collaborated on the topic of teaching as a research-rich profession. Their final report argues for the integration of research literacy into teacher education, for making research activity inclusive of more members of the profession and for greater collaboration and partnerships between the various stakeholders in developing teaching as a research-rich profession (White et al. forthcoming).

We are seeing greater calls for international collaboration in policy, practice and research, and there are an increasing number of comparative research projects. The past tendency for teacher education to be contained within nations—or even within states—had tended to discourage more ambitious wider ranging studies, albeit with a few notable exceptions, such as Tatto (2007) and Darling-Hammond and Lieberman (2012). Many but not all of these studies are primarily concerned with policy. It will also be important in the future to encourage more research that examines practice. One study that has sought to operate at three levels is the study of policy and practice in England and the USA undertaken by a team at the University of Oxford collaborating with a leading teacher education researcher from the USA (Tatto et al. 2018). This study adopted an explicitly sociocultural theoretical framework and developed a methodology that seeks to examine policy and practice at macro-, meso- and micro-levels. This means examining how teacher education works at national, institutional and personal levels and the interaction between the three. The study reveals just how complex the task of making sense of teacher education can be.

A study of a different kind which is perhaps best described as multinational rather than comparative as such is the work undertaken by an International Research Network of the World Educational Research Association (Tatto and Menter forthcoming). This network invited colleagues in twelve different national settings[1] to examine what knowledge is involved in learning to teach in each context and to review the research that has been undertaken towards creating an effective approach. It quickly became apparent that there were great variations in the amount, quality and types of research being carried out in these twelve nations, but an overview of the twelve cases led to the identification of six themes which appear to be important in describing any teacher education system. These six themes create a typology through which any national system of teacher education may be characterised.[2]

The Professionalisation/Universitisation Trajectory Versus the Deprofessionalisation/De-Universitisation Trajectory

In every one of the twelve cases, we noted some forms of institutional reorganisation taking place. In many cases, this involved transforming separate teacher education institutions into constituent parts of universities, through mergers. Sometimes, this has involved the majority of institutions in the country (e.g. Israel), in other countries only a selection of the institutions (e.g. Russia). In Mexico, which has seen the most recent developments of this nature, we have seen teacher education moving from 'normal schools' into higher education over the past few years. These moves have generally reflected both an 'academicisation' and a 'professionalisation' of teacher education, responses to the policy problem of teaching and teacher education. The former process has tended to mean that there has been greater attention given to education sciences or education studies in the program by the beginning teacher and the latter has been manifested by an increasing length of study and sometimes by raising the academic credentials to at least degree level and sometimes to master's level (as in Finland).

But in a small number of countries, we have seen evidence of a reversal of this trend, at least in part, what might be seen as a countervailing tendency. This is most apparent in England, where an apprenticeship model of teacher 'training' has been promoted and universities have experienced some sense of marginalisation in these matters. In Australia too, we have seen the emergence of Teach for Australia, an employment-based route and in the USA, programs such as 'urban residencies' have followed a similar pattern (as well as Teach for America).

---

[1] The twelve countries are Australia, Czech Republic, England, Finland, Hong Kong, Israel, Italy, Japan, Mexico, Russia, South Korea and USA.

[2] Parts of what follows are adapted from Menter (forthcoming).

The Positioning of Research in Relation to Policy and Practice

The extent to which research underpins policy and practice in teacher education varies greatly in the twelve cases. All the researchers were able to identify a range of research that has been carried out within their contexts, but the influence of that research appears to be extremely variable. Moreover, it would seem to be a reasonable generalisation that teacher education is significantly under researched as a whole. In one or two settings, we can see a large amount of research activity (notably in the USA, see Cochran-Smith et al. 2008; Cochran-Smith and Zeichner 2005) but it is still remarkably difficult to identify sustained programs of teacher education research that are large-scale and/or longitudinal. It may be that the amount of turbulence on policy and practice in many countries makes the creation of such a program an insuperable challenge, but given the considerable public expenditure involved and the political sensitivity of the topic of 'teacher quality', this remains astonishing.

Settings where there is a positive relationship between research, policy and practice communities include Finland, Korea and Russia. In these countries, we have seen evidence of a much more respectful set of relationships than, for example, in England or Italy. There are other countries where there appears to be growing awareness of the need for research to underpin developments, as for example in Australia and Israel.

Nevertheless, it is important to acknowledge, as many of the researchers do, that a considerable range of localised research activity does take place and there can be little doubt that such work does have a significant positive effect on practice, if less on policy. Such research 'in' teacher education will remain important and indeed is closely linked to the notion of teaching itself as an enquiry-based profession (see BERA-RSA 2014). Research 'on' or 'about' teacher education (Menter 2017) is equally important, but generally far less evident.

Partnership and Roles in Teacher Education

The respective contributions of specialist institutions, whether they be freestanding 'colleges of education' or departments/schools within universities, on the one hand, and schools, on the other, has been an enduring theme in teacher education since its inception. As we noted above, institutional arrangements have themselves varied over time and context but the particular relationships between higher education and schools have also been subject to much change. As the processes of universitisation developed in most countries during the twentieth century, so the input to teacher education programs of those based there has generally increased. Thus, we saw the emergence of a cadre of higher education-based 'teacher educators' developing. The educational and professional backgrounds of these people varied. In Italy, for example, the emphasis in recruiting these staff was on their academic background, with an expectation that they would have a strong profile in a discipline such as sociology or psychology. However, in some other settings, such as Australia or England, priority tended to be given to the professional experience of people appointed. In other words, they were expected to have been successful school teachers.

Nevertheless, as we have seen in the USA, Australia and England at least, the dual expectations on such staff that they would be both professionally skilled and experienced and capable of fulfilling an 'all-round' academic role in higher education has created considerable pressures. Many staff working in faculties of education have found it very challenging to develop successful research profiles at the same time as committing themselves fully to teaching on their teacher education programs (Menter et al. 2012).

As these pressures on university-based staff have increased, the growing emphasis on the contribution made to teacher education by those based in schools has also had a significant impact. What some have called 'the practicum turn' in teacher education (Lawn and Furlong 2011; Mattson et al. 2011) has led to increased attention being paid to the nature of the contribution made by teachers. There has been a massive expansion of the mentoring role of school teachers in teacher education (Heikennen et al. 2012). In programs in Finland and England, for example, training in the development of mentoring skills has been a key element of provision for at least twenty or thirty years now. Of course, some of the school-led or school-based schemes offered in England or the USA rely almost entirely on such mentoring by school staff.

The nature of partnership between higher education and schools is therefore not only about the sharing of resources or indeed of contracts between the two, but has become a key pedagogical element of the programs (Mutton 2016). This has been clearly demonstrated in a number of research studies including Tatto et al. (2018) and Mutton et al. (2018).

However, it must be acknowledged that such partnership arrangements and the development of mentoring practices by school-based staff are far less visible in a number of settings, such as the Czech Republic, Italy and Japan.

Power and Control in Teacher Education—Questions of Governance

As teacher education has become a 'policy problem' in so many settings it is no surprise that not only have the providers been restructured and reorganised, but the involvement of government agencies has also become a matter of change. The first point to note here, however, is that in different settings, there are different governmental levels with responsibility for teacher education. Ranging from Hong Kong, which is a special administrative region (SAR) of the Republic of China, but where the major responsibility for teacher education lies with the SAR, we can observe the importance of states within a federal system, for example in the USA, Russia and Australia. It is notable that in the USA and Australia, the federal government has made recent attempts to intervene in teacher education, arguably with more success in

Australia than in the USA. There are many other countries where a single unified government is the main policy body for teacher education. These would include Israel, Korea, Japan, Finland, the Czech Republic and Italy. England is again something of an oddity, in that the nationally elected government is at the United Kingdom level, but as mentioned above, responsibility for education, including teacher education, lies at the level of the four separate jurisdictions, England, Northern Ireland, Scotland and Wales and so policy and practice are quite different in the four constituent parts of the UK (Teacher Education Group 2016).

So, the level of government with responsibility varies and is sometimes shared between different levels, but this does not directly connect with the degree of involvement in controlling policy and practice in teacher education. There are in other words varying levels of power and control exercised in different settings by central or regional government. In many countries, now the required outcomes of teacher education programs are defined as a series of standards (see below) and these are sometimes determined by government agencies (as in England) and sometimes by professional bodies (as in Finland) or by accreditation boards that represent a collaboration of government and professional bodies (as in the US).

The significance of these variations is that the particular arrangements may be seen to represent the extent to which professionals—teachers and teacher educators—are trusted by the wider society, represented by politicians, to make decisions and to take control of their own work. In other words, the level of professional agency may be seen as being in proportion to the level of trust given to them. In some settings, there may be a professional body that has been established, which plays a major role in these matters, as for example in Australia, with their Institute for Teaching and School Leadership (AITSL). In England, the General Teaching Council which had been established in 2001 was closed down by the government in 2010 but is now in the process of being replaced (after a fashion) by a Chartered College of Teaching.

The arrangements for the governance of teacher education connect closely with some of the previous themes discussed, including the role and use of research and the arrangements for partnerships and indeed the institutional provision of teacher education. In particular these arrangements may be seen to have a determining influence on the key question of who defines teachers' professional knowledge (the key theme under investigation in the trans-national study from which these points are drawn).

The Impact of Performativity and Accountability and the Rise of 'Standards'

One of the key elements of Sahlberg's concept of the 'GERM' is the spread around education systems of accountability measures (Sahlberg 2010). These take many forms in schools, including heavy reliance on assessments of pupil performance, but they also reach into most teacher education systems, in some shape or form. Most frequently, they are very visibly manifested through the adoption or imposition of a series of published standards that define what it is a teacher should know and be able to do. Teaching standards have indeed spread around the world like an epidemic and so, although the details of what is regarded as important in each setting may vary to some extent, the idea that the quality of teaching should be judged against an observable set of behaviours and knowledge has become commonplace. The suggestion that there are elements of teaching that are in some senses ineffable beyond measurement has become seen as a romantic or idealist notion. Technical rationalism has become the common unifying principle of what it is to be a teacher around the world. That is not to say that there is no scope for creativity and imagination in the performance of teaching, but it is to confirm that there are now 'baselines' almost everywhere that determine what is entailed in qualifying as a teacher.

The common features of most sets of standards include lists of knowledge, skills and dispositions. These now tend to form the basis not only of the judgements about teachers' performances but play a major part in shaping the content of teacher education programs. Thus, the standards become in essence the definition of the professional knowledge required in any particular setting. Again, thinking back to the previous point above, we may see how the more open ended the standards are then the more agency we may see as being available to the teacher educators in shaping and determining their program. However, conversely, we may also see how the more tightly standards are defined, the less flexibility there may be in determining the nature of the learning experiences made available for beginning teachers.

Indeed, more generally, the standards may be seen as a statement of the values of the people who have determined them. So, while it is common for all standards to have a statement about preparing teachers to support learners in overcoming disadvantage, the ways in which this is defined may vary. The emphasis may be on 'learning disabilities', on inequalities associated with ethnicity or gender or indeed may be on social disadvantage. Similarly, the positioning of educational research in lists of standards may well indicate the extent to which teachers are encouraged to engage with the available evidence (for example about teaching and learning) or to engage in their own enquiry in the classroom.

Technology and Communication—The Impact of Digitisation

The final theme is one that is perhaps more speculative than the previous five. It is widely acknowledged that we now live in a networked society (Castells 2010) in which information technology (IT), including social media plays a very significant role. The extent to which these technological developments have as yet had an impact on teacher education is questionable. Clearly, there are some global developments that are far less likely to have happened without the availability of rapid forms of communication. Two examples of this that are very pertinent to this volume would be the global spread of standards, just discussed in the previous section and the development of the 'Teach for All' brand, now operating in more than 35 countries (see:

Teachforall.org). More generally, the rapid spread of performativity and accountability measures has been highly dependent on electronic communication. From the administration of assessment procedures through to the consultation between ministers of education and their staff, the GERM has clearly been facilitated by the use of IT.

But in terms of learning to teach, it seems that while student teachers are being encouraged to make use of IT in their classrooms and in preparing to teach their lessons, the adoption of electronic forms of learning for the students themselves has not been developing rapidly. We may note some reference to the use of video technology and microteaching (for example in Australia) but the standard use of e-learning as a means of communication for learning to teach is not visible. While higher education internationally has seen a phenomenal growth of massive open online courses (MOOCs) and there have been some attempts at 'distance learning' in teacher education, for example in Scotland and in sub-Saharan Africa (Moon 2013), we have as yet seen little evidence of the use of these technologies.

Conclusion

So, if we take these six themes as criteria by which to depict and evaluate a teacher education system, it is apparent that what the depiction will reveal is a sense of the underlying values that currently shape the particular system. We have already noted throughout that we cannot assume any sort of stasis in the situation—teacher education is dynamic and continuously changing. It is indeed a 'crucible of change' (see Chap. 1 of this book, p. 3).

There is a very clear need for research not only to make sense of what is currently happening but in order to inform future developments. Much of this research will necessarily be carried out within each system but there is also much to be gained from transnational and comparative research. As has been argued elsewhere (Menter 2017) we should also be aware of the possible different approaches to teacher education research—all of which are very important and each of which will provide different insights. Research is needed **in**, **on** and **about** teacher education. Research in teacher education is typically carried out with teachers and teacher educators themselves in the lead and will include self-study, action and practitioner research as well as evaluations of particular schemes and approaches. Research on teacher education, by contrast, will typically be carried out by external researchers and will often concern itself with policy, not just nationally but also institutionally, and may well also have an international dimension as suggested above. Finally, we do need to see more research that is about teacher education. That is, we need research that offers a more distanced analysis of teacher education in its wider context. This will include research that draws on a range of social science disciplines, including anthropology, sociology and history. Much of it is likely to be interdisciplinary in nature, and it is this approach—research about teacher education—that is most difficult to find strong examples of.

Finally, we must note how important it is in any of this work that the voices and experiences of teachers and teacher educators themselves are at the centre of investigation. It is only through grounding research in the real lives and experiences of those undertaking the crucial work of educating the citizens of tomorrow, as well as their teachers, that the critical edge and insight can be assured, that are so important in establishing research that is meaningful and valuable now and in the future.

References

Alexander, R. (2000). *Culture and pedagogy*. Oxford, England: Blackwell.
BERA-RSA. (2014). *Research and the teaching profession: Building the capacity for a self-improving education system*. London, England: BERA.
Carter, A. (2015). *Carter review of initial teacher training*. London, England: Department for Education.
Castells, M. (2010). *The rise of the network society* (2nd ed.). Chichester, England: Wiley-Blackwell.
Clarke, J., & Newman, J. (1997). *The managerial state*. London, England: Sage.
Cochran-Smith, M., Feiman-Nemser, S., McIntyre, D., & Demers, K. (Eds.). (2008). *Handbook of research on teacher education: Enduring questions in changing contexts*. New York, NY: Routledge.
Cochran-Smith, M., & Fries, K. (2008). Research on teacher education: Changing times, changing paradigms. In M. Cochran-Smith, S. Feiman-Nemser, D. McIntyre, & K. Demers (Eds.), *Handbook of research on teacher education: Enduring questions in changing contexts* (pp. 1050–1093). New York, NY: Routledge.
Cochran-Smith, M., & Zeichner, K. (Eds.). (2005). *Studying teacher education: The report of the AERA panel on research and teacher education*. New Jersey, NJ: Lawrence Erlbaum.
Craven, G., Beswick, K., Fleming, J., Fletcher, T., Green, M., Jensen, B., et al. (2014). *Action now: Classroom ready teachers*. Retrieved May 9, 2018 from https://docs.education.gov.au/system/files/doc/other/action_now_classroom_ready_teachers_accessible.pdf.
Darling-Hammond, L., & Lieberman, A. (Eds.). (2012). *Teacher education around the world*. London, England: Routledge.
Department for Education [DfE]. (2010). *The importance of teaching (White Paper)*. London, England: DfE.
Green, A. (1990). *Education and state formation: The rise of education systems in England, France and the USA*. London, England: Macmillan.
Green, A. (1997). *Education, globalization and the nation state*. Basingstoke, England: Macmillan.
Heikennen, H., Jokinen, H., & Tynjala, P. (Eds.). (2012). *Peer-group mentoring for teacher development*. London, England: Routledge.
Lawn, M., & Furlong, J. (2011). The disciplines of education: Between the ghost and the shadow. In J. Furlong & M. Lawn (Eds.), *Disciplines of education*. London, England: Routledge.
Mattsson, M., Eilertson, T., & Rorrison, D. (Eds.). (2011). *A practicum turn in teacher education*. Rotterdam, The Netherlands: Sense.
Menter, I. (2017). Teacher education research. *In Oxford encyclopedia of education*. https://doi.org/10.1093/acrefore/9780190264093.013.275.
Menter, I. (forthcoming). The interaction of global and national influences. In M. T. Tatto & Menter, I. (Eds.), *Knowledge, policy and practice in teacher education: A cross-national study*. London, England: Bloomsbury.
Menter, I., Hulme, M., & Sangster, P. (2012). Performance in teacher education and research—A double whammy for teacher educators? In B. Jeffrey & G. Troman (Eds.), *Performativity in*

education in the UK: Effects, consequences and agency (pp. 23–40). Stroud, England: E&E Publishing.

Moon, B. (2013). *Teacher education and the challenge of development.* London, England: Routledge.

Murray, J., & Mutton, T. (2016). Teacher education in England: Change in abundance, continuities in question. In Teacher Education Group (Eds.), *Teacher education in times of change.* Bristol, England: Policy Press.

Mutton, T. (2016). Partnership in teacher education. In Teacher Education Group (Eds.), *Teacher education in times of change.* Bristol, England: Policy Press.

Mutton, T., Burn, K., Hagger, H., & Thirlwall, K. (2018). *Teacher education partnerships: Policy and practice.* Northwich, England: Critical Publishing.

Mutton, T., Burn, K., & Menter, I. (2017). Deconstructing the Carter review: Competing conceptions of quality in England's 'school-led' system of initial teacher education. *Journal of Education Policy, 32*(1), 14–33.

Paterson, L. (2003). *Scottish education in the twentieth century.* Edinburgh, Scotland: Edinburgh University Press.

Rizvi, F., & Lingard, B. (2010). *Globalizing education policy.* London, England: Routledge.

Sahlberg, P. (2010). *Finnish lessons.* Columbia, SC: Teachers' College Press.

Sorenson, N. (Ed.). (forthcoming). *Diversity in teacher education in England.* London, England: IoE/Trentham Press.

Tatto, M. T. (Ed.). (2007). *Reforming teaching globally.* Didcot, England: Symposium Books.

Tatto, M. T., Burn, K., Menter, I., Mutton, T., & Thompson, I. (2018). *Learning to teach in England and the United States.* London, England: Routledge.

Tatto, M. T., & Menter, I. (Ed.). (forthcoming). *Knowledge, policy and practice in teacher education: A cross-national study.* London, England: Bloomsbury.

Teacher Education Group. (2016). *Teacher education in times of change.* Bristol, England: Policy Press.

White, S., Nuttall, J., Down, B., Shore, S., Woods, A., Mills, M., et al. (forthcoming). *Strengthening a research-rich teaching profession for Australia.* ATEA/AARE/ACDE.

Whiting, C., Whitty, G., Menter, I., Black, P., Hordern, J., Parfitt, A., et al. (2018). Diversity and complexity: Becoming a teacher in England in 2015–16. *Review of Education, 6*(1), 69–96.

Wigdortz, B. (2012). *Success against the odds.* London, England: Short Books.

Ian Menter is an Emeritus Professor of Teacher Education at the Department of Education, University of Oxford. He is a former President of BERA, 2013-2015. At OUDE, he was the Director of Professional Programmes and led the development of the Oxford Education Deanery. Before moving to Oxford, he was a Professor of Teacher Education at the University of Glasgow. Prior to that, he held posts at the University of the West of Scotland (Dean of Education and Media), London Metropolitan University (Head of School of Education), University of the West of England, and the University of Gloucestershire. He was the President of the Scottish Educational Research Association from 2005 to 2007 and chaired the Research and Development Committee of the Universities' Council for the Education of Teachers from 2008 to 2011. He is a Fellow of the Academy of Social Sciences and a Fellow of the Royal Society of Arts, is a Visiting Professor at the University of Nottingham; at Newman University, Birmingham; at Bath Spa University; and at Ulster University, and is also an Adjunct Professor at Southern Cross University in Australia.

Index

A
Access, 67, 82, 83, 86, 118, 135, 190, 203, 207–209, 249, 260, 315, 316
Accountability, v, vi, xi, 1, 4–9, 12, 13, 19, 22, 24, 28–33, 37–39, 41–48, 51, 52, 54, 56–59, 61, 116–118, 127, 160, 167, 172–175, 181, 186, 195, 210, 212, 231, 243, 244, 253, 262, 268, 294, 313, 321, 323
Approach, 2, 5, 7, 31, 33, 43, 46, 47, 52, 56, 57, 62, 66, 67, 69–73, 76, 77, 87, 98, 104, 119, 120, 125, 127, 135, 137, 141, 144, 146, 147, 150, 165, 172, 177–180, 186, 195, 206, 228, 249, 261, 273, 281, 295–297, 301, 303, 304, 306, 314–316, 318, 323
   developmental approach, 298
   differentiated approach, 179
   equitable approach, 179
   hierarchical approach, 67
   instructional approach, 297
   pedagogical approach(es), 65, 118, 166, 189, 236
   programmatic approach, 259
   summative approach, 179
   thematic approach, 137, 300, 302
Approaches to assessment, 9, 172, 173, 176, 179, 180, 182
Assessment, vi, xi, 1, 4, 5, 8–12, 19, 23, 25, 27, 28, 35, 41, 43, 53, 65–68, 71, 73–77, 97–99, 101–104, 106, 109, 115–117, 119, 121–127, 136, 138, 139, 141–143, 145, 148, 150, 162–164, 167, 172–182, 186, 191, 192, 204, 208, 227, 228, 234, 236, 244, 249, 250, 255–257, 261, 262, 264, 267, 268, 270, 272–274, 279, 281, 283, 285, 288, 289, 294, 306, 314, 323
Assessment for Learning (AfL), 171, 174, 179, 180, 261–264
   Assessment for Learning (AfL) module, 261, 263
   assessment literacy, 172, 174, 175, 177, 178, 181
   assessment reform, 1, 116, 189
   formative assessment, 77, 126, 174, 175, 178–180, 261, 263
   summative assessment, 119, 126, 174
Australia, v, vi, xi, 3, 8, 9, 11, 66, 71–73, 97, 104, 110, 115–119, 121, 122, 124, 127, 128, 156–162, 165–167, 175, 190, 191, 202, 204, 207, 210, 213, 224, 233, 234, 243, 244, 248, 249, 252, 294, 297, 317–321, 323
Australian, 3, 8, 9, 99–101, 103, 105, 106, 108–110, 115, 118, 119, 128, 155, 156, 158, 160, 162, 165, 166, 201, 202, 213, 214, 225, 230, 294, 296, 315, 317

B
Beginning teacher experiences, 245
Beginning teachers, vi, 3, 7, 8, 11, 37, 42, 52, 54, 81, 82, 84–94, 105, 106, 108, 174, 180, 190, 193, 195, 223–236, 243–253, 322

C
Canada, v, 9, 71, 172–177, 181, 186, 204, 207, 213, 297
Childhood, vi, 155, 157, 158, 160, 163, 165, 166

Childhood (*cont.*)
  early childhood, vi, 9, 135, 148, 159, 166, 186, 206, 296
  early childhood education, vi, 9, 135, 143, 158–161, 165, 166, 186, 206
  early childhood teachers, 156, 160, 162, 166, 167
Children, 9, 27, 39, 40, 43, 58, 67, 68, 87, 123, 135–138, 141–151, 155, 157–160, 162, 163, 165, 166, 194, 205, 214, 230, 234, 286
Classroom, vi, 5, 9, 12, 59–61, 73, 75–77, 86, 88, 91, 100, 101, 103, 104, 106, 107, 109, 117, 119, 124, 126, 137, 150, 151, 172–174, 179–181, 186, 191, 194, 201, 224, 226–235, 249, 250, 263, 264, 273, 274, 287, 295, 301–303, 305, 306, 322
  classroom assessment, 9, 172, 174, 176, 180, 181
  classroom management, 53, 57, 192, 249, 250, 258
  classroom practice(s), vi, 8, 11, 59, 91, 117, 118, 122, 125, 151, 203, 233, 251, 274, 296, 303, 304
  classroom readiness, vi, 101–108, 110, 118, 119, 243, 244, 304
Competence, 5, 20, 23–26, 32, 42, 43, 65, 74, 83, 102, 109, 110, 115, 117, 121, 127, 150, 188, 191, 256, 260, 280, 281, 283, 287
Connection(s), 1, 6, 10, 87, 141, 151, 189, 196, 261, 283, 304
Content, vi, 12, 20, 22, 23, 26–28, 52, 56, 57, 59, 65, 67, 72, 100, 105, 107, 118, 119, 122, 136, 138, 139, 141, 142, 146–150, 165, 166, 210–212, 215, 217, 224, 228, 230, 233, 236, 250, 261–263, 273, 279, 295, 322
  content knowledge, 11, 20, 21, 27–29, 31, 41, 53, 76, 106, 122, 141, 144, 194, 224, 231, 237, 304
  Pedagogical Content Knowledge (PCK), 11, 28, 106, 176, 195, 232, 237, 300, 303, 304
Context, v, vi, 1, 6, 8, 9, 11–13, 19, 31, 33, 37–39, 41, 43, 51–54, 56, 57, 59–62, 66, 85, 88, 99, 100, 102, 103, 105–110, 115, 123, 136, 155, 157, 162, 175, 181, 186, 191, 193–196, 208, 210, 212, 223, 224, 227, 228, 230, 233, 236, 243, 246, 249, 252, 255, 258, 259, 262, 278, 279, 281, 284, 288, 295, 298, 301, 302, 313, 318, 323
  assessment context, 174
  learning context(s), 124, 286
Control vs. Autonomy, 22, 30
Cultural-historical theory, 156
Curriculum, vi, 2, 7, 9, 10, 12, 38, 40, 41, 54, 58, 59, 61, 68–72, 75, 77, 81, 83–87, 107, 120, 122, 135–143, 145–147, 149–151, 162, 166, 174, 175, 186–196, 203, 213, 216, 223, 226, 230, 231, 249, 250, 260, 270, 285, 294, 298, 301–306, 314
  curriculum design, 9, 141, 146–148, 150, 151, 189, 296–298, 303
  curriculum development, 69, 76, 135–138, 298
  curriculum framework, 9, 83, 86, 138, 143, 145, 149, 150, 162, 298
  curriculum guide, 9, 135–137, 142, 147, 150
  curriculum orientations, 9, 136, 138–141, 144, 149–151
  curriculum philosophy, 297
  curriculum reform, 12, 137, 143

D

Data, 1, 2, 4, 6, 9, 11, 32, 39, 41, 47, 51, 54, 60, 66, 68, 69, 74, 77, 98, 99, 118, 119, 121–124, 139, 141, 148, 164, 174, 175, 176, 191, 192, 194, 206, 208, 209, 211, 212, 225, 227–229, 248, 250, 251, 262, 264, 265, 273, 316
Develop, vi, ix, 10, 11, 24, 27, 30–32, 41, 43, 44, 58, 67–69, 71, 75–77, 90, 105, 107, 110, 118, 123, 126, 138, 141, 142, 144–146, 148, 149, 160, 164, 166, 172, 175, 182, 187–190, 192, 204, 216, 225, 227, 228, 230, 231, 235, 236, 248, 250, 252, 261, 262, 264, 268, 272, 300–302, 314, 320
Development, 4, 7, 9, 27, 40, 43, 45–47, 65, 75–77, 83, 89, 92, 106–110, 117, 120, 125, 126, 135, 137, 138, 143, 146–149, 156, 159, 160, 162, 164, 165, 178, 190, 191, 193, 195, 206, 215, 223–232, 234, 235, 237, 255, 257, 259, 261, 263, 266, 268, 270, 273, 278, 287, 288, 297, 298, 300, 302, 304–306, 314, 315, 320, 322
  professional development, vi, 5, 25, 35, 46, 76, 82, 108, 120, 127, 135, 193, 203,

Index

213, 215, 230, 251, 256, 275, 282, 285, 286, 288, 294, 298, 314
Dispositions, 4, 10, 103, 106, 110, 117, 122, 124–126, 166, 193, 215, 225, 232, 235, 258, 321

E
Education, v–vii, ix, xi, 1, 2, 5, 9, 11, 19–22, 24, 26, 27, 29, 31, 35, 37, 39, 40, 42, 44, 53, 54, 58, 59, 66–71, 75, 81, 89, 99, 105, 116, 118, 122, 138, 143, 156, 160, 161, 164, 165, 173, 174, 186, 193, 201, 203, 206, 208, 210, 216, 229, 247, 252, 253, 255, 257, 275, 277, 278, 287, 289, 296, 314, 315, 320, 321, 323
  education policy, 2, 3, 6, 9, 37, 38, 40, 41, 72, 116, 136, 155, 156, 158, 203, 253, 294, 315
  education reform, 10, 29, 116, 137, 138, 203, 206–212, 215–217, 243, 313
  education research, 3, 13, 115, 316, 319, 323
Educational, 2, 6, 8, 19, 21, 29–31, 37–42, 45, 46, 51, 60, 68, 70, 71, 74, 92, 97, 98, 100–102, 105, 106, 108–110, 119, 135, 138, 150, 151, 163, 172–174, 176, 178, 181, 205, 210, 214, 245, 261, 280, 281, 285, 298, 300–304, 313, 314, 316, 319, 322
  educational assessment, 9, 275
Educators, vi, vii, 5, 9, 10, 13, 21, 23–25, 33, 43, 47, 53, 61, 65, 73, 75, 77, 81, 90, 91, 105, 108, 110, 127, 128, 141, 158, 160, 162, 165, 171–173, 176, 177, 179, 180, 186, 187, 189–193, 195, 216, 229, 230, 252, 260, 278, 282, 295, 301, 304, 305, 321, 324
  initial teacher educators, 122, 189
Equity, 2, 10, 11, 52, 84, 171, 188, 190, 201, 203, 206, 208, 210, 212, 214, 215, 217, 275, 300, 301
Evidence, v, vi, 1–3, 5, 7–9, 13, 26, 38, 39, 41, 43, 45, 47, 62, 68, 70, 71, 77, 88, 89, 93, 97–99, 110, 115–124, 126, 128, 145, 148, 156, 158, 160, 163, 165, 173, 176, 181, 191, 193, 215, 225–227, 229, 233, 236, 243, 253, 264, 273, 280, 283, 316, 318, 322, 323
  evidence-based, 4, 10, 92, 118, 194, 211, 236, 296, 297, 317
Experience(s), vi, 3, 9, 11, 12, 45, 52, 54, 56, 83, 85, 87–93, 123, 126, 139, 142–144, 146, 147, 150, 151, 164, 171–173, 175, 176, 178, 180, 182, 187, 193, 203, 224, 226–230, 232, 235, 236, 244–251, 253, 256, 259, 263, 265, 266, 268, 274, 281, 284–286, 290, 294, 301, 302, 313, 322, 324
  classroom experiences, 9, 179
Experiential Learning (EL), 257, 298, 304

F
Fairness, 122, 125, 127, 172, 177–180
Fidelity, 8, 115, 116, 124–127
Futures, 2, 5, 8, 81, 90, 253
  futures thinking, 8
Future-focused education, 8
  future-focused, 8, 90, 93
  future-oriented, 81, 88

G
Government, 20, 22, 39–42, 44, 46, 47, 51, 69, 100–102, 104, 108, 118, 119, 135, 155, 156, 158, 159, 161, 206, 213, 315, 316
Graduate, 8, 10, 11, 23, 30, 41, 99, 102–104, 108, 109, 115, 117–119, 121, 122, 126, 156, 162, 163, 165, 188, 189, 190, 192, 195, 223–237, 244, 246, 248–253, 255, 277, 289, 298, 316
  Graduate Teacher Performance Assessment (GTPA), 8, 115, 122
Guide, 55, 86, 89, 117, 135–138, 141, 148, 215, 259, 260, 300

H
High-stakes testing, 6, 51
Hong Kong, vi, 12, 71, 73, 135, 136, 138–141, 146, 151, 295, 297, 298, 303, 306, 320

I
Identity, 10, 11, 39, 72, 92, 121, 205, 215, 226–228, 230–232, 235, 245, 298, 315
Impact, 1–3, 5, 6, 8, 11, 12, 32, 37–39, 41, 44–46, 54, 88, 91, 97, 99, 103, 105, 107, 109, 110, 117–119, 123–125, 128, 151, 156, 161, 163, 166, 187, 193, 194, 201, 205, 214–216, 224, 225, 230, 233, 234, 236, 243, 244, 257, 260, 263, 268, 273, 274, 286, 306, 316, 320–322
Inclusive, vi, 10, 39, 46, 188, 203, 205–208, 210–216, 258, 281, 317
Inclusive education, 10, 201, 203, 206, 207, 210–217

Initial teacher education (ITE), 2–4, 8–12, 20, 21, 42, 45, 46, 81, 82, 87, 90, 92, 97, 115–117, 119, 127, 155, 156, 159, 160, 166, 188, 191–195, 210, 211, 213, 214, 243, 248, 255, 277, 295
  ITE reform, 297
Inquiry, vi, 5, 7, 24, 52, 54, 60–62, 76, 84, 98, 141, 146, 189, 193, 195, 229, 233, 246, 284, 285, 294, 298, 300–302, 304
  critical inquiry, 125, 195, 235
  inquiry-based, 12, 141, 285, 296, 297, 300–302, 306
  inquiry-based learning, 141
  inquiry mindset, 150
Intelligent accountability, 6, 22, 33, 121, 181, 182
International, v, vi, xi, 1, 6, 10–12, 19–21, 24–26, 28, 29, 31, 38–40, 46, 47, 97, 98, 111, 115, 116, 162, 181, 186, 190, 191, 201, 206, 207, 209, 212, 217, 234, 275, 277, 278, 290, 296, 314, 317, 323
  Programme for international student assessment (PISA), 165, 190, 234, 280, 314
Ireland, v, vi, 3, 12, 97, 165, 211, 277–279, 281–286, 288–290, 294, 315, 321

K

Kindergarten
  kindergarten curriculum, 135–138, 141, 149, 150
  kindergarten education, 135, 136, 138, 141, 146, 147, 150, 151
Knowledge, ix, xi, 2–5, 7, 9, 11, 12, 19, 21, 23, 26, 28, 31, 38, 40, 53, 56, 59–62, 66, 67, 75, 83, 84, 86–88, 90, 91, 98, 103, 105, 106, 110, 117, 120–122, 124, 125, 137, 141–143, 145, 151, 176, 181, 188, 189, 192, 193, 195, 213–216, 223, 225, 226, 228–236, 244, 246, 250, 255, 257–259, 261, 263, 264, 270, 272–274, 278–281, 284–287, 296, 298, 300, 303, 305, 318, 321, 322
  pedagogical knowledge, 10, 22, 106, 107, 150, 216, 223, 257, 264, 273, 303, 304

L

Learning, v, vi, xi, 1–7, 9–11, 20, 23, 25–28, 35, 40–42, 44, 47, 48, 52–54, 57–62, 66–68, 71, 73, 74, 76, 77, 81–83, 85–88, 90–93, 103, 108, 118, 119, 121–124, 136–139, 141–143, 145–150, 162, 164–166, 172–176, 178, 181, 182, 187–190, 192, 194, 196, 201, 203, 206, 210, 212, 217, 223, 225–233, 235–237, 250, 252, 256, 258–262, 264, 266, 274, 275, 279, 281, 283–286, 288, 290, 295, 297, 298, 301, 302, 304, 305, 322, 323
  learning needs, 60, 82, 118, 122, 124, 177, 178, 189, 204, 209, 210, 231, 234, 274
  learning progressions, 7, 74, 77
  learning to teach, 6, 52, 54, 58, 59, 61, 91, 125, 250, 252, 253, 259, 260, 294, 318, 322
  lifelong learning, 10, 40, 135, 188, 190, 192, 215, 225
  school-based learning, 2, 117, 151
  student learning, v, xi, 2, 3, 5, 10, 20, 28, 57, 60, 61, 91, 97, 98, 107, 110, 117, 118, 121, 123–125, 128, 151, 172, 173, 175, 176, 178, 181, 182, 186–189, 193, 194, 204, 211, 214, 216, 232, 243, 244, 249, 250, 295
  theoretical learning, 118

M

Mathematical thinking, 10, 190–193
Mentoring, 7, 27, 35, 45, 53, 59, 93, 126, 164, 251, 279, 280, 285, 287, 288, 294, 320
  mentoring beginning teachers, 7
Metacognition, 76
Mistrust and trust, 6, 20–22, 24, 26, 28–31, 33

N

National, v, vi, xi, 1–3, 11, 19, 20, 23, 25–29, 31, 33, 38, 39, 44, 47, 69–71, 73, 77, 83, 99, 108, 116, 120, 127, 161, 181, 186, 188, 201, 206, 207, 227, 234, 262, 264, 275, 277, 278, 283, 314, 315, 318, 321
  national guidelines, 99, 127
  national policy, 68, 71
  national regulatory requirements, 116
Need(s), vi, 2, 3, 7, 10, 12, 13, 19, 25–28, 31, 38, 40, 43, 44, 47, 53, 55, 57, 59–62, 65, 68, 69, 74–77, 81, 84, 85, 87–90, 93, 101, 104–108, 110, 122, 123, 125, 127, 128, 138, 141–143, 145, 149, 150, 158, 159, 166, 171, 179, 180, 187–191, 193–196, 203, 205, 210–212, 214, 216, 217, 224–228, 230, 232, 233, 235–237, 244, 248, 250, 255, 258, 259, 273, 281, 285, 288, 295, 300, 301, 319, 323

Index

New Zealand, v, 7, 10, 31, 81, 84–86, 88–90, 165, 175, 188, 191–193, 205
Norway, v, 5, 6, 19–22, 24, 25, 27–29, 31–33, 35

P

Pedagogical practices, xi, 7, 73, 264
Pedagogy, vi, 6, 29, 41, 45, 53, 68, 77, 81, 85, 86, 89, 166, 181, 186, 193, 204, 229, 231, 249, 250, 263, 305, 314
Perceptions, vi, 11, 67, 98, 102, 139, 151, 223, 225, 227, 233, 235, 237, 244–253, 271, 272, 296
Phenomenology, 11
  phenomenology of perceptions, 11
Policy, xi, 2, 3, 6, 8, 9, 11, 19, 29, 31, 33, 38, 43–47, 70, 71, 74, 97, 99, 110, 115, 116, 128, 151, 155, 156, 159, 160, 165, 167, 174, 187, 201, 203, 206, 213, 214, 217, 228, 255, 261, 262, 278, 280–282, 287, 294, 314, 315, 317–319, 321, 323
  policy reform, 8, 9, 166
  teacher education policy, 9, 253
Practice(s), vi, 2, 4, 5, 8, 11–13, 22, 24–27, 30, 31, 33, 38, 39, 42–44, 46, 47, 51–54, 56–61, 75–77, 81, 84, 86–93, 99, 100, 103, 107, 109, 110, 116–126, 128, 151, 156, 159, 162, 165, 172–174, 180, 181, 188, 189, 193, 194, 196, 201, 203–205, 210–216, 225–227, 231–233, 237, 244, 246–248, 250, 255–264, 266, 318
  professional practice, 42, 119, 194, 244
  teacher practice, 76, 203, 214, 257, 259
Practicum, 22, 255, 257, 258, 261, 286, 320
  Professional Practicum (PP), 298, 302, 304
Pre-service education, 75
Professional, vi, xi, 2, 4, 5, 11–13, 23, 29, 30, 32, 35, 37, 41, 42, 44–46, 52, 54, 59, 60, 76, 82, 88, 90, 98, 99, 105, 106, 108–110, 117–121, 125, 127, 128, 135, 162, 172, 175, 176, 181, 182, 190, 191, 194, 203, 204, 213, 214, 216, 224–227, 229–232, 235, 236, 243–245, 247–251, 253, 256, 261, 275, 277, 281–285, 287–289, 294, 296, 297, 300, 303, 317, 321, 322
  professional competence, 115, 117, 150
  professional experience, vi, ix, 107, 108
  professional learning, 5, 7, 44, 52–54, 59, 60, 86, 89, 92, 106, 110, 121, 190, 229, 230, 246, 247, 249, 250, 253, 261–263, 278, 283

professional standards, vi, 2, 4–6, 8, 37, 42, 44–47, 116–118, 120, 121, 124, 128, 173, 177, 203, 204, 206, 244, 246, 294
Program(s), vi, 2–4, 6, 10–12, 20–26, 28, 30, 32, 51, 52, 54, 56–59, 61, 62, 66, 86, 89, 93, 94, 97–99, 102, 105, 106, 116–120, 125–128, 162, 166, 172, 173, 175, 176, 180, 182, 190–196, 203, 214, 216, 217, 224, 226, 227, 230, 231, 233–237, 244, 246, 248, 250, 251, 255–261, 264–266, 270, 273, 275, 277, 278, 281, 283, 290, 302, 304, 305, 316, 318–320, 322
  academic program, 2, 12, 99, 117, 123, 125, 126, 128, 265
  teacher education program(s), 5, 6, 11, 23, 31, 32, 35, 90, 119, 120, 171, 173–175, 211, 215–217, 243, 315, 321, 322

Q

Quality, v, vi, xi, 2–4, 6, 8, 10, 11, 13, 19, 20, 23–25, 27–30, 32, 37, 41, 51, 74, 90, 97, 98, 102, 105, 107, 108, 116, 117, 119, 126, 128, 135, 159, 173, 188, 203, 212, 217, 223, 225, 226, 228, 230, 233–236, 244, 258, 275, 280, 289, 294, 296, 314, 318, 321, 322
  quality assurance, 20, 30–32, 107, 118, 306
  quality control, 117
  teaching quality, 32, 117, 124, 224, 225

R

Reform, v, 3, 5, 8, 9, 12, 20, 22, 24, 26, 28, 32, 39, 65, 71, 76, 100, 105, 106, 108, 110, 115, 116, 119, 135, 138, 155, 156, 176, 203, 206–209, 215, 217, 252, 280, 284, 296–298, 303, 304, 306, 315, 316
  international teacher education reform, 208, 210, 211
Relationships, vi, 6, 47, 52, 84, 92, 101, 104, 128, 158, 163, 226, 230, 232, 236, 244, 250, 253, 260, 268, 279, 283, 284, 287, 288, 314, 319
Report, 20, 27, 37, 38, 42–48, 65, 66, 73, 74, 77, 89, 99–102, 104, 105, 108, 110, 118, 119, 122, 138, 158, 163, 172–174, 188, 191, 192, 203, 206–210, 212, 217, 224–226, 228, 231–234, 236, 245, 249, 256, 257, 272, 273, 280, 281, 296, 306, 315–317
Research, vi, xi, 3, 4, 8–10, 13, 20–27, 31, 32, 35, 47, 54, 59, 60, 62, 69, 71, 76, 81, 84, 85, 87, 89, 94, 98, 100, 101, 105, 108,

115, 116, 118, 122, 123, 128, 136, 139, 141, 151, 155, 156, 158, 160, 164–167, 173–177, 181, 186, 188, 191–196, 206, 215–217, 224–229, 233, 245, 246, 248, 253, 260, 261, 263, 264, 274, 275, 282–286, 288–290, 294, 297, 301, 315–324
international research, 47
Review, v, 3, 8, 10, 38, 40, 42, 43, 45–47, 65, 81, 97, 99–104, 109, 110, 116, 117, 122, 128, 136, 138, 148, 151, 155, 156, 164, 166, 175, 195, 203, 206, 207, 211–215, 228, 248, 252, 255, 256, 259, 261, 263, 268, 280, 282–285, 294, 296, 303, 315, 316, 318
Roles and responsibilities, 12, 102, 279, 282, 284

S

School(s), vi, vii, xi, 2–4, 8–13, 21–23, 25–29, 32, 35, 39–42, 44–46, 51, 52, 54, 56, 57, 60, 67, 71, 73, 74, 77, 82, 83, 85–89, 91, 92, 97, 100–102, 107, 108, 116–118, 122, 124, 128, 135–140, 143, 146, 147, 149, 150, 155–158, 162, 163, 165, 166, 172–174, 177, 181, 182, 186–191, 193–195, 202, 203, 211, 213, 214, 216, 224–227, 230, 231, 234, 235, 246, 247, 249–253, 255–258, 260, 262–264, 266, 268, 274, 275, 278–290, 294, 296, 301–305, 316, 317, 319–321
school experience (SE), 298, 301–304
school leadership, 4, 8, 235, 250, 251, 284
school partnerships, 284, 286, 287
school systems, 118, 213, 214
school-university partnerships, 12, 278, 279, 285, 294
Scotland, v, 3, 6, 37–48, 71, 203, 211, 212, 296, 297, 315, 316, 321, 323
Singapore, v, 66, 71
Skills, 2–5, 7, 11, 12, 23, 24, 26, 27, 29, 40, 52, 55, 56, 58–61, 65–72, 74–77, 88, 90, 102–104, 106, 107, 110, 117, 118, 120, 121, 124–127, 137, 138, 141, 143, 145–150, 164, 175, 188, 189, 191, 210–213, 216, 223, 224, 227, 228, 230–235, 257, 260–265, 268, 270, 272–274, 277–279, 281, 283, 285, 288, 289, 298, 303, 305, 306, 317, 320, 322
Social, 5, 9, 33, 39, 41, 42, 52, 60, 66, 67, 69, 83, 84, 92, 97, 123, 127, 137–143, 146, 147, 149, 156–158, 164, 165, 188, 190, 195, 196, 201, 214, 217, 227, 228, 258, 277, 279, 286, 290, 298, 300, 301, 305, 306, 315, 322, 323
social context, 66
South Africa, v, vi, 11, 76, 206, 233, 255–258, 262–264, 270, 273
Stance, 7, 10, 52, 60–62, 120, 121, 164, 166, 176, 182, 195, 280, 286, 295, 298
cultural stance, 9, 166, 195
Standards, vi, xi, 1, 4, 8, 10, 19, 20, 23, 37, 42–46, 58, 59, 97, 99, 100, 105, 108, 115, 117, 119–122, 127, 156, 163, 172, 175, 178, 181, 186–188, 191, 195, 203, 214, 216, 232, 233, 244–246, 280, 282, 306, 321, 322
graduate teacher standards, 99, 102, 108, 119
Student(s), v, vi, xi, 2, 3, 5–8, 10, 12, 13, 21, 23, 24, 26, 28, 46, 51, 52, 54–58, 61, 67–69, 71, 74–77, 82–86, 88, 92, 98–101, 107, 118, 119, 121–125, 128, 139, 171–174, 177–179, 181, 182, 186–196, 201–204, 211–213, 215, 216, 223, 224, 226–228, 230–234, 236, 249, 255–258, 260–265, 268, 270, 273, 274, 279, 280, 283, 285–289, 294, 295, 298, 303–305, 314, 323
student teachers, 2, 10, 12, 21, 27, 85, 90, 91, 122, 191, 193–195, 216, 256, 257, 259, 260, 264, 268, 270, 273, 278, 280–283, 285–290, 295, 300–302, 304–306, 323
Study, xi, 5, 7, 9–11, 20, 24–27, 30, 42, 43, 45, 71–76, 81, 88, 89, 93, 125, 136, 140, 141, 150, 151, 165, 175, 176, 180, 188, 191, 193, 195, 213, 216, 233, 243, 247–249, 251, 253, 257, 261, 264, 270, 273, 284, 298, 316–318, 321, 323
Support, 5, 10, 39, 41, 42, 44, 46, 47, 51, 58–61, 66, 67, 71, 74, 75, 82, 84–86, 88, 91–93, 108, 119, 121, 122, 128, 135, 148, 149, 155, 160, 166, 172, 173, 176, 180, 186, 187, 190, 193–195, 203–206, 211–215, 224, 226–228, 232, 233, 235, 236, 250–253, 256, 259–261, 268, 269, 279, 283, 285, 288, 289, 297, 298, 300, 302, 306, 314, 322
System, v, xi, 2, 6–8, 12, 19, 20, 22, 23, 28, 30–33, 38–41, 43–48, 52, 55–57, 60–62, 65, 67–71, 73, 74, 76, 77, 81, 82, 84, 89, 115, 116, 118, 122, 124, 128, 141, 159, 160, 163, 164, 167, 171, 173, 181, 189, 211–214, 217, 225, 227, 233, 247, 252, 275, 277, 282, 289, 294, 295,

Index

298, 302, 303, 305, 313–316, 318, 320, 321, 323
system and site validity, 8, 115, 116, 124, 125, 127, 128

T

Teach, 7, 9, 21, 27, 52, 54–62, 67, 69, 82, 88–90, 92, 98, 99, 103, 104, 117, 119, 123, 125, 171, 172, 180, 189, 192, 224, 230, 231, 244, 252, 260, 266, 270, 280, 289, 294, 301, 303, 304, 314, 316, 318, 322, 323

Teacher(s), v–vii, ix, xi, 1–13, 19–24, 26–33, 35, 37–39, 41–46, 51–54, 56–62, 65, 73–77, 81–93, 97–111, 115–128, 135–137, 139–143, 145–151, 155, 156, 158–164, 166, 171–177, 179, 180–182, 186–191, 193, 194, 196, 203, 204, 206, 208, 210–217, 223–236, 243–253, 256–258, 260, 261, 263, 265, 268, 270, 273, 275, 277–290, 294–306, 313–324
teacher beliefs, 136, 139, 141, 151
teacher capacity, 7, 66, 190, 192
teacher education, v–vii, ix, xi, 2–13, 19–33, 35, 37–39, 41–46, 51, 52, 62, 75, 76, 81, 82, 87, 88, 90–93, 98, 99, 101, 105, 108, 110, 116–121, 125–128, 155, 156, 158–161, 163–167, 171, 172, 174–176, 186–188, 191–196, 203, 206–217, 223, 225–227, 229, 233, 234, 243, 246–248, 250, 252, 253, 255, 257, 259, 264, 275, 277, 278, 280, 281, 285, 289, 290, 294, 296–298, 302, 304, 305, 313–323
teacher education reform, 207, 208, 216, 217
teacher educator learning, 189, 193, 195
teacher educators, vi, vii, 3, 9, 10, 13, 21, 23–25, 32, 33, 46, 47, 61, 81, 90, 91, 110, 122, 127, 128, 172, 173, 176, 177, 179, 180, 182, 186–196, 216, 227, 229, 244, 252, 253, 259, 260, 278, 282, 301, 306, 319, 321–324
teacher training, 65, 75, 76, 157, 210–213, 257, 316, 317

Teaching, vi, xi, 1–5, 8, 13, 15, 38, 41–48, 66, 91, 96, 99, 119, 121, 122, 141, 147, 156, 186, 194, 204, 213, 215, 217, 224–226, 232, 244, 253, 257, 259, 260, 277, 278, 281–283, 301, 306, 310, 311, 316, 321
teaching performance assessment (TPA), vi, xi, 8, 115, 116, 119, 121–124, 126, 127, 244
teaching practicum, 11, 255–269, 273

Test-based accountability, 6, 51, 52, 54, 55, 59–62
Thinking, 5, 8, 10, 13, 52, 55, 67, 69, 70, 72, 75, 76, 83, 88, 89, 107, 124, 137, 138, 145, 182, 188, 189, 190–193, 214, 252, 260, 270–272, 285, 286, 288, 297, 314, 316, 321
futures thinking, 8
Time, 2, 6, 19, 21, 23, 25, 29, 30, 32, 43, 51, 55–58, 60, 69–71, 73, 88, 91, 120, 124, 125, 127, 128, 142, 147, 149, 155, 161, 165, 172, 178, 182, 189, 192–194, 215, 226, 246–248, 250–252, 256, 266, 270, 284, 306, 319, 320
Transformative, 82, 90, 91, 93, 283, 305
transformative learning, 91
transformative student learning, 91
Transition from university to work, 11
Transversal competencies, 7, 71–74, 77, 189
Trust and mistrust, 19, 23
Twenty-first century learning, 7, 8, 82, 87, 90
Twenty-first century skills, vi, 7, 65–68, 71, 75–77

U

United States, 6, 51, 52, 58, 116, 117, 128, 139, 157, 177, 202, 207, 233, 279, 295
Universal Design for Learning (UDL), 203, 213, 214
University, vi, vii, xi, 5, 11, 23, 25, 88, 117, 140, 186, 194, 206, 253, 257, 262, 263, 273, 275, 294, 295, 298, 302, 316, 317

V

Validity, 8, 115, 116, 122, 124, 125, 127, 128, 139, 140, 164, 178, 179, 180
system and site validity, 8, 115, 116, 124–128
Values, 1, 5, 6, 10, 13, 37, 38, 40, 42, 45, 46, 48, 52, 65, 69, 72, 75, 83, 88, 135, 142–145, 148, 149, 151, 165, 194, 203, 204, 215–217, 245, 281, 282, 303, 305, 314, 322, 323

W

Work, vi, ix, xi, 3, 4, 7, 10–12, 20, 21, 26, 28–33, 42, 45, 52, 53, 55, 57–61, 74, 75, 81–87, 90, 92, 93, 101, 102, 105, 108–111, 119, 120, 123, 126–128, 139, 157–161, 176, 182, 186, 188–191, 193, 195, 211, 225, 227, 228, 231–236, 243–251, 253, 256, 258, 262, 263, 270, 273, 278–281, 284, 285, 287–289, 297, 301, 302, 305, 314, 317, 319, 321, 324

CPSIA information can be obtained
at www.ICGtesting.com
Printed in the USA
LVHW021438300619
622785LV00004B/113/P